D0732544

THE
MYSTERY-RELIGIONS

A STUDY IN THE RELIGIOUS BACKGROUND
OF EARLY CHRISTIANITY

BY

S. ANGUS, Ph.D., D.Lit., D.D.

SOMETIME PROFESSOR OF NEW TESTAMENT AND HISTORICAL THEOLOGY
ST. ANDREW'S COLLEGE, SYDNEY

DOVER PUBLICATIONS, INC.
NEW YORK

This Dover edition, first published in 1975, is an unabridged and unaltered republication of the second (1928) edition of the work originally published by John Murray, in London, in 1925 under the title *The Mystery-Religions and Christianity*.

International Standard Book Number: 0-486-23124-0
Library of Congress Catalog Card Number: 74-12657

Manufactured in the United States of America
Dover Publications, Inc.
180 Varick Street
New York, N.Y. 10014

καὶ νοοῦμεν ἐκεῖνα οὐκ εἴδωλα αὐτῶν οὐδὲ τύπους
ἔχοντες, εἰ δὲ μὴ τοῦτο ὄντες ἐκεῖνα.

Plotinus, Enneades, VI. 5, 7.

τὸ σοφὸν δ᾽ οὐ σοφία.

Euripides, Bacchae, 395.

Uno itinere non potest pervenire ad tam grande Secretum.

Q. Aurelius Symmachus, Rel. III (Seeck's ed. p. 282).

FOREWORD

FOR over a thousand years the ancient Mediterranean world was familiar with a type of religion known as Mystery-Religions which changed the religious outlook of the Western world, and which are operative in European civilization and in the Christian Church to this day. Dean Inge, e.g. in his *Christian Mysticism*, p. 354, says that Catholicism owes to the Mysteries " the notions of secrecy, of symbolism, of mystical brotherhood, of sacramental grace, and, above all, of the three stages in the spiritual life : ascetic purification, illumination, and ἐποπτεία as the crown." These Mysteries covered an enormous range, and manifested a great diversity in character and outlook, from Orphism to Gnosticism, from the orgies of the Cabiri to the fervours of the Hermetic contemplative. Some of them, e.g. the Eleusinia, were Greek, but the majority were of Oriental provenance and all were infected by the spirit of the Orient. The most important were the Greek Eleusinia, the cults of the Cappadocian Mên, the Phrygian Sabazios and the Great Mother, the Egyptian Isis and Serapis, and the Samothracian Cabiri, the *Dea Syria* and her satellites, the Persian Mithra. For over eleven centuries Eleusis supported the hope of man till destroyed by the fanatic monks in the train of Alaric in 396. The Orphic gospel was heard in the Mediterranean for at least twelve centuries. For eight centuries Queen Isis and the Lord Serapis swayed their myriads of devotees in the Greek world, and for five centuries in the Roman. The Great Mother was passionately revered for six centuries in Italy. For over half a millennium the approach to religion for thoughtful minds was by the *Gnostic* path. Such facts—since no religion persists by its falsehood, but by its truth—entitle the ancient Mysteries to due consideration. As an important background to early Christianity and as the chief medium of sacramentarianism to the West they cannot be neglected ; for to fail to recognize the moral and spiritual values of Hellenistic-Oriental paganism is to misunderstand the early Christian centuries and to do injustice to the victory of Christianity. Moreover, much from the Mysteries has persisted in various modern phases of thought and practice.

As we attempt to re-live the experiences or to recapture the mentality of the past, to break upon the inexorable silences of perished centuries, to give heed to those who laboriously devoted themselves to the everlasting human problem, and to understand the old emphases which have shifted, our attitude must be that of sympathy as also of appreciation of every effort made by the human spirit toward reality and toward the attainment of—

> " that blessed mood,
> In which the burthen of the Mystery,
> In which the heavy and the weary weight
> Of all this unintelligible world
> Is lightened."

Every endeavour to secure " news from the inner court of things " and to bring man into touch with the Eternal is of worth in our human story. Without undue generosity we may have patience with men who set out for a goal which they never reached, realizing that the failures of former generations are as interesting, and often more instructive, than their successes.

In estimating the Mysteries we must not judge them, any more than any other religions, by their lowest forms, but, as Cicero recognized, we must take the example from the highest and judge them rather by their ideals. It is an historic injustice to compare the Bacchi of one religion with the thyrsus-bearers of another. If there is only one River of Truth, into which tributaries from all parts flow, as asserted by the most readable of the Christian Fathers, Clement of Alexandria, who lived in the heyday of the

Mysteries, we need not disdain the tributaries.   The pagan misunderstandings of primitive Christianity are a warning to the student of religious history.   Celsus in all good faith viewed his equally honest opponent's religion as gross superstition.   The holiest rite—Agape—of the first believers was travestied as the occasion of immoralities and 'Thyestean banquets.'   The absence of image, sacrifice, and temple seemed to lead to the obvious conclusion that Christians were 'Atheists.'

This disability of the adherent of one religion to understand the adherent of another religion is an unlovely fact in the history of religions and by no means antiquated to-day. Men are separated in their religious sympathies by culture, tradition, era, individual and group experiences.   The saintly John Wesley saw in Catherine of Genoa "a fool of a saint."   A late Dean of Westminster, Dr. Farrar, spoke disparagingly of one, whose death-scene in the interests of moral integrity has appealed to the imagination of twenty-three centuries, as "the ugly Greek."   A cultured Greek like Herodotus was astonished at the aniconic worship of Persia, and the Romans were bewildered to find no image in the temple of Jerusalem.

In the study of the Mysteries we shall see truth and error side by side, the spirituality of the true *epoptes* and the magic sacramentarianism of the literalist, the inability to distinguish between the cult act and the religious experience. We shall detect the conjunction of faith and credulity, the degeneration of mysticism into occultism, the revivalist phenomena and mass-psychology, and those pathological conditions of illusion, suggestion, and hypnotic hallucination and emotional excitations which too easily issue in moral aberrations.   We shall meet the extravagances and extremes which are the concomitants of every great movement, and which in healthy creative periods are kept in restraint, but waiting to force their way to the front with any weakening of the originating conception or native power.

On the other hand, the Mysteries stood for much of permanent value.   Above all they emphasized the perfect

humanity and passion of the Deity, and suggested a fellowship of suffering as the pre-condition to participation in the
divine victory.   This *Sympathia* was more akin to the
mediaeval desire to share the sufferings of the Saviour in
extreme forms, as in the marks of the Cross or the wounds
of Christ.   They offered a gospel of salvation by means of
union with Saviour-Gods, and of a Hereafter of blessedness
for initiates.   As trans-social organizations they furthered
personal religion.   In their general trend they made for
monotheism.   In their emotional triumphs they satisfied
the need of exaltation and escape.   By their cosmic outlook
they made men comfortable in an uncomfortable Universe.
Never was there an age which heard so distinctly and
responded so willingly to the call of the *Cosmos* to its
inhabitants.   The unity of all Life, the mysterious harmony
of the least and nearest with the greatest and most remote,
the conviction that the life of the Universe pulsated in all its
parts, were as familiar to that ancient cosmic consciousness
as to modern biology and psychology.   By the articulation
of their symbolism they adumbrated that indefinable aspect
of man's religion of which Otto has so excellently taken
account in his *Das Heilige,* as they also witnessed, if feebly,
with Bonaventura: " If you would know how these things
come to pass, ask it of desire, not intellect ; of the ardours
of prayer, not of the teaching of the schools."

The Mysteries can no more be studied in isolation than
can early Christianity.   Hence a study of the Mysteries
demanded a prolonged study of their background of ancient
magic and sorcery in all their varieties, theosophy, theurgy
and occultism, daemonology, astrology, solar monotheism
and Element-Mysticism ; also of their kindred philosophies,
Stoicism, Neo-Pythagoreanism, and Neo-Platonism.   The
reading, therefore, of e.g. Sextus Empiricus, Plotinus, the
Commentaries of Proclus, the magic papyri, the *Astronomica*
of Manilius, is directly relevant to an understanding of the
world of the Mysteries.

Quotations from ancient sources are enclosed in single
quotation marks ; those from modern authorities in the

usual double marks. Translations from both are, unless otherwise specified, by the writer.

A Selected Bibliography has been added, restricted to accessible works, which, it is hoped, will enhance the value of the book to students. The chief ancient sources are also given.

To my colleague Principal G. W. Thatcher, of Camden College, Sydney, and to Professor Leslie H. Allen, of Royal Military College, Duntroon, thanks are due for having read the manuscript and given me the advantage of useful criticisms and suggestions. I am especially indebted to Professor Vittorio Macchioro, of the Royal University and National Museum of Naples, for the care with which he read the manuscript, and for the great privilege which he afforded me of examining important archaeological remains of the Mystery-Religions under his expert guidance. As on a former occasion I would once more record my gratitude to Professor H. A. A. Kennedy, New College, Edinburgh, for valuable suggestions in revision of the manuscript. It is fair to add that in such a wide and controversial field the writer alone is responsible for the views expressed.

As a Britisher I would take this occasion of expressing my grateful appreciation of American hospitality extended unstintingly during visits to Western Theological Seminary, Pittsburg, Southern Baptist Seminary, Louisville, the Presbyterian Seminary of Kentucky, the Union Theological Seminary, New York, and Chicago University, where the material of the volume was delivered, wholly or partially in lecture form since November 1920. I would also make grateful mention of a memorable week as guest of Manitoba College, Winnipeg, Canada, in October 1923, and of a visit to the University of Toronto.

S. A.

EDINBURGH,
September 18, 1924

CONTENTS

CHAPTER II

WHAT IS A MYSTERY-RELIGION ?

CHAPTER III

THE THREE STAGES OF A MYSTERY

CHAPTER IV

THE APPEAL OF THE MYSTERY-RELIGIONS

CHAPTER V

THE APPEAL OF THE MYSTERY-RELIGIONS

CHAPTER VI

THE DEFECTS OF THE MYSTERIES AND THEIR ULTIMATE FAILURE

CHAPTER VII

THE VICTORY OF CHRISTIANITY

THE
MYSTERY-RELIGIONS

CHAPTER I

ORIENTATION : THE HISTORICAL CRISES OF THE GRAECO-
ROMAN WORLD IN THEIR BEARING UPON THE MYSTERY
RELIGIONS AND CHRISTIANITY

'Magnus ab integro saeclorum nascitur ordo.'—VIRGIL.

IN order to a proper understanding of the strange
phenomenon presented by the rapid spread of the Eastern
Mystery-cults in the Graeco-Roman world, the conflict of
Christianity with, and ultimate triumph over, its competitors,
the gradual and finally almost complete subjugation of the
West to Oriental ways and thoughts and modes of worship,
we must take into account the political, social, and religious
history of the Mediterranean world during the period of
approximately seven centuries, from the invasion of the
East by Alexander the Great in 334 B.C. until the foundation
of Constantinople by the first Christian emperor in A.D. 327.
We must also review the means by which the new order
inaugurated by Alexander arose out of the old order which
had dominated the peoples of the Eastern Mediterranean.

This period is of enthralling interest to the student of
the history of religion. In these centuries the vital forces
of old and ripe civilizations were brought to a focus. New
ideas were implanted in human society which have been
productive of much good—and evil—for all subsequent
history. If these centuries cannot boast of anything so
sublime as Hebrew prophecy or anything so perfectly

I

finished and perennially beautiful as the classics of the Periclean age, they present, in their chequered story, themes that rival in human interest those of the Christianizing of Western Europe, the rise of the Holy Roman Empire, the Crusades, the Renaissance, the discoveries of the fifteenth and sixteenth centuries, the Reformation and Counter-Reformation, and modern social reconstruction. During the ages stretching between the teaching of Aristotle and the baptism of Constantine mankind witnessed the fall of the *polis*—that most wonderful and fruitful of the political experiments of ancient history [1]; the meteor-like appearance of Alexander the Great ; the rapprochement between East and West such as has never since been achieved ; the growth and influence of the Jewish Diaspora, the chief path-finder for Christianity ; the political supremacy of the West over the East for the first time and the establishment of the first western empire ; the dissemination of Oriental mysticism and with it a world-renouncing ethic in the West ; the prevalence for half a millennium of the *Gnosis* conception of religion which left its indelible mark on Christian theology ; the beginning and rapid spread of those voluntary associations for religious purposes and mutual support which have done so much to shape human society ; the rise of the Roman Empire, the culminating factor in the consummation of ' the fulness of the time.'

This period witnessed also the rise of a problem very similar to that which the Great War has accentuated for us—that of internationalism and nationalism. All the previous empires of the Orient had been based upon the principle of internationalism : some of them, e.g. the Assyrian, attempted to crush nationalism, others, e.g. the Persian, adopted a liberal policy toward subject nationalities. This liberal policy Alexander the Great expanded and transmitted to Rome. The ancient solution of the problem was instructive. Empire and Church and Oriental religions alike aimed at internationalism and achieved it to a degree unknown

[1] Cf. Kaerst, *Gesch. des hellenist. Zeitalters*, I, p. 408.

hitherto or since, so that internationalism prevailed in the world for about two millennia. It did not endure. During the Middle Ages racial, linguistic, and climatic factors reasserted the national or enchoric principle.

The economic life of the West was also profoundly affected by the introduction of the industrial and commercial spirit of the Asiatics, who, whether Syrians, Egyptians, Phoenicians, Carthaginians, or Jews, were adepts in barter and trade of all kinds. This spirit, once introduced, found a congenial soil in the practical West, which has in this respect outstripped its teachers (except perhaps the Jews) and carried competitive commerce to such an extent that Western society now seems to Oriental eyes to rest on a material civilization. The Western political life was also in this period orientalized by the spread of the Eastern monarchical principle of government as against native Western democracy, and the consequent rise of a court-life which played a leading part in history for fifteen centuries in the West and has to this day maintained a shadow of its influence.

In the third century B.C. Greek civilization was seriously threatened by the incursions of the Northern Keltic barbarians into the Hellenic peninsula and Asia Minor. Had they succeeded, Greek culture would have disappeared and thus the Roman masters of the world would have missed the refining influence of Greece.[1] Early in the third century A.D. the East again threw down the political challenge to the West in the rise of the Sassanid dynasty of Persia. Near the end of our period we read of the first appearance of the Franks on the Rhine, and the first invasions of Spain and Africa by these peoples who were destined to carry Roman civilization and Latin Christianity northward. Many other events of world importance might be mentioned from this period of human history. Never did mankind pass through more decisive crises, or drink a fuller cup, or witness greater social upheavals than during these centuries.

[1] Mahaffy, *Progress of Hellenism in Alexander's Empire*, pp. 43–6.

Throughout this long period, but particularly in the first Christian centuries, religious interests occupied the dominant place in the lives of the men and women who made the history of the Graeco-Roman world, with the result that for the ensuing thousand years, down to about A.D. 1300, " the basis of human organization is the religious motive, and human society is ecclesiastical in its primary inspiration." [1] Men were in quest of a religion of redemption with an adequate theology and a satisfying and stimulating worship. On this point students of the Graeco-Roman world are in agreement. Thus Legge [2] affirms of the six centuries from Alexander to Constantine : " There has probably been no time in the history of mankind when all classes were more given up to thoughts of religion, or when they strained more fervently after high ethical ideals." Aust,[3] speaking of the imperial age, says : " The hero is less honoured than the saint ; the religious movement puts its seal upon the century; " while Dill asserts of the same era : " The world was in the throes of a religious revolution, and eagerly in quest of some fresh vision of the Divine, from whatever quarter it might dawn." [4]

That such statements are correct will appear from even a superficial acquaintance with the literature and thought of the Hellenistic and Roman age. In the ever-increasing asceticism and other-worldliness ; the sustained efforts made to surmount Dualism; the rapid spread of Mysteries which taught men to find symbols of the spiritual in the material ; the *theocrasia* which sought satisfaction for spiritual longings from whatever quarter ; the urgent call for salvation and appeals for redemption-religions ; the active religious missionary spirit and street-preaching ; the

[1] E. Barker in *Legacy of Rome*, p. 77.
[2] *Forerunners and Rivals of Christianity*, I, p. xlix.
[3] *Die Religion der Römer*, p. 107.
[4] *Roman Society from Nero to Marcus Aurelius*, p. 82. Cf. also Lake, *Stewardship of Faith*, p. 75 f. ;   Case, *Evolution of Early Christianity*, p. 31, " Christianity arose in a very religious world " ; Hatch, *The Influence of Greek Ideas and Usages*, p. 292 ; Deissmann, *Licht*, p. 242, " Ein tiefer religiöser Zug durch diese ganze Welt hindurchging."

burdensome sense of sin and failure ; the earnest attempts
to solve the enigmas of life and penetrate the mystery of the
grave : in these and other features familiar to the student
of the Graeco-Roman period are revealed the aspirations
of this ancient world for a pragmatic view of God and the
world upon which, in the phrase of Cicero, men might
'live with joy and die with a better hope.' The themes
which most engaged the minds of men were the nature and
unity of the divine, the origin of evil, the relation of Fate
and Fortune to Providence, the nature of the soul and the
problem of immortality, the possibility of purification from
moral stains, the means of union with God, and spiritual
support for the individual life. Hellenistic philosophy
became less scientific [1] and speculative, addressing itself
directly to the practical business of the moral life until in
Philo and Neo-Platonism it ended in a profound religion of
unio mystica.

From the days of Aristotle onwards numerous treatises
were written on prayer,[2] as, e.g., by Persius, Juvenal, the
author of *Alcibiades II*, Maximus of Tyre. Practically every
moralist of later paganism—Cicero, Seneca, Epictetus,
Lucian, Marcus Aurelius, Porphyry, Plotinus—devoted
attention to this expression of the religious life. Many of
their declarations upon this topic are marked by deep spiritual insight. Some of the language is of supreme beauty
and might be used by Christian hearts. The many en-
deavours made by statesmen, poets, and philosophers, to
bring about a revival of religion indicate that religion
was viewed as the imperative necessity of society.
After the close of the Roman civil wars there was a genuine
outburst of religious feeling and thanksgiving, of which, it
is true, Augustus shrewdly took advantage for political
and dynastic purposes. Even the apotheosis of Hellenistic

---

[1] Cf. Mahaffy, *What have the Greeks done for Modern Civilization ?* pp.
168–71.

[2] Cf. Schmidt, *Veteres philosophi quomodo iudicaverint de precibus*
(Giessen, 1907) ; A. W. Mair, *Prayer,* in Hastings' *E.R.E.* ; C. Ausfeld,
De Graecoram precationibus quaestiones, in Fleckeisen's *Jahrb.* Supp.
XXVIII, '03.

kings and Roman emperors showed that far-sighted rulers recognized in religion the best bond of social cohesion and the best means of promoting loyalty. There is also abundant evidence that the numerous and terrible calamities of the period were generally attributed to neglect of worship for which some religious observance must atone. The history of the Punic wars furnishes a conspicuous instance. During that protracted struggle the populace, discouraged by defeats and terrified by *prodigia*, turned coldly away from their national gods toward new cults.

The outbreak and universal prevalence of Superstition throughout the Graeco-Roman world is another index of its religious interests. As nationalistic religions decayed, individualistic tendencies were given freer play. Men did not cease to believe in the Supernatural or in divine interference in the affairs of the world, but there was a profound change in belief as to the nature of the Supernatural and the means of placating demonic powers. The ritual means offered by the Western states were distrusted : individuals sought means of their own. Hence popular beliefs that had been kept under during the halcyon days of state-religion emerged once more, and methods of approach to deity formerly looked upon as not respectable or even prohibited came into vogue. Superstition was in its first stages the continued belief of the masses in deities toward whom the cultured were agnostic or atheistical. The first marked impetus to the spread of superstition was given by the breaking up of the priestly colleges of Mesopotamia by Alexander and the opening up of Egypt, the land of fascinating mystery, to the West, through Alexandria. From the days of the Second Punic War superstition grew apace, first among the lower classes, but gradually penetrating the higher classes until under the Empire it became universal. In eagerness to lose no liturgic formula or ceremonial secret men looked with admiration toward the East, and thus the way was opened to magic, astrology, demonology, theosophy, and physico-psychical experiments. The greatest

of the emperors, such as Augustus, fell a prey to superstition, while Nero and Domitian lived under ghostly
terrorism. Certain forms of superstition, viewed as politically dangerous, were so popular that no legal enactments
and no police investigations could exterminate them. Star-
readers, necromancers, and purveyors of magical
incantations drove a thriving trade. Governing circles were
thwarted in their attempts to secure a monopoly of illicit
means of forcing the hands of Deity by the tenacity with
which their subjects clung to them. " People could no longer
take a bath, go to the barber, change their clothes, or
manicure their finger-nails without first awaiting the
proper moment." [1]

The rise of *Superstitio* or religiosity as a species of nonconformity against *Religio* was a symptom of the age,
so that in post-Augustan literature the terms were often
(as in Seneca) used synonymously, and *Religio* was given
a bad name, as in Lucretius' famous verse (1,101) :

'tantum religio potuit suadere malorum.'

The literature of the time teems with references to this
religiosity. Cicero [2] contrasts superstition as *timor inanis
deorum* with religion as *deorum cultu pio*, and draws the
distinction between the adjectives 'superstitious' and
'religious' as *alterum vitii nomen alterum laudis*.[3] The
rise of Epicureanism was a protest against current superstition. The chief aim of Epicurus, for which he was
acclaimed a 'Saviour' by his disciples, was to deliver mankind from the terrors of superstition here by affirming the
apathy of the gods, and hereafter by negating its existence.
This passion inspired Lucretius [4] to his majestic *De Rerum
Natura*, in which he characterizes *superstitio* as

'omnia suffundens mortis nigrore.'

[1] Cumont, *Religions orientales*, Eng. tr. p. 165.
[2] *N.D.* I. 47, 117.
[3] *Ib.* II. 28, 72.
[4] Cf. Sellar, *Rom. Poets of the Repub.* (3rd ed.), pp. 295, 309, 364 ff.

To cure the *terrorem animi tenebrasque* he applies the *naturae species ratioque*, while beyond the *flammantia moenia mundi* there are no terrors of hell but only darkness and nothingness. Seneca, as a man of his age and a student of religious pathology, recognized the power and the danger of this *error insanus*, which he endeavoured to exorcise by his Stoic principles. According to Augustine [1] he wrote a book *Contra superstitiones*. Lucian's satiric pen exposed the religious foibles of his day, especially in his *Philopseudes*. The most readable account has been given us by Plutarch in his essay *On Superstition*. He describes superstition as a moral and emotional disorder as compared with Atheism which is an intellectual error.[2] Fear is the motive of superstition. The atheist believes that there are no gods ; the superstitious wishes there were none,[3] while he flees for refuge to the gods whom he fears. The dreadful presence of the Deity allows the superstitious man no respite by land or sea. Slaves may in sleep forget their tyrannous masters, but the superstitious man meets them in terrifying dreams.[4] Even in the exercise of his religion there is no comfort, for at the very altar he is tortured. For guidance he has resort to fortune-tellers and other impostors who relieve him of his cash. He bathes in the sea, sits the live-long day on the bare earth, besmears himself with mud, rolls on the dung-hills, observes sabbaths, prostrates himself in strange attitudes, passes time in silent contemplation before the god, employs absurd addresses and barbarous invocations, and makes religion an expensive affair, like the folk in the comedy who bestrew their beds with gold and silver while sleep is the only thing given gratis by the gods.[5] There is one world common to waking men, while in sleep each wanders into worlds of his own. The *deisidaimon*, on the contrary, when awake fails to enjoy the rational world, and when asleep cannot escape the world of terrors. The power of superstition extends beyond the grave in attaching to death eternal torments—the yawning gates of Hell,

----

[1] *De Civ. Dei*, VI. 10.   [2] 165 C.   [3] 170 F.
          [4] 165 D.   [5] *Ib.* 166.

flaming rivers, the dismal Styx, and ghostly shapes. In physical maladies and family and political misfortunes the conduct of the superstitious contrasts unfavourably with that of the atheist. The former is unmanned by what he calls the 'plagues of the god,' or 'the attacks of the demon ': he denounces himself as hateful to gods and demons, and clad in miserable rags he makes public confession of his sins and negligencies. Atheism is not responsible for superstition, though the latter has conduced to the former. Plutarch concludes :

' No disease is so full of variations, so changeable in symptoms, so made up out of ideas opposed to, nay, rather, at war with one another, as is the disease called Superstition. We must therefore fly from it, but in a safe way and to our own good—not like those who, running away from the attack of highwaymen, or wild beasts, or a fire, have entangled themselves in mazes leading to pitfalls and precipices. For thus some people, when running away from Superstition, fall headlong into atheism, both rugged and obstinate, and leap over that which lies between the two, namely, true Religion.'

In the complementary essay *On Isis and Osiris* [1] Plutarch speaks of those who can transmute myths into symbols of religious truth as opposed to those who in their desire to shun the quagmire of Superstition slip unwittingly over the precipice of Atheism.

The religious spirit, even the religiosity of the age, is further marked not only by the beginnings and spread " of those great associations of mankind for religious purposes, henceforth the principal factors of world-history," [2] but by an aggressive religious propaganda such as no other age has surpassed. Each religion in the Roman world became a missionary religion ; to enlarge its prestige and increase its adherents was an obligation and a privilege resting upon the humblest member. The shrewdest Syrian merchant was not satisfied with the exchange of the wares

[1] Cf. Oakesmith, *The Religion of Plutarch*, p. 200.

[2] Legge, I, p. 27.

which produced his profits ; he was equally zealous to exchange his spiritual wares, and did so with considerable
success, as we know from the diffusion of the Syrian cults.
Although there is rhetorical hyperbole in the statement that
the Pharisees compassed sea and land to make one proselyte,
there is ample evidence that the ubiquitous Jew was a
successful missionary.   The rapid and amazing dissemination
of Mithraism throughout the West remains one of the
outstanding phenomena of religious propaganda.〕

Let us consider the antecedents of this religious world
into which Oriental cults rushed like an irresistible tide ;
what were the conditions which influenced and informed the
spirit of this period ; what were the crises through which
the Mediterranean nations passed which drove them loose
from their old moorings ; and in what respects the Greek
and the Roman, the Jew and the Oriental, reacted upon
one another.   We may summarize the decisive historic
moments which opened the way for the Oriental religions
and Christianity thus :

I. Bankruptcy of Greek Religion and the Disintegrating Influence of Greek Philosophy

Greek religion [1] was the expression of a highly gifted and
imaginative people which mirrored their social and
intellectual development.   The main features of the old
Homeric faith were pantheistic polytheism and anthropomorphism which made religion rich in humanized personalities.   The Olympian gods were clearly defined
personalities, each with his assigned function and with his
peculiar iconic representation.   They were merely men
of a larger growth who loved and quarrelled and lived a life
of careless ease.   Even Zeus was only a *primus inter pares*,
unable to trench upon the province of associate or satellite
deities, or to deflect the fixed course of Fate.   A Greek
pantheon was constituted in order to admit a dozen gods of
different conquering races who entered Greece from the

[1] Cf. Angus, *Greek Religion* in *Standard Bib. Dict.* (2nd ed.), '25.

North. The worship of these deities was as joyous and restrained as everything Greek, the characteristically Greek μηδὲν ἀγάν being inscribed upon a temple architrave. The Olympian religion was never conspicuously ethical : the morals of the Greek gods did not keep pace with the developing ethical consciousness of the Hellenes. It was not from their cults, but from their philosophy that moral ideals came to the Greeks. Greek thought in its laborious striving for a synthesis of the Many easily grasped the conception of the unity of the Deity, and the Greeks—the first higher critics—never hesitated to apply relentlessly any truth at whatever cost to their religion or institutions or mental comfort. A fatal blow was thus struck at polytheism. Guided by this intuition that the Divine is one, the Greek mind pursued its way through henotheism and abstract monotheism toward a truer personal monotheism which it never quite attained. Both pillars of the temple of old Hellenic religion—polytheism and anthropomorphism —fell before the assault of criticism. There was a growing sense that religion must be rational and also satisfy the highest moral ideals. The myths became repulsive and were either repudiated as fables or interpreted symbolically by means of that maid of all work, Allegory. It is not Greek religion, except so far as it inspired art, but Greek ethical and mystical philosophy which has left an enduring heritage to mankind. Greek religion succumbed before " man's meddling intellect." In the period of the Enlightenment philosophy was coldly critical toward the popular religion, whilst in the last period Hellenistic philosophy itself assumed the character of a religion or a religio-ethical system, and in Neo-Platonism ended in contemplative mysticism. In the former period art and religion parted company, or, rather, art retained the religious myths as suitable subjects on which to exercise its aesthetic powers.

The national character of Greek religion disappeared.[1]

[1] Cf. G. Murray, " By the time of Plato the traditional religion of the Greek states was, at least among educated Athenians, a bankrupt concern." *Hib. Jour.* Oct. 1910, p. 16.

The Greeks began to abandon their religion, which they believed came from the North, and to look with favourable regard upon religions coming from the East. Hence, particularly from the fourth century B.C. onwards, Oriental cults gained access into Greece, especially into Boeotia, Attica, and the Islands, the entrepots of a busy commerce, and this susceptibility to foreign religious influences increased in the Greek world till Greek minds began to devote themselves to the metaphysics of Christian theology. Greek logic had acted as a solvent on Greek faith. To the Greek ethical sense—

" Two questions arose naturally to the minds of all who thought about the common religion : first, what was the relation of Zeus to the other gods, and how could will and power in them be reconciled with his omnipotence ? And, second, what was the relation of Zeus to that overpowering Fate that seemed at times to control even his will ? " [1]

The former was met by an answer which conduced to monotheism, that Deity is one and that all the gods are but manifestations of the One. To the latter men began to reply that Fate was merely the will of God executed in an intelligent Providence.

While the " conflict of religion and science, which had begun in the fifth century or even earlier, was the prominent fact in the fourth century," [2] in the final stages of Greek religion philosophy and religion attempted a rapprochement. Scepticism from the third century B.C. until the first century A.D. was even stronger than in the previous period, but this was the counterpart to a sturdier faith. Euhemerism might declare that the gods were merely deified men. Epicureanism might benignly grant the existence of gods while affirming their indifference to mortal affairs. The New Academy might affect a complacent superiority to the superstition of the masses. Nevertheless faith persisted

---

[1] Ramsay, *Greek Religion*, Hastings' *D.B.* extra vol. p. 147
[2] *Ib.*

and men looked heavenwards for support in the ills of life. The national Hellenic religion was dead beyond hope, but with it were not buried the faith and the hope of Greece. Its failure made place for more satisfying cults. This failure was inevitable from the rise of European philosophy among the Greeks of Ionia, whose criticisms were furthered by the eristic methods of the Sophists. Greek religion was doomed in the collapse of the *polis* which had given it its life and form.[1] Recuperative and propagating power there was none. Stereotyped in rich myths, classic verse, and artistic creations, it could ill adapt itself to the demands of a perplexing age. And Greek religion had one serious congenital defect—it appealed only to one side of man's nature, the aesthetic. A religion of Beauty and Joy, it offered no message to men in the perplexities and sorrows of life ; it was almost dumb as to a hope beyond death. Its most typical god was the bright, youthful, and many-talented Apollo. But the dark things of human life and destiny cannot be for ever kept in the background, and this was especially the case when the corporate ideal of the city-state was displaced by that of a sensitive individual life. Besides philosophy there were two other influences which made mighty impacts on Greek religion, particularly in the Graeco-Roman period succeeding the Classic age—Oriental mysticism and Chthonic conceptions. For a thousand years B.C. Greek religion was not wholly lacking in the mystic strain. Indeed, throughout the whole history of Greek thought there ran two concurrent and often conflicting tendencies, the ' scientific ' and the ' mystical,'[2] the Olympian and the Dionysian, the philosophical and the intuitional. That the division cannot be made absolute will be obvious to readers of Prof. Macchioro's *Eraclito*.[3] Dionysus with his mysticism, doctrine of incarnation, divine passion, and sacramental grace, had found

---

[1] Rohde, *Rel. der Griechen*, p. 28 (*Kl. Schr.* II, p. 338).

[2] Cf. Cornford, *From Religion to Philosophy*, pp. viii, 110 ff. ; Harrison, *Proleg.* p. 474.

[3] *Eraclito : Nuovi Studi sull' Orfismo* (Bari, '22).

entry into the Greek peninsula about the tenth century B.C.[1]
Mysticism made its next powerful attack upon Greece in the
Orphic movement [2] of the seventh and sixth centuries,
from the sacerdotalism and vagueness of which—fortunately
for Europe—the intellect of Ionia and Athens delivered
Greece. But from the fourth century B.C. the Greek
spirit gave way with increasing docility to the mystic and
psychic cults of the East. Greek philosophy, notably
Platonism, Stoicism, Neo-Pythagoreanism, and Neo-
Platonism, attempting the task in which Greek religion had
failed, became in its last expression—Neo-Platonism—a
religion of the 'spirit in Love'[3]—which has appealed to the
noblest minds through the ages and which through Augustine
found entry into Christianity which it has influenced to this
day. In this mystic religion of Redemption "the ancient
Greek religion sank. It was extinguished without much
struggle, like an exhausted light as a new dawn broke upon
it in power from the East."[4]

Still more amazing among the least ghost-ridden of ancient
peoples was the resurgence—from aboriginal strata or from
whatever quarter—of chthonic notions about Earth- or
Underworld-Powers. These views precipitated the mind
toward the Mystery-Religions, which, originally nature
cults, had conserved elements of chthonic and telluric ritual
and which also were professedly eschatological religions.

Such was the religious experience of the Greek people, the
first of Mediterranean peoples to experience the fascination
of a mystic religion of Redemption, who first essayed the
adaptation of the Oriental spirit to the West which was
completed in the triumph of Christianity, and who were to
play such a part in giving expression to that great complex
of Hellenistic-Oriental theology and to Christian thought.
They went forth to hellenize East and West after they had
witnessed the wreck of their city-state, after they had

[1] Farnell, *Cults*, V, p. 85 ff.
[2] Gruppe, *Mythologie*, II, p. 1016 ff.
[3] *Enn.* VI. 7, 35.
[4] Rohde, p. 29 (*Kl. Schr.* II, p. 339).

themselves become conscious of spiritual needs which could be satisfied only by religions of a more emotional and individual character. In their last genuinely Greek philosopher they furnished a tutor to Philip's son : for their talents Alexander opened a boundless vista, and they supplied a *lingua franca* for the widely-scattered cult-brotherhoods of the Mystery-Religions and the house-churches of early Christianity.

II. ALEXANDER THE GREAT

The appearance of Alexander forms a turning-point in the history of the race with which may not be compared even the rise of the Roman empire, the coronation of Charles the Great at Rome in 800, or the Renaissance, or the Reformation. Alexander made all things new : the results of his work have affected all the religious history of the Mediterranean world and the civilizations descended therefrom.

Alexander's greatness does not merely rest on his marvellous military exploits—though in this field he has had no equal—nor in his arresting the encroachments of Eastern despotism upon Western liberties, nor on his propagation of Greek culture (which has proved an inestimable boon to the progress of mankind), nor on his having antiquated previous political systems of East and West. Alexander did all this and much more. Although the words of *Daniel* XI. 4 were literally fulfilled, little of the work of this ' mighty king ' has been undone. He did much to facilitate and inspire the exploits of the Romans, whose empire was the consummation of his work.

" As a pioneer of Hellenic cultivation he became in the end the pioneer of Christianity. He paved the way for the intellectual empire of the Greek and for the political empire of the Roman. And it was the extent of that empire, intellectual and political, which has marked the lasting extent of the religion of Christ." [1]

[1] E. A. Freeman, *Hist. Essays*, 2nd series, Lond. 1880, p. 225.

Wherein did his work affect vitally the religious life of the Hellenistic world and open the way for the adoption by the West of Oriental mystery-cults and finally for Christianity ?

(a) *Cosmopolitanism and the unity of the human race.*— Because of Alexander's conquests and wise statesmanship it was easier for the Mystery-Religions, Stoicism, and Paul to declare ' he made of one every race of men.' Alexander translated into a reality what Greek philosophy had fitfully advocated. He first broke down national barriers and set the nations free for international relationships. Well might the author [1] of *The Fortune of Alexander* say :

" Considering himself appointed by God as a universal ruler and reconciler . . . he brought together everything from every quarter. He mixed as in a loving-cup men's lives and their customs and their marriages and modes of life. He commanded all to regard the world as their fatherland, the good as their kith, and the wicked as aliens ; . . . for the Hellenic spirit was manifested only in virtue and the barbarian only in vice."

Alexander was the inaugurator of that comprehensive cosmopolitanism which reached its apogee in the Roman Empire. Though favouring Greek culture, his larger aim was to accomplish " the marriage of East and West," as was symbolized in striking fashion by the espousals of the fête at Susa. There was in a true sense to Alexander neither barbarian nor Scythian, Greek nor Jew. He was the first of ancient conquerors by whom the conquered were conceded any rights, and in this humane outlook he surpassed his Persian predecessors and the Roman conquerors of a later age. Neither Greek nor Macedonian was immune from the severest punishment if found guilty of oppression. The backbone of his army was the Macedonians, but multitudes of Greek mercenaries and adventurers thronged into his ranks, which were open also to Asiatic recruits. His army was thus an image of his empire in its cosmopolitan character.

[1] Pseudo-Plutarch, I 6 (329, C.D.).

" The generation which had seen Alexander face to face was hardly in its grave before the Marriage of Europe and Asia had become a very real and pregnant fact." [1]

The exclusivism and particularism of the ancient world were broken up : in the new situation created by Alexander each race was challenged to contribute of its peculiar genius for the good of all.   Henceforth East and West continue to approximate in their moral and spiritual progress until they converge in the Christian era.   This interaction of East and West, which has never ceased since Alexander's day, was destined to be fruitful for good to all subsequent ages in enlarging life.   Hebrew revelation, and Greek thought, and Oriental mysticism could never again be isolated.   From this time date the diasporae of all the Eastern peoples [2]—Jews, Syrians, Persians, Egyptians— which became so active in proselytizing propaganda in the Roman Empire.

In speaking of this cosmopolitanism it is impossible strictly to separate cause and effect.   It may be said to have been promoted by Alexander's deliberate policy of intermixing diverse populations ; his studied fair treatment of all peoples under his sovereignty ; the commercial activity [3] which was stimulated by opening up new fields of enterprise and by putting millions of hoarded Persian bullion into circulation ; by religious tolerance ; and in a conspicuous manner by providing the first universal tongue for the whole civilized world in the Greek *Koiné*.

(b) *The Koiné.*—The spread of the *Koiné* or common Greek tongue deserves special mention as a potent factor in the religious propaganda of the following centuries.   Before Alexander's day Athens had chiselled for herself her dialect into that classic perfection which is the wonder of students, but Greece never had a uniform national language.   Each separate city-state had its own patois, which in most cases

[1] Legge, *Ip.* 8.
[2] Cf. Lake, *Earlier Epp. of St. Paul*, p. 41 f.
[3] Cf. for the new economic situation, Wilcken, *Alex. d Grosse u. d. hellenist, Wirtschaft* in Schmoller's *Jahrbuch*, XLV, p. 349 ff.

was as distinct from that of its neighbour a couple of leagues distant as are Spanish and Italian. The term ' Hellas ' never became a national or linguistic unity, the chief bond of union being a more or less catholic religion. While there was no uniform language in which Greek could converse with Greek it was impossible for Greece to exercise her intellectual hegemony. And if a man must learn a dozen Greek patois and half a dozen Oriental tongues before he could travel and exchange ideas with men of other races, he would prefer to remain at home. That Aramaic which had for centuries served as the diplomatic [1] language between the powers of the Nile and those of the Euphrates and Tigris [2] was no longer adequate,[3] and the perfect precision of Attic Greek was as impossible for the ordinary man as it seems now to a schoolboy in his first year. The other Greek dialects failed through poverty of vocabulary or rudeness of expression.

By stress of circumstances—the collapse of the *polis* and with it the end of Greek jealousies and exclusivism, the indifference to patriotic interests engendered by individualism, the demand for Greek mercenaries in the armies of the East, but above all through the adoption of Greek culture and language by the Macedonians under Philip and Alexander, there arose out of the babel of Greek dialects and amid competition with Asiatic tongues a Greek language [4] intelligible to every Greek and easy of acquirement by foreigners. It is important to realize what a stimulus to

---

[1] Cf. *Aramaic Papyri discovered at Assuan*, ed. Sayce and others (Lond. '06) ; E. Sachau, *Drei aramäische Papyri aus Elephantine* (in *Abh. d. Kgl. Preuss. Akad. d. Wiss.*) (Berlin, '07) ; W. Staerk, *Aram. Urkunden* in *Kleine Texte*, 22, 23, 32 (Bonn, '07–8).

[2] Cf. Schwyzer, *Die Weltsprachen des Altertums* (Ber. 1902).

[3] And as official and business language of the Arsacid Kingdom, cf. 1st cent. B.C. documents (2 Greek and 1 Aràmaic) in E. H. Minns, *Parchments of the Parthian Period from Avroman* (in *J.H.S.* XXXV, pp. 22–65).

[4] Cf. A. Thumb, *Die griech. Sprache im Zeital. d. Hellenismus*, p. 238 ; A. Deissmann, *Hellenistisches Griechisch* in *R.E.*, 3rd ed. VII, p. 627 ff. ; A. T. Robertson, *Grammar of the Greek N. T.* ch. III ; P. Kretschmer, *Die Entstehung der Koine* in *Sitzb. der kais. Akad. d. Wiss., Wiener Studien*, vol. 143, 1900, X Ab.

intellectual advancement [1] and what an excellent medium
for the missionary activity of the subsequent centuries the
Koiné proved, in which men could exchange ideas from
Mooltan to Syracuse and from Macedonia to the cataracts
of the Nile. It became the ordinary language of the liturgy
and ritual of those cult-brotherhoods which promoted the
equality of mankind. And this Greek *lingua franca* " was
a better medium for the transmission of metaphysical theories
than the founder of any world-religion has ever had at his
disposal before or since." [1]

(c) *Theocrasia*, or religious Syncretism,[2] on a stupendous
scale was an immediate outcome of Alexander's intermingling
of races, and for the next seven centuries proved a potent
factor in the religious history of the Graeco-Roman world,
reaching its apogee in the III and IV centuries A.D. Every
Mystery-Religion was syncretistic. Before the time of
Alexander there are instances of the equating of their
respective gods by different peoples, but from his day
Theocrasia both became a universal practice and gained
increasing momentum. Religious syncretism was abetted
by the almost complete absence of intolerance, by the
universal demand for Saviour-gods, by the medium of a
common tongue, and by that mixture of races such as could
be found to-day only in the United States. Alexander's
general policy of wedding East and West and of treating
Persians, Greeks, and Macedonians on an equality [4] conduced
to equality of deities. He set the example in his foundation
of Alexandria and pointed the three races in the same direction by establishing a temple of Isis alongside a temple to
Hellenic deities.[5] In the same capital a Ptolemy inaugurated
on his successful career the syncretistic Serapis,[6] who was

[1] Cf. Butcher, *Aspects of Greek Genius*, p. 43.
[2] Legge, I, p. 9.
[3] Cf. *Synkretismus in Altertum*, in *R.G.G.* V. 1043 ff.
[4] Mahaffy remarks " the studied equality of the three races " on the
Sidonian sarcophagus (*Survey*, p. 237).
[5] Arrian, III. 1.
[6] Dieterich regards the creation of Serapis as the greatest event in
syncretism, *Kl. Schriften*, p. 159.

identified with Osiris-Apis, Zeus, Helios, Mithra, and Aesculapius.

This syncretistic tendency increased in intensity under the Roman Empire. It prepared the way for the long sway of Oriental cults over the West and for the success of Christianity itself. Alexander's empire suggested as its counterpart a world-religion, which the Roman Empire rendered imperative. Religious syncretism was carried to such an extent as to render it hazardous or impossible to define the differing features of any one of the numerous faiths competing for adherents in the ancient world.

The Persian Mithra-cult was at least partially egyptianized [1]; the Egyptian Isiac cult largely hellenized.[2] Stoicism exerted an immense modifying influence upon Gnosticism.[3] The Hermetic literature is such a blend that scholars are not agreed as to the relative proportion of Egyptian, Babylonian, Stoic, Platonic, Neo-Pythagorean, and even Christian ingredients. We often cannot tell from sepulchral inscriptions to which cult the deceased belonged ; the language would sometimes point equally to membership in the Christian Church or in a mystery-cult. One need merely cite as an example the famous Abercius inscription.

(d) The *apotheosis* of Alexander deserves mention because of its far-reaching consequences for the next 2000 years both politically and religiously in introducing an entirely new conception of the Divine into the European world.[4]

Deification during Alexander's lifetime has been disputed, but without reason. Alexander was far too astute a statesman to forgo the advantages offered by religious uniformity and loyalty to his person based on religious authority. He was too anxious to cement the diverse parts of his world-empire to neglect a device of his predecessors in Persia and Egypt. As a consequence of Alexander's adoption of this Oriental custom the apotheosis of kings and emperors

---

[1] Cf. Dieterich, *Mithrasliturgie*, 3rd ed. pp. 75, 81.
[2] Cf. Scott-Moncrieff, *J.H.S.* XXIX, pp. 79–90.
[3] Dieterich, *Abraxas*, p. 83 ff.
[4] Legge, I, p. 17.

became familiar to the West through the Diadochi [1] and the Romans. With this Oriental obsequiousness came the idea of the divine rights of kings which engaged pagan theologians for seven centuries and Christian theologians for another thousand years ; the alliance of throne and altar through which Christianity was destined to suffer in prestige ; the adoption of religious uniformity as an instrument for political unity—a device of government adopted by Antiochus Epiphanes, dear to the Roman and the early Christian emperors, to some of the occupants of the throne of the Holy Roman Empire, to Elizabeth and the Stuarts of England, and to the Valois and Navarre dynasties of France.

Alexander's assertion of his divinity, advantageous as a political device, proved disastrous to morality and religion. The wearers of these divine honours often vied with the Olympian gods in placing themselves above the recognized laws of morality. Their assumption of divine dignity accentuated their arrogance and cruelty, and contributed to the conversion of the principate of Augustus into the absolute despotism of Diocletian. This practice of deification was a retrograde step in the conception of the Divine and issued in the sceptical belief of Euhemerus that the gods were but deified men, a view which had a special fascination for educated Romans. It should be remembered, however, that such deification did not appear as strange to the ancients as it appears to us, nor would it have gained much recognition had it not expressed in a concrete form the " Man-God " idea which had emerged in some form in every religion of the period, an idea which we find, e.g., in the Osiris legend of Egypt and the Mithra legend of Persia. Apotheosis also found a point of vital contact with the prevalent demand for intermediaries—priests, hypostases like the Logos or Sophia, demons, *heroes*—between God and man.

(e) If Alexander in claiming divine honours took a step

[1] On apotheosis of Hellenistic kings *v.* Ferguson, *Hellenistic Athens*, p. 108 f.

which was fraught with more evil than good, in another
direction his appearance promoted a worthier conception
of the Divine by furthering monotheism, toward which
Greek philosophy had been tending. His commanding
personality aided by the universal religious syncretism
accelerated a unitary conception of God. One obstacle to
monotheism was removed by the political blow given by
Alexander to the enchoric or parochial conception of Deity.
The relation between kingship and divinity was of the closest
order in antiquity, the king or superman being the visible
incarnation of deity. The ancients instinctively sought
visibility in their religion, a ' God manifest,' and in Alexander
they beheld one who bestrode " the narrow world like a
Colossus," unimpeded by the tutelage of national gods and
overthrowing systems immemorially under their patronage.
Monarchy visible in state made the monarchic principle
more accessible to theology. If the world was united under
one ruler, why should men not believe in the rule of one
God ? This would be in accordance with Aristotle's statement that the form of religion in a state is fashioned after
the form of the government.

III. Appearance of the Jews in World-History

The appearance of the Jews on the horizon of universal
world-history has had vast consequences for the history of
religion in antiquity and to-day. This obstinate people,
with a thirst for righteousness and a passion for monotheism,
stepped out of its long seclusion to deliver its perennial
message and to realize its own prophetic ideals. In the
Greek period commenced its long missionary career, which
did not abate for half a millennium, until late in the second
Christian century, as a consequence of the wars of extermination under Hadrian and the success of Christianity.[1]
Previous to the Graeco-Roman period, Israel had come in
contact successively with Egypt, Syria, Assyria, Babylonia,
and Persia, but by none of these except the last was she much

[1] Harnack, *Hist. of Dogma*, Eng. tr. I, p 108.

influenced in her faith. Her attitude toward Persia was more docile than to the other suzerain powers. Of the two centuries (539–333 B.C.) under Persian domination, the first (539–444) was marked by attempts to recolonize Judaea, restore the Temple worship, and purge the nation of foreign accretions, and so create a second centre of Jewish thought beside that of Babylon where the best of the nation remained. During the next century (444–333) " Judaism " developed and Israel became a people ' fenced in by the Law.' Alongside the spirituality of the exilic or post-exilic prophets appeared the ritualism, legalism, and traditionalism, so conspicuous in later periods. There is, however, another side to what appears hard in Judaism. The Law was necessary to conserve the national consciousness and coherence of Israel in face of the disintegrating tendencies of Hellenism and the centrifugal forces menacing inner unity, chiefly the rise of antagonistic parties and a growing cleavage between Palestinian and Hellenistic Judaism.

In 333 B.C. the Jews passed under vassalage to Alexander ; from his death in 323 they were subjects of the Lagids of Egypt until Antiochus the Great annexed Palestine, under whose suzerainty they remained until 167 B.C. Then, taking advantage of the difficulties of Syria, they asserted their independence, 167–63 B.C., until Pompey interfered in the affairs of Palestine. With the rise of the Arsacid kingdom of Parthia by secession from Syria in 249 B.C. the Eastern Jews came under Asiatic rather than Greek influence, and with the rise of the Sassanid power and the rehabilitation of Persia in A.D. 226 the Eastern Dispersion was left to pursue its own course.

Alexander's conquests were epoch-making for the Jews. He realized the wisdom of conciliating this stubborn people who, perhaps, had earned his gratitude by acting as spies and guides in his campaigns.[1] His example of liberal treatment, followed generally by the Lagids and the Seleucids and lastly by the Romans, increased the momentum of the Diaspora. There had been deportations of the Jews by

[1] Mahaffy, *Empire of the Ptolemies*, pp. 85–6.

Assyrians, Babylonians, and Persians from Tiglath-Pileser (middle of VIII c. b.c.) until Artaxerxes Ochus (middle of IV c. b.c.). These dispersions had been due to compulsion and were eastwards. Moreover, Israel had not yet been sufficiently consolidated to resist the action of her new environment, as shown by the absorption of the ten tribes. A new era for the Jewish Diaspora began with the foundation of Alexandria in 331, whither Alexander transported many Jews, bestowing upon them equal municipal rights with Macedonians and Egyptians. This act and its influence upon Greek and Roman statesmen accelerated Jewish migration. Henceforth the Dispersion was mostly westwards and voluntary. Attracted by the favour of rulers, new opportunities for commerce,[1] and facilities of intercommunication, the Jews settled in ever larger numbers among alien populations. Now for the first time they came in contact with the Western spirit and were exposed to all the syncretistic influences of the Hellenistic world. They were neither to remain what they had been before the " marriage of East and West," nor to lose their peculiar character in the new world, but were destined henceforth to prove the main link between East and West, and so a unifying factor in world-history. In their collision with Hellenism they did not succumb, though they were profoundly affected by it and as profoundly left their impress upon it. Protected by the fence of the Law, their ritual, their services of the synagogue, and the Greek Bible, they faced the temptations of the Graeco-Roman world without losing the sense of righteousness which distinguished them among ancient peoples. The loss of their nationhood and political autonomy strengthened the spiritual bonds of cohesion and equipped them to become a leavening power in the alien world in which their future lay. They became a missionary nation to all nations. They promoted the growth of that monotheism which increasingly marks the centuries between Aristotle

---

[1] Friedländer (*Roman Life and Manners*, Eng. tr. III, p. 172) maintains that Jewish emigration was not to an appreciable extent determined by commercial motives.

and Constantine. The Septuagint in the *lingua franca* made pagans familiar with a holy book superior to anything that any other religion could offer. The synagogue was the centre of the life of the Diaspora. In every large town and city pagans were reminded of the presence of a pious people by a house of prayer or by several. ' There are opened on the Sabbaths in every city thousands of places of instruction in which wisdom and self-restraint and courage and justice and the other virtues are taught,' says Philo.[1] Those who thronged the streets to the markets, the law courts, the baths, the theatres, the museums, or the amphitheatre, beheld on fixed days the open doors of a synagogue, and overheard the music of praise and the solemn intonation of prayers. How many of these passers-by entered the house of prayer and were arrested by the message of the LXX and the preacher we may not tell. The missionary enthusiasm of Israel, which she bequeathed to nascent Christianity, the example of a sober people amid the looser morals of paganism, the open door of a house of prayer, the existence of voluntary associations of men and women to cultivate the spiritual life, the promises and the denunciations of the synagogue pulpit, the reading of a holy book in the common tongue, could not fail to produce fruit. We have abundant evidence that the Jews not only remained loyal to their religion but won multitudes of converts and adherents. The *odium humani generis* hurled against the Jew from the beginning of the migrations under Alexander till the time of Hadrian is of importance in the history of Jewish propaganda. There were four main causes of this anti-semitism : (1) The success of the Jews in trade competition. (2) Religious scruples exposed them to the charge of being unsocial and unpatriotic. They could not be present at public banquets because of association with pagan cults ; they could not join with their fellow-citizens on festal occasions for fear of contamination ; they could not evince loyalty by complying with the imperial cult ; they were averse to public games and the exercises of the gymnasium ; the

[1] *De Sept.* 6, M II. 282.

theatre [1] they could not frequent because it drew largely on heathen mythology ; to them the spectacles of the amphitheatre were loathsome. The mart was the only scene of public life which permitted close contact with pagans. (3) The spirit of revolt [2] which characterized the race from the conquest of Palestine by the Seleucids, 205 B.C., until the wars of extermination under Hadrian, A.D. 132. They took advantage of every perplexity in the affairs of the empire, the advantages of which they in no small measure reaped. When Syria was pressed on the east by Parthia and on the west by Rome, they seized the opportunity of asserting their brief independence which in the end threw them into the arms of their most hated suzerain. Their national hate flamed forth against Rome during the turmoil of the wars of the Neronian succession. When Rome was involved in conflict with her inveterate enemy, Parthia, in A.D. 113-114, this insurgent people found occasion to revolt in the East. When Hadrian was occupied with frontier trouble in North Britain, Dacia, North Africa, and the East, Bar Cochba led the last revolt which ended in prodigious bloodshed for both Jews and Romans. (4) The success of Jewish propaganda in non-Jewish homes. In his zeal to influence the greatest possible number, the Jew recognized two degrees among those who were attracted to the synagogue. First, the converts who, by submitting to circumcision and so taking upon themselves the obligations of the Mosaic system, became full members of the Covenant. [3] These proselytes, we may well conceive, were more zealous propagandists than Jews by birth, and were probably the bitterest opponents of the Christian mission. Secondly, the ' Godfearers ' who in a loose way connected themselves with the Jews, attended the services of the synagogue, observed Sabbaths, and in other ways imitated the Jews, but refused

---

[1] That there were exceptions is proved by the Jewish inscription in the theatre of Miletus : τόπος τῶν 'Ειουδέων τῶν καὶ θεοσεβίον (sic), Deissmann, *Licht*, 4th ed. p. 391.

[2] Cf. Hastings, *D.B.* extra vol. 104*b*.

[3] ' Transgressi in morem eorum idem usurpant ' (Tac. *Hist.* V. 5).

to submit to circumcision or to undertake the full obligation of the Mosaic law. These were the first to rush into the Christian Church, which declared that in Christ there was neither Jew nor Greek. Conversions caused just such family and social disturbances as we are familiar with in the early Christian mission. Families were divided. The pagan whose wife or son became attached to Judaism hated this proselytizing people, of whom Tacitus asserts that they inculcate nothing so much as ' to despise the gods, renounce one's country, and hold parents and children and brothers as of no account.' [1] The heathen held the Jew in derision but could not thwart the Jewish mission. Tacitus, while speaking in the strongest terms of reproach of this *genus hominum invisum deis*, witnesses to its increase of converts. Juvenal [2] testifies to the number of those who by looking favourably on Judaism brought upon themselves the derision of their friends, while Seneca says that this cursed race, ' though conquered, imposed laws on its conquerors.' [3] John Hyrcanus forcibly proselytized the Idumaeans and Aristobulus the Itureans. The majority of the women of Damascus were addicted to the Jewish cult. [4] The rapid increase of the Jewish population at Rome between the date of the earliest contact of the Romans and Jews—the embassy of Judas in 161 B.C.—and the first expulsion of the Jews from Rome by the praetor Hispalus in 139 B.C. was partly due to proselytizing which, according to Valerius Maximus, [5] was commenced by those who came in the train of the embassies from Judaea. [6]

The religious destitution of the Western peoples, the divorce between the religion of the State and that of the citizen, the taste for Oriental cults which seized the Greek world in the days of Alexander and the Roman world in the Second Punic War, facilitated the task of the Jewish missionaries. For this task the Jew was pre-eminently

[1] *Ib.*   [3] Augustine, *De Civ. Dei*, VI. ii.
[2] *Sat.* XIV. 96 ff.   [4] Jos. *B.J.* II. 20, 2.
[5] I. 3, 2 ; cf. Hastings, *D.B.* extra vol. p. 97 b.
[6] Cf. further, Jos. *c. Apionem*, II. 29 ; Philo, *Vita Mosis*, II. 4, C.-W. 17 ff.; Horace *Sat.* I. 4, 142 f.; Persius, *Sat.* V. 179-84.

qualified because of his adaptability to environment, his capacity for assimilating alien ideas without weakening his racial consciousness, or losing his ancestral faith, and his ability to turn to advantage every change of government or national fortune.[1] Schürer attributes the conspicuous success of their propaganda to three main causes—first, Judaism always presented its most attractive side to paganism ; secondly, it pursued the practical aim of securing a moral and happy life ; thirdly, it profited by the general trend toward Oriental faiths in monotheism, in discovering a cathartic for sin, and in the promise of blessedness.[2]   This mission made a threefold appeal—the general witness of a moral people in the markets and in ordinary business, and that of the synagogue, the main focus of proselytism, and an energetic literary apologetic.[3]

The Jew was quick to realize that he was living in a world that had attained a remarkable degree of culture, and that he must attempt to persuade thinkers as well as the thoughtless masses.   Hellenism was the heaviest counterweight to Judaism.   In the Greek tongue spoken by all there was a religious and philosophical literature which he could not afford to overlook.   When the merits of all the competing religious movements were being freely discussed the Jew was compelled to enter the lists for Judaism.   Jewish literary propaganda was both offensive, directed against that idolatry which was always in Jewish eyes the chief sin of paganism, and defensive, demonstrative of the originality and priority of the Mosaic cult.   The stock arguments of this apologetic were the divine origin of Judaism through supernatural revelation, its historicity, its antiquity, its impressive code of morality, and the coming of a future Deliverer to fulfil the promises.   Its method was generally eclectic ; its main instrument, allegory.   The authorship was of two kinds—pseudonymic, the *nom de plume* being chosen either from conspicuous pagan names or from worthies

---

[1] Cf. Legge, I. 150.

[2] *Gesch. des jüd. Volkes*, 4th ed. III, p. 155 ff.

[3] For Jewish apologetic cf. Schürer, III. 545 ff. and Edersheim, art. *Philo* in Smith's *D.C.B.* IV. 360 b.

of Jewish history, and authentic authorship when the writers came out into the open. The book of Jonah, written at the end of the Persian or the beginning of the Greek period, was a tocsin to national proselytism. Among the earliest Jewish-Greek propagandist literature was the work of the eclectic Aristobulus, the first Judaeo-Greek philosopher. He too was apparently the first Jew to adopt that device of allegorical interpretation, which he applied alike to Jewish history and Greek philosophy. He claimed —a claim often repeated subsequently—that Greek philosophy took its rise from the fountain of Mosaism. The Hermippus [1] who asserted that Pythagoras had borrowed from the Jews was probably a Jew. Pseudo-Aristeas similarly advocated the originality of the faith of the synagogue. By manipulation of the Sibylline oracles Jewish versifiers imposed upon the heathen by ostensibly citing their own poets and warning the Greeks that 'the great-hearted Immortal One' would intervene, after signs in heaven and earth, through the Messiah to exalt the chosen race over Hellas. In the *Wisdom of Solomon* the futility of idolatry is shown, and both Jews and Gentiles are pointed to the source of all wisdom in the Law and the fear of God. Other examples are found in the Pseudo-Justinian *Cohortatio ad Graecos* and *De Monarchia*, and in the *Contemplative Life* of Philo. Josephus, indirectly in his *Histories* and especially in the *contra Apionem*, occupies an important place in Jewish apologetic, defending his faith against current calumnies and making prominent its chief attractions.

Mention should be made of the momentous attempt to fuse Greek philosophy and Hebrew revelation at Alexandria, of which the outstanding figure, but not the first, was Philo. When we endeavour to reconcile in a synthesis the diverse faculties of our personality, when we seek to bring together mysticism and knowledge, intuition and reason, objective and subjective authority, when we hold fast God's transcendence without exiling Him from His world, and God's immanence without being engulfed in pantheism, when we

[1] Jos. *c. Apionem*, I. 22.

unite religion and culture, we are continuing the work which was commenced in the museums of Alexandria. The Jews of the Diaspora read Greek literature, spoke Greek, used Greek in the services of the synagogue and in family worship,[1] while the inquisitive Greeks were not averse to studying a new cult. These two spiritual forces, the religion of Israel and the thought of Greece, confronted each other in Alexandria, the capital of the Western Diaspora and of Hellenism, and the results of their interaction permeated the whole Mediterranean world. With enlarged sympathies Jew and Greek became eclectic. Both were propounding the same question : How does God come into relations with the world and men ? Both applied the same method to modernize their traditions ; both were attempting to apply religion to life.

The Jews whetted the appetite for Oriental faiths, while Judaeo-Hellenism fostered that religious syncretism in which the Oriental cults throve. In voluntary associations for the cultivation of personal religion, in appointed days for worship, in enthusiastic missionary impulse, in proclaiming the forgiveness of sins and offering the means of purification, in teaching the habit of prayer, in furnishing sacraments and holding out future rewards, in serving as a nexus between East and West, Judaism marched in line with the Mystery-Religions.

IV. The Romans in Contact with the East

The contact of the Romans with Greece and the East, their religious condition during the centuries of their conquests, and the moral effect of their victories were destined to have far-reaching results for the religious history of Europe.

Rome became acquainted with Greek civilization in Magna Graecia from 281 B.C. onwards, and in the last quarter of the same century she interfered in the affairs of Greece. The victory of Cynoscephalae, 196 B.C., gave Rome the upper hand over Macedonia, and the victories of Thermo-

[1] Cf. Smith's D.C.B. IV. 359 a.

pylae and Magnesia forced Antiochus of Syria to yield the hegemony in the Greek world to Rome. From this date Rome disposed of the countries of Asia Minor as she deemed best. Early in the first century B.C. her conquests brought her into conflict with the military power of Pontus, which issued in three Mithridatic wars. Mithridates, the protagonist of Orientalism against Western encroachments, was the predecessor of those rulers of Parthia and Persia who were to maintain the struggle with Rome until the fall of her empire.

Roman religion was that of a practical, unimaginative, and patriotic [1] people, fostering domestic and civic virtues, and adapted to an agricultural society, but continually being overcome by ceremonial and elaborated by foreign accretions. It was essentially a family religion.[2] Each family constituted a little church, on the religion of which that of the State was modelled. What was initially its strength—its intimate connexion with the political life—became its weakness on the degradation of religion into a part of the political machinery. Unlike the religion of Israel, that of Rome had never in it that vital principle of evolution which would enable it to meet the needs of different eras of spiritual experience. Consequently there was, to a far greater extent than in Greek religion, an atavism, or attempt to return to unintelligible formulae and customs of the past, while on the other hand the inadequacy of the Roman *Numina* was felt, and from the beginning of the sixth century B.C. onwards the Roman *di indigetes* were displaced by *di novensiles*. Roman animism was displaced by Greek anthropomorphism. Aniconic *powers* became *persons*. Greek High Churchism, with its love of ritual and pomp, sacrament and aestheticism, encroached upon the simpler Roman cult. The foundation of the Capitoline temple in 509 B.C. to the Trinity, Jupiter, O.M., Juno, and Minerva, marked a distinct epoch [3] by opening the floodgates of

[1] Cf. Mommsen, cited in Aust, *Die Religion der Römer*, p. 14.
[2] Cf. Giles, *Rom. Civilization*, p. 45.
[3] Wissowa, *Religion u. Kultus der Römer*, p. 34 n. ; Aust, p. 48.

innovation. Etruscan and Greek rites and theology found entry ; the *ritus graecus* supplemented the *ritus romanus*. Early in this period, 496 B.C., belongs the first collection of the Sibylline Oracles, which were used by their custodian priests to introduce from time to time Greek and Oriental innovations. On their advice in 493, at a time of military disasters and famine, a temple was built in the Circus Maximus to the Greek Trinity, Demeter, Dionysus, Persephone, under the Latin names of Ceres, Liber, Libera. Through them too, in 431, the cult of Apollo, most typical of Hellenic deities, was introduced owing to a pestilence. In similar circumstances the Healing God, Aesculapius, became settled in Rome in 291. Previously the twin Greek deities, the Dioscuri, had found entry. At some uncertain date the Greek Hercules had been admitted to the Roman pantheon.

The great crisis in Rome's religion began during the Hannibalic Wars, which proved more disastrous to Roman religion and morality than the Peloponnesian War had been to Hellas. During this period [1] Rome's spirituality reached its lowest ebb. The distress and terror caused by Hannibal, the thirst for conquest, the luxury arising from abundant spoliation, the civil wars with their proscriptions and confiscations, the tolerance of Greek thought, and infection of Greek scepticism, brought about a religious anaemia for which the state religion offered no remedy. Old Roman simplicity disappeared before boundless extravagance and heartless selfishness. Roman piety was buried under Greek culture. Political interests gained the right of way over religious interests because politics now opened the path to self-aggrandizement.[2] Henceforth the religion of the State

---

[1] The history of Roman religion falls into four clearly marked periods : (1) from the earliest times till the Capitoline temple, 509 B.C. ; (2) from 509 B.C. till Second Punic War, 218 B.C. ; (3) from Second Punic War till end of the Republic, 218–31 B.C. ; (4) the imperial period. So, in general, Wissowa, Aust, Chantepie de la Saussaye, Fowler.

[2] " Ancient venerable cult-usages surrounded the Roman religion with a strong dike, but the waves of the Hannibalic War overflowed it " (Aust, p. 59).

and that of the people go their own ways. Every effort was made to lessen the distance between the *di indigetes* and the *di novensiles*, but the former continue to retreat until they retain their place only so far as they have been identified with the foreign deities, or survive in the pages of poetry or in the lore of antiquarians. The laws were repealed to permit the settlement of *peregrina numina* within the precincts of the pomoerium. Some Roman *auguria* and *haruspicia* fell into desuetude. The masses paid no attention to the public divination, but had recourse to private consultations with Etruscan soothsayers or Eastern astrologians. Venerable priesthoods ceased through lack of candidates : national feasts were neglected or celebrated *graeco ritu*.

Throughout this period we must distinguish the state religion, the religion of the educated, and popular superstition. The first was cold and formal and, from the Second Punic War, had become an instrument of government in the hands of the nobility. Those entrusted with its administration, while recognizing its social value, no longer believed in it. Its observation was very perfunctory ; its ceremonies were often neglected. Even during the first Punic War Appius Claudius Pulcher had thrown the sacred fowls overboard before the battle of Drepanum because they refused to eat auspiciously, an act which the deity avenged. C. Flaminius, consul for 217, neglected the customary observances before taking the field. Caesar makes no mention of *divinatio* in the history of his campaigns. The learned were sceptical about the value of the official religion. Scaevola, Pontifex Maximus in the first century B.C., enumerates three kinds of gods : those of the poets, who are futile ; those of the philosophers, who do not suit the State owing partly to their being superfluous and partly to their being injurious to the people ; and those of the statesmen. Cato wondered how two haruspices [1] could pass each other on the street without laughing at the inanity of their profession. Cicero was astonished that anyone could believe in the office of augur. The philosophies by which the educated

[1] Cicero, *De Div.* II. 24, 51.

were guided increased the scepticism. The populace, having lost faith in their ancestral gods, looked toward the East for the satisfaction of their yearnings. Popular religion, so long repressed, now welled up in an overflowing flood of superstition. It revealed itself in a strong desire to satisfy personal needs without reference to the State, in a new sense of sin which called for atonement, in a demand for union with the deity, which could then be accomplished only by the Mystery-Religions.

In the stress of the Second Punic War the Senate recognized that the restless populace, depressed by defeats and with their imagination excited by *prodigia*, must be granted some means of religious support to maintain their morale. The masses must be amused while the State must make a show of keeping up its paternal interest by putting forward a popular cult and diverting their minds from disasters by imposing public spectacles. In reality the Senate was not guiding the people, but merely sanctioning the official entry of foreign cults to which the masses had betaken themselves. New *ludi* were added : henceforth there was a rapid growth both in the number and length of these religious festal days, which among other objects were intended to induce the people to look to the State for everything. In 217 *lectisternia* were decreed in honour of the twelve official Greek gods with whom the Roman gods were equated. Roman rites, *a ver sacrum*, and human sacrifice, were tried in vain. In 207 the Senate met the position created by Hasdrubal's entry into Italy and the occurrence of a hermaphrodite birth at Frosinum by decreeing a grand festal procession in Greek style with a Latin hymn sung by a choir of twenty-seven maidens in honour of Juno. A momentous step was taken in 205—on the advice of the Sibylline books—the transportation of the black monolith of the Magna Mater from Pessinus. Livy marks the importance of this event by his detailed description of the solemn procession in which the noblest matrons and the whole body of citizens went forth to meet the new goddess and request her to enter the city garlanded in her honour.

In 191 a stately temple was dedicated to her on the Palatine. " With the entry of the Magna Mater of Ida the orgiastic and enervating Oriental worship found entrance into Rome and took up its place within the pomoerium in the very heart of the city." [1] The Great Mother won her way to popular favour immediately and her worship whetted the appetite of the Romans for emotional cults. Rome's interference in the affairs of the East, more energetic after the defeat of Carthage, brought her armies and merchants and officials increasingly into contact with that type of religion of which the Great Mother was the first example. The thousands of Orientals who travelled westward brought their mystery-gods with them. The multitudes of slaves from the East not only formed private religious associations, but became propagandists to their Roman masters.

When the Romans went forth to conquer the earth, the Roman gods remained at home to be forsaken. When Rome became a world-power she was in a position similar to the Greeks when, under Alexander, they undertook the education of the world. The Romans, like the Greeks of a century and a half before, had lost faith in their national religion, while their faith in themselves increased. They were even in a worse position than the Greeks, since their religion made no appeal to the imagination by a rich mythology nor to the aesthetic taste by a pantheon of lovely anthropomorphic divinities. The ignorant had recourse to superstitions and foreign cults ; the learned turned to foreign philosophies, the noblest form of which was that Stoicism of Roman type founded by Panaetius and Posidonius, taught later by Seneca, and lived by Marcus Aurelius. In personal necessities men fled to strange gods. Religious indifference infected all ranks. A Pontifex Maximus questioned the very existence of the deities with whose cult he was entrusted. Roman audiences applauded the sentiment of Ennius that the gods live a careless existence heedless of mortal concerns, or approved of Euhemerus' view that the gods were merely deified men.

[1] Aust, *ib.* p. 64.

Early in this period Oriental mysticism and emotionalism had gained official entry, but not to the liking of the governing orders. For at least a century the worship of foreign deities was discouraged within the precincts of the pomoerium. Astrology, which in the second century B.C. was confined to the lower classes, won adherents in the next among the highest society.[1] Political confusion and the increasing religious restlessness of the masses hastened the collapse of the Roman religion. Nonconformity grew apace toward the close of the republic. Rome had now gained the whole world and lost her own soul.

" How thoroughly religious sentiment had disappeared from the heart at the end of the republic is evident from the fact that the leading men of the State did not hesitate to scorn openly venerable usages in the most shameless fashion. . . . We see the state religion degraded to a menial of politics, the educated filled with the spirit of unbelief, or of scepticism, the masses serving foreign gods or sunk in superstition. A degenerate age stands unintelligent before the ruins of its faith and the usages of its forbears. Such is the picture of the religious condition of Rome about the time when Jesus was born." [2]

The fears of Varro had been realized : ' Dicat se timere ne pereant [dii] non incursu hostili sed civium neglegentia.' [3]

The imperial period is from the religious standpoint more interesting as marking the return of the Romans to religious earnestness. After the unspeakable suffering caused by the republican wars of conquest in the provinces, which furnished battle-fields for Roman civil strife, the whole world was weary of war and longed for a cessation of bloodshed and a return to settled social and economic conditions. Hence the rise of the empire was universally hailed as the dawn of a better era. The *Pax Romana*, the first settled peace since the days of Alexander's conquests, called forth a chorus of profound thanksgiving, which in that age was necessarily of a religious character. Emperors were hailed as Saviours, sons of the Divine, Protectors of the human race. Incense

---

[1] Cf. Aust, p. 80.   [2] Aust, p. 90.   [3] Augustine, *De Civ. Dei*, VI. 2.

rose once more in peace from a thousand ruined altars. The imperial government was more at leisure to devote attention to the religious condition of the people. Augustus cleverly took advantage of the universal spirit of thanksgiving to foster a revival of religion in dynastic interests.[1] His religious reforms were dictated by a practical aim. He wished to impress upon all minds the superiority of one-man rule, to revive republican religious forms so as to conceal his own imperial position, and to unite Church and State in such a way as to subserve the unity of the State and foster loyalty to himself by giving to it religious sanction. Ruined temples were rebuilt, altars were repaired, religious endowments were restored, or payments made with princely generosity, priesthoods were elevated in rank, and vacant religious offices filled. In 13 B.C. Augustus took the title of Pontifex Maximus, which gave to his person a halo of sanctity and proved so effective that subsequent emperors, pagan and Christian, retained it. In 17 B.C., on his initiative, the magnificent *ludi saeculares*, for which Horace wrote the *Carmen Saeculare*, were celebrated with impressive solemnity.

Men cannot long rest in unbelief or agnosticism. Everywhere efforts were being put forth to find new religious supports and new objects of faith. Hence in the empire that religious syncretism, inaugurated by Alexander, increased in momentum until it reached its might in the third and early fourth centuries. The sense of sin, emerging during the Hannibalic struggle, grew more acute, and with it the demand for means of cleansing and expiation. Men were in search for salvation from whatever quarter. Rome had no Redemption-religion to offer, while Greece had been looking to the Orient or to her own philosophies now saturated with Orientalism. The Orientals were offering the dissatisfied Romans the religious comforts which they could not find elsewhere.

The imperial era is marked by the rapid increase in the power and prestige of Eastern religions, most of which had been introduced under the republic either officially, like

---

[1] Cf. Chantepie de la Saussaye, p. 636.

that of the Great Mother, or illegally, like those of Isis, Serapis, and Mithra. Attachment to Oriental cults in the Republican period obtained, generally speaking, among the masses, and the spread of private associations was strenuously prohibited by the government.[1]

Under the empire, excepting the reigns of Augustus and Tiberius, the situation is reversed, and Eastern religions ascend the imperial throne successively or simultaneously. Augustus and Tiberius shared the republican disinclination to the warmer and politically dangerous cults of the East. Though Egypt had become a province in 30 B.C. Augustus, in 28 B.C., ordered that all temples of Isis and Serapis should be outside the pomoerium, and his minister, Agrippa, inhibited the celebration of the Isiac rites within one mile of the walls. In A.D. 19 Tiberius expelled Orientals, including Jews, from Rome, dismantled the temple of Isis, and instituted a bloody persecution against her devotees. But with the accession of Caligula the imperial policy changed in favour of Orientalism, until in 304 Mithra was declared Protector of the Empire, and in 321 the Galilean religion became the state religion.

The rise of the empire promoted the growth of monotheism because of the close relation between the form of religion and polity. One supreme ruler on earth made it natural and inevitable that men should believe in one Supreme Being in the universe. The empire also proved a levelling force in breaking down the racial and national and linguistic barriers, thereby promoting the idea of a common humanity, and it should be remembered that it was to man as man that Mystery-Religions and Christianity appealed. The paternal policy of the imperial government also released men from public affairs and afforded leisure for the cultivation of personal interests for which the private religious associations of the Mystery-religions and Christianity catered. The general drift of the imperial era was toward Oriental ways. The empire thus brought the ancient world into a condition which made it a fertile soil for Eastern faiths.

[1] Cf. Boissier, *La Religion romaine*, II. p. 248 ff.

CHAPTER II

WHAT IS A MYSTERY-RELIGION ?

Φοβεροὶ δὲ βροτοῖσι μῦθοι
Κέρδος πρὸς θεῶν θεραπείας.

EURIPIDES.

IN spite of the fact that, since the publication of the pioneer work of Sainte-Croix in 1784 with revised edition by Silvestre de Sacy in 1817, Creuzer's *Symbolik* in 1810, and especially of Lobeck's *Aglaophamus* in Königsberg in 1829, so much study has been devoted to the Mystery-Religions, it is very difficult to convey to modern minds an adequate idea of what a Mystery-Religion was in the Greek or Roman era.[1] Several causes contribute to this difficulty. In the very nature of the case the secrecy [2] to which initiates were pledged rendered it impossible for outsiders to become acquainted with the inner history of the religious societies : such history could be written only by those whose vows forbade them to divulge the *mysteria*. Of course, there were certain things in connexion with these cults which the members were allowed to publish as freely as they wished. Also, the adherents of the Mysteries, in daily contact with their fellow-men and actuated by a desire to make converts, discussed their religious views and pointed to some advantages of their worship. There was no injunction against referring to the blessedness accruing from initiation. There were also educated men like Plutarch, Porphyry, Iamblichus, Julian, and Proclus, who had partaken of the sacraments of the Mysteries and expressed the religious ideas

---

[1] For the various opinions regarding the nature of the ' Mystery,' cf. Macchioro, *Zagreus*, p. 185, and his criticisms in *Orfismo e Paolinismo*, pp. 119–45 (*L'Essenza del Mistero*).

[2] Cf. Lysias, *c. Andoc.*, 104 ; Cic. *N.D.* III. 37 ; Lobeck, *Aglaophamus*, pp. 67 ff., 1202 ff. ; Dibelius, *Die Isisweihe* in *Sitzb. d. Heid. Akad.* '17, p. 15 ff. ; Anrich. 31 f.

of those Mysteries in their philosophic teaching without disclosing the details of initiation. Some features of the religious guilds and of the lives of their members were patent to all ; e.g. that there was at least in some of the cults a more or less regular congregational worship, that there was a strong bond of fellowship among the members which made the burdens of life more tolerable, that the guild was supported by the free-will offerings of its members, that they had sometimes a common burial-ground, etc. The *mystae* were apparently permitted to confess their faith publicly in certain *symbola*, or *signa*. Such formulae, accessible to, e.g. Demosthenes, Clement of Alexandria, or Firmicus Maternus, betrayed neither the ritual nor liturgy, nor the nature and use of the *sacra*, and were unintelligible except to those equipped with the mystery *gnosis*. ' I have become a mystes of Attis ' would reveal no more to the outsider than the confession ' Jesus is Lord ' would convey of the inner meaning of the *agape*. Apuleius' procedure is instructive. Having asserted that he dare not disclose *quid deinde dictum, deinde factum* in his initiation at Cenchreae, he repeats a long *symbolum* (*Acessi confinium Mortis*, etc. XI. 23) and then informs the reader, ' Behold, I have told you things of which, although you have heard them, you cannot know the meaning.' [1] Only to the Orphic mind would ' A kid, I fell into milk ' speak of mystic identification with *Dionysos Eriphos*, of resurrection and rebirth.[2] Yet we are in a worse position with regard to these ancient cults than a present-day historian would be in regard to Freemasonry. A mason may not disclose the secrets, while an outsider could record only such usages of Freemasonry as are obvious to all or such features as are openly spoken of by the brotherhood.

We have extant but a few literary works dealing with the Mysteries, many scattered references, verses of poetry,

---

[1] Cf. his request at his trial for magic practices to a possible fellow initiate, ' signum dato ' (' let him repeat the formula ') with his ' for my part I shall be forced by no possible danger to disclose to the uninitiated what I received under vow of secrecy ' (*Apologia*, 56).

[2] Cf. Macchioro, *Zagreus*, pp. 80–6.

fragments of hymns and prayers, mutilated inscriptions, damaged papyri, cult emblems, bas-reliefs, frescoes, painted vases, ruined chapels and temples. These are the varied and imperfect material out of which we have to attempt reconstruction. Our difficulties are much heightened by the insecurity of chronological sequence, and the uncertainty as to the particular usages or beliefs of a cult at a particular period of the long history of the Mystery-Religions from the sixth century B.C. to the fifth century A.D. During the centuries from Alexander the Great until Constantine these Mysteries have undergone marvellous remodelling to adapt them, as they were constantly adapted, to the demands of the day. Further, when literary notices, inscriptions, and monuments begin to increase in volume, the Mysteries have each and all been affected by religious syncretism in doctrine and cult, and so, by borrowings and mutual interaction, have approximated to each other so as to be in many respects indistinguishable.

Another problem is that of reconciling our fragmentary notices in any reconstruction. Some of our information comes from sympathetic sources, some from sources avowedly hostile, and some from professed apologists of the Mysteries. Christian iconoclasm not only destroyed the shrines, overthrew the altars, and effaced, as far as possible, all trace of the literature and liturgy of the Mysteries, but, in their apologetic, Christian writers represented, or rather misrepresented, the Mystery-cults in such a way that one is sometimes compelled to question how these ever exercised such a potent spell over ancient religious minds. Ancient writers [1] are not agreed as to the effects of initiation, though the majority maintain that participation in the Mysteries was salutary. Indeed, it would have been no easy task even for an ancient adherent to give an account of his cult which would have been accepted by his ' brothers,' because the Mysteries were so indefinite in form and vague in outlook that much was left to the individual imagination. Hence the ancient worshipper found in his Mystery-

---

[1] Cf. Creuzer, *Symbolik*, p. 849 f.

Religion what he sought [1] or what he brought to it. Of these, as of all religious observances, we may say, with Goethe :

"Ein jeder sieht was er im Herzen trägt."

Men entered the Mystery-cults for different purposes : there were all degrees of belief and unbelief, morality and laxity, mysticism and realism. The carnal could find in orgiastic processions and midnight revels opportunities for self-indulgence ; the superstitious would approach because of the magical value attributed to the formulae and sacraments ; the educated could, in the material and physical, perceive symbols of the truth dear to his heart ; the ascetic would look upon initiation as a means of buffeting his body and giving freedom to the spirit ; the mystic would in enthusiasm or ecstasy enjoy the beatific vision by entering into communion with God or by undergoing deification. Then, as always, ' many are the wandbearers, but few are the mystae.' This divergence in the point of view of the *epoptae* was easy because of the heterogeneous elements, or perhaps, rather, the various strata of religious history embedded in the Mysteries. Every note in the religious gamut might be struck, from the crassest materialism of Phrygia to the purest yearnings of Neo-Platonism. The Mysteries had a sensuous and at times even a sensual side, but they could never have entered into competition with Christianity had they not also presented a pronounced religious character. Freed from the national and political restraints of the state churches, they in a wonderful measure adapted themselves to the needs of every age by casting off what was repulsive or flagrantly offensive ; but they never succeeded in wholly divesting themselves of primitive naturalism and the magic in which superstition throve.

History cannot give us back the psychology of those who assembled for matins or vespers at the shrine of Isis, who took part in the orgiastic processions of Cybele, who met in silent contemplation in the Mithraic chapel, who pored deep over the Hermetic Revelation in quest of a satisfying know-

[1] So Philo, *De Vita Cont.* p. 473 M., C.-W. 12.

ledge of God. Anthropology and the science of Comparative Religion have come to our aid, and historic study has guided us by showing how essentially modern was the Graeco-Roman epoch in its strivings and intuitions. We may, therefore, with a considerable measure of assurance, trace our way backwards from the religious psychology of our own day, and in the light of it read the sacred liturgies of the past.

The Mystery-Religions offer a fascinating study [1] for those who believe that " through the ages one increasing purpose runs," and that the march of mankind is Godward. This study reveals that on the larger view the spiritual prevails, that there is in man a religious instinct the satisfaction of which but quickens that instinct and lays bare the greater need, that there is a native idealism and spirituality in our being which transmutes the crudest acts of worship into uplifting sacraments, and which leaves behind rude naturalism to behold in the material symbols of the divine.

The Mystery-Religions were lowly and simple enough in their origin. They arose from the observation of the patent facts of recurring death and subsequent rebirth in nature, and from the attempt to see in these alternations of winter and spring, decay and generation, sunset and sunrise, a symbol of the life and hope of man and a replica of the divine life, which in primitive thought was conceived merely as the all-vitalizing energy resident in nature. Their origin belongs apparently to a remote period of civilization which was pastoral rather than agricultural. Two centres of the ancient Mysteries, the wild plateau of Phrygia with its

[1] Cf. the judgment of Sir W. M. Ramsay, ". . . The elaborate and artificial products of a diseased religion. . . . The development has been a depravation " (Hastings' *D.B.* ex. vol. p. 124 a), with his more favourable judgment in *C. and B.* I. p. 92 f.: " The Oriental, and especially the Phrygian, Mysteries met the natural and overwhelming desire for a rational system by their teaching of the divine unity-in-multiplicity. . . . The Phrygian Mysteries must always remain one of the most instructive and strange attempts to frame a religion, containing many germs of high conceptions expressed in the rudest and grossest symbolism, deifying the natural processes of life in their primitive nakedness, and treating all that veiled or modified or restrained or directed these processes as impertinent outrages of man on the divine simplicity."

emotionalism, and Thrace, the homeland of the Dionysiac-Orphic Mysteries, have exercised an enormous influence in the religious history of Europe.

There were probably four stages in the history of the Mysteries from the earliest naturalistic period to their popularity and imperial recognition in the Roman Empire. (1) There was a time when the Mysteries, in their crudest form, were not ' mysteries ' for initiates only, but were the religion of a whole pastoral or primitive agricultural people.[1] (2) A period during which this primitive religion, with necessary modifications, was the religion of the lower stratum of population which adhered to the customs of the auto-chthons. This lower stratum would be the aborigines who survived the successive waves of conquest.[2] (3) A period during which the Mysteries were the concern of private religious associations, which might be dated from the first introduction of Orphic cults into the Greek world until the reign of Caligula.   These *thiasoi*, or *sodalitates*, though they represent what Gardner has called " Hellenic Noncon-formity," did not necessarily refuse conformity with the national public worship, but found their chief religious activity in the small brotherhoods. During this period they attracted, on the whole, the lower orders and the foreign population. They were legally on the footing of *religiones licitae*.   (4) The imperial period.   Though Augustus favoured the cult of the Great Mother, he and Tiberius were not well disposed toward Oriental religions. With Cali-gula's dedication of a temple to Isis Campensis, and more particularly from the accession of the Flavian emperors, the Oriental religions came into universal favour until under the Syrian emperors they were elevated to the rank of state religions. What were once local worships cultivated in private associations became universal religions, only that men were not born into them but entered by an initiation, or rebirth.

---

[1] " In primitive religion all men were religious, and mysteries were the religion of the whole people, and not confined to chosen mystae " (Ramsay, 124 a, *ib*.   Cf. Farnell, *Cults*, III, p. 132).

[2] Cf. Gardner, *Relig. Exper. of St. Paul*, p. 58 *f*.

Turning now to the prominent features of a Mystery-Religion, we may say that a Mystery-Religion was (I) a religion of symbolism which, through myth and allegory, iconic representations, blazing lights and dense darkness, liturgies and sacramental acts, and suggestion quickened the intuitions of the heart, and provoked in the initiate a mystical experience conducing to *palingenesia* (regeneration), the object of every initiation. In such symbolism was removed the offence of what were originally vulgar tokens of life and generation and birth, tokens which received a spiritual meaning consonant with the stage of moral education reached by the age. This in itself not only marked a stage in moral evolution, but pointed, vaguely it is true, toward that modern view of the world in which the spiritual interpenetrates and unites all things. In every religion ritual precedes symbol and symbol precedes language and prompts the articulation of feelings and needs so vague for the time being as to elude expression. In the symbolism of the Mysteries, often unintelligible and sometimes offensive to us, men were blindly grasping for the truth and reality of things. The imagination was quickened and deep emotions were stirred, which might lead the spiritual Godwards and might at the same time be the occasion to the unspiritual of moral aberrations or fruitless psychopathic conditions. Language is at best only an inadequate expression of spiritual experience, as mystics in all ages testify, and has often to take refuge in metaphor or to apply the speech of daily life in a domain for which it is inadequate. Symbolism may convey to mind and heart the significance of impalpable experiences and so hasten the formation of a religious phraseology. In this respect the Mysteries promoted religious growth. Thus, in lustrations with water, the ancient saw the sacramental cathartic which washed away his sins and opened the way to approach the deity.[1] In the enacted passion-drama of the resurrection of Osiris

---

[1] Lustrations were originally not symbolic at all, but exorcistic or apotropaic.

the initiate read the promise of his own triumph over death :
' as truly as Osiris lives shall he live ; as truly as Osiris is
not dead shall he not die.'   The cult meal was in some
mystic sense a means of communion with the deity.   In the
bath in bull's blood (taurobolium) the participant believed
that through the impartation of the divine life he was ' born
again for eternity.'   The soldier of Mithra in silent contemplation of the tauroctony [1] read his own conquest over
the ills of life, and especially over the darkness of death.

' All things are opposite the one to the other ' was a principle universally observed by the ancient worshipper of
the Mysteries.   To understand the Mysteries we must
endeavour to recapture the ancient mind which in religious
matters expressed itself spontaneously in symbolism where
we would speak more concretely.   The line of demarcation
between symbol and fact, the objective and subjective,
was not distinctly drawn.   In fact in ancient realism [2]
the identity of subjective and objective was not questioned.
If the writer of our ' spiritual gospel,' distinguished for the
spirituality of his treatment of Baptism and the Eucharist,
does not strictly discriminate between the outward ritual
and the inner experience, it is not astonishing that adherents
of the Mysteries failed to separate the physical and the
spiritual.

" The contradiction which our analytic thought is accustomed to find between the nature of an inner spiritual
process and its mediation through an outward sensible act,
has for ancient thought in general, and the period of the
Mysteries in particular, no existence.   Instead, we may say,
that our difficulties on this point would have been quite
unintelligible to the men of that time, for it appeared to them
self-evident that a real inward experience must also be

---

[1] Cf. Statius, Theb. I. 717 ff.

[2] " E indiscutibile che il popolo greco non superò mai completamente i
confini della mentalità prelogica e non arrivò se non in età tarda, dopo
Platone, a una mentalità razionale vera e propria.   Nella filosofia greca
bisogna scendere fino agli stoici per trovare la distinzione ovvia per noi,
di rappresentazione subbiettiva e obbiettiva " (Macchioro, Zagreus, p. 165 ;
cf. Orfismo e Paolinismo, p. 159 ff.)

visibly represented by a corresponding outward event, and that just in this mystic interplay of inward and outward consisted the significance of all cultus-ceremonies." [1]

A splendid example of the idealizing power of religious symbolism is presented in the treatment of the Zagreus-myth of the wild Thracian Dionysiac religion by the Orphic Mysteries. No more unpromising material could have been chosen than this repulsive story, which, told in various forms, represents Zeus as seducing in the form of a serpent his ' only-born ' daughter, Persephone, from which amour was born the Cretan Dionysus-Zagreus with the horns of a bull. This infant god, destined by his father to be world-ruler, was kidnapped by the envious Titans, sons of Earth, torn limb from limb, cooked and eaten. His heart, rescued by Athene, was brought to Zeus, by whom it was swallowed, and became reborn as the Theban Dionysus, son of Zeus and Semele. Zeus then blasted with lightning the earth-born Titans, from whose ashes arose mankind. The Orphics moralized this myth into a symbol of man's composite nature, consisting of the evil, or Titanic, elements and the divine or Dionysiac elements. From the former man must, through self-renunciation, liberate himself and return to God, with whose life he may be united. The body is the tomb of the soul : salvation consists in rescuing the divine, Dionysiac, spark from the enveloping evil matter, and so securing escape from the round of reincarnation to which the soul is subject.

There were two factors in particular which abetted the symbolism of the Mysteries, and both factors, most pronounced in Stoicism, attained a powerful influence in Hellenistic-Oriental theology—materialistic pantheism or divine immanence, and allegorical interpretation.

1. The Stoics, in their efforts to conceive the unity of all things, produced a strange materialistic pantheism according to which the divine interpenetrated all in such a way as to admit of no essential difference between God and the World.

---

[1] Pfleiderer, *Primitive Christianity*, Eng. tr. IV, p. 231.

Cornutus, in his *Compendium of Greek Theology*,[1] says : ' just as we ourselves are controlled by a soul, so the world possesses a soul holding it together, and this soul is designated God, primordially and ever living and the source of all life.'

" We can therefore think of nothing which is not either immediately deity or a manifestation of deity. In point of essence God and the World are therefore the same. . . . The same universal Being is called God when it is regarded as a whole, World when it is regarded as progressive in one of the many forms assumed in the course of development." [2]

As a result of this immanent unity there is a natural correspondence, or ' sympathy ' among all things. Epictetus [3] asks, ' Don't you think that all things have been brought into a unity ? ' ' Certainly.' ' Well, don't you suppose that the things of earth are in sympathy with the things of heaven ? ' ' Yes.' The elements are shot through by the Spermatic Logos, or Generative Reason, and become divine by the interpenetrating attenuated fiery breath. This Stoic view is expressed in such a line as

' Juppiter est quodcunque vides, quodcunque moveris,'

and by Virgil :

' Deum namque ire per omnis
Terrasque tractusque maris caelumque profundum ;
Hinc pecudes, armenta, viros, genus omne et ferarum,
Quemque sibi tenues nascentem arcessere vitas,
Scilicet huc reddi deinde ac resoluta referri
Omnia, nec morti esse locum, sed viva volare
Sideris in numerum atque alto succedere caelo.' [4]

With this pantheism Posidonius linked a semi-philosophical, semi-astrological doctrine of nature-mysticism [5] which never died out of ancient theology. According to this Posidonian conception, men have in themselves the same

---

[1] Lang's ed. (Teubner, 1881) ch. ii. ; cf. Cic. *N.D.* I. 14, 37.
[2] Zeller, *Stoics, Epicureans, and Sceptics*, p. 157 f.
[3] *Dis.* I. 14, 1.
[4] *Georg.* IV. 221 ff.
[5] Cf. quotation from Posidonius in Sext. Empir. *Math.* VII. 93.

' elements ' which exist in principle in the deity and through which they are in ' sympathy ' with the deity. Wherefore the religious mind is quickened to perceive that ' the things of earth are in sympathy with the things of heaven,' that the natural is but the manifestation of the divine, and that through the contemplation of material objects, especially the heavenly bodies,[1] the soul may be elevated toward God. The writer of the Fourth Gospel, familiar with these views, says, ' if I spoke to you about things on earth, and you do not believe, how will you believe if I speak to you about things in heaven ? '[2] Herein we find an anticipation of the words from the mystic chorus of *Faust* :

> " Alles Vergängliche
> Ist nur ein Gleichnis."

2. The Mysteries preserved much in ritual that was archaic, the original significance of which was lost in antiquity and the prima facie character of which was repulsive to a developing ethic. In order to retain these elements it was necessary to have recourse to allegory. This method of interpretation arose among the Greeks and the Jews from the same cause—the maturer moral sense,[3] which revolted against the literalism of some stories in their religious classics : " In the absence of any kind of historic sense, it was perhaps the only way in which the continuity of religious thought could then be maintained."[4] Allegory was the application of philosophy to mythology, which sought in the myths, however crude, a hidden spiritual meaning. Allegory was probably developed earlier among the Greeks than among the Jews. The Stoics, deriving this method from the Cynics, brought it to perfection as a theological weapon, by means of which they were able to conserve the form of popular religion while transforming the content. We have abundant examples of the employment of allegory, e.g. in Cornutus' *Compendium of Greek Theology*

---

[1] Cf. Cumont, *Mysticisme Astrale*, p. 262 ff.

[2] Cf. Origen's statement of the law of correspondence, *In Cant. Cant.* (Lom. xv. 48).

[3] Cf. Dill, pp. 422–3. [4] Glover, p. 184.

and in the probably pseudonymous *Homeric Allegories*.[1]
In Plutarch's essay, *On Isis and Osiris*, the most commonplace myth is by the use of allegory tuned to lofty morality.
Similarly, Maximus of Tyre can use the crassest myths to
suggest the purest spirituality.   How early the allegoric
method was adopted by the Jews it is difficult to determine
with certainty.   It certainly would be in demand as early
as the translation of the Septuagint in Egypt.   Aristobolus
used it freely in his exposition of the Pentateuch, and
Schürer believes that allegoric exegesis was in vogue in
Palestine a considerable time before the days of Philo,[2]
who applied it wholesale to the Hebrew Scriptures.   He was
followed by Paul, through whom allegory entered upon its
long career in Christian theology.

The allegorical method enabled writers to link the present
with the past ; it could bring any ritual or drama into line
with current ethics.   It utterly ignored the intention of the
writer or the original and obvious significance of a mystery
ceremonial, and replaced these by the reader's or observer's
own interpretation.   It idealized what was said into what
should have been intended.   Abundant scope was afforded
to this prevalent allegorism by the symbolism of the
Mysteries.[3]

II. A Mystery-Religion was a religion of Redemption
which professed to remove estrangement between man and
God, to procure forgiveness of sins, to furnish mediation.
Means of purification and formulae of access to God, and
acclamations of confidence and victory were part of the
apparatus of every Mystery.   It is necessary here to dwell
only briefly on this aspect of the Mysteries which made them
so popular.   We must recall the intellectual and spiritual
perplexities of those who lived in the Graeco-Roman age
in order to understand the religious refuges to which they
fled ; we must understand the heavy burdens which they

    [1] Ed. by Mehler (Leiden, 1851).
    [2] *Gesch. des jüd. Volkes* (3rd–4th ed.), III, p. 702.
    [3] Cf. Hatch, *Influence of Greek Ideas and Usages*, p. 39.   Bacon's *Wisdom
of the Ancients*, and Ruskin's *Queen of the Air* give the reader unfamiliar
with Greek a fairly adequate idea of the ancient hermeneutics

sought to lay down in the shrines of the Oriental cults. Life was threatened and made wretched by the tyranny of Fate, the caprice of Fortune, the malice of ubiquitous demons, the crushing weight of Astralism, the dread of Magic, the deepening sense of sin (which was part of the Orientalization of the Western mind), and the mystery of Death. The first thing that Alexander the Great did in Babylon was to consult the Chaldaei.[1] Men and women moved nervously in a world where at any moment they might fall under the evil of sorcery. Pliny [2] informs us that there was no one who did not dread being bewitched. F. C. Burkitt calls attention to a homily,[3] written probably by Isaac of Antioch (A.D. 450), who complains that Christian people and clergy alike,

' Instead of the blessings of the saints, lo, they carry about the incantations of the magicians ; and instead of the holy cross, lo, they carry the books of devils . . . one carries it on his head, another round his neck, and a child carries about devils' names and comes [to church].'

Now, the propagandists of the Mysteries never denied the reality and terrors of magic, but professed to impart the correct name of a deity or precise formulae to thwart incantations. Similarly, Fate might not be wholly evaded, but by union with the mystery-gods its blows would not crush man. The initiate of the gods could not be overwhelmed by *Fatum irrevocabile* or by *Fors inopinata*, for the mystery-gods were lords of the baleful powers. Deliverance from malefic demons was found in becoming a devotee of a deity more potent than they. Even the planets, which exercised such a momentous influence over man's destiny, lost much of their terror when the mystery-deity became a heavenly deity, with whom the soul of the deceased initiate would mount through all the spheres to the highest heaven.

[1] Arr. *Anab.* III. 16. 5 ; Q. Curtius, V. 3.
[2] *H.N.* XXVIII. 4.
[3] *Proc. Soc. Bib. Arch.*, 1901, p. 77. Cf. Le Blant, *L'accusation de magie dirigée contre les premiers chrétiens* in *Mém. de la Soc. des antiq. de France,* XXXI.

The mystery ritual supplied for distressed consciences a cathartic to remove the stain of sin. The *mystes* did not die without hope. He believed that in some mysterious way he was brought in initiation into fellowship with the eternal life of his god ; he not only saw in the death and resurrection of the cult-deity a symbol of his own deathlessness, but also experienced a real inner *henosis*.[1] These redemption-religions thus promised salvation and provided the worshipper with a patron deity in life and death. This salvation consisted in release from the tyranny of Fate, alleviation from the burdens and limitations of existence, comfort in the sorrows of man's lot, a real identification with his god guaranteeing *palingenesia* (rebirth), and hope beyond. We should judge of this aspect of the Mysteries by the language of the hymns and prayers [2] of the devotees, rather than by our modern views. In every act of worship the blessing is ' according to your faith.'

III. The Mystery-Religions were systems of *Gnosis* akin, and forming a stage to, those movements to which the name of Gnosticism became attached. They professed to satisfy the desire for the knowledge of God which became pronounced from at least the second century B.C. and increased in intensity until the acme of syncretism in the third and fourth centuries of our era.[3] The Mysteries brought men into contact with that god ' who wishes to be known and is known to his own.' [4] They offered an esoteric equipment by which the initiate might ward off the attacks of demons, thwart the menace of Fate, and after death reach the abodes of the blessed mysteries. There was something, whether doctrine, symbol, or divine drama, which could not be imparted except by initiation to those duly qualified to receive, a supernatural revelation which gave the recipient a new outlook upon life, the world, and the deity, and a security denied to the uninitiated. The ' mystery ' con-

---

[1] Cf. Macchioro, *Zagreus*, p. 159 ff.

[2] See pp. 99, 119, 139, 230, 238 ff., 263.

[3] Usener attributes the beginning of the Gnostic movement to the propaganda and syncretism of the Oriental cults (*Weihnachtsfest*, 2nd ed., p. 25 ff.).   [4] *Corp. Herm.* I. 31.

sisted in an objective presentation of the history of the cult-deity in his or her struggles, sorrows, and triumphs, repeated subjectively by the initiate in sacramental acts together with prayers and liturgic formulae, or it was a profound intuition of the ' Spirit in Love,' or foretaste of that mystic experience in which ' we know as we are known,' in the progressive satisfaction of the two eternal passions of selfhood—the desire for Love and also for Knowledge. The ' secret,' when imparted, rendered men superior to all the trials of life and ensured salvation.

There were many grades of Mysteries, some of which were crude and almost wholly symbolic, with but little doctrine, and in which *rerum magis natura cognoscitur quam deorum,*[1] while others provided a more elaborate liturgy and a fuller theology. A considerable distance separated popular magic, which was the Gnosis of the masses,[2] from the cult of Isis, whose name was a favourite among magicians and in whose cult magic was freely employed ; and again there is a considerable step from the Isiac religion which moved among demonic hierarchies to the Hermetic, which undertook to ' preach to men the beauty of Knowledge,'[3] and in which Gnosis is ' the religion of the Spirit (*Nous*),' and as such is synonymous with ' the vision of things divine.'[4] Every Mystery-Religion imparted a ' secret,' a knowledge of the life of the deity and the means of union with him. There was a sacred tradition of ritual and cult usages expounded by hierophants and handed down by a succession of priests or teachers. Plato informs us that the Orphic mysteries promised escape from ills beyond death and foretold an awful future for the uninitiated.[5] Sophocles likewise limits eternal felicity to initiates.[6] The adherents of the Mysteries pitched heir claims high, and their faith in the possession of an esoteric doctrine and way of salvation was not the smallest factor in the success of their propaganda. They struck the chords of both hope and terror in the heart of man.

[1] Cic. *N.D.* I. 42, 119.
[2] Cf. Dieterich, *Abraxas*, p. 2.
[3] *Poim.* I. 26
[4] *Corp. Herm.* IV. 6.
[5] *Repub.* 365, A.
[6] Frag. 719 Dind., 348 Didot.

In pointing the way of communion with deity in a 'mystery,' the Mystery-Religions were preparing the way for the orientalization of the Western religious thought [1] known as Gnosticism; but also, as religion became universally recognized as a definite *Gnosis*, they accommodated themselves to this new demand.   In the prevalent syncretism the Mysteries approached in varying degrees the religious movements and revivals called Gnostic, so dissimilar in many aspects, but all linked together by the identification of religion with ' Knowledge ' (*Gnosis*, not ἐπιστήμη, conceptual knowledge) or rather, that view of religion which gave to *Knowledge* a central place in asserting the realization of deity by union, not by faith.   Common to the Mysteries and Gnosticism were certain ideas, such as pantheistic mysticism, magic practices, elaborate cosmogonies and theogonies, rebirth, union with God, revelation from above, dualistic views, the importance attaching to the names and attributes of the deity, and the same aim at personal salvation.   As Gnosticism took possession of the field East and West, the Mysteries assumed an increasingly gnostic character.   The dividing line is sometimes difficult to determine.   Thus, Hermetic may be viewed as a Mystery-Religion or as a phase of Gnosticism.

This aspect of the Mysteries brings us in touch with a factor in the development of the Western religious thought of far-reaching influence in the history of the Mysteries, Christianity, and philosophy, namely, the belief that God is unknown save so far as He manifests Himself in special revelation to faith ;   that, defying comprehension and being far above man, He is apprehended only by an ineffable mystic experience and passive attitude of the soul.   This was no less than an Oriental reaction against the epistemology of the West.[2]

Behind the expression ' to know God ' or ' the knowledge of God,' so familiar to us, there lies a long history, during which

---

[1] Cf. Mead, *Quests Old and New*, p. 182.

[2] Cf. Clem. Alex. *Strom.* VII. 11. 68, ἡ ἁγιωτάτη κ. κυριωτάτη πάσης ἐπιστήμης ἀγάπη (' The most holy and potent of all knowledge is Love ').

Orient and Occident gradually approached in their thinking until the Occident adopted the point of view of the Orient. Greek Intellect and Oriental Revelation, the lay and the sacerdotal, met, and as a result the world became convinced of the need of a Revelation,[1] but not without some modification of the conception of revelation.

In Hellenic thought God was neither ' unknown ' nor ' unknowable,' since the Greek intellect believed that it could penetrate the adyta of all knowledge, and since, being essentially pantheistic, it saw God in the world and the world as the sensible manifestation of a God that could be comprehended by reason ($\nu o\eta\tau\grave{o}\varsigma$ $\theta\epsilon\grave{o}\varsigma$). But as weariness overtook Hellenic thought and it gave way to Hellenistic, as the nature and certainty of knowledge were doubted, and as scepticism as to the ability of reason to attain ultimate reality gained ground, the demand for authority and for revelation, or ' a sure word,' increased. This momentous outlook dawned only gradually,[2] and with it the conviction that " the $\gamma\nu\hat{\omega}\sigma\iota\varsigma$ $\theta\epsilon o\hat{v}$ cannot be an acquisition of the intellect, but a gift of God's grace to a soul conscious of its sinfulness, and therefore, receptive of divine grace." [3] The time had arrived when, in the words of Seneca, *adscendentibus Di manum porrigunt.*

Three men stand out conspicuously in this epoch-making transition from Western to Eastern religious conceptions— Plato, Posidonius, and Philo. Plato, though admitting that the Creator and Father of the world is apprehensible by thought,[4] yet asserts ' to discover the Maker and Father of this universe is both an arduous task, and, having discovered Him, it is impossible to speak of Him to all.' This warning of a master-mind of Greece, and one whose thought entered into every subsequent religious and philosophical system of the Graeco-Roman world, was prophetic. It seemed to suggest that to find God or speak of Him was not the prerogative of every man, but required special qualifications. This, taken with Plato's view of the need of a safe raft

---

[1] Cf. Reitzenstein, *Poim.* p. 158 f.   [2] *Ibid.* p. 87.
[3] Cf. Norden, *Agnostos Theos*, p. 85.   [4] *Tim.* 28, c.

or sure word, pointed toward the Oriental Revelation-Theory of religious knowledge. Nor did Plato stop here. He inoculated Greek thought with that transcendentalism which entered henceforth to contest the field with indigenous Greek immanence and finally to triumph in Neo-Platonism. In the Hellenistic era this element of Platonism proved a convenient bridge to the Oriental conception of deity which necessitated a condescension in the form of a special revelation.

Plato having thus prepared the way, Posidonius was the first, so far as our evidence goes, who definitely introduced to the Western religious mind [1] the conception of ' the knowledge of God ' as something transcending conceptual thought and eluding intellectual grasp. It is noteworthy that this idea of the knowledge of God, so faint in Greek literature, grows *pari passu* with the increasing religious syncretism of the Hellenistic-Roman era, to which no one contributed more than did Posidonius, who influenced Lucretius, Virgil, Cicero, Seneca, Philo, the Hermetic writers, and practically every subsequent religious writer.

In Philo we come nearest to the later conception of God being not only unknown, but also defying comprehension (ἀκατάληπτος), though Philo struggles hard to hold together the Greek view of God as comprehensible by reason and the Hebraic idea of divine transcendence, the latter of which he carried far beyond Plato and nearer to the position of Plotinus. While asserting that the knowledge of God is ' the summit of happiness and blessedness,' he says ' the Creator made no soul in any body capable by its own powers of seeing the Creator.' [2] His tendency is further illustrated in the following passages : God says to Moses,[3] ' As to the comprehension of Me, human nature is unequal to the task, for not even the whole earth nor the world is able to contain it '; and again he asks, ' Is it to be wondered at if the Being [God]

---

[1] Norden, p. 99.

[2] *Quod det. potiori insid*; XXIV, Mang. I. 208, C.-W. 86.

[3] *De Monarchia*, I, ch. VI ; Mang. II. 218.

defies the comprehension of men, when the spirit that is in each one is unknown ? ' [1]

Subsequently, especially in the second and third centuries of our era, the intermixture of Greek thought and Oriental mystic speculation grew apace, the latter element becoming predominant, in the attempt to release the spirit from the realm of matter, the way to which was a *Gnosis*, or special revelation. The quest for the knowledge of God which would ensure salvation became the occupation of an intensely religious age, a quest upon which the Orient sent the Occident.[2] Every religion, in order to survive and compete successfully, was obliged to assume in some degree the character of a *Gnosis*, a necessity from which even Christianity did not escape and of which we find traces in the Epistles of the Imprisonment and in the Fourth Gospel. Whence this radical change in ancient outlook ? Norden[3] has answered thus :

" The Greek sought his *Weltanschauung* by way of speculation. With his unique clearness of conceptual thinking he knocked at the gate of knowledge ; he aimed at intellectual apprehension by his logical faculties, the mystic-ecstatic element being at least in principle excluded. The Oriental acquires his knowledge of God not by way of speculation, but his emotional life, slumbering in the deeps of his soul, and awakened through religious needs, brings him to a union with God. Such a union issues in a complete ascent to God, so that knowledge is acquired in a supernatural fashion to the exclusion of the intellect, because God of His grace manifests Himself to the soul that strives after Him.

" Hence, faith and enlightened vision supersede scientific knowledge and understanding, a profound inner experience supersedes reflection, pious surrender to the Absolute takes the place of that proud sense of enquiry which prescribes its own bounds. Only through union with God (*Poim.* I. 22) is a knowledge of the world and man made possible ; consequently this knowledge of the world and man is rated as of merely secondary importance."

---

[1] *De mut. nom.* II, Mang. I. 579, C.-W. 10
[2] Cf. Norden, p. 113.   [3] *Ibid.* pp. 97–8.

IV. A Mystery-Religion was a Sacramental Drama which appealed primarily to the emotions and aimed at producing psychic and mystic effects by which the neophyte might experience the exaltation of a new life. In saying this we must once more bear in mind the numerous and marked differences obtaining among the Mysteries, and the very different presentations given of the nature of the Mystery.[1] The old and purely objective view of a Mystery as an external representation or ritual transaction to the neglect of the inner experiences and ecstatic conditions, prevalent since the days of Lobeck, is no longer tenable. Had the Mysteries and their *dromena* been merely such an external spectacle one fails to find any explanation why they quickened religious life for so many centuries and how they fostered mysticism. Moreover, a visit to the *telesterion* of Eleusis is convincing evidence that a *drama*, in the scenographic sense of the word, could not have been enacted there. Neither can we suppose that at the numerous small centres of the Mysteries there was available the apparatus for staging a passion-play of mediaeval character. Such dramatic performances would be out of the question for individual initiations, such as were possible in some of the Mysteries. The strongest reaction from the old objective idea is that of the Dutch scholar, De Jong, who, in his valuable *De Apuleio Isiacorum mysteriorum teste* and *Das antike Mysterienwesen*, stresses the connexion between the Mysteries and Magic, collects ancient and modern occult phenomena parallel to those of the Mysteries, and eliminates the objective for the subjective. Macchioro, in his *Zagreus* and *Orfismo e Paolinismo*, reads the ancient evidence in favour of the Mysteries as real subjective experiences[2] accompanying sacramental acts,

[1] For conspectus of views cf. Macchioro, *Zagreus*, p. 184 f.

[2] " La novità . . . delle mie ricerche intorno ai misteri sta nell' aver concepito il *dromenon* come drama subbiettivo invece che come drama obbiettivo, nell' aver trasportato cioè il dramma dall' esterno all' interno e averlo posto non come fatto naturale ma come un processo spirituale. In fondo potremmo dire che ciò equivale a ridurre il *dromenon* da conoscenza a esperienza : e come tale la mia teoria si connette alla corrente religiosa odierna che tende a concepire il fatto religioso come *azione* " (*Orfismo e P.* p. 115 ; cf. his summary, p. 190).

as religion in action. On our view—most nearly approaching that of Macchioro—the objective cannot be lightly
eliminated. Though the subjective estate, with its mystic
experiences, visions, and auto-suggestion, was the real
' mystery ' sought after and, by many, attained, meticulous
importance was attached to the formality of the *dromena*,
or cult transactions, which, for many, remained liturgical
representations, and nothing more. The *action* was to the
ancient mind, as it is to many modern minds, a sacramental
constituent of the whole spiritual experience. The dramatic
representations assumed varying proportions according to
the spiritual maturity or genius of the particular Mystery.
The sensuous appeal varied according to the cult and the
individual worshipper. There were all degrees of excitation
—the drunken frenzy of the Bacchanalian rites, the maddening and bloody ritual of Cybele or Mên, the imposing pomp
of the Isiac cult, the silent contemplation of the Mithraic
brethren. On the other hand, the syncretistic Hermetic
religion has practically outgrown the dramatic representations and sensuous attractions, making its appeal primarily
to the *Nous*, or Spirit. But, speaking generally, the Mysteries
made their appeal not to the intellect, but through eye, ear,
and imagination to the emotions. What Farnell has said
of the Eleusinian Mysteries applies in a measure to all :

" To understand the quality and intensity of the
impression we should borrow something from the modern
experiences of Christian Communion Service, Mass, and
Passion Play, and bear in mind also the extraordinary
susceptibility of the Greek mind to an artistically impressive
pageant." [1]

A Mystery-Religion was thus a divine drama [2] which portrayed before the wondering eyes of the privileged observers
the story of the struggles, sufferings, and victory of a patron
deity, the travail of nature in which life ultimately triumphs
over death, and joy is born of pain. This was impressed

---

[1] Art. *Mystery, Ency. Brit.* 11th ed. XIX, p. 121 b.
[2] Cf. Athenagoras, 30 B, Clement, *Protr.* II, 12.

on the beholder by a solemn mimic representation. Thus,
at the spring festival (*Megalensia*) of the Great Mother
the myth of Attis was rehearsed in a passion-play. The
sacred pine-tree under which the unfaithful youth had
mutilated himself was cut down. The tree then, prepared
like a corpse, was carried into the sanctuary, accompanied
by a statue of the god and other symbols. Then followed
the lamentation of Attis, with an appropriate period of
abstinence. On the *Day of Blood* the tree was buried, while
the *mystae* in frenzied dances gashed themselves with knives
to prove their participation in the sorrows of the god that
they might have fellowship in his joy. Next night the
Resurrection of Attis was celebrated by the opening of the
grave. In the darkness of the night a light was brought to
the open grave, while the presiding priest anointed the lips
of the initiates with holy oil, comforting them with the
words : [1] ' Be of good cheer, ye *mystae* of the god who has
been saved ; to you likewise there shall come salvation from
your trouble.' The initiates gave vent to their emotions
in a wild carnival : they made their confession that by
eating out of the *tympanum* and drinking out of the *cymbalum* they had been rendered communicants of Attis.[2]

Examples of the enactment of these symbolic passion-
plays could be multiplied, as for instance, the Finding of
Osiris,[3] emblematic of man's immortality, or the slaughter
of the mystic bull so familiar on the sculptures of the Mithraic
chapels.[4] Plutarch [5] depicts the myth of the rending of
Osiris by Typhon and the ensuing struggles of Isis as a
passion-play in which Isis ' did not forget the struggles
and trials which she had endured, nor permit oblivion
and silence to overtake her wanderings and many deeds
of wisdom and courage, but by associating images and
suggestions and representations of her erstwhile sufferings

[1] Minucius Felix, *De err. prof. relig.* XXII.
[2] Cf. Hepding, *Attis*, pp. 147–67.
[3] Cf. Cumont, *Relig. orient.*, p. 146 ; Min. Felix, II ; Statius, *Silvae*,
V. iii. 3, 241.
[4] Cumont, *The Mysteries of Mithra*, Eng. tr. p. 130 ff.
[5] *De I. et Os.* XXVII. 361 D.

with the holiest mysteries she thereby consecrated a lesson in piety and a consolation for men and women who are overtaken by similar misfortunes.' Firmicus Maternus [1] states, in reference to the legend of Dionysus: ' Cretenses . . . festos funeris dies statuunt, et annum sacrum trieterica consecratione componunt, *omnia per ordinem facientes quae puer moriens aut fecit aut passus est.*'

The whole ritual of the Mysteries aimed especially at quickening the emotional life, and in this respect Cumont affirms that " they refined and exalted the psychic life and gave to it an almost supernatural intensity such as the ancient world had never before known." [2] No means of exciting the emotions was neglected in the passion-play, either by way of inducing careful predispositions or of supplying external stimulus. Tense mental anticipation, heightened by a period of abstinence, hushed silences, imposing processions and elaborated pageantry, music loud and violent or soft and enthralling, delirious dances, the drinking of spirituous liquors,[3] physical macerations, alternations of dense darkness and dazzling light, the sight of gorgeous ceremonial vestments, the handling of holy emblems, auto-suggestion and the promptings of the hierophant—these and many other secrets of emotional exaltation were in vogue. Apuleius [4] avers of his initiation : ' I approached the confines of Death ; I trod the threshold of Proserpina ; after being carried through all the elements, I returned to earth. At midnight I beheld the sun shining with its bright splendour : I penetrated into the very presence of the gods below and the gods above, where I worshipped face to face.'

Thus the Mysteries, with the exception of the Hermetic theology and Orphism, were never conspicuously doctrinal or dogmatic [5] : they were weak intellectually and theologically. Aristotle's statement that it was not necessary for

[1] VI. 5.
[2] *Religions orient.* p. xxv ; cf. p. 43 f.
[3] Cumont, *T. et M.* I, p. 323 ; *Relig. orient.* 2nd ed. p. 45.
[4] *Metam.* XI. 23.
[5] Reitzenstein, *Mysterien-rel.* 2nd ed. p. 14.

the initiated ' to learn anything, but to have their emotions stirred,' does not prove the absence of all instruction, but indicates that such occupied a secondary place. Things were ' said ' as well as ' done.' According to Apuleius certain secrets too holy for utterance were imparted by the priest : his reader might rightly enquire *quid dictum, quid factum.* But the symbolic representations, the handling of the *sacra,* and the emotional exaltation were the chief matter. Some interpretation was necessary in order to assure the participant that he had found a redemptive religion. The τελετῆς παράδοσις was accompanied by a ἱερὸς λόγος, or sacred exegesis.

The secrecy with which the Mysteries terminated behind the veil of the temple,[1] compared with the publicity with which they generally commenced in the streets, is explicable from the fact that the things ' done ' or ' said ' were not the things actually to be revealed but merely symbolic means of conveying the intended truth to the minds of the votaries. The sacramental acts and religious legends, based on naturalism, would have been repellent to the moral sense of the votaries. The true votary, however, like every true worshipper, believed that the letter killeth and the spirit quickeneth. We can well conceive how the sacramental representations of the Sacred Marriage and Rebirth were fraught with grave difficulty even to the participant equipped with an esoteric exegesis. The same religious idealism was demanded from him as that by which Christian mystics and the Church hymnology have transmuted the prothalamium or epithalamium of the Canticles into an expression of the passion of the soul for God. Some of the acts and portions of the legends were, taken literally, frankly indecent, and gave justification to the strictures of Clement of Alexandria,[2] Arnobius,[3] Minucius Felix,[4] and other

---

[1] Cf. Slade Butler, *XIXth Cent.,* 1905, pp. 490–9.

[2] *Protrept.* II. 16, et passim

[3] *Adv. Gentes,* V. 21, of the Sabazian mysteries, ' in quibus aureus coluber in sinum dimittitur consecratis et eximitur rursus ab inferioribus partibus atque imis.'

[4] *De err. prof. rel.* X, XII, XIX.

Christian apologists, against the Mysteries as provocative of lust. On the other hand, Iamblichus, no mean philosopher, and one who has written from personal experience one of the finest passages in literature on the joy brought to the soul by the divine presence,[1] defends with all his religious earnestness even the exhibitions of sex emblems[2] in the Mysteries as veritable means of grace to overcome fleshly appetite. In estimating these dramatic representations, so strange and even offensive to us, we should as students of the history of religion, hear both sides. Alongside of Clement of Alexandria we should read what the father of European idealism, Plotinus, found in their symbolism. " The great problem of Idealism is symbolically solved in the Eleusinia " is the conclusion of an early nineteenth century writer.[3] Each Mystery-Religion had an idealistic tendency.[4]

V. The Mysteries were eschatological religions having to do with the interests and issues of life and death. Their chief charm was that they brought an evangel of life and immortality to confront the mystery of the grave. The religion of Greece might satisfy while life was joyous ; it offered no rod and staff to men entering the valley of the Shadow. The religion of Rome, in which the domestic hearth and the continuity of the family bulked so large, could hold forth nothing better than the dreary Manes-cult. Philosophy brought to many great souls a blessed hope and in later phases employed the symbolism of the Mysteries to reinforce the faith in immortality. But for the multitude it was the Mysteries which illuminated the Hereafter.[5] Earth's smoothness had been turned rough ; the mind was directed from the state-religions, which had failed to save the State, to eschatological cults in which individuals found

---

[1] *De Mysteriis*, II. 6 and 9.   [2] *Ib*. I. 11, 12.
[3] Cited in Taylor, *Eleus. and Bacchic Mysteries*, p. vii. Cf. Inge, *Phil. of Plotinus*, I. p. 56 : " These strange institutions combined naturalistic tradition and mystic theology, the realism of a legendary divine drama and philosophical idealism, the religion of the senses and that of the heart."
[4] Cf. Cornford, *From Religion to Phil.* p. 114 ; Ramsay, *Cities and B.* I. p. 93.
[5] Cf. Lake, *Stewardship of Faith*, p. 69.

salvation. The Mysteries responded to the prevalent *appetit d'un monde meilleur*, to that world-renouncing and world-weary spirit which demands another sphere [1] wherein the wrongs of the present are righted, to that ancient desire for the ' rebirth for eternity ' with its escape from the ' cycle of generation.'

An eschatological religion entails an ethic by maintaining a moral nexus between this life and the next. Hence the Mysteries, by asserting that man's hereafter is in some way conditioned by conduct here, definitely ranged themselves with that religious faith in a future life which had been increasing since the day when Plato made " the noblest single offering that human reason has yet laid upon the altar of human hope." [2]   In alliance with Neo-Pythagoreanism and Neo-Platonism, they appealed to that spirit of other-worldliness which became so characteristic of the religious syncretism of the third and fourth centuries. The *mystae* were witnesses against religious agnosticism, which would view the question of immortality as a *bellum somnium*, and against the doctrine of annihilation, which would assert that ' beyond the grave there is no opportunity for either anxiety or joy.' [3]   What a contrast this profession of faith of the *mystae* must have presented to the unbelieving world ! [4]   Carved on the tombs in the cemetery of the Mystery ' brothers ' the passer-by would be arrested by such triumphant words as ' Reborn for eternity ' or ' Be of good cheer,' while on those of the uninitiated he might read such a frivolous confession as ' I was not, I became : I am not and I care not,' or ' Hold all a mockery, reader ; nothing is our own.' [5]   The Orphic dead were cremated in hope of a blessed hereafter ensured by the tablets deposited with them,[6] just as the *Apocalypse of Peter* was deposited in a Christian grave in Egypt.

---

[1] What Inge calls " The ' ought-to-be '—the not-given complement of our fragmentary and unsatisfying experience " (*Ib.* I. 51).

[2] Geddes, *Phaedo of Plato*, p. xxvii.   [3] Sallust, *In Cat.* LI.

[4] Cf. ' sweet hopes,' Aristides, *Eleus.* I. 421 (Dind.) ; *C.I.G.* 6562.

[5] Cf. Angus, *Environment of Early Christianity*, p. 103 ff.

[6] For Orphic funerary rite, cf. Macchioro, *Orf. e Paol.*, p. 274 ff.

VI. A Mystery-Religion was a personal religion to which membership was open not by the accident of birth but by a religious rebirth. The hereditary principle of membership known to the state-religions of Greece and Rome and to the church-state of Israel was superseded by that of personal volition which has been the dominating principle in religious history since the days of Alexander the Great. The religion of the *thiasos* had replaced that of the *polis*.[1] Consequently the Mysteries, with their pronounced subjectivity and variety of impression, responded to and augmented the individualism inaugurated in the Mediterranean world by Alexander and consummated by the Roman Empire.

That religion is primarily a personal matter is a commonplace to us ; it was an epoch-making discovery to the leading peoples of the Roman Empire. So strong was the racial consciousness of the Jews that they for the most part conceived God's dealings with them as moving within the Covenant. Individualism was at any time but a passing phase in their religious experience.[2] It is true that Jeremiah and Ezekiel rescued the individual, and that Ezekiel carried individualism to such an extent as to overlook the effects of heredity and the constitution of society by which we are members the one of the other. It was in the services of the Synagogue that the personal religion and piety of Israel attained fullest expression.[3] The religions of Greece and Rome were corporate entities—the religious experience of their social and political systems. Men worshipped for the good of all collectively rather than for the good of their own souls. These religions, like every religion that allies itself with temporal power, collapsed with the state systems which they had buttressed. In the ensuing confusion and amid the welter of centuries of strife personal needs became more clamant. These needs were at least partially satisfied by

---

[1] Cf. Kaerst, II. 1, pp. 280–3 : " Die private Initiative tritt an die Stelle der von der Polis hervorgerufenen Veranstaltungen."

[2] Cf. Charles, *Eschatology*, 2nd ed. pp. 59–69, 78–81, 129 ff.

[3] Cf. Fairweather, *Background of the Gospels*, 2nd ed. pp. 30–8.

the Mysteries,[1] which contemplated man irrespective of the polity or social conditions under which he lived. " With them," says Cumont, " religion ceases to be bound to the State in order to become universal; it is no longer conceived as a public duty, but as a personal obligation; it no longer subordinates the individual to the city-state, but professes above all to ensure his personal salvation in this world and above all in the next." [2] To Orphism must be attributed in no small measure this shifting of religious emphasis.[3] Athens, too, took a momentous religious step [4] in the abolition before the sixth century B.C. of gentile privileges in the Eleusinian Mysteries in favour of free choice. Unlike the state religions the Mysteries as personal cults produced saints and ascetics,[5] and martyrs. Livy records how ' a multitude ' of the members of the Dionysiac brotherhoods lost their lives in an attempt by the Government to extirpate them. Many and severe were the persecutions to which the Isiac faith was subjected about the beginning of the Christian era.[6] The presence of skeletons in the Mithraic chapels testifies to this day to the martyrs who, as devoted *milites Mithrae invicti*, suffered at Christian hands.[7] In these personal cults the worshippers were united by the ties of fellowship with the deity of their choice, by the obligation of common vows, by the duty of personal propaganda, and by revivalistic enthusiasm. The pious could in ecstasy feel himself lifted above his ordinary limitations to behold the beatific vision,

---

[1] Cf. Bousset, *Kyrios Christos*, p. 152 ff.; *Religion in Gesch. u. Geg* V, p. 1043 ff.; Mackintosh, *Originality*, p. 19.

[2] *Religions orient.* p. xxii; cf. pp. 68–9.

[3] Rohde, II, p. 121; Macchioro, *Zagreus*, p. 263 f.; Eisler, *Weltenmantel u. H.* II. p. 679.

[4] Farnell, *Cults*, III. p. 155.

[5] Cf. Reitzenstein, *Hell. Mysterien-rel.* 2nd ed. p. 79 ff.; Bouché-Leclercq, *Mélanges Perrot*, p. 17 ff.; Preuschen, *Mönchtum u. Sarapis Kult*, p. 5 ff.; K. Sethe, *Sarapis u. d. sogen. κάτοχοι d. Sarapis* in *Abh. Ges. Wiss. Gött.* XIV. '13. Cf. Porph. *De Antro Nymph.* 15.

[6] Cf. Dill, *Rom. Society*, pp. 563–6; Aust, p. 157; Lafaye, *Isis* in Daremberg-Saglio, p. 577.

[7] In Cumont's *T. et M.* II, p. 519, there appears a photo of the chained skeleton found in the Mithraeum of Sarrebourg. Cf. also his *Mysteries of Mithra*, 3rd ed. p. 215, Eng. tr. pp. 203–5.

or in enthusiasm believe himself to be God-inspired or God-filled—phenomena in some respects akin to the experiences of the early Christians on the outpouring of the Spirit.

One reason why the Mysteries were so long anathema to the rulers of the West was that, as personal religions, they concerned themselves little with public life, centring their attention on the individual life. They accentuated that indifference to citizenship in society at large which was charged against the Jews, and not without some justification against the Christians,[1] and which proved one of the chief factors in the disintegration of ancient civilization.[2]

VII. A Mystery-Religion, as a personal religion, presents another side, which is the necessary complement of an individualistic religion ; that is, it takes on the character of a cosmic religion. The ancients lived in a world in which the primitive association of man's life with the earth and plant and animal life [3] was axiomatic, in which the stars [4] were ensouled as deities, in which the Universe itself was a rational living being,[5] in which man by his good deeds might be elevated to a *demon* as a stage on the path to divinization.[6] This comprehensive cosmic consciousness made what Emerson calls " the linked purpose of the whole " the object both of speculative [7] and religious thought, which derived from

<hr/>

[1] Cf. A. C. McGiffert, *The Influence of Christianity upon the Roman Empire* in *Harv. Theo. Rev.* Jan. 1909 ; J. Geffcken, *Der Ausgang des griech.-röm. Heidentums* in *N. Jahrb. f. d. klas. Alt.* XLI, pp. 93-124 ; and a series of arts. by Ferrero on *La Ruine de la civilisation antique* in *Rev. des deux mondes*, Sep. '19 ff.

[2] This is sometimes viewed by historians as the nemesis for the ostracism of early Christianity by Paganism. Cf. Lavisse et Rambaud, *Hist. générale du IVᵉ. siècle à nos jours* (Paris '96) vol. I. pp. 31-5.

[3] Hence Pythagoras, like St. Francis of Assisi, preached to animals. Iamblichus, *V. Pyth.* 13 ; Porphyry, *V. Pyth.* 24. Cf. what Sextus Emp. (*Math.* 9, 127) says of the Italian School : φασὶ μὴ μόνον ἡμῖν πρὸς ἀλλήλους καὶ πρὸς θεοὺς εἶναί τινα κοινωνίαν, ἀλλὰ καὶ πρὸς τὰ ἄλογα τῶν ξῴων. ἐν γὰρ ὑπάρχειν πνεῦμα τὸ διὰ παντὸς τοῦ κόσμου διῆκον ψυχῆς τρόπον, τὸ καὶ ἐνοῦν ἡμᾶς πρὸς ἐκεῖνα.

[4] Cic. *N.D.* II. 15, 39 ; II. 21, 56 ; 44, 115 ; Seneca, *Benef.* VII. 313 ; II. 41, 126 ; Philo, *De Opif. Mundi*, 24, M.I. 17.

[5] Cf. Arnold, *Rom. Stoicism*, p. 184 f. ; Murray, *Four Stages*, p. 119.

[6] Cf. Plutarch, *De I. et Os.* 27, *Rom.* 28 ; Pseudo-Apul., *Asclepius*, 6.

[7] Cf. the ps.-Arist. treatise *De Mundo*, and Capelle thereon in *N. Jahrb. f. d. klas. Alt.* '05, pp. 529-68.

this universal kinship the postulate that like is apprehended by like [1] in a harmony in which Plato said that God Himself ' geometrizes.' [2]

This cosmic interest—the craving of man for order within as without—was one of the most prominent notes in the Hellenistic age, not only in the Mysteries but in the philosophies, and in Christian theology, which was obliged to include cosmological speculation in its Christology. It rested upon the true instinct that religion must put man right with the totality of things by removing desolating antitheses. As with one acclaim there arose from the hearts of the men of the Graeco-Roman period the cosmic prayer : παῦε παῦε τὴν ἀσυμφωνίαν τοῦ κόσμου.[3]   In many ways utterance was given to presages of Whittier's verses :

> " So sometimes comes to soul and sense
> The feeling that is evidence
> That very near about us lies
> The realm of spiritual mysteries,
> The sphere of the supernal powers
> Impinges on this world of ours."

The naïveté of a primitive naturalistic monism had been succeeded by a consciousness of a breach between Man and Nature, and by the conception of a Chaos beside a Cosmos. To the problem thereby created the Mysteries addressed themselves. Only the few contemplatives could remain permanently persuaded that the centripetal forces of the soul expressed in Mysticism make up the totality of spiritual life.

Cosmic religious interest was stimulated by a variety of factors : (1) The breaking up of the ecclesiastical colleges of the Euphrates Valley, whose disestablished priests directed attention to the study of the heavens and asserted the

---

[1] Perhaps the best expression of this is Plotinus, *Enn.* I. 6, 9: τὸ γὰρ ὁρῶν πρὸς τὸ ὁρώμενον συγγενὲς καὶ ὅμοιον ποιησάμενον δεῖ ἐπιβάλλειν τῇ θέᾳ. οὐ γὰρ ἂν πώποτε εἶδεν ὀφθαλμὸς ἥλιον ἡλιοειδὴς μὴ γεγενημένος, οὐδὲ τὸ καλὸν ἂν ἴδοι ψυχὴ μὴ καλὴ γενομένη.

[2] Cf. *Sapientia*, II. 17 ff.

[3] Hippolytus, *Philosoph.* V. 8, 75.

indissoluble connexion between heaven and earth in magic, astrology, and divination. (2) The invasion of polytheism by a subtle and mystical pantheism which altered the whole outlook of Hellenistic-Oriental theology by making cosmic interests and speculations henceforth organic to all theology. (3) The frightful social evils which may be dated from the Peloponnesian War and became increasingly oppressive until respite was granted in the Roman Peace. In these distresses and upheavals the spirit of Orphism revived and with it the Orphic speculations in cosmogony and eschatology which had retreated to the background in days of joy.[1] (4) The missionary propaganda of the Oriental religions which, being originally nature-cults, retained and enlarged their interest in cosmic speculation. (5) The widening of the intellectual horizon by which men were regarded as denizens of a cosmos rather than as citizens of a State. (6) The immense progress made in the scientific study [2] of astronomy, mathematics, medicine, and other sciences, which disclosed harmonies and universal laws by which the human mind appeared as participant in, and in alignment with, the all-ordering *Nous*, or World-Soul.

The manifold religious phases of cosmic thought [3] in the Hellenistic-Roman period are reflected in its cosmogonies, theogonies, theosophy, astralism, magic, pantheistic element-mysticism, solar monotheism, doctrine of reincarnation, and in all systems of Gnosticism. Such cosmic speculation did good service in vindicating a unitary conception of the universe. In the *Timaeus* Plato discovered evidence of an ordering Mind in all things, and Aristotle emphasized the fact that all formed a rational whole interpenetrated by reason and unveiling its secrets to reason. Posidonius, by uniting Platonic and Oriental mysticism and by infusing into scientific studies religious fervour, did more than anyone

---

[1] Cf. Dieterich, *Abraxas*, p. 1.

[2] Cf. Th. H. Martin, *Astronomia* in Daremberg-Saglio, *Dict.* p. 501 ff. ; Legge, I, pp. 116–19.

[3] Cf. M. Dibelius, *Die Christianisierung einer hellenist. Formel* in *Jahrb. f. das kl. Alt.* XXXV, pp. 224–35.

else to make cosmology a religion.[1] In his teaching γνῶσις
θεοῦ and *rerum cognoscere causas* were practically
synonymous. The cosmos, so far from being a chaos, is on
deeper knowledge perceived to be a soul-permeated magni-
tude. It was an image of God as was also man.[2] God is in
all and through all, and by a knowledge of the All one
attains to the knowledge of God, whose nature is revealed
in the mysteries of creation, generation, decay, rebirth,
universal law. Stoic monism was emphatic on the unity of
things. God was conceived as the World, or again as the
spiritual element or vital fire of the World. Thus, Marcus
Aurelius frequently returns to the thought of the unity of
the world, his most explicit statement being :

' All things are intertwined, the one with the other, and
sacred is the bond : there is practically nothing alien the
one to the other, for all things have been marshalled in order
and constitute the one Cosmos. For there is both one
Cosmos of all things, and one God through all, and one
Substance, and one Law, and one common Reason of
intelligent beings, and one Truth.' [3]

Such a unitary conception of the world was a fixed article
of faith in the Mysteries. They professed to bring the
initiand into union with the God of the All and to impart
to him a knowledge of the secrets of Nature in all its phases
from before birth to the other side of the grave. ' Every
initiation aims at uniting us with the World and with the
Deity,' says Sallustius.[4] These religions not only prompted
cosmic speculation, but adjusted themselves to prevalent
cosmic views, which for a time increased their popularity
but ultimately militated against them. By their sacraments
they undertook to deliver man from the Necessity inherent

[1] Cf. W. Kroll, *Die gesch. Bedeutung des Posidonios* in *N. Jahrb. f. d. kl.
Alt.* XXIX, pp. 145–57.

[2] *Asclepius*, 10.

[3] *Meditations*, VII. 9 ; cf. IV. 40, 45, VI. 38.

[4] *De diis et mundo*, 4 (Mullach, *F.P.G.* I, p. 33), with which Mullach
compares Jamb. *De Myst.* V. 23.

in a fixed world-order. The Mysteries made terms with polytheism and pantheism by making their respective deities all-comprehensive, and with monotheism by equating the gods of competing religions with their cult-deity, and in later stages of more advanced monotheism [1] by identifying in some measure their deity with the Sun-god,[2] until the solar cult became the concentration of vital paganism.[3]

The cult-titles used in prayers of invocation will reveal the cosmic character of the Mystery-gods. The god of the Mystery is not like the Jahweh of the Hebrews, whose is the earth and the fulness thereof. The Mystery-god had other functions besides those of creation and providence. He was both the One and the All. An Orphic [4] verse declares ' Zeus was first, Zeus last, and Zeus head and middle.' In answer to Lucius' invocation Isis manifests herself as ' rerum naturae parens, elementorum omnium domina, saeculorum progenies initialis, summa numinum, regina manium, prima caelitum, deorum dearumque facies uniformis, quae caeli luminosa culmina, maris salubria flamina, inferum deplorata silentia nutibus meis dispenso.'[5] The same goddess is addressed as Una quae est omnia,[6] and on the inscription in the shrine of Neit in Sais recorded in Plutarch [7] Isis appears as ' I am all, that which has been, is, and shall be.' Attis appears as the ' Most High and bond of the Universe.'[8] Serapis is ' as the Coryphaeus of the universe, holding the beginnings and the ends.'[9]

The doctrine of man as a microcosm of the macrocosm— *hominem quasi minorem quemdam mundum*[10]—is one to which frequent expression is given in the mystic-astrological

---

[1] Cf. ' One is Zeus, one Hades, one Helios, one Dionysos, one God in all ' (Abel, fr. 7).

[2] Cf. Proclus' *Hymn to the Sun*.

[3] Cf. Boissier, *La Fin*, I. pp. 129–36 ; Allard, *Julien*, II. pp. 232–45.

[4] Abel, fr. 46, 123.

[5] Apuleius, *Metam.* XI. 5 ; cf. also *ib.* 2 and 25.

[6] Dessau, 4362 ; cf. Orelli-Henzen, 1871.

[7] *De I. et O.* 9.

[8] *C.I.L.* VI. 509 ; Hepding, *Attis*, p. 83 : Ἄττει ὑψίστῳ καὶ συνέχοντι τὸ πᾶν.

[9] Aristides, *Or. sacrae*, VIII. 53 ; Dind. I. p. 91.

[10] Firm. Maternus, *Math.* III. *init.*

theology.[1] It is a corollary of the kindred doctrine of Element-mysticism, viz. that man is constituted of the same elements as the heavenly bodies, which are viewed as animate beings.[2] No one has given clearer expression to such microcosm-theology than Manilius[3] :

> ' An dubium est, habitare deum sub pectore nostro
> In caelumque redire animas caeloque venire ?
> Utque sit ex omni constructus corpore mundus
> Aetheris atque ignis summi terraeque marisque,
> Spiritus et motu rapido, quae visa, gubernet,
> Sic esse in nobis terrenae corpora sortis,
> Sanguineasque animas, animum, qui cuncta gubernat.
> Dispensatque hominem ?　Quid mirum noscere mundum
> Si possunt homines, quibus est et mundus in ipsis,
> Exemplumque dei quisque est in imagine parva ? '

A very practical application was made of the cosmic view of the microcosm and the macrocosm both by philosophy and mystic theology, namely, that the contemplation of the cosmos, particularly the resplendent starry heavens, proved to the devout soul an efficient means of grace.　Such sentiments are frequently met in Posidonius, Vettius Valens, Philo, Cicero, Seneca, Manilius, and Plotinus.　Thus Philo, in answer to the question why man was created last, replies that God provided previously all things necessary for him not merely to live but to live nobly : for the latter purpose the contemplation of the heavens induces in the mind a love of and desire for knowledge, which gives rise to philosophy, by which ' man, though mortal, is rendered immortal.'[4]　Similarly, Plotinus argues that the reverent contemplation of the world brings the soul into contact with the God of the cosmos.[5] Manilius discovers man's distinguishing dignity in the fact that he—

> ' Stetit unus in arcem
> Erectus capitis victorque ad sidera mittit
> Sidereos oculos propiusque adspectat Olympum

---

[1] Cf. Dieterich, *Mithraslit.* 2nd ed. p. 55 ff. ; J. Kroll, *Die Lehren des Hermes Trismegistos*, p. 233 f. ; Mead, *Quests*, p. 158.

[2] Cf. Cumont, I, p. 117.　　　[4] *De mundi opif.* XXV (Mang. I. 18).

[3] *Astronomica*, IV. 886 ff.　　　[5] *Ennead.* V. 8, 9.

Inquiritque Iovem ; nec sola fronte deorum
Contentus manet et caelum scrutatur in alvo
Cognatumque sequens corpus se quaerit in astris.'[1]

The purifying effect of such an exercise is beautifully expressed by Vettius Valens : ' I desired to obtain a divine and adoring contemplation of the heavens and to purify my ways from wickedness and all defilement.'[2]

The Mystery-Religions, which were ever sensitive to the *Zeitgeist*, offered to their votaries abundant satisfaction in an extensive cosmology. Above all, they afforded means whereby the harmful influences of the heavenly powers might be averted, and their beneficent energy turned to advantage. In that troubled age of cosmological perils it was no mean merit of the Mysteries that they made men comfortable in the universe. Discussing what were the new and worthy elements contributed by the Oriental Religions to the Hellenistic age, Dibelius asserts that, in addition to claiming to establish a close relation between the mystes and his God, founded upon the personal choice and devotion of the mystes, " the Oriental Religions, in a much more marked degree than those of the West, take into account cosmic interests . . . so that in these cults religious development keeps pace with the knowledge of the universe."[3] In other words, their purpose was " to make men at home in the universe," the phrase in which Bevan[4] so exquisitely sums up the work of Posidonius.

Seeing that " a man's religion is the expression of his ultimate attitude to the universe, the summed-up meaning and purport of his whole consciousness of things,"[5] it is not strange that Christian theology shared with the Mysteries an interest in cosmological speculations. The apocalyptic hope, so integral to primitive Christianity, embraced the ultimate relations of God to the present world order as much as to the individual believer. As soon

---

[1] *Astronomica*, IV. 905–10.

[2] Ed. Kroll, p. 242 ; Kennedy, *St. Paul and the Mystery-Religions*, p. 7. ' The shining stars purge the soul ' (M. Aurelius, VII. 47). Cf. Lucretius' noble passage, V. 1204–40.　　　　[4] *Stoics and Sceptics*, p. 85.

[3] *Op. cit.* p. 227.　　　　[5] E. Caird, *Evol. of Religion*, I, p. 30.

as Christianity was carried beyond the pale of Judaism
the growth of its theology was inevitably marked by an
increasing cosmological interest, as we discover in the
Christology of Paul.[1] The work of Christ, according to
Paul, extends to the vanquishing of demons and the subjugation of all hostile celestial hierarchies, and aims ultimately
at nothing less than ' the complete reconciliation of the
universe to Him [i.e. God] ' (*Col.* I. 20).[2] The writer of the
Fourth Gospel, though he has eliminated demonology, con-
ceives Christ's work in its effects upon the hostile ' world '
and particularly upon a personal spirit of evil, ' the ruler of
this world.' The retreat of the Messianic categories in favour
of the Logos Christology corresponded to the universal
necessity for a religion with a cosmic outlook.[3]

Thus, to the merit of the Mystery-Religions be it said
that they anticipated that modern view which holds that
theology must have a cosmic scope, i.e. must profess to
present an adequate conception of God in relation to the
universe and of man in relation to his complete environment.
Ritschl may be claimed as the father of this modern view-
point in his notable supplementing of Schleiermacher's great
truth of an inner world by that of an equally important outer
world with which man has relations. " No religion," he
asserts rightly [4]—

" can be properly understood unless it be interpreted on
some other principles than the most usual one, that religion
consists in a relation between man and God. Three points

---

[1] Cf. J. Weiss, *Urchristentum*, II. pp. 464–70.

[2] Cf. Morgan, *Religion and Theology of Paul*, p. 68 ff.

[3] " We need to remember that no salvation strictly confined to man's
interior life could have won the adhesion of that old world. . . . What
vexed men was not merely guilt and moral slackness ; they also longed,
perhaps still more passionately, to be redeemed from fate, from this
unintelligible world, from devils and death. Possibly the salvation they
prayed for was nearly as much physical or political as spiritual. But it
is a true instinct which contends that redemption covers life in the world
as really as life within " (Mackintosh, *Originality of the Christian Message*,
pp. 25–6).

[4] *Justif. and Rec.* Eng. tr. pp. 26–30.

are necessary to determine the circle by which a religion is completely represented—God, man and the world."

Modern Christian idealism has solved for us the cosmic problem on which the Mysteries and the ancient mystic philosophies laboured with but partial success.

CHAPTER III

THE THREE STAGES OF A MYSTERY-RELIGION

Ζητήσατε χειραγωγὸν τὸν ὁδηγήσοντα ὑμᾶς ἐπὶ τὰς τῆς γνώσεως θύρας ὅπου ἐστὶν
τὸ λαμπρὸν φῶς, τὸ καθαρὸν σκότους ὅπου οὐδὲ εἷς μεθύει ἀλλὰ πάντες νήφουσιν
ἀφορῶντες τῇ καρδίᾳ εἰς τὸν ὁραθῆναι θέλοντα.

Corpus Hermeticum, Poimandres
VII. 2 (Parthey).

THE Mystery-Religions present immense varieties in detail
and emphasis.[1] In order, however, to exhibit a pragmatic
view of a Mystery in operation and set in relief its differential
features we may, in a general way, analyse such a religion
into three parts or stages having to do respectively with
candidacy for membership, reception into the religious
brotherhood, and the privileges and blessings resultant
therefrom. These divisions we shall consider under (1)
Preparation and Probation, *Katharsis*; (2) Initiation and
Communion, *Muesis*; (3) Blessedness and Salvation,
Epopteia.

Somewhat similarly Proclus [2] gives the three divisions
of a Mystery as τελετή, μύησις and ἐποπτεία. Olympiodorus,[3]
on the other hand, gives *five* stages, thus: ' In the
Mysteries the public purifications precede ; then the more
ineffable; after these the introductory rites (συστάσεις),[4]
followed by initiation (μυήσεις); finally, the culminating
act of initiation (ἐποπτεῖαι).' In Theo Smyrnaeus [5] we
find also *five* stages, but dissimilar from those of Olympiodorus : ' There are five stages in Initiation (μύησις).
First of all Purification (for participation in the Mysteries

[1] Anrich, *Das antike Mysterienwesen*, p. 24.
[2] Προηγεῖται γὰρ ἡ μὲν τελετὴ τῆς μυήσεως, αὕτη δὲ τῆς ἐποπτείας.
[3] Cited Lobeck, p. 41. Anrich, p. 25.
[4] Cf. K. Preisendenz, in *Wiener Studien* (Kl. phil.) '18, pp. 2–5. " The
rites and sacrifices which preceded and prepared the way for the actual
celebration " (Gardner, *New Chapters*, p. 386).
[5] P. 14, ed. Hiller ; p. 15, ed. Herscher.

is not possible for all who wish it, some being excluded beforehand by proclamation, such as those whose hands are impure and whose speech is unintelligible, while it is required of those not so excluded that they previously undergo purification); after the purification the second step is the communication of the rite (τελετῆς παράδοσις); the third is what is termed ἐποπτεία [the contemplation of the symbols and ecstatic vision]. The fourth act, closing the *Epopteia*, is the binding and decking with garlands, qualifying the initiate to communicate to others the rites delivered to him either as a torch-bearer, hierophant, or in any other sacred capacity; the fifth, arising from the preceding, is Blessedness according to the grace and fellowship with the Deity.'

These differences indicate that the terminology was not hard and fast, and that the boundary lines of the above threefold division [1] were not rigid. We should remember also that a considerable length of time separates the above writers; that each may have had a particular Mystery in mind; and that developments may have introduced differences.

I. PREPARATION AND PROBATION

1. Vows of Secrecy and deterrent Formulae. The Mysteries were personal religions whose adherents were volunteers admitted on evidence of their sincerity and fitness for membership. The obligation resting upon worshippers was personal, and not legal. If one desired to enter the fellowship of a religious brotherhood and share its privileges he was called upon to undergo examination, and disciplinary preparation. As against the national cults, the individual

---

[1] " Plerosque duas facere mysteriorum partes, μύησιν et ἐποπτείαν, nonnullos tres, τελετὴν, μύησιν, ἐποπτείαν " (Lobeck, p. 41). " The successive stages or acts of initiation are variously described and enumerated, but there were at least four : κάθαρσις, the preparatory purification ; σύστασις, the initiatory rites and sacrifices ; τελετή, or μύησις, the prior initiation ; ἐποπτεία, the higher or greater initiation which admitted to the παράδοσις τῶν ἱερῶν, or holiest act of the ritual " (Hatch, *Influence of Greek Ideas*, p. 284, n. 3).

and religious motive predominated arising out of a vague sense of sin, defilement, and weakness, which caused disabilities in approach to the Divine. Initiands must therefore submit to a cathartic process whereby the defilements of the flesh and ritual uncleanness were removed, and an expiation for sin duly made. The cathartic, if too often of a ceremonial and external character, was, as in the religion of Israel, a step toward a spiritual outlook. In the imperfect ritual the religious-minded would find sacramental means of grace, while the superstitious would think only of magical efficacy. Crude forms from a naturalistic past did survive to mar spiritual symbolism, but even these yielded, however obstinately, to the developing moral sense and innate spiritual idealism of mankind. The preparatory purification was of a liberal character, adapted to candidates of every level of spirituality.

Thus, the Mysteries antiquated the state-church theory of the native equality of all in the privileges of a religion by the introduction of a religious distinction between the ' pure ' and the ' impure,' with corresponding rewards and disadvantages. By the creation of such a distinction " the race of mankind was lifted to a higher plane when it came to be taught that only the pure in heart can see God." [1]

An awful obligation to perpetual secrecy as to what was said and transacted behind closed doors in the initiation proper was imposed—an obligation so scrupulously observed through the centuries that not one account of the secrets of the holy of holies of the Mysteries has been published to gratify the curiosity of historians.[2] Apuleius [3] would disclose what was ' said ' and ' done ' at the Isiac initiation if it were lawful for the reader to hear and for himself to disclose it, but such a disclosure would inflict upon the reader and himself *parem noxam*. It was a crime of the most heinous character [4] to divulge the Mystery-secrets. Alcibiades was

[1] Hatch, p. 285.

[2] On the principle stated by Strabo (X. 3, 9, p. 467): ἡ κρύψις ἡ μυστικὴ τῶν ἱερῶν σεμνοποιεῖ τὸ θεῖον μιμουμένη τὴν φύσιν αὐτοῦ ἐκφεύγουσαν ἡμῶν τὴν αἴσθησιν.

[3] *Metam.* XI. 23.   [4] Cf. Lobeck, p. 48 ff.

saved from the consequences of his profanation of the Eleusinian Mysteries only by his popularity with the marines of the fleet.[1]

This vow of secrecy did not extend, of course, to all the elements of a Mystery.[2] ' It is unlawful to communicate the details to the uninitiated.'[3] Apuleius gratifies the reader ' quod solum potest sine piaculo ad profanorum intellegentias enuntiari.'[4] Pausanias[5] narrates of the Mysteries of the Kabiri : ' Demeter deposited something in their hands, but what that object was, together with the subsequent procedure, my conscience forbids me to disclose.' The secrecy kept inviolate the details of the ceremonial transactions of the revelation in the shrine, the exact enactment of the cult drama, and perhaps the esoteric interpretation of its legend,[6] the inner meaning of the watchword (*symbolum*) of the brotherhood, the solemn formulae of the enlightenment, taboos, and we know not how much more.

The vow of secrecy having been administered, there fell upon the ears of the excited neophyte the proclamation of some awful deterrent formulae, which were accompanied, in some cases at least, by terrifying sights, as we infer from Nero's alarm at the preliminaries of initiation at Eleusis.[7] Olympiodorus informs us that not all who desired initiation were granted it. The candidate had to face a religious ceremony [8] of an admonitory character corresponding to the now almost extinct " fencing of the tables " at a Presbyterian Communion Service. Celsus quotes two or three such proclamations : ' whosoever has clean hands and an intelligible tongue ' ; ' whosoever is holy from

---

[1] Plutarch, *Alcib.* XIX-XXII, which he expiated, Xen. *Hell.* IV. 20, 21.
[2] Cf. Anrich, p. 31 f.   [4] *Ib.*
[3] Diodorus, III. 61.   [5] IX. 25.
[6] Cf. Seneca, *Ep.* XCV. 64 : ' Sicut sanctiora sacrorum tantum initiati sciunt, ita in philosophia arcana illa admissis receptisque in sacra ostenduntur, at praecepta et alia eiusmodi profanis quoque nota sunt,' and Plutarch, *Quomodo qui suos sent,* 82 E. Proclus constantly refers to the Orphic interpretation of the Dionysiac myth, which in this case does not seem to have been subject to secrecy.
[7] Suet. *Nero,* 34 ; cf. Aristoph. *Frogs,* 354 f.
[8] Cf. Farnell, *Cults,* III. 355.

every defilement and whose soul is conscious of no evil ';
' whosoever has lived a righteous life.' [1] Orphic formulae
barred the doors to the profane.[2] Homicides were
particularly precluded. A more exacting proclamation
required ' that no one should approach unless he was
conscious of his innocence.' [3] Even a saintly man like
Apollonius of Tyana was excluded by the hierophant from
initiation into the Eleusinian Mysteries because reputed
to be a magician.[4] In the days of Libanius [5] initiation was
for ' the pure of soul.' Lucian's parody of the Mysteries
represents his false prophet as beginning with the utterance :
' If any Atheist, or Christian, or Epicurean has come to
spy upon our festival, let him begone,'[6] followed later by
' Christians, avaunt.' ' Epicureans, avaunt.'

2. *Confession.* The entrance to the Mysteries being
guarded so scrupulously, it may be inferred that some sort
of confession of sin was required of the neophyte. It will
not surprise us, whose sense of sin has been quickened by
Hebrew prophetism and the spiritual ideals of Jesus, that
the consciousness of sin played a small part in ancient
paganism. But even in the scanty remnants of the Mysteries
we have ample evidence that at least several of these—the
Samothracian, Lydian, Phrygian, Syrian, and Egyptian—
anticipated Catholicism in the establishment of a Confessional [7]—but less rigid—with the elements of a penitential
system and absolution for uneasy devotees. The priests
acted as representatives of the Mystery-god, exacting
auricular confession, which the sensitive *deisidaemon*
sometimes supplemented by public [8] confession or by a
written record even on a public stone.

The Samothracian Mysteries possessed such a system of

[1] Origen, *con. Cels.* III. 59.
[2] Kern, *Orph. frag.* pp. 257, 261.
[3] Lamprid. *Sever.* XVIII.
[4] Philos. *Vita Apoll.* IV. 18.
[5] *Or. Cor.* IV. 356.
[6] *Alex.* 38.
[7] Cf. Steinleitner, *Die Beicht im Zusam. mit der sakralen Rechtspflege in der Antike*, pp. 110–23.
[8] Cf. Plutarch, *Deisidaemon*, VII. 168 D.

confessional.[1]   Plutarch [2] tells that when a certain Lysander was asked by the mystagogue to confess the most heinous sin lying on his conscience, he asked, 'Whether am I to do so at your bidding or at divine command ? '   ' By the Gods.' ' Well, then, if you leave me alone I will confess to them, if they want to know.'   An Antalkidas, asked to make a similar confession at initiation into the Samothracian Mysteries, replied, ' If I have done such a sin the gods themselves will know of it.' [3]

Juvenal records an interesting case [4] of confessional in the cult of Isis at Rome.   The Roman lady devotee of the Egyptian religion, having failed to observe the prescribed abstinence, consults the priest with a view to conciliate Osiris.   The priest lays her request before the deity and prescribes the offering of a goose and a cake as means of absolution.   Such cases were by no means isolated.[5]

3. Baptisms, or lustral purifications according to carefully prescribed forms, were required.   Says Tertullian [6] : ' In certain Mysteries, e.g. of Isis and Mithra, it is by baptism (*per lavacrum*) that members are initiated . . . in the Apollinarian and Eleusinian rites they are baptized, and they imagine that the result of this baptism is regeneration and the remission of the penalties of their sins.'   Similarly Clement of Alexandria [7] : ' It is not without reason that in the Mysteries current among the Greeks lustrations hold the premier place.'   At Eleusis the *mystae* cleansed themselves in the sea.   Apuleius, after prayer for pardon, underwent a bath of purification, and, after the vision of the deity, a baptism of sprinkling.[8]   After ten days' *castimonia* the Dionysiac candidate was thoroughly cleansed before

[1] Cf. Farnell, art. *Mysteries, Ency. Brit.* 11th ed. XIX, p. 119, who adds somewhat inaccurately, " in this respect unique in the world of classical religion " ; Ramsay, *Cities and B.* I, pp. 134, 152.

[2] *Moralia*, 229 D.

[3] *Apophth.* 217 D.

[4] *Sat.* VI. 532 ff.

[5] Cf. Porph. *De Abst.* IV. 15 ; Apuleius, *Met.* VIII. 28.

[6] *De Bapt.* 5 : cf. *De Praes. Haer.* 40.

[7] *Strom.* V. 11 ; cf. *ib.* 4.

[8] *Metam.* XI. 20, 23.

initiation.[1]   Ritual ablutions were originally assigned apotropaic efficacy ; but, as the centre of gravity shifted from magic to religion, the symbolic and sacramental aspect of ablutions became more obvious than the apotropaic ; but this did not arrest development in theories of baptism. The union of ' water ' and ' spirit ' was a conception current in ancient religion which did not dissever the sign and the inner experience.   The evidence for such baptisms and the importance attached thereto by antiquity,[2] especially in religions of the Mystery type, has been greatly increased by recent discoveries.   In the Hall of Initiation of the temple of Mên at Pisidian Antioch there was found an oblong depression, of which the most obvious explanation is that it was *lacus*[3] for baptism, not by bathing or immersion, as at Eleusis, but slighter.   In the underground pagan shrine, discovered a few months ago on the Via Salaria,[4] the most striking feature is a tank sunk deep in the floor which may well have served as a baptistery[5] in some Mystery-religion. Baptism was also viewed as a means or sacrament of regeneration,[6] as clearly expressed by Tertullian above.   Firmicus Maternus knew this conception in the Mysteries, but ' there is another water, whereby men are renewed and reborn.' [7] Conspicuous among such baptisms was the *Taurobolium*, which was to the *renatus* his ' spiritual birthday.'   In *Titus* III. 5 baptism is already the ' bath of regeneration ' accompanying *renewal* by the Spirit.[8]   In Hermas (*Sim.* IX. 16, 4) ' the seal of the Son of God ' is water, ' into which they descend dead and come up alive.'   In Gnosticism baptism

[1] ' *Pure lautum*' (Livy, XXXIX, 9).

[2] Cf. Hubaux, *Le plongeon rituel*, *Musée Belge*, XXVII, pp. 1–81.

[3] Ramsay, *Athenaeum*, Jan. '13, p. 106 f.

[4] Described in *Not. degli Scavi*, '23, p. 380 ff. by Sig. R. Paribeni, to whose kindness the writer owes the opportunity of inspecting the shrine.

[5] Not a Christian baptistery, as maintained by Wilpert; *v.* Paribeni, *ib.* p. 396.

[6] For an allied conception of baptism as the means of attaining divine sonship *v.* Usener, *Weihnachtsfest*, p. 160 ff.

[7] *De Err. Prof. Rel.* 2.

[8] Cf. *Acts* XXII. 16 ; *Eph.* V. 26 ; *Heb.* X 22.

was more important than even in orthodox Christianity.[1]
For the highest Mysteries a threefold baptism was required,
of Water, Fire, and Spirit.[2]

4. Sacrifices were not overlooked in the Mysteries. In
spite of the philosophic protest against bloody sacrifices,
the prevailing view in the theology of antiquity was that
' without shedding of blood there is no remission of sin,'
so that the ancients were familiar with what has been
termed " blood-theology." According to Jerome, to reverence the gods with offerings was one of the three precepts
carved in the shrine of Eleusis.[3] Olympiodorus [4] mentions
συστάσεις between purification and initiation : these
introductory rites are naturally sacrifices. The Eleusinian
ritual required the sacrifice of a young pig after the bathing
in the sea.[5] The inscription of Andania [6] in Messenia,
91 B.C., is the most explicit statement about mystery-sacrifices. The ceremony begins with the sacrifice of two white
lambs, followed at the purification by that of a healthy ram ;
then in the shrine the priest offers three young pigs, and
finally on behalf of the society one hundred lambs. In
addition to the common sacrifice of the mystery-community
each candidate at initiation would be obliged to offer an
individual sacrifice. The number and character of the
sacrifices doubtless varied with each Mystery. The
regulations [7] of the mystery society of the Iobacchi of Athens
include sacrifices. The instructive inscription of Lycosura [8]
specifies for the mysteries of the Mistress white female
victims. In the apse of the subterranean basilica outside
the Porta Maggiore are two sacrificial pits close to which
have been found sacrificial remains which have been identified
as skeletons of a dog and a pig—animals sacred to the cult

---

[1] Bousset, *Hauptprobleme*, p. 278 ff.   [3] *Adv. Iov.* II. 14
[2] Schmidt, *Kop.-Gnost. Sch.* I, p. 303.   [4] Lobeck, p. 41.
[5] Cf. Aristoph. *Frogs*, 338 ; *Achar* 764 ; *Peace*, 374.
[6] Cf. Sauppe, *Die Mysterieninschrift von Andania* ; Prott-Ziehen, I,
p. 166 ff. ; Michel, *Recueil*, no. 694 ; Cauer, 47.
[7] Greek text in Maas, *Orpheus*, pp. 18–32.
[8] Ditt. *Syll.* 2nd ed. 939; Prott-Ziehen, II. 63. Cf. Pausanias, VIII.
37, 3, and Frazer's notes.

of the Chthonians. By the impluvium of the atrium the
bones of a second pig were found. In a chest in a chamber
giving entrance to the hall of initiation in the basilica of the
Fondo Gargiulo (Villa Item) were discovered bones of birds,
probably remnants of the mystery-sacrifices. Similar discoveries in some Mithraea point to the usage of bird
sacrifices.[1]

5. Ascetic preparations of all kinds and degrees of rigour
were practised—prolonged fasts, absolute continence, severe
bodily mutilations and painful flagellations,[2] uncomfortable
pilgrimages to holy places, public confession, contributions
to the church funds—in fact, nearly every form of self-
mortification and renunciation practised by the saints and
mystics of all ages. Some of these were of such severity
as to be expected only from the priests or saints of a Mystery :
they were often signs of growth in grace rather than mere
acts of preparation, but they never lost in the estimation of
antiquity their purificatory virtue. That adherents of these
religions were induced to undergo tedious and painful rites
and renew them after initiation may seem strange in our age
of comfortable religion. The motives prompting may have
been as disparate as human motives have ever been :
spiritual or worldly, or both—the sense of sin, the desire to
escape the clogging weight of the body, or to enter into the
felicities of the religious exaltation enjoyed by others (as
Paul discovered in his Corinthian communities), to attain a
pre-eminence which would entail both honour and profit,
to facilitate the ascent of the soul.

Rigorous ablutions were practised which must have taxed
the robustest health, an example of which is given by Juvenal
of a devotee of Isis : ' She will break the ice and descend into
the river in winter ; thrice a morning she will bathe in the
Tiber and lave her tumid head in its very depths. Then,
with bleeding knees, she will creep, naked and shivering, over
the whole length of the Campus Martius.'[3]

---

[1] Cumont, *T. et M.* I. p. 322.
[2] Graillot, *Le Culte de Cybèle*, p. 301 ff. ; Macchioro, *Zagreus*, p. 121 ff.
[3] *Sat.* VI. 521 ff. ; cf. Seneca, *De Vita Beata*, XXVI. 8.

Abstinence from food was a feature common to the entrants into all the Mysteries. Fasting may not be due in its origin to ascetic reasons arising from dualism, but was partly a self-discipline and partly a reversion to primitive customs,[1] but the purpose of it as a constituent rite in the Mysteries was partly to avoid conveyance of evil and impurities into the body, partly as a due preparation for the reception of the holy food of the sacramental meal,[2] and partly through the weakening of the body to give the spirit the upper hand and induce the pathological conditions for the ecstatic exaltation. Sometimes the injunction to abstinence extended to all foods, but mostly only to specific, especially luxurious and flesh foods and wine. There was a prescribed period of fasting varying according to the different Mysteries, but eager initiands frequently, in the ardour of their faith, exceeded the prescription as a supererogatory merit ; such was the case of Lucius—' lege perpetua praescriptis illis decem diebus spontali sobrietate multiplicatis.' [3]

The Mysteries, in demanding abstinence from candidates, were introducing and promoting the Oriental ascetic ideal into the religious practices of the West, which was alien to the brightness of Greek worship and the practical form of Roman piety. Of course, Greece had her Eleusinian Mysteries, but modified by Oriental influences, and Rome had her vestals ; but neither Greeks nor Romans looked upon the reduction of the body and the renunciation of the external things of life as part of religion until they came under the influence of the Oriental asceticism, especially in the Mysteries. Fasts, either partial or absolute, were so characteristic of alien cults that Seneca gave up vegetarianism to avoid suspicion of being a member of a foreign religion. In the Eleusinian legend Demeter fasted nine days, thus setting an example to initiates. ' I have fasted ' was part of the *symbolum* of such initiates.[4] On the third day of the

---

[1] Cf. Hall in Hastings' *E.R.E.* III, p. 63 f.
[2] Cf. W. R. Smith, *Religion of the Semites,* new ed. pp. 434–5.
[3] *Metam.* XI. 30.
[4] Clem. Alex. *Protrep.* 2.

Thesmophoria the women fasted sitting on the ground.[1] The *Day of Blood*, preceding the *Hilaria*, was observed as a fast-day in the festival of the Great Mother.[2] Apuleius has recorded the thrice-repeated ten-day fasts of Lucius.[3] Long abstinences were also practised by the Mithraic celebrants.[4]

Absolute continence was requisite during the holy season, especially on fast days. In the festival of the Thesmophoria the women took an oath that they were free from contact with men.[5] The Eleusinian initiands were forbidden sexual intercourse during the holy season.[6] The Orphic Hippolytus protests his chastity.[7] In this respect the Mysteries bear the birth-mark of their Eastern provenance or modification through Eastern influences. Such cult encratism contrasts strangely with some survivals of phallism and with the occasional eroto-religious excesses which too often were the concomitants of mysticism.[8]

6. Another feature of preparation for the full privileges of the Mysteries were the pilgrimages of a penitential nature, thus satirized by Juvenal : ' If the white-robed Io [Isis] commands, the devotee will go to the confines of Egypt and will carry back the desired waters from cold Meroe, that she may sprinkle them in Isis' shrine.' [9] Apuleius has left a vivid account of his wanderings from shrine to shrine by which his purse was depleted. These pilgrimages were repeated after initiation as tokens of devotion when the worshipper could afford the heavy expense, and in the world-wide religious revival commencing in the first century of our era such religious pilgrimages became increasingly fashionable.[10]

[1] Plutarch, *De Is. et Osir.* 69. [4] Cf. Hepding, p. 182 f.
[3] *Metam.* XI. 23, 28, 30.
[4] Cf. Cumont, *Mysteries of Mithra*, p. 160 ff.
[5] Demosth. *Con. Neaerch.* 78.
[6] Porphyry, *De Abstin.* IV. 16. [7] Eurip. *Hipp.* 100 ff.
[8] Cf. Hartland, *Phallism*, in Hastings' *E.R.E.* IX, p. 827.
[9] VI. 525 ff.
[10] Cf. Aust, 9, 60. " Throughout the world of St. Paul we see a mighty wandering of pilgrims desirous to wash away their sins at the great shrines and to be delivered of their need " (Deissmann, *St. Paul*, p. 44).

7. Both in preparation for initiation and in the practice of the Mysteries obligations of painful self-mortification were laid upon those celebrants who would excel in the cult, or become hierophants, or reap the fullest advantages of adherence. The period was past when men offered the fruit of their bodies for the sin of their souls, but was succeeded by another epoch when men, by personal bodily torture and discomfort, would expiate their sins and placate the deity.[1] The naturalistic origin of the Mysteries, with violent and sanguinary survivals, rendered it too easy to retain repulsive self-mutilations against which the moral consciousness of a humaner era struggled with only partial success. The cruel elements were never wholly eliminated, though some Mysteries took on a more humane aspect than others, notably Orphism and the Hermetic Revelation Religion. Those of Phrygia and the related Anatolian cults were among the bloodiest ; next came the Syrian cults, but these were gradually refined by the development of a solar monotheism. That of Isis was the most respectable, while that of Mithra was the most sober. But in each and all it was, by a true religious instinct, perceived that man must enter into fellowship of the deity's sufferings if he would participate in the deity's joy.[2] In studying the cruel side of the Mystery-cults we must remember that the religious thought of the world was struggling with the twofold problem of the relation of the material to the spiritual, with but dim rays of that light which Christian idealism has shed upon the enigma, and of the means whereby man can most securely enter into union with God. In an era of religious excitation no price was too high to pay to attain quietude of heart. The worst forms of self-mortification were generally performed by, but by no means restricted to, the priesthood.

The religious self-mutilations were of Oriental provenance.[3] The most familiar are those of the Galli of the Great Mother

---

[1] Cf. Keats' Dionysiac hymn in *Endymion*.

[2] Cf. Paul's view of the Christian life as in one aspect a replica of that of Jesus (*Rom.* VI. 1 ff. ; *Phil.* II. 5 ff.).

[3] Cf. Gray, art *Eunuch* in Hastings' *E.R.E.* V, p. 580

(contemptuously called *semi viri* by Juvenal and *Gallae* by Catullus), which consisted in the laceration of their flesh with broken pottery, gashing of their limbs with knives during delirious dances and processions, self-flagellations or mutual floggings, and finally the perpetration of the culminating act of self-effacement in imitation of the act of their patron Attis under the pine-tree.[1] The male servitors of the Ephesian Artemis were eunuchs, as were also the priests of Atargatis, the *dea Syria*. The rites of Bellona, identified with Ma, Isis, and Cybele, were equally bloody with those of the Great Mother. Her black-robed *fanatici* made offerings of their own blood and slashed their bodies while raving ecstatically with a sword in each hand.[2] Blood drawn from the lacerated thighs of the priests and partaken of by the candidates was the seal of initiation.[3]

The probation for entry into the Mithraic communion was more prolonged and the degrees of preparation more numerous and exacting than for other cults, though not so orgiastic as those of Anatolia. The number, however, and nature of the Mithraic grades are somewhat uncertain, perhaps owing to the disturbance of the original economy— whatever it was—by the introduction of the astral theology of the seven planets and the still later solar theology of the twelve signs of the zodiac. Students of Mithraism [4] usually follow Jerome [5] in affirming the existence of seven grades : *Raven*, *Hidden* or *Secret One* (? *Cryphius*), *Soldier*, *Lion*, *Persian*, *Sun-runner* (*Heliodromus*) and *Father*, of which the *Lion* is the most frequently met and that of *Father* the most coveted. Phythian-Adams contends for the number six as being correct and original.[6] On the other hand, Celsus [7] would indicate perhaps eight grades when he states

---

[1] Hepding, p. 158 ff.   [2] Lactantius, *Inst.* I. 21.

[3] Tert. *Apol.* 9.

[4] E.g. Cumont, Dill, Legge, Toutain, Dieterich.

[5] *Ep. ad Laetam*, CVII. 2.

[6] *The Problem of the Mithraic Grades* in *Jour. of Roman Studies*, vol. II (1912), pp. 53-64. ' Soldier,' he holds, was not a grade, but a designation which any Mithraist might apply to himself, *militia* being a frequent religious metaphor.

[7] Origen, *Con. Cels.* VI. 22.

that in the Persian Mysteries there is a ladder with seven [1] gates with an eighth gate at the top. The first three stages, according to Porphyry,[2] preceded initiation, so that the subsequent grades marked degrees of spiritual rank after initiation. Either the communicant himself or the officiating priest or those present, were obliged to wear masks corresponding to the *Raven* and *Lion*, and a garb corresponding to the other characters. By the strictest kind of freemasonry the initiate was tested at each stage, and his spiritual career was marked by ordeals, feigned or real, and by an austere discipline which demonstrated his courage, sincerity, and faith. He submitted to a baptism of total immersion.[3] He was called upon to pass through flame with hands bound and eyes blindfolded, or to swim rivers. In some cases at least the neophyte jumped down a precipice [4] : whether this was done in symbol merely or was an actual leap we cannot tell. If an actual jump it must have taken place outside the Mithraic chapels, which were too small to permit of such a gymnastic feat. A Heddernheim relief [5] represents a neophyte standing in snow.[6] Animal sacrifices, mostly of birds, were made in the chapels. At some stage the neophyte was obliged to witness or even to take part in a ' simulated death to produce reverence.' [7] A case is recorded [8] in which the emperor Commodus, on initiation, polluted the chapel by perpetrating an actual murder upon a celebrant. What was the nature of this symbolic death we may not be certain, though theologically it was perhaps viewed as vicarious rather than sacrificial, as we may infer from the evidence of the practice of animal sacrifices.[9] Suggestive symbolic ceremonies were enacted

---

[1] Reading ἑπτάπυλος for ὑψίπυλος.   [3] Porphyry, *De Antro Nymph.* 15.
[2] *De Abstin.* IV. 16.   [4] *Ibid.*
[5] Cumont, *T. et M.* II, pl. VIII.
[6] Gregory of Nazianzen, with exaggeration, makes the candidate pass through eighty tortures, after which, if he is alive, he is initiated (*In Julianum*, Migne, *P.G.* XXXVI, pp. 989, 1010).
[7] Lamprid. *Commod.* 9 in *Script. hist. August* 1, p. 105.
[8] *Ibid.*
[9] Cumont, *T. et M.* I, p. 322.

at each stage of initiation. Tertullian [1] records that the neophyte, on attaining the degree of 'Soldier,' was offered, at the point of a sword, a crown or garland, which was then put upon his head only to be thrust away with the confession 'Mithra is my crown.' Such a soldier was 'signed' on the forehead with a hot iron. Thenceforth he renounced the social custom of wearing a garland even at a banquet. According to Porphyry,[2] on entry upon the next degree, that of 'Lion,' the initiate's lips were purified with honey.

8, Other admissory rites or customs are often mentioned in our sources, e.g. smearing the body with mud [3] and subsequent washing, cleansing with gypsum in Orphic usage, incubation, the reception of a new name, the reading of scriptures,[4] and the mastery of some foreign expressions, or secret formulae, enthusiastic pantomimic dancing ('for there is no mystery without dancing'),[5] enforced silences, veiling, the donning of new robes, offering incense, roaring like a wild animal—perhaps the original totemistic animal—the wearing of masks, the drinking of spirituous liquors.

Special importance attached to wearing the proper vestments [6] and generally white robes—because of the 'holy marriage' with the deity. At initiations—as seen in the Villa Item frescoes—a special priestess supervised the robing, particularly for the Eleusinian Mysteries.[7] In the Bacchic ceremonies a special vestment, the *sindon*, was essential.[8] The strict regulations of the Andania inscrip-

---

[1] *De Corona*, 15.

[2] *De Antro Nymph.* 15.

[3] Cf. Harpocration, ἀπομάττων.

[4] On the use of books cf. Lobeck, p. 193 ; Paus. IV. 27, 5 ; Dem. *De Cor.* 259, *De Falsa Leg.* 199 ; Manetho, II. 197 ; Diog. Laer. X. 4. 'Let the priests hand the books to those appointed therefor' (Andania inscr. l. 12). The *catechesis* scene is well illustrated in the frescoes of the Villa of the Mysteries (Macchioro, *Zagreus*, p. 73). Cf. Cook, *J.R.S.* III, p. 170. A similar reading of a divine liturgy is recognizable in the ceiling of one of the aisles in the underground basilica at the Porta Maggiore (*J.H.S.* XLIV, p. 95).

[5] Lucian, *On Dancing*, 15 ; cf. Dieterich, *Kl. Schr.*, p. 465.

[6] Macchioro, *Zagreus*, p. 44.

[7] Foucart, *Mystères*, p. 210.

[8] Cf. Strabo, XVI. 58, 712 C ; Meinike, and Suidas, σινδονιάζειν διονυσιάζειν.

tion [1] regarding the garments and their maximum prices are evidence of the value attached to correct ritual dressing in antiquity. Another inscription [2] records the appointment of a special priestess to prevent zeal or rivalry in such robing being carried to excess.

Initiates were 'crowned.' The Orphics crowned themselves with flowers. The Graeco-Roman vase of Monaco [3] shows, amid some eschatological scenes, an initiate with a crown on his head. The *pinax* of Ninnion [4] and the relief of Lacratides [5] represent the Eleusinian candidate crowned with myrtle, the nuptial plant sacred to Aphrodite.

In all the Mystery-Religions the candidate was 'seated on a throne,' *thronosis* being, as defined by Hesychius, [6] ' the first step in initiation,' so that to be 'enthroned' was synonymous with 'initiated.' [7] According to Dio Chrysostom, 'initiators are accustomed, in the so-called enthroning, to set up the candidates and dance around them in a circle.' [8] Aristophanes, [9] in his burlesque on Socrates, parodies the Dionysiac *thronosis*. The Orphics practised the same rite as *thronismos*, or *enthronismos*, [10] which is recognizable in one of the scenes in the Villa Item. [11]

II. INITIATION AND COMMUNION

After due probation the neophyte was solemnly received into membership of the Mystery cult and into fellowship with its members and its tutelar deity. Naturally, we know less about the process of the initiation proper than about any

[1] l. 16 ff.
[2] Foucart, *Assoc. relig.* no. 4, 7 f.
[3] Baumeister, *Denkm. d. klass. Alt.* III, fig. 77.
[4] *Journal internat. d'arch. numism.* IV. '01, tab. I ; Harrison, *Proleg.* fig. 158.
[5] Reinach, *Répertoire des reliefs*, II, p. 348 ; cf. schol. on *Oed. Col.* 715.
[6] θρόνωσις καταρχὴ περὶ τοὺς μυουμένους.
[7] Rohde, *Kl. Schriften*, I, p. 298 ; cf. Plato, *Euthyd.* VII. 277 D.
[8] XII. 387 Dind. de Arnim. I. 163, 33.
[9] *Clouds*, 254 f.
[10] Lobeck, p. 368 f
[11] Macchioro, *Zagreus*, p. 32 ff.

other part of the Mysteries [1]: the rites could not be divulged. Hence some stages of initiation are unknown, or so obscure as to be unintelligible : e.g. we cannot be sure as to the place or meaning of the symbol ' A kid, I fell into milk,' in the Orphic confession. The nearest approach to an unveiling of the Isiac initiation is found in Apuleius' enigmatic words : ' Hear, therefore, but believe what is true. I approached the confines of Death and trod the threshold of Proserpina : I was carried through all the elements and returned again : in the middle of the night I saw the sun gleaming in radiant splendour. I approached into the presence of the gods below and the gods celestial and worshipped before their face ' ; and he significantly adds : ' Behold, I have told you things which, although you have heard them, you must not understand.' [2]

Initiation (*traditio sacrorum*) included ' things exhibited,' ' acts done ' and ' things said,' the emphasis being put on the exhibition of the *sacra* and the symbols of the divine passion rather than on specific teaching, of which it is impossible to speak with certainty.[3] Clement of Alexandria assigns to the Lesser Mysteries (Eleusinian) a basis of instruction and preparation for the subsequent Greater Mysteries, of which he asserts that nothing remains to be learned of the universe, but only to contemplate the vision and comprehend nature and things,[4] and again, that the Mysteries were revealed only ' after certain purifications and preliminary instructions.' With a view to initiation Apuleius speaks of a reading from the Isiac scriptures and several (ten) days' preliminary *culturae sacrorum ministerium*.[5] Of at least an elementary catechumenate for initiands there is ample evidence. In the Orphic frescoes of the Villa Item the scene of the toilet and veiling of the initiand is succeeded by one in which she stands attentively listening while a child priest reads from a roll under the supervision of a

---

[1] Cf. Foucart, *Mystères d'Éleusis*, p. 389 ff.
[2] *Metam.* XI. 23.
[3] Cf. Lobeck, p. 141 f. ; Macchioro, *Zagreus*, p. 74.
[4] *Strom.* V. 11 (689 ; 71, 1) ; cf. Lobeck, p. 140 f.
[5] *Metam.* XI 22, 23.

seated female figure holding another roll in her left hand. In the cult of Demeter of Pheneus holy books were employed to give a basis of instruction for the greater Mysteries.[1]

That there existed any elaborate dogmatic system of esoteric doctrines is improbable.[2] Synesius[3] asserts: 'Aristotle maintains that it is not necessary for the initiated to learn anything, but to receive impressions and to be put in a certain frame of mind by becoming worthy candidates.' The 'things said' consisted not so much in a *disciplina arcani* as in ritual directions regarding cult symbols,[4] liturgical forms, esoteric formulae, the annunciation of the candidate's obligation to suffer in the passion of the god, the authorized version of the cult legend,[5] the *propria signa, propria responsa.*[6] The appeal was to the eye, the imagination and the emotions rather than to the intellect, the main purpose being to induce the initiand through the substitution of personality[7] (by hallucination, hypnotism, or suggestion) to *experience* his identification with deity.

It was inevitable, however, as the Mysteries developed an apologetic and linked up with the speculation of the age, that theory and interpretation should develop *pari passu*, but such *praecepta et alia eiusmodi* were common property.[8] The addition of the words *religionis secreta perdidici* in the Attis formula given by Firmicus Maternus, but not found in the parallel Greek originals, may indicate a later stage when more instruction was imparted.[10] This increasing demand for explanation is well illustrated in both Hermeticism and Gnosticism, and was accentuated by the cosmic pretensions of the Mysteries.

[1] Pausanias, VIII. 15, 1.
[2] Cf. Anrich, p. 31 ; Hatch, p. 289 ; Kennedy, *St. Paul*, p. 83.
[3] *De Dione*, 10.
[4] Cf. Apul. *Apol.* 53 ff.
[5] Cf. Farnell, *Ency. Brit.* 11th ed. XIX, p. 121.
[6] Firm. Mat. *De Err. Prof. Rel.* 18.
[7] Macchioro, *Zagreus*, p. 135 ff.
[8] Seneca, *Ep.* XCV. 64.
[9] *Ib.* 18.
[10] Cf. Dibelius, *Die Isisweihe*, p. 10.

Taurobolium

The most impressive sacrament of the Mysteries was the *taurobolium*,[1] or bath in bull's blood—a rite so costly that sometimes the expense was borne by the whole brotherhood.[2] The *taurobolium* formed part of the ritual of the Cybele-Attis cult [3] from at least the second century, from which it may have been borrowed by the Mithraists.[4]   The earliest form and idea of the rite are uncertain : it is familiar to us only in its latest developments in connexion with the religious conception of regeneration.   " In the *taurobolium* there was developed a ritual in which, coarse and materialistic as it was, paganism made, in however imperfect a form, its nearest approach to the religion of the Cross." [5] The fullest account has been left by the Christian poet, Prudentius,[6] to whom, as to the other Christian apologists, it was an object of special detestation both because of the supposed benefits accruing thereto and because of its affinity in redemptive conception with the sacrifice of Calvary, of which it was viewed as a travesty.   A trench was dug over which was erected a platform of planks with perforations and gaps.   Upon the platform the sacrificial bull was slaughtered, whose blood dripped through upon the initiate in the trench.   He exposed his head and all his garments to be saturated with the blood ; then he turned round and held up his neck that the blood might trickle upon his lips, ears, eyes, and nostrils; he moistened his tongue with the blood, which he then drank as a sacramental act.   Greeted

---

[1] First mentioned in the West in an inscription from Puteoli, *C.I.L.* X. 1596 (A.D. 134).

[2] *C.I.L.* XII. 4321.

[3] Cumont contends that the worship of the Great Mother derived this rite from the Persian, or Cappadocian, cult of Anahita (*T. et M.* I, p. 194 ff. ; *Revue arch.* XII. 1888, p. 132 ff. ; *Religions or.*, 2nd ed., pp. 99 ff., 332–3) with whom agree Dill, p. 556 ; Kennedy, p. 95. Hepding on the other hand claims pure Phrygian origin for the *taurobolium*, p. 201.

[4] So Dill, pp. 556, 609 ; Legge, II, p. 259 ; denied by Cumont (*T. et M.* I, p. 334, II. p. 179 n. ; *Mysteries of M.*, pp. 180–1, 3rd ed. p. 192 ; Roscher, II. 3064) ; Toutain, p. 138.

[5] Dill, p. 555.

[6] *Peristeph.* X. 1011 ff. (Hepding, pp. 65–7).

by the spectators, he came forth from this bloody baptism believing that he was purified from his sin and ' born again for eternity.' The efficacy of this consecration was such as to last for twenty years,[1] and was rated so high that many of those who had undergone the baptism have left testimony on their sepulchral stones of having been *renati in aeternum*.[2] It cleansed from the past and endowed with the principle of immortality. However crude this rite may have been in its inception, it was, in its later phases, used of God to give men peace in this life and hope beyond the grave.

A similar sacrament, but less frequent and held in less esteem, was the *criobolium*, or sacrifice of a ram, to which was attached the same ritual blood-baptism, with its spiritual interpretation. Sometimes it was performed in conjunction [3] with the *taurobolium*, sometimes as an alternative. The chief difference between these kindred rites, according to Showerman,[4] lies in this, that the *criobolium* was a sacrament instituted subsequently and on analogy of the *taurobolium* in order to give due prominence to the increasing importance of Attis in the myth, whereas the *taurobolium* had a previous history as a sacrifice before it became such a conspicuous rite of initiation.[5]

Regeneration (Palingenesia)

Since the great revival of the sixth century B.C. the idea of Regeneration [6] had become familiar, and with it a new sacramental conception, attested in Orphism, and in the cults of Isis, Attis, Dionysos, and Mithra. Every Mystery-Religion, being a religion of Redemption, offered means of suppressing the old man and of imparting or vitalizing the spiritual principle. Every serious *mystes* approached the solemn sacrament of Initiation believing that he thereby became ' twice-born,' a ' new creature,' and passed in a

[1] *C.I.L.* VI. 512.
[2] Cf. *C.I.L.* VI. 510 ; VIII. 8203.
[3] Hepding, p. 199.
[4] *The Great Mother of the Gods.*
[5] Hepding, *ib.*
[6] Cf. Lobeck, *Aglaoph.* p. 797 ff. ; Dieterich. *Mithraslit.*, p. 157 ff. ; Rohde, *Psyche*, II, pp. 421 ff. ; Reitzenstein, *Hell. Mysterienrelig.*, pp. 26, 31 ff. ; Kennedy, pp. 69 ff., 107 f., 209 ff. ; Macchioro, *Zagreus*, pp. 80 ff., 127.

real sense from death unto life by being brought into a mysterious intimacy with the deity. ' There can be no salvation without regeneration ' [1] was emphatically asserted in the Hermetic revelation. This regeneration was conceived in various ways, as realistic, physical-hyperphysical, symbolic, or spiritual. The conception went back ultimately to a crude and even physical belief in a divine ' begetting,' [2] by which men became sons of God : into this primitive region it is not necessary for our purpose to enter. The co-efficients of regeneration may not have been clear to the *mystes*—how much of faith, how much of magic resting upon *ex opere operato* potencies. The universal religious law of ' according to your faith ' obtained for the ancient worshippers, for whom regeneration might signify a solution of the pressing problem of dualism, or transformation of character, or the basis of spiritual exaltation, or mystic sympathy with the divine undying life which secured deathlessness.

Initiation proper was considered as a ' death ' from which believers arose through rebirth : probably for this reason the hour of midnight was often chosen as the most appropriate hour for initiation. There was a familiar word-play on the words for ' initiation ' (τελεῖσθαι) and ' dying ' (τελευτᾶν) : ' to die is to be initiated ' says Plato. Stobaeus [3] has preserved a fragment of Themistius (or Plutarch ?) which runs : ' then [the soul] suffers a passion, such as that of those who are undergoing initiation into great Mysteries ; wherefore also there is a correspondence of word to word and act to act in τελευτᾶν τελεῖσθαι with reference to the Dionysiac or Eleusinian Mysteries. Apuleius underwent ' a voluntary death ' (*ad instar uoluntariae mortis*) and ' approached the realm of Death ' in order thereby to attain his ' spiritual birthday ' (*natalem sacrum*) [4] in the service of a goddess whose followers were ' as it were

---

[1] *Corp. Hermet. Poim.* ch. XIII. (XIV.) 1.

[2] Cf. Windisch, *Die Katolischen Briefe*, pp. 118–20 ; Frazer, *G.B.* 3rd ed. II, p 247 ff.

[3] *Flor.* 120, 28 IV, p. 107 M. ; cf. Dieterich, *Mithraslit.*, pp. 163–4 ; Hatch, p. 289.

[4] *Metam.* XI. 21, 24, reading *sacrum*.

reborn ' (quodammodo renatos). This drama commemorated the death and resurrection of Osiris. In the rites of the Great Mother a trench or grave was dug in which the mystes was symbolically buried : [1] the tauroboliatus arose from the trench into a new life. According to Firmicus Maternus [2] the intending mystes of Attis was admitted as moriturus, ' about to die.' Perhaps some such death is indicated in Tertullian's enigmatic expression sub gladio redimit coronam, which he describes as ' in mimicry of martyrdom.'[3] An interesting example of symbolic burial in the Dionysiac-Orphic [4] rites is given by Proclus [5] : ' The priests command that the body should be buried except the head in the most secret of all the initiations,' as a result of which ' the Spirit in us is Dionysiac [divine] and a veritable image of Dionysos.'[6]

To such a death a new life succeeded by a spiritual resurrection. In the Mithraic initiation, after baptism, the branding on the forehead, and a sacred meal, Mithra, or the presiding priest, introduced imaginem resurrectionis,[7] and the supposed result of baptism in the Apollinarian and Eleusinian Mysteries was regeneration and the forgiveness of sins.[8] Hippolytus has preserved a valuable statement [9] of this doctrine of a rebirth in the Eleusinian Mysteries :

ἱερὸν ἔτεκε πότνιακοῦ ρον βριμὼ βριμόν, τουτέστινἰσχυρὰ ἰσχυρὸν

of which he explains πότνια as ' the spiritual begetting, which is heavenly, from above ' and the ἰσχυρὸς as ' he who is thus begotten.' That the mystes of Attis participated in the resurrection of his tutelar is stated by Damascius, who, with Isidorus, entered the Ploutium at Hierapolis : ' I dreamed that I had become Attis, and that I was being initiated by the Mother of the Gods in the

[1] Hepding, p. 196.
[2] De Err. Prof. Rel. 18.
[3] De Praes. Haer. 40 ; De Corona, 15.
[4] Dieterich, ib. p. 163.
[5] In Plat. Theol. IV. 9, p. 139 (Dieterich, ib. ; Hepding, p. 196).
[6] Ad Craty., p. 82.
[7] Tert. De Praes. Haer. 40.
[8] Id. De Bap. 5, 'in regenerationem et impunitatem periuriorum.
[9] Phil. V. 8, p. 164 ; Dieterich, Mithraslit, p. 138.

festival called *Hilaria,* inasmuch as it was intended to signify that our salvation from death had been accomplished.' [1] Sallustius [2] informs us that in the same Phrygian rites the newly initiated ' received nourishment of milk as if they were being reborn.' For the *tauroboliatus* the sacrament marked his religious birthday, *natalicium.* [3]

The more spiritual and mature a Mystery became, the more clamant grew the demand for regeneration, and the more the intuitions found expression in words rather than in symbol. Hence in the Hermetic revelation the mode, content, and results of regeneration occupy much attention. One interesting section [4] of the *Corpus Hermeticum* deals with this topic. Tat reminds his father, Hermes, that the latter had asserted that ' no one can be saved without regeneration,' the manner of which he had promised to reveal to him. Purified from worldliness, Tat now begs the boon, to which Hermes replies : ' Spiritual wisdom is found in silence, and the seed [birth] is the true good ' (2). By the will of God the new birth is accomplished by which the ' begotten ' of God becomes ' divine ' and ' Son.' Tat thereupon beholds the supersensual Vision and undergoes a transformation in his body by which he becomes other than he was. The author of the new birth is ' the Son of God,' ' the One Man ' by the will of God (4). The supersensual Truth is then revealed (6), after which he is released from twelve deadly sins (7) by ten divine Powers (11). Spiritual rebirth is an escape from the delusions of the body (13) in order by ' the essential birth ' to become ' divine and Son of the One ' (14).

Tat attains the Ogdoad, home of the Divine, or the Spiritual World, [5] where he hears from his father ' the Hymn of Regeneration,' which cannot be taught :

' Let all Nature hear the Hymn . . . let every bar of the

---

[1] Cited Hepding, p. 197 : ὅπερ ἐδήλου τὴν ἐξ Ἅιδου γεγονυῖαν ἡμῶν σωτηρίαν.

[2] *De Diis et Mundo,* 4.

[3] *C.I.L.* II. 5260.

[4] *Poimandres* XIV. (XIII.) ; text in Reitzenstein, pp. 339–48.

[5] Cf. Bousset, *Himmelreise* ; Kroll, *Lehren d. Hermes Trismegistos,* p. 362.

Abyss be opened. . . . I will hymn the Lord of Creation, the All and One. Let the heavens open . . . let the immortal Cycle of God receive my praise. . . . Let us all together give praise to him. . . . He is the light of my spirit ; his be the blessing of my powers. Ye powers of mine hymn the One and All ; join all of ye in song with my will. Holy Knowledge, enlightened from thee and by thee the spiritual light.[1] I rejoice as I raise my hymn in spiritual joy. . . . Hymn, O Truth, the Truth, O Goodness, the Good. Life and Light, from you comes as to you returns our thanksgiving. I give thee thanks, O Father, thou potency of my powers : I give thee thanks, O God, the power of my potencies. Thine own Word through me hymns thee : through me receive the all by thy Word, my reasonable (spiritual) sacrifice. . . . Accept from all reasonable sacrifice. Thou pleroma in us, O Life, save us ; O Light, enlighten us ; O God, make us spiritual. The Spirit guards thy Word. . . . Thou art God, and thy Man thus cries to thee. . . . From the Eternal I received blessing and what I seek. By thy will have I found rest.'

To which Tat responds with a Thanksgiving (21) :

' By thy Spirit, O Father, I declare what I perceive. To thee, author of my new birth, I, Tat, offer reasonable [spiritual] sacrifices. O God and Father, thou art the Lord, thou art the Spirit. Accept from me the reasonable sacrifices which thou requirest : for by thy will all things are accomplished.'

Hermes closes the Dialogue with the significant words which contain the gist of the whole experience : ' thou hast come to a spiritual knowledge of thyself and our Father.' [2]

A similar Thanksgiving is found at the close of the *Perfect Word*, the translation of which is given on p. 242.

Such a spiritual regeneration (νοερὰ γένεσις, ἡ γένεσις τῆς θεότητος) is also prominent in the so-called *Liturgy of Mithra*, which undoubtedly betrays Hermetic kinship. It will suffice to translate the Prayer of Invocation [3] :

---

[1] Text corrupt : cf. Reitzenstein's note.

[2] νοερῶς ἔγνως σεαυτὸν καὶ τὸν πατέρα τὸν ἡμέτερον.

[3] Dieterich, *Mithrasliturgie*, 2nd ed. p. 10, l. 34.

'O Lord, if it please thee, announce me to the greatest God, . . . I, a man, son of A. and born of the mortal womb of B. and of spermatic substance, that he to-day, having been born again by thee, out of so many myriads rendered immortal, in this hour according to the good pleasure of God in his surpassing goodness, seeks to worship thee and prays to thee to the utmost of his human powers.'

And the Hymn of Regeneration in the same Liturgy [1]:

'Hail, Lord, potentate of water ; hail, ruler of earth ; hail, master of spirit. . . . Lord, having been regenerated, I depart in exaltation, and having been exalted I die. Born again for rebirth of that life-giving birth, and delivered unto death, I go the way, as thou hast established, as thou hast decreed, as thou hast created the sacrament.'

Communion and Identification with God

Closely allied with Regeneration and common to all the Mysteries was the faith in communion, or identification with God. "It was the great merit of the Mysteries that they established and cultivated a communion between the human and the divine, and that they opened ways in which man could draw nearer God." [2] The relationship to deity was imperfectly conceived, and the co-efficients and issues often of a too sensuous and magical character. But that the Mysteries offered a certain satisfaction to the religious instinct [3] which seeks to know God and come near to Him is attested by their remarkable success and by the testimony of the initiates. The union with God effected by the Mysteries was vouchsafed, expressed, and maintained in various ways.

(a) The *mystes* was brought into a mystic ineffable condition in which the normal functions of personality were in abeyance [4] and the moral strivings which form character

---

[1] *Ib.* p. 14, l. 27.
[2] Gardner, *Relig. Exper. of St. Paul*, p. 100
[3] Cf. Mackintosh, *Originality*, etc. p. 19.
[4] Cf. Macchioro, *Zagreus*, p. 152 ff.

virtually ceased or were relaxed, while the emotional and intuitive were accentuated. These states were Ecstasy (ἔκστασις) and Enthusiasm (ἐνθουσιασμός), both of which might be induced by vigil and fasting, tense religious expectancy, whirling dances, physical stimuli, the contemplation of the sacred objects, the effect of stirring music,[1] inhalation of fumes, revivalistic contagion (such as happened in the Church at Corinth), hallucination, suggestion, and all the other means belonging to the apparatus of the Mysteries. These two kindred abnormal states of consciousness, often indistinguishable, are united by Proclus when he speaks of men 'going out of themselves to be wholly established in the Divine and to be enraptured.'[2]

In ecstasy[3] the devotee was lifted above the level of his ordinary experience into an abnormal consciousness of an exhilarating condition in which the body ceased to be a hindrance to the soul. Ecstasy might be of a passive character resembling a trance, or of an active orgiastic character of excitation resembling what Plato calls 'divine frenzy.' According to the means of induction, the temperament of the initiate, and his spiritual history, ecstasy might range anywhere from non-moral delirium[4] to that consciousness of oneness with the Invisible and the dissolution of painful individuality which marks the mystics of all ages.

" In ecstasy, in the freeing of the soul from the hampering confinement of the body, in its communion with the deity, powers arise within it of which it knows nothing in the daily life hampered by the body. It now becomes free as spirit to hold communion with spirits : also released from transiency, it is endowed with capacities to behold what only the eyes of the spirit can behold, that which is removed beyond time and space."[5]

Physically the condition was one of anaesthesia, uncon-

---

[1] Cf. Aristotle, *Pol.* VIII. 55.
[2] *In Rempub.* II, p. 108 (Kroll).
[3] Cf. Rohde, *Psyche*, II. 14–22 ; Inge, *Phil. of Plotinus*, II. 132–62.
[4] Cf. Philo, *Quis rer. div. haeres ?* 51, C.-W. 249, M. 508.
[5] Rohde, II, p. 20.

scious of pain or of anything hostile or disconcerting in the surroundings. There is ample evidence that the Bacchae, for example, were insensate to pain and endued with preternatural strength [1]; so also were the priests of Cybele and the priests and priestesses of Ma. This anaesthesia to pain [2] is a religious phenomenon known in all ages, especially in great revivals, and in many forms, from that of the Indian Yogi to the Christian martyr whose ecstasy took away the terrors of agonizing death by imparting miraculous fortitude. We may assume that this semi-physical, semi-psychic state was much coveted by the initiates, as the ' pneumatic ' condition was among the Christians of Corinth. To be lifted above sense to behold the beatific vision and become " incorporate in " God was the end sought in ecstasy, and the satisfaction sought, or derived, was of various kinds, physical or sensuous, aesthetic and intellectual.

In the more spiritual Mysteries the profoundest expression is given to the idea of ecstasy. In the *Liturgy of Mithra* the suppliant prays ' abide with me in my soul : leave me not,' and ' that I may be initiated and that the holy Spirit may breathe within me.' [3] The communion becomes so intimate as to pass into identity : ' I am thou and thou art I.' [4] Through such religious experiences men learned to seek that *coniunctione deorum qua homines soli eorum dignitate perfruuntur.*[5]

In this respect of communion we are able particularly to observe a tendency which obtrudes at so many points in the historic course of the Mysteries, namely, that Mysteries conduce to Mysticism, that through the spiritualizing of the interpretative faculty the purely symbolical recedes before the deepening of intuition and experience. The Mysteries held, in common with most religious philosophy of the time,

---

[1] Cf. Eurip. *Bacchae*, 757.

[2] Cf. Inge, Hastings' *E.R.E.* V. 158 b. Such anaesthesia is described by Nonnus, *Dionysiaca*, XIV. 384–5, and in striking words by Iamblichus. *De Myst.* III. 4, p. 110 (Parthey).

[3] *Mithraslit.*, p. 14, l. 24 ; p. 4, l. 13.

[4] *Pap. Graeci Musei Lugd.* II. 141 ; Kenyon, *Greek Papyri*, 116 f.

[5] Ps. Apuleius, *Asclepius*, VII.

the doctrine of an Ascent of the Soul [1] as a phase of salvation toward which ecstasy was valued as one important step. On the experience of ecstasy the philosophic thought of later paganism laid hold by a revulsion from arid doctrinaire dialecticism to a self-attesting experience of truth, corresponding to Schleiermacher's revolt from theological scholasticism. The Orphic and Dionysiac notes sounded louder as the West turned increasingly toward the East for new life. If the Mysteries supplied the phenomena of ecstasy philosophy attempted to analyse the psychology of a condition which it confessed to be ineffable. But ecstasy in its highest form has always been a rare experience even to cultivated mystics. Plotinus, than whom there never lived a more earnest mystic, was favoured with the beatifi vision only four times during the years of Porphyry's residence with him.[2] Porphyry himself confesses that he enjoyed the ecstatic state only once, and that not until his sixty-eighth year; and with that most practical of all mystics, St. Paul, ecstasy was an exceptional favour (2 *Cor.* XII. 2 ff.). In Philo's religious philosophy this much-coveted mystic condition occupies an important place.[3] But Philo knows also another species of ecstasy akin to inspiration or enthusiasm exemplified in Hebrew and early Christian prophetism and in the prophetic inspiration of ethnic religions.[4] Of such an experience, which Philo had himself experienced a thousand times, he has left an interesting account.[5]

Finally, if the mysticism of the Mysteries seems to us sometimes crude and unedifying, it gains in interest when we remember that it was in some degree the harbinger and later the ally of that rich philosophic-religious mysticism of closing paganism, which, in sublimated form, has become the perennial possession of Christianity through Philo,

---

[1] Cf. Bousset, *Archiv f. Religionswiss.* IV, p. 145 ff.

[2] Porph. *Vita Plot.* 23.

[3] Cf. Bousset, *Religion des Judentums*, 2nd ed. pp. 516 f. ; Kennedy, *Philo's Contribution*, p. 221 ff. ; Inge, II. p. 154 f.

[4] Cf. Reitzenstein, *Poim.* p. 220 ff.

[5] *De Migrat.* Abr. 7 (M.I. 441, C.-W. 34).

Plotinus, and the Neo-Platonists, Dionysius the Areopagite, Augustine, and the Christian Platonists.

Enthusiasm was the kindred state of communion often accompanying and confused with ecstasy,[1] but " *enthousiasmos* was from the first mainly a theological conception, while *ekstasis*, on the other hand, comes from the domain of medical terminology, and, so far as known, was not applied till long after Plato's day to the rapturous state of a soul delivered from earthly conditions."[2] Enthusiasm was the immediate ' inspiration ' or replenishing of the personality by the deity, defined by Plutarch[3] as ' an affective condition of the soul produced by some divine power.' The subjects became ἔνθεοι, ' in God,' κατεχόμενοι ἐκ τοῦ θεοῦ, ' possessed of the deity,' and ' full of God.' The term *enthousiasmos*, with its cognate *enthousiasis*, was probably first employed by Plato, and the verb ἐνθουσιᾶν first by Aeschylus[4] as a synonym of βακχεύειν. But to these terms and their correlatives a new prominence was given by the rapid spread of the Mysteries (with the doctrine of union with deity so fundamental to their theology), by the increasing prevalence of the ecstatic experiences cultivated in these individualistic religions,[5] and finally by the mystic theology of closing paganism. The idea of ' inspiration,' not unknown before the rise of the Mysteries, had a very wide application especially in the prophetic theology of the ancients. Under Enthusiasm were included by the Greeks all forms of Mantic, or prophecy and soothsaying, also revelations in dreams and visions, such revelations being the direct utterances of the deity. The songs of inspired poets are the product of enthusiasm, according to Plato ; while the Latin poets, e.g. Lucretius, are emphatic in claiming the inspiration of a *furor poeticus*. Plutarch[6] enumerates the varieties of enthusiasm as

---

[1] Cf. Rohde, II, p. 19 : Dieterich, *Mithraslit.*, p. 98.

[2] Radermacher, in Hastings' *E.R.E.*, V. 316.

[3] *De Amore*, 16 ; cf. Aristotle's definition of it as ' an emotional condition of the character of the soul ' (*Pol.* VIII. 1340 a, 11).

[4] Radermacher, *ib.*

[5] Cf. Reitzenstein, *Poim.*, p. 200.

[6] *De amore*, 16.

ENTHOUSIASMOS 105

prophetic, Dionysiac, the frenzy produced by the Muses, and amatory. In all forms of enthusiasm there is the same underlying idea that " the *entheos* is wholly in the power of the god, the god acts and speaks with him : his own self-consciousness has disappeared." [1]

These ideas found congenial soil in the Mysteries. Plutarch has likened the Bacchic frenzy to prophecy, and says that ' the rites of Cybele and Pan very much resemble the orgies of Dionysos.' [2] It is significant that the music of Phrygia— the homeland of orgiastic-mystic cults—was regarded as specially appropriate for the Bacchic and Corybantic dances. [3] Aristotle declares that the strains of the Phrygian musician, Olympus, ' make souls enthusiastic,' and refers to the flute as an instrument ' not affecting character, but orgiastic.' [4]

That the Mysteries cultivated these abnormal psychopathic conditions such as were manifested in Hebrew prophecy and later in the psychological phenomena of the three pre-eminent centuries of Christian mysticism, the first, fourteenth, and seventeenth, cannot be disputed. The spiritual nature of man in seeking union with God progressively purified and elevated the conception of ecstasy and enthusiasm from physical and artificial conditions to be channels of divine truth—from that enthusiasm too truly symbolized in the wine-god, Dionysus, to that of Philo, in which the thankful spirit ' is intoxicated with the sober intoxication,' [5] and that of Plotinus, in which the soul, elevated above the shadows of earth, ' returns to its Father ' and ' enjoys possession of the Heavenly Love.' [6] Orgiasm was forced to retreat before quietism.

Against an original dissociation of ecstasy and enthusiasm from ethical demands or a precarious alliance therewith the religious genius of the great mystics made ethical considera-

---

[1] Rohde, II. 19.   [2] *Ib.*
[3] *Ib.* ; cf. Proclus, *In Plat. Alc.* I, p. 479 ; *In Plat. Remp.* I. 84 ; Cicero, *De Div.* 1. 114.
[4] *Pol.* VIII. 1340 a, 10 ; 1341 a, 21.
[5] *Leg. alleg.* I. 26, Mang. 60 ; C.-W. I. 84.
[6] *Enn.* VI 9, 9

tions a requisite condition for a true enjoyment of these religious privileges. Thus, Plato says that the divinely possessed 'take on the character and qualities of the divine, so far as man may participate in God '[1]; and Philo asserts that it is impossible for a worthless man to become an interpreter of God, 'for, properly speaking, no wicked man can be inspired, which is appropriate only for a wise man.'[2]

(b) The Mystery-cults introduce us to another conception of communion with God at first sight very alien to our ideas, but one of far-reaching importance in religious history and finding a counterpart in modern Christian philosophy, viz. Deification, Demortalizing, or Apotheosis (ἀποθέωσις, ἀπαθανατισμός, θεοποίησις, θεωθῆναι).[3] It is rather the form than the content of the idea that appears so strange to moderns. Clement of Alexandria employed a language intelligible alike to pagan and Christian ; he writes :

'If anyone knows himself he shall know God, and by knowing God he shall be made like unto Him '[4]; and again 'that man with whom the Logos dwells . . . is made like God and is beautiful . . . that man becomes God, for God so wills it '[5]; and 'the Logos of God became man that from man you might learn how man may become God.'[6] Further, that the true (Christian) Gnostic 'has already become God.'[7]

In the same strain Lactantius[8] affirms that the chaste man (calcatis omnibus terrenis) will become 'identical in all respects with God' (consimilis Deo). Even more emphatically the Greek father, Methodius, taught 'every believer must through participation in Christ be born a

---

[1] *Phaedr.* 253 A.
[2] *Quis rer. div. her. sit.* LII. (Mang. I. 510, C.-W. III. 259).
[3] Cf. Reitzenstein, *Hell. Mysterienrelig.* p. 29 ff. ; Dieterich, *Abraxas*, 104 ; Wendland, *Hell.-röm. Kultur*, p. 73 ff. ; Fowler, *Rom. Ideas of Deity*, p. 98 ff.
[4] *Paed.* I. iii.
[5] *Ib.* 5.
[6] *Strom.* IV. 23 (p. 632).
[7] *Protr.* VIII. 4.
[8] *Div. Inst.* VI. 23.

Christ,'[1] and the master of orthodoxy did not hesitate to
say dogmatically, 'He was made man that we might be
made God.'[2]   We should remind ourselves that though
'God' is the literal rendering of θεὸς or *deus*, 'Divine'
might better convey to our minds what these terms conveyed to the minds of men living in the Graeco-Roman
world, to whom they were of a more fluid nature than
they have since long become in scholastic theology. The
conception of divinizing steadily took on more concrete
form, a process accelerated by the many lines of approach
between Oriental and Occidental ideas of the relation of
human and divine.   Even in Greece and Rome there
were legends of men who, by conspicuous deserts, had been
promoted to gods, as there were also legends of gods who
had descended to earth.   The Roman dead became *Manes*,
and so divine.   Greek heroes, like Brasidas, had after death
been accorded divine honours.   But in Hellenistic-Oriental
thought the essential unity of man and God was enforced
by, first, Orphic mystic speculations[3] as to the Descent
and Ascent of the soul, emphasizing the native divinity of
man, and professing to make initiates divine instead of
mortal through sacraments which enabled the soul to make
Ascent. Secondly, the spread of Egyptian-Hellenistic rationalism[4] as to the origin of the accepted deities, dating back
from the time of Alexander the Great, who was informed by
Leo, an Egyptian priest, that heroes and gods alike had been
elevated from the ranks of humanity,[5] a theory to which
later Hecataeus, under Ptolemy I, gave more definite
expression by asserting that the original gods were the
heavenly gods, sun, moon, etc., while the earthly gods, such
as Zeus and Isis, had been mortals divinized because of their
beneficent deeds to mankind.   It remained for Euhemerus
to systematize and popularize this theology in his epochal

[1] Cited, Inge, *Christian Mysticism*, p. 357.
[2] *De Incarn.* 54, ἵνα θεοποιηθῶμεν ; cf. *Orat. c. Arianos*, I. 39.
[3] " Die Mystik hat den Glauben an die Göttlichkeit der Menschenseele
gestärkt " (Wendland, p. 71).
[4] Fowler, p. 100, calls Egypt " The well-head of all these notions."
[5] Augustine, *De Civ. Dei*, VIII. 5.

Sacred History: he "simply denied their [gods'] existence as a species, so to speak, distinct from man."[1] This doctrine, in union with Greek anthropomorphism, spread like contagion and worked a revolution in the Roman conception of deity. What had happened before might be repeated : heaven was opened to candidates from earth. Thirdly, the attraction of pantheism and the philosophic teaching, especially of the Platonists and Stoics, that man is truly divine. In fact, "through the course of Greek religious thought a single thread may be traced, in the essential unity of man and God."[2] The pantheistic tendency is most pronounced in the Hermetic theology, and, in a less degree, in Orphism, while the later view of the essential kinship of God and man meets us in such Stoics as Seneca and Epictetus, and in an eclectic like Cicero. 'We are his offspring' was a Stoic sentiment cited with approval by Paul. Seneca says that ' a good man differs only in point of time from God, whose disciple and imitator he is.' Epictetus speaks eloquently of the security accruing to man from the fact that God is his Father : ' Do you suppose that God would suffer His own son to be enslaved ? ' ' Know, then, that thou art a god,' says Cicero,[3] ' and inferior in no whit to the celestials save in immortality.'[4] Fourthly, Daemonism, which contributed to facilitate the passage from human to divine. Lastly, above all was the God-Man conception, which, rising in the East, and advancing from vague intuitions and impalpable premonitions, and assuming diverse forms, modified all ancient pagan and even Christian theology. The steps by which such a conception acquired universal prevalence elude us. The primitive belief in the divine origin and function of kings, the practice of divinizing the dead or living rulers of the Ptolemaic dynasty and the Diadochi and the subsequent imperial cult familiarized men with acknowledging in individuals who rose above ordinary

---

[1] Fowler, *ib.*

[2] Mrs. Adam, *Greek Ideals of Righteousness*, p. 67.

[3] *De Repub.* VI. 17 ; *N.D.* II. 61.

[4] Cf. Oakesmith, *Religion of Plutarch*, pp. 120 ff., 171 f.

human stature a certain divinity and regarding them as visible deities, or god-men. The increasing importance of outstanding individuals in Hellenistic and Roman times was one of the most marked features of the new age which reacted directly upon theology. These individuals, of whom Alexander was the first, manifested in such an unmistakeable fashion their godlike capacities for bestowing universal tangible blessings upon mankind that they were inevitably after death, and sometimes during their lifetime, *in deorum numerum relati*. Amid the distress of the pre-Christian centuries who shall say how far the wish was father to the thought ? Men were craving for a *praesens deus*, a visible manifestation of deity, such an epiphany as should right the wrongs of the world, heal its bleeding wounds, and give social peace and economic security. Prayers and thanksgiving were directed to these incarnate Benefactors as visible gods. In the year 48 B.C. the Asiatic cities set up an inscription to Julius Caesar hailing him as ' God manifest and universal Saviour of human life.' [1] Similarly, Augustus was recorded as ' Ancestral God and Saviour of the whole human race,' [2] whose name Ovid in a prayer for grace couples with the gods with the significant words ' than whom *he* is more tangible.' [3]

The Mystery-Religions did not overlook such fruitful conceptions, which they had anticipated. They undertook to effect such apotheosis not merely for outstanding personalities but for the humblest candidate. Divinizing was conceived in the main in three ways, which, however, cannot be treated separately : (1) mystic identification with the tutelar ; (2) endowment with deathlessness and transformation into the divine substance ; (3) in a more refined form, in the divine indwelling, by which the material man became spiritual. By mystic identification Lucius, after the sacrament of initiation, was ' arrayed like the sun

---

[1] Dittenberger, *Sylloge*, 2nd ed. I. 347 ; 3rd ed. 760.
[2] *Greek Inscriptions in the British Museum*, 894 ; cf. *Praesens Divus habebitur Augustus*, Hor. *Carm*. III. 5, 2.
[3] *Ep Ponto*, I. 1, 63 : ' quibus est manifestior ipse.'

and set up like an image of the god' before the spectators.[1]
The *mystes* of Attis became himself Attis.[2] On an Orphic
tablet, found at Petelia and now in the British Museum, the
deceased declares, ' I am a child of Earth and Starry Heaven ;
but my race is of Heaven.' On a Compagno tablet, now in
the Museum of Naples, the deceased is addressed as ' Happy
and blessed one, thou shalt be god instead of mortal.'[3]
In a more elevated form we meet the same thought in the
Hermetic religion. A Greek papyrus has preserved a
magical prayer based on Hermetic theology, in which occur
the words : ' Enter thou into my spirit and my thoughts my
whole life long, for thou art I and I am thou ; thy name I
guard as a charm in my heart '[4] ; in a similar prayer we read :
' I know thee, Hermes, and thou knowest me : I am thou,
and thou art I.'[5] The second mode of divinizing, by
endowing with immortality, was first popularized by Orphism,
and became during the Graeco-Roman era one mode of
conceiving immortality. According to Greek, and even
Latin, theology, the gods differed from men only in being
immortal.[6] Consequently, to render a mortal immortal was
to deify him. Such was the significance of the triumphant
Orphic faith—' a God instead of mortal.' This demortalizing (ἀπαθανατισμός) is the subject of a thanksgiving in
the so-called *Liturgy* of *Mithra :* ' I a man . . . born of
mortal womb . . . having been this day begotten again by
thee, out of so many myriads rendered immortal in this
hour by the good will of God in his abounding goodness.'[7]
' This is the good end for those who have attained knowledge, namely, Deification,' we read in the Hermetic
literature,[8] which recalls the famous statement of Clement of

[1] *Metam.* XI. 24.

[2] Hepding, p. 197.

[3] Harrison, *Proleg.* p. 586 f.

[4] Leemans, *Papyri Graeci Musei Lugd.* II. 141 ; cited also Dieterich,
Abraxas, p. 196, Reitzenstein, *Poim.* p. 17.

[5] Kenyon, *Greek Papyri in the British Museum*, I. p. 116 ; Reitzenstein,
ib. p. 20.

[6] Cf. Rohde, *Griech. Religion*, p. 11 (*Kl. Schr.* 322) ; *Psyche*, II, p. 2

[7] *Mithraslit.*, p. 12, 2.

[8] *Poim.* I. 26.

Alexandria that the true Gnostic 'practises being God.'[1]
In the thanksgiving prayer of the *Perfect Word* occurs the
expression ' Saved by thee . . . we rejoice that even in our
mortal bodies thou didst deify us by the Vision of Thyself.'[2]
The same thought is familiar in an Orphic ritual prayer.[3]

A third phase, the divine indwelling, expressed a religious
experience which formed a ground common to the Mysteries
and Platonic and Stoic philosophy and to Christianity. The
experience and modes of expression admitted of great
varieties. The devotee in the *Liturgy of Mithra* prays :
' abide with me in my soul : leave me not,'[4] and ' that I
may be initiated and that the Holy Spirit may breathe
within me.'[5] A magical prayer in the British Museum runs,
' Come to me, Lord Hermes, as babes to women's wombs,'[6]
a phase of mysticism which recalls many of the seemingly
exaggerated cravings of some of the Christian Mystics.[7]
This condition of divine indwelling is the counterpart to that
of enthusiasm whereby the mystic is in a real sense ' in God '
by substitution or interpenetration of personality. The
Mysteries were thus familiar with that mutual indwelling
of human and divine so conspicuous in the mystical aspects
of Paulinism, and still more in the thought of the Fourth
Gospel, and in the highest reaches of Christian experience.
To Paul ' in Christ,' ' in the Spirit,' and ' Christ in you '
were synonymous expressions of a psychological reality.
The language of the Fourth Gospel, ' I in you and you in
Me,' conveyed a familiar meaning to a world saturated in
mystic thought. A London papyrus[8] has preserved a

---

[1] μελετᾷ εἶναι θεός.

[2] Greek text in Reitzenstein, *Hell. Mysterienrelig.* 114.   The Latin
translation (*Asclepius*, 41) weakly renders : ' Numine salvati tuo . . .
gaudemus quod nos in corporibus sitos aeternitati fueris consecrare
dignatus.'

[3] Comparetti, *Laminette orfiche*, p. 25; cf. *I.G.S.I.* 642, Diels, *Frag.*
3rd ed. p. 177 n. 20.

[4] *Mithraslit.*, p. 14, 24.

[5] *Ib.* p. 4, 13.

[6] Kenyon, *ib.* ; Dieterich, *Mithraslit.*, p. 97.

[7] As Madame Guyon, in a trance or ecstasy, became married to Christ.

[8] Wessely, *Gr. Zauberpapyri*, 122, 37 f.

magical (Hermetic) prayer : ' for thou art I, and I am thou ; thy name is mine, for I am thy image (*eidolon*).' If the language of the ancient initiates seems to us very impalpable, elusive, and exaggerated, so also is frequently the language in which those who have seen the Vision Beatific have endeavoured to label religious experiences, the reality and power of which cannot be doubted. Philosophy came to the aid of the Mysteries in asserting, ' God is nigh thee, is with thee, is within thee. . . . A holy spirit dwells within us, a scrutinizer and guardian of our good and evil.'[1] Epictetus teaches : ' You are bearing a God with you though you know it not. Do you think I mean some external god of silver or gold ? It is within yourself you carry him, and you do not perceive that it is he whom you profane by impure thoughts and unworthy actions. If even an image of God were present you would not dare to act as you do, but when God himself is within you, hearing and seeing all, are you not ashamed of such conduct and thoughts, ignorant of your own nature ? '[2]

(c) Another conception of communion with the deity in the Mysteries was a religious Marriage[3]—a conception the roots of which can be traced back to the Egyptian and Asiatic belief and practice of copulation with deity. When we compare the remote origins of this religious idea with its expression in Christian mysticism and hymnology we see how potent spiritual idealism has been in religious evolution. Other obvious human relationships being employed to represent the union of man and God, it was inevitable that the marriage relationship should be pressed into like service. Mystics of all ages have seen therein the most adequate symbol of the ineffably intimate union of the soul with God.[4] Such *synousia* had a double underlying idea : first,

---

[1] Seneca, *Ep.* 41, 2.

[2] *Disc.* II. 8.

[3] Cf. Lobeck, pp. 608, 649 ff. ; Dieterich, *Mithraslit.* 3rd ed. pp. 121–34 ; Macchioro, *Zagreus*, p. 70 ff. ; Reitzenstein, *Poim.* 226 ff. ; *Hel. Mysterienrel.* p. 21 ff. ; Foucart, *Mystères d'Éleusis*, p. 475 ff. ; Bousset, *Hauptprobleme*, ch. VI ; Anrich, p. 77.

[4] Cf. Underhill, *Mysticism*, p. 495 f.

an erotic-anthropomorphic, in which *synousia* has the character of an offering or sacrifice (of purity) ; secondly, the magical, whereby the worshippers participated in the god's *Mana* and secured life and salvation. There were three stages of growing refinement whereby the early worshipper joins hands across the centuries with the great mystics.[1] First,[2] the ' holy marriage ' corresponded to a literal act of *synousia* with the deity through his priests, or phallos, or otherwise. Such a ceremonial could not persist in face of an increasingly worthy sense of man and God. As society regulated the relations between the sexes phallic ideas were forced to retreat. At first the difference between legend and poetry was not marked. Of a form of communion which excluded males Plutarch records that the Egyptians believe ' it is not impossible for the Spirit of God to have intercourse with a woman ' καὶ τίνας ἐντεκεῖν ἀρχὰς γενέσεως, ἀνδρὶ δ' οὐκ ἔστι σύμμιξις πρὸς θεὸν οὐδ' ὁμιλία σώματος.[3] This limitation to women shows that the time had not yet come when the soul could be regarded as the spouse of God. The curious story of Josephus about Paulina indicates how a lady of rank and education could be induced to enter an Isiac temple to hold intercourse with Anubis.[4] This was probably not an isolated case, but so realistic was the antiquated formula that the danger for devout and credulous minds was obvious. The wife of the King-Archon at Athens was joined in a ritual marriage at the festival of the Anthesteria with Dionysus, commemorating a more literalistic period.

[1] " It seems to be a fact of religious history that the most primitive and crude conceptions of a union with God and those of the most exalted mysticism always meet in those religious images in which men think " (Dieterich, p. 134).

[2] Originally sacred marriages occurred with animals, e.g. Pasiphae, Europa, Leda. Then came the connexion between human beings and animals, e.g. Alexander's mother dreamt that she had copulated with a snake. Misgivings arose, since Pasiphae seems to have been a criminal in Greek, if not in Cretan eyes, and the Minotaur an abortion. A refinement is the story of Danaë, wherein Jupiter is a golden shower.

[3] *Numa*, IV ; cf. Reitzenstein, *Poim.*, p. 229.

[4] *Antiq.* XVIII. 3, 4, the historicity of which is disputed by Lafaye, *Culte de Divinités*, p. 54.

Secondly, such realistic union could not be tolerated by a maturer age. Men must stand on equality with women in the intimacy with deity, but the conception of *synousia* had become too venerable to be wholly discarded. The act was not repeated but exhibited in sacramental symbols and emblems in a form as far removed from the original theory as an observance of the Lord's Supper is from the cult meal in which the *mystae* of Dionysus tore asunder and ate the raw flesh of the mystic bull. Phallic associations never became quite extinct in the Mysteries. We must not, however, receive the language of the Christian apologists too literally. Their horror of phallic survivals caused them to use language which must be discounted by their tendency to hark back [1] to customs and beliefs which were antiquated to all thinking pagans, and by their construing the ' spiritual marriage ' as if the *mystae* had not outgrown the original stage. When all is said, enough remained of offensive symbolism to afford Christian controversialists cause for scorn [2] and even a pagan for his witticism.[3] On the other hand, the great Mystery-apologist, Iamblichus, defends the sacramental marriage at initiation as calculated to liberate men from evil passions. Lastly, the sacramental marriage became the profoundest symbol of the most intimate union known to religious experience.

The Mysteries contributed largely to the conservation of the material which Christianity has recast. But in the Mysteries it was and remained more than a symbol : it was pre-eminently the sacrament of ἕνωσις, guaranteeing the communion which assured regeneration by imparting the divine nature. The terminology and usages of marriage were transferred to initiation.[4] An ancient fresco has fortunately preserved scenes of preparation for initiation in the fashion of a bride.[5]

---

[1] As Augustine charges his pagan contemporaries with believing primitive theology and rites which Varro had great trouble in rescuing from oblivion.

[2] Cf. Clem. Alex. *Protr.* II. ; Lactantius, *Div. Inst.* I. 17.

[3] Lucian, *Alex.* 38 f.

[4] Harrison, *Proleg.* p. 533 ; Diels, *Sib. Bl.* p. 48.

[5] Macchioro, *Zagreus*, p. 69 f.

Several *symbola* of the holy marriage have survived. Firmicus [1] has related a Dionysiac *symbolum*, (ἰ)δὲ νυμφ(ί)ε χαῖρε νυμφ(ί)ε, χαῖρε νέον φῶς, in which the god is addressed at his epiphany, ' Hail, Bridal one; hail, new Light.' [2] In the Sabazian initiations 'the god in the bosom' (ὁ διὰ κόλπου θεός) had a conspicuous rôle thus described by Arnobius [3]: ' *aureus coluber in sinum dimittitur consecratis et eximitur ab inferioribus partibus atque imis.*' To the Orphics who addressed their god as ὑποκόλπιε the bridal idea was familiar, especially in the *hieros gamos* of Zeus and Hera,[4] and in the union of Dionysus and Ariadne.[5] The confession on one of the tablets from Magna Graecia, δεσποίνας δ' ὑπὸ κόλπον ἔδυν χθονίας βασιλείας, has been interpreted of such a union.[6] To the same effect is the Phrygian ' I entered the chamber,' which Clement characterizes as indecent. An inscription [7] commemorates the dedication of a *porticum et cubiculum* to the Great Mother. The ἐργασάμενος [8] in the Eleusinian formula ('I fasted,' etc.) may be a euphemism for the ritual marriage. Pausanias [9] testifies to the presence of a bridal chamber (*nymphon*) in the sanctuary of Demeter and Kore near Phlieus. Examples need not be multiplied.

The conception was borrowed and further spiritualized by the Hermetic brethren and their kindred, the Gnostics. In the Hermetic prayer, ' Come to me, Lord Hermes, as babes to women's wombs,' [10] mysticism seeks expression in words

---

[1] *De Err. Prof. Rel.* XIX ; Dieterich, pp. 122, 214.

[2] Also interpreted as an address to the newly initiated, the initiate, irrespective of sex, being bride to the bridegroom god (Anrich, p. 77).

[3] *Adv. Nat.* v. 21 ; cf. Clem. Alex. *Protr.* II. 16, Firm. Mat. xxvi.

[4] Abel, 220 ; Proclus, *In Tim.* ; Macchioro, *Orf. e Paol.* 224.

[5] Cf. Macchioro, *Orf. e Paol.* pp. 209–16.

[6] The meaning is rather ' I entered the womb ' for rebirth. For other interpretations cf. Olivieri, p. 7, and scholiast on Plato, *Gorgias*, cited Farnell, *Cults*, III, p. 187.

[7] *C.I.L.* X. 6423.

[8] Retained by Foucart, *Mystères*, p. 379, and Dieterich, p. 125, against Lobeck's ἐγγευσόμενος, p. 25, which Farnell (*Cults*, III, 185) supports, but which is as unnecessary as his change of *moriturus* to *oraturus* in the Attis formula.   [9] II. 11, 3.

[10] Which may admit of interpretation rather of rebirth; cf. Reitzenstein, *Zwei Relig. Fragen*, p. 20 ff.

that have long since parted company with their original connotation. In Gnosticism the heavenly marriage was the favourite conception of bliss.[1] One group, the Marcossians, ' prepare a bridal chamber and perform an initiatory rite for the *mystae* with certain formulae, and they term this a spiritual marriage.'[2] Another sect, the Valentinians, practise the rite of a spiritual marriage with angels[3] in a nuptial chamber, while another sect, the Naassenes, teach that the spirituals ' must cast off their garments and all become brides pregnant by the Virgin Spirit.'[4] In the *Hymn of the Soul* the conception has been given its highest expression. It was also the Gnostics that brought into prominence the individual[5] soul rather than the group, as partner in this union.

The idea of a mystic marriage, found in the earliest documents of Christianity, was not implanted by the Mysteries. It is familiar in Jewish-Christian documents, as in those written in Gentile environment. The form, too, is different from the individualistic marriage in the Mysteries, since it was rather the society which was the Bride of Christ, a collective conception which was the direct heritage of Jewish thought in which Israel was the spouse, faithful or faithless, of Jahwe. But the Mysteries reacted upon the use of this common religious idea by exalting the individual as the bride of Christ beside the Church, the consummation of which is found in mediaeval and modern mysticism, and by intensifying the realism and concreteness of the idea. Thus the Church became not only the Bride but the Flesh of Christ, against whom the marriage of the individual was a breach of contract.[6] How realistically this could be conceived is illustrated by Jerome,[7] who, writing to Eusto-

---

[1] Liechtenhan, *Offenbarung im Gnosticismus*, p. 143.

[2] Iren. *Adv. Haer.* I. 21, 3.

[3] Bousset, *Hauptprobleme*, p. 315 ff.; Pauly-Wissowa, *R.-Ency.* VII, p. 1522.

[4] Hippolytus, *Phil.* V. 8.

[5] Cf. *Acta Thomae*, 11 ff., Hennecke, *N.T. Apokr.* p. 484 ff.

[6] Cf. Harnack, *Lehre d. zwölf Apostel*, p. 44 ff. (ref. from Dieterich); *Dogmengesch.* 4th ed., p. 27.   [7] *Ad Eustochium*, XXII, 20.

chium's mother on her daughter's decision not to marry a soldier when she could marry the King himself, comforts her, ' She has done you a great service : you have begun to be mother-in-law to God.' In the early Church virgins were encouraged to dedicate their members and their flesh to Christ [1] (*tam carne quam mente deo se vovere*). Clement of Rome had already interpreted *Gen.* I. 27, as ' the male is Christ, the female the Church ' and ' the flesh is the Church, the spirit Christ.' [2] Examples of the ardent *noces spirituelles* in the experience of mystics could be multiplied, e.g. Saint Catharine's betrothal to the infant Christ. A curious document of October 8, 1900, relative to the canonization of Crescentia Hoss reads : " Jesus Christ, our Lord, has espoused the virgin Crescentia . . . by the giving of a ring in the presence of the most holy Mother, her guardian Angel presenting her to her Spouse." [3] The language of the ancient Mysteries is not dead. One may recall how fervently Abelard urges upon the superior soul of Héloïse that his place as husband has been vacated for her Lord.

(*d*) *Sympathia* with the Mystery-god. The bond of ' Sympathy '—in its literal sense—between the deity and the worshipper was a powerful attraction in the Mystery-Religions. In the sacrament the communicant witnessed and participated in the sorrows of his tutelar as a step to participation in the triumphant issues. The Oriental gods were not passionless and joyous abstractions or personifications : they were beings who suffered and rejoiced, struggled and conquered, died and rose again,[4] and in these aspects came nearer to the experiences of man. This fellowship in the deity's sorrows as a means of ensuring

---

[1] Wilpert, *Die gottgeweihten Jungfrauen*, p. 7 ; Heiler, *Das Gebet*, 3rd ed., p. 331 ff.

[2] *Ad Cor.* II. 14, 2, 4.

[3] Dieterich, p. 132, who also cites the cases of Adelheid Langmann and Margaret Ebner.

[4] Cf. Baudissin, *Adonis und Esmun* ; Macchioro, *Zagreus*, p. 120 ff. Ps.-Apuleius, 14, remarks, ' uti Aegyptica numina ferme plangoribus, Graeca plerumque choreis.' ' Men are objects of concern to me, even in perishing ' (*Iliad*, XX. 21), was not characteristic of the Apolline religion.

the deity's fellowship in man's sorrows and of attaining apotheosis was a comparatively new idea in the West, which, once introduced, gained a powerful hold on the imagination.

A great revolution had passed over the Mediterranean world in the conception of God. There spread a universal craving for a God of the heart to be approached with a warmth of affection and emotion. Larger scope was sought for the moral and spiritual life of man in the incessant world-struggle in which the deity was engaged. Only a god whose life could be the example and model for that of his worshippers could suffice ; as a corollary the life of man was ideally a replica of that of his god. In the all-pervading sympathy which bound heaven and earth together man was linked with God. The Apolline religion of Beauty and Joy and the Roman religion of abstract Virtues were supplanted by a religion of Sorrow. That religious instinct was quickened which points to the only fulfilment of divine joy along the path of ' fellowship of sufferings.'

It was the preaching of Orphism which first popularized the idea that the repetition of the deity's passion must precede fellowship in his resurrection, so that each reborn Orphic had passed through the fate of Zagreus. The Orphic dead is greeted, ' Hail, thou who hast suffered the passion ; hitherto thou hadst not suffered it. Thou didst become a god instead of mortal.' [1] Philosophic expression was given to Orphism by Heraclitus, who, in reference to the doctrine, speaks of ' immortal mortals, mortal immortals, living his death, having died their life.' [2] The frescoes of the Orphic chapel of the Villa Item reveal, in the terror of the initiand and in the flagellation, that such a repetition of the divine passion was not a dumb-show. There too is displayed the looking-glass which, from its tragic association with the death of Zagreus, became to these mystics the symbol of divine passion, as the Cross to Christianity.[3] An examination

[1] Olivieri, *Lamellae orph.*, p. 16.
[2] Diels, Fr. 62 : cf. Macchioro, *Eraclito*, p. 88 ff.
[3] Macchioro, *Zagreus*, p. 105 ff. . . .

of the rich symbolism of the underground basilica [1] outside
the Porta Maggiore will deepen the impression that the
Mysteries uttered no uncertain note as to the passion of the
soul with saviour-gods on the path to apotheosis and throw
light on the statement of Plutarch [2] that virtuous souls
‘ returning as from exile to their homeland, taste a joy such
as is experienced especially by initiands, mingled with
alarm and terror together with a sweet hope,’ and on the
well-known comparison [3] of the passion of the dying soul
to the experiences of initiation.

In the Greek rites of Eleusis the devotee contemplated
and entered into the trials of Demeter in her sorrowful quest
for the lost Persephone; but these Greek rites had been
touched by Asiatic influences, inasmuch as the scene of
Demeter’s sorrows is laid partly in Asia. In the Phrygian
Mystery the sorrowful quest of the Great Mother for the
unfaithful Attis was portrayed and found a response among
the assistants. [4] On a certain night an image of the deity
was laid upon a bed accompanied by an antiphonal lamentation, after which the priest anointed the throats of all those
who had joined in the wailing and *lento murmure susurrat* :
‘ Be of good cheer, ye *mystae* of the saved deity : to you
too there will be salvation from your sorrow.’ In the
Egyptian cult pre-eminently this religion of sorrow found
its highest pagan expression : Isis was the *mater dolorosa*
who sympathized with all the trials and afflictions of mortals.
Reading Lucius’ sacramental prayer [5] : ‘ O thou holy and
eternal Saviour of the human race . . . thou bestowest a
mother’s tender affections on the misfortunes of unhappy
mortals . . . thou dispellest the storms of life and stretchest
forth thy right hand of salvation,’ we regret that Time has
dealt so harshly with the Mystery liturgies. The Isiac
communicant, after the period of grief, rejoiced with Isis in

[1] Cf. Mrs. Strong in *J.H.S.* XLIV, p. 65 f.; Cumont, *Rev. Arch.* ’18, pp.
52–73.

[2] *De facie in orbe lunae,* 28, 943 C.

[3] Themistios (?), cf. Maas, *Orpheus,* 303 ff.; Stob. *Flor.* IV. 128; Mein.
p. 107.

[4] Firm. Mat. *De Err. Prof. Rel.* 22.   [5] *Metam.* XI. 25.

the *inventio Osiridis* according to the symbolum ' we have found : we rejoice together.' [1] In Mithraism, the most virile of Oriental cults and therefore most attractive to the Roman soldiery, the conception of the sympathy of God and man was prominent. Men saw in the struggles of Mithra the Unconquered the prototype of their daily life. The tauroctonous Mediator,[2] so familiar on the revolving slab in the chapels, the champion of Light against Darkness, of the weak against the strong, of men against the dominion of demons and cosmic powers, was a human figure whose triumphant struggle encouraged men to higher endeavour. Mithra, moreover, compensated for any apparent deficiency in sympathetic communion by alliance with other Eastern cults, particularly that of the Great Mother,[3] and, in its latest stages, with that of the Egyptian mother of sorrows.

Of course into this communion of Sympathy, as in every act of worship, the communicant entered only so far as his spiritual capacities and achievement permitted. Probably only a small proportion of the initiates really comprehended the full spiritual meaning of the ceremonies and derived moral support therefrom. But who in any age may say what is the proportion of the Bacchi to the thyrsus-bearers ? When, arising out of a sense of utter dependence on the help of the deity, there was a universal demand for spiritual support, for manifestation of the ' philanthropy ' of saviour-gods, we can understand the fascination which the Mysteries, as religions of suffering and struggle, exercised upon spiritual minds. In their weakness men and women—particularly women [4]—believed that the gods from the sunrise could really sympathize with their human lot, and in this faith were fortified for the business of life. Such were those to whom it was given to grasp the real meaning of the Mysteries.[5] We shall see how Christianity was called upon to face the same

---

[1] Firm. Mat., *ib.* 2 ; Augustine, *De Civ. Dei*, VI. ii.

[2] Plutarch, *De Is. et Os.* 46.

[3] Cf. Cumont, *Mystères*, 3rd ed. p. 189 ff.

[4] Cf. Boissier, *Rel. rom.* 7th ed. I. p. 359 ; Diog. Laert. *Vita Pythag.* VIII. 1, 10; Foucart, *Assoc. relig.*, p. 61 ff.

[5] Cf. spirituality of Plutarch, *De Is. et Os.* 3, 352 C.

problem of human existence, and how it outstripped the Mysteries in reading " the holy hieroglyph of pain."

(e) Divine Services.   This communion of sympathy, effected at initiation, was renewed and fostered by divine services of a congregational as also of a private character. The weekly services in the Jewish synagogues and the festivals of the Jewish calendar were familiar to the Graeco-Roman world, as were also the regular meetings of the Christian *ecclesiae*.

The public service of the Great Mother was usually reserved for special occasions such as the annual spring festival, or *Megalensia*,[1] first officially recognized by Claudius, but the history of which stretches back to an early date, spring being the season which from time immemorial spoke of new life.   The celebration opened on the Ides (15th) of March (a day marked in the calendar of Philocalus [2] as *Canna intrat*) with a procession of the college of the *Cannophori* (Reed-bearers).   A week later (22nd)—marked *arbor intrat* in the same calendar—the college of the *Dendrophori* (Tree-bearers) marched in solemn procession carrying the sacred pine wrapped in woollen fillets and decorated with fillets, commemorating Attis' act.   The 23rd was probably,[3] at least in later times, observed as the day of the Cleansing of the Trumpets.   The 24th, the *Dies sanguinis*, was the high day of the festival, observed by strict fasting and lamentation and by participation in a sacrament during the night ; it was further marked by the self-flagellation and laceration of the frenzied Galli.   This day of grief—the third after Attis' death—was succeeded on the 25th by the *Hilaria*, or wild jubilation over the Resurrection of Attis.   Such had been the emotional strain of these two days of tense grief and joy that the 26th was observed as a day of rest—the *Requietio*.   The festival closed on the 27th with the *Lavatio*, or the bathing of the silver image of the Mother and the *articles de culte* in the Almo by the college of the *Fifteen*. Thereafter the sacred objects were conducted back to the

[1] Cf. Hepding, pp. 145–75 ; Aust, p. 155 f.
[2] Hepding, p. 51.   [3] *Ib.* p. 158.

temple by the priests, accompanied by a wildly jubilant carnival in which considerable licence was permitted, and during which the Galli took up the collection.

The nature of the divine services and their frequency in Mithraism are very imperfectly known to us.[1] We know of the existence of an *ordo sacerdotum*, but whether the sacerdotal succession could be strictly maintained in the Western countries as in the homelands of Mithraism is a moot question. The duty of such a clergy was to celebrate the daily offices,[2] maintain—at least in the Eastern chapels [3]— the perpetual holy altar fire, invoke the planet of the day, offer the frequent sacrifices for the adherents, and preside at initiations. The great festival of the Mithraic calendar was held on December 25, the *Natalis Invicti*, which in the lands of the Occident probably took the place of the *Mithrakana* [4] in the East. The first day of the week was dedicated to the Sun, to whom prayers were recited thrice daily, morning, noon, and evening.[5] Special services were probably held on the Sunday. The sixteenth was kept holy to Mithra. " The small size of the Mithraea, and the scanty number of the members of the associations supporting each, make it extremely unlikely that there was anything like regular congregational worship, or that the faithful assembled there except for initiations or meetings for conferring the different degrees," says Legge.[6] No doubt the soldiers with the colours, who formed the majority of the adherents, could not observe a regular attendance at fixed hours, nor could the slaves with their long and irregular hours of toil. But, despite difficulties, opportunities were found for worship, both fraternal and private devotion. The ' brothers ' met in the artificially lighted ' Cave ' or ' Grotto,' where they

[1] Cf. Cumont, *T. et M.* p. 313-30 ; Toutain, II, p. 132 ff.
[2] Cf. Cumont, *ib.* I, p. 324 f.
[3] Cumont, *ib.* " No proof is forthcoming that a fire was kept perpetually burning on the altar in the European chapels of Mithras, as perhaps was the case with the temples of the faith in Asia Minor, or that daily or any other regularly repeated services were held there " (Legge, II. p. 268).
[4] The Parsee *Mithragan* ; cf. Cumont, *ib.* pp. 230, 325.
[5] Cumont, *ib.* pp. 325, 342.   [6] II, p. 269.

seated themselves on the stone benches running along both sides of the chapel [1] separated by a central aisle. The service consisted chiefly of the contemplation of the holy symbols, prayer (for which they knelt at the benches [2]), participation in the chanting of a litany to instrumental music, mostly flutes. Bells were sounded, perhaps mostly before the exposure of the Tauroctony. Sacrifices were offered, on great occasions a bull, on ordinary occasions birds. The two chief objects of adoration in these services—the one speaking of victory and the other of reconciliation—were the carved altarpiece representing the Tauroctony, or bull-slaying scene, and the other the carved plaque representing the sacred *agape* of Mithra and the Sun reconciled after their struggle. At these services candidates completed their catechumenate, and the tried 'soldiers' of Mithra joined in the sacrament of bread and water mixed with wine, which to Christians appeared a travesty of the Last Supper. In such a communion service the Mithraist believers were strengthened in their faith that Mithra would assure them victory here,[3] and would come again from heaven to bring forth the dead from their graves for a judgment at which their Mediator would be the Advocate of the initiated soul, which, purified through his rites, would ascend through the seven planetary spheres to Paradise.[4]

Concerning the public services of the Isiac Church we are better informed [5] by the narrative of Apuleius and the two frescoes from Herculaneum. Like the other deities, Isis too had her public festivals to cater for popular taste, of which the two chief were the *Navigium Isidis*, or Blessing of the Vessel of Isis, on March 5, and the *Isia, Inventio Osiris*,

---

[1] See photograph of the Mithraeum under church of St. Clement in Rome (Cumont, no. 63).

[2] So Cumont, I. p. 61, and Toutain, II, p. 135. Others believe that the initiates reclined on the benches in partaking of the *agape*.

[3] " La religion mithraique fournissait à ses adeptes des réponses précises et consolantes aux plus graves questions que peuvent suggérer le spectacle de l'univers matériel, la conscience de l'activité morale, les incertitudes et les angoisses inspirées par la mort " (Toutain, II, p. 132).

[4] Cumont, *ib.* I. 309 f.

[5] Cf. also Porphyry, *De Abst.* IV. 9 ; Arnobius, VII. 32.

or Passion and Resurrection of Osiris, celebrated from October 28 to November 1. Of the first, the ' peculiar procession of the saviour-goddess,' a vivid account is given by Apuleius,[1] who witnessed it at Corinth. Women in white raiment led the procession, strewing the road from the city to the sea with flowers, followed by a crowd of men and women with torches and lanterns. Bands played instrumental music. A ' beautiful hymn ' was rendered by a special choir of youths, and the special flute-players of Serapis chanted the hymn usual in his temple. Then thronged the initiated, the women transparently veiled, the men tonsured. The priests closed the procession ; the first carrying a golden boat-shaped lamp, the second the altars of Succour, the third a golden palm and wand of Mercury, the fourth a left hand, emblem of Equity, and a golden vase, the fifth a winnowing-fan, the sixth an amphora ; another personated Anubis, followed by a cow as emblem of fertility ; another carried the chest with the venerable mysteries ; another in his bosom the image of the Supreme Deity in the form of a curious urn with Egyptian hieroglyphs. On reaching the water the vessel of Isis was consecrated by the chief priest with solemn prayers, laden with offerings by the multitude, loosed from its moorings, and, with prayers inscribed on its sails, wafted out of sight by a breeze which seemingly arose of express purpose. Prayers being offered for the success of the year's navigation, the holy things were borne in solemn procession back to the temple.

The chief public festival of the Alexandrine cult was the Passion and Resurrection of Osiris,[2] ' God of great Gods.' [3] The celebration began with a fast of ten days—a fact not to be overlooked in the psychopathy of the festival. In a passion-play Isis sorrowfully sought the dismembered Osiris, a quest in which the priests and initiates joined with loud wailing. Finally, Isis' grief is turned to joy by the Finding

---

[1] *Metam.* XI. 9-16; cf. Lafaye, *Hist. du Culte*, p. 126 ff. ; Legge, I. p. 71 f. ; Dill, p. 579.

[2] Cf. Minucius Felix, *Octav.* 21 ; Plutarch, *De Is. et Osir.* 16 f. 39 ; Herod. III. 27-8. [3] *Metam.* XI. 30.

of Osiris, which the initiates exultantly celebrate with the cries, ' We have found him : we rejoice together,' after which follow banquets in the temples and public games. ' Thus,' says Minucius Felix, ' they never cease year by year to lose what they find and to find what they lose.' [1]

It was not, however, these public festivals which lent such fascination to the Egyptian cult ; it was rather its regular daily congregational services,[2] of which there were two—*bisque die* [3]—Matins and Vespers: Matins, ' the morning opening of the temple' (*templi matutinas aper- tiones*),[4] at ' the first hour,' and Vespers ' at the eighth hour,' [5] or 2 o'clock in the afternoon, the chants of which were audible to passers-by.

These services were performed by white-robed priests with tonsured heads, by whom they were made very impressive. Apuleius describes the morning service, which consisted of hymns, adoration, sacrifice and prayers, at which a liturgy was used. The worshippers are assembled before the door of the Isaeum awaiting the ' opening of the temple.' At the hour a priest withdraws the white curtains that concealed the statue of Isis who in the glory of her rich robes was exposed for the adoration of the faithful as an Egyptian Madonna. A sacrifice—*matutinum sacrificium*—was then offered, during which the priest made the circuit of the altars reciting the morning litany and sprinkling before them the holy water from the sacred well within the temple precincts, and solemnly proclaiming the hour of prayer. The office concluded with the chanting of the morning hymn by the temple choir, in which probably the congregation participated antiphonally, and with a Mass or dismissal of the worshippers.

The Vespers at two o'clock are not so fully known to us. There was a chant by the priests or temple-choir. As at the morning service the opening hour was announced, it is probable that a similar ceremony marked the closing of the

[1] *Ib.*
[2] Cf. Lafaye, *Hist. du Culte*, p. 113 f.
[3] Tibullus, I 3, 31.
[4] *Metam.* XI. 20.
[5] Martial, X. 48, 1 ; II. 14, 8.

temple. As Isis was unveiled at the Matins it is likely that at the Vespers her statue was robed and withdrawn within the shrine, after her feet had been kissed by the most ardent devotees.[1]

The fresco from Herculaneum in the Museum of Naples evidently portrays the morning service or rather portions of it. In a grove of trees a Serapeum stands in view—perhaps a copy of that of Alexandria [2]—to the porch of which a row of steps rises. At the top of the stairs before the portal stands the tonsured Alexandrian priest lifting in both hands breast-high an urn containing probably the holy Nile water. Behind him stand two figures—one shaking a sistrum and the other tonsured. At the foot of the stairs stands another priest with a sistrum in his left hand and some emblem of authority in his right, while on the stairs the initiates are ranged. Three altars appear in view, on the central one of which a sacrifice is smoking, attended by an acolyte. On the right is seated a flute-player evidently leading the tune ; on the left stand a man and woman shaking the sistrum, while on the right a priest with a wand acts evidently as choir-conductor to the chanting choirs. Lafaye [3] has conjectured that this fresco scene depicts the adoration of the holy water, the representative symbol of Osiris as the giver of life and ' Lord of Eternity.' The other fresco,[4] also from Herculaneum, is equally noteworthy both in its similarities to and differences from the previous. In a sacred enclosure stands an open temple, flanked with Doric columns ornamented with garlands and reached by five steps. In the centre is a dark-bearded figure with head crowned with lotus and a chaplet, the one hand resting on his hip, the other raised in the air in the poise of a dance. Behind him stand two women, two children, and a shaven priest nude to the waist and in the act of shaking a sistrum. In the foreground at the foot of the steps there is seen

[1] Apuleius, *Metam.* XI. 17.

[2] Which was to the Isiac Church what the Temple at Jerusalem was to the Jewish Church.

[3] *Hist. du Culte*, etc. p. 115 ; Plut. *De Is. et Os.* XXXVI.

[4] Lafaye, pp. 115, 328 ; Legge, I, p. 68 f.

an altar smoking with sacrifice, at the base of which are two ibises ; on the right a priest with a musical instrument in each hand, a flute-player, a child, a kneeling man, a draped woman bearing a sistrum and a branch. On the left is a priest shaking a sistrum, an indistinct figure, a child with a basket and an urn, and, at the top of the steps, a kneeling woman supporting in her left hand a basket of fruits and holding a sistrum in her right. The whole scene is evidently one of great joy. Lafaye [1] has conjectured that the swarthy figure personates Osiris, and that the scene is the closing pantomimic representation of the Passion of Osiris at the joyful moment of his resurrection before the jubilant spectators. If this conjecture is correct, the dramatic scene could not have formed part of the esoteric initiation, which would preclude it from being chosen as the subject of a fresco on which uninitiated eyes might gaze.

(*f*) Sacramental Meals. Sacred meals played an important part in the Mysteries as sacraments of union with the deity,[2] but the precise significance of these meals is disputed. Common meals of a religious character were in vogue in antiquity, such as the Greek συσσιτία, and such meals were in some sense of a sacrificial character in forming part of a sacrifice or following a sacrifice. Guild meals were also a common feature of the ancient life, one particular class of which, that of the funerary guilds, appear frequently in Roman inscriptions. These guilds held commemorative banquets in honour of departed members of the household, at which the dead were regarded as present to participate in the feast and to whom offerings of food and drink were made. These meals furnished occasions of family reunions, at which, through religious ceremonies, the living maintained fellowship with the dead and satisfied that craving so deep-seated in the Roman heart and so clamant on Roman sepulchral stones for an immortality of remembrance.

---

[1] *Hist. du Culte*, pp. 115–16.
[2] Cf. Clemen, *Prim. Christianity*, p. 260.

We have abundant evidence that in the cult meals of the Graeco-Roman age the deity was viewed sometimes as guest and sometimes as host, or indefinitely as both guest and host, as in the religious conception, ' I will come in and sup with him, and he with Me.' As instances of the deity as host, we may cite the dinner-invitation of a second-century papyrus,[1] ' Chaeremon invites you to dine at the table of the Lord Serapis, to-morrow, 15th, at nine o'clock,' and a similar one from the same century :[2] ' Antonius, Ptolemaeus' son, invites you to dine with him at the table of the Lord Serapis, in the Serapeum of Claudius, on the 16th at nine o'clock.' An inscription from Kos [3] has preserved an interesting ritual for the entertainment of Hercules, in which occurs the expression ' the table of the God ' (τρπέζαν τὴν τοῦ θεοῦ). Aristides tells how the worshippers of Serapis partake in the full communion with him by ' inviting him to the hearth as guest and host.' [4] Paulina was lured to a Serapeum on an invitation to sup with Anubis. In Paul's expression, ' the cup of demons,' ' the table of demons,' there is implied the same view of divine hospitality.

There is also evidence that the deity was viewed as guest. Rohde [5] gives examples from Greek inscriptions in which the formula κλίνην στρῶσαι, ' spread the table for,' is found in connexion with several deities, Pluto, Aesculapius, and Attis. The Roman Iovis Epulum became, at least in the closing republic, a banquet at which the worshippers served the god with food and invited the Capitoline Trinity to partake thereof.[6] Valerius Maximus expressly states : ' At the banquet of Jupiter he himself was invited to the table, and Juno and Minerva were invited to dine.' [7] The lectisternia and later sellisternia for female deities were examples of entertainment of the celestials.

In nearly all the Mysteries an agape, or sacramental meal,

---

[1] Oxyrhy. Pap. I. 110.   [2] Ib. III. 523.

[3] Dittenberger, Sylloge, 3rd ed. no. 1106, l. 100 ; Paton and Hicks, Inscr. of Cos. 36 ; Prott-Ziehen, 144.

[4] δαιτυμόνα αὐτὸν καὶ ἑστιάτορα, 97 (Dind. I, p. 94).

[5] Psyche, I. 130.

[6] Cf. Wissowa, p. 357.   [7] II. 1, 7 (cited in Rohde).

preceded initiation. At Eleusis the sacrifice to Demeter and Kore was followed by a banquet on the flesh of the victims. Tertullian [1] records a *coquorum delectus* at the Dionysiac Apaturia and Attic Mysteries. In the Mysteries of Mithra ' bread and a cup of water are offered in the rites of initiation accompanied by certain explanations,' [2] to which Pliny [3] refers in *magicis cenis initiaverat*. Extant *symbola* attest the sacramental meal in the cult of the Great Mother. The inscription of Andania and one from Messenia [4] prove the same for Demeter, while for the Samothracian Mysteries an inscription from Tomi [5] relates that the priest ' shall break and offer the food and pour out the cup to the *mystae*.' In the remains of ancient sculpture and painting are preserved such scenes, of which a striking example is that of the Villa Item.[6]

But in what sense did the participant of the sacramental meal become κοινωνὸς of the god ? Was he conceived as feeding on the god by eating his totem or sacrifice, that is, by the entry of the deity into the believer in a magical fashion ? That there was a firm belief, in the earlier stages of religion, of such participation in the god by eating him in a sacramental meal cannot be questioned. In the Thracian-Dionysiac Mysteries, e.g., the celebrants by such a meal obtain a share in the divine life of the god, and so are called by his name, *Saboi, Sabazioi*.[7] And in the Dionysus-Zagreus cult the communicants rushed madly upon the sacrificial animal, tore it to pieces and ate it raw, believing that the god was resident in the offering.[8] Cumont believes that the original significance of the eating of a sacred animal in the Phrygian cults was that " it was believed that thus there took place an identification with the god himself, together with a participation in his substance and qualities," and that in certain mystic meals of the Syrian cult the priests

[1] *Apol.* 39. [3] XXX. 1, 6.
[2] Justin, *Apol.* 166. [4] *J.H.S.* '05, p. 50.
[5] *Arch. epig. aus Öst.* VII. '82, p. 8 ; Prott-Ziehen, 84 ; Michel, 704.
[6] Photo by De Petra in *Not. d. Scavi*, '10.
[7] Cf. Rohde, II, p. 14.
[8] *Religions orientales*, 2nd ed. pp. 104, 174.

and the initiates, by eating the fish sacred to Atargatis, considered themselves to be devouring the life of the deity. But Dieterich,[1] Lietzmann,[2] and Heitmüller[3] admit that the examples are scanty, though they incline to believe that this crude conception was not extinct in the days of St. Paul when the Mysteries were enjoying a career of success. On the other hand, it is affirmed by Gardner,[4] " In his [Paul's] time we cannot trace in any of the more respectable forms of heathen religion a survival of the practice of eating the deity," with which Kennedy[5] agrees while affirming " at least as probable an explanation is the notion that the god himself is present and shares with his worshippers in the sacrificial meal "; that is, deity and worshippers are commensals.

The evidence for the persistence of such a crude semi-physical idea of communion in the later stages of the Mysteries is too scanty to permit us to see in the sacramental meals of these cults the means whereby the communicant sought union with the god by partaking of him or feeding upon him. The chief evidence on which a magical view of fellowship is based are some mystic formulae preserved by Clement of Alexandria, Minucius Felix, and Arnobius. According to Clement the following confession was repeated by the Eleusinian communicant after the sacred meal: ' I fasted, I drank the *cykeon*, I took out of the chest ; having done the act I put again into the basket, and from the basket again into the chest,'[6] words which appear in Arnobius as ' ieiunavi atque ebibi cyceonem : ex cista sumpsi et in calathum misi ; accepi rursus, in cistulam transtuli.'[7] Clement likewise gives the *symbolum* of the Attis-*mystes* as ' I ate out of the tympanum ; I drank out of cymbalum ; I carried the κερνός ; I entered the chamber.'[8] These

---

[1] *Mithraslit.* 2nd ed. p. 105.
[2] *Handb. Z.N.T.* III. 1, p. 125.
[3] *Taufe u. Abendmahl*, p. 40 ff.
[4] *St. Paul*, p. 121 ; cf. Morgan, *Relig. and Theology of Paul*, p. 214.
[5] *St. Paul*, pp. 256-9.
[6] *Protrep.* II. 21.   [7] *Adv. Nat.* V. 26.
[8] *Ib.* II. 15 : cf. Firm. Mat., *De Err. Prof. Rel.* XVIII.

sacramental confessions are clearly not determinative. Besides, it is a well-known fact that in all religions rites become stereotyped and formulae remain unchanged while the interpretations and the symbolism are constantly expanding in spirituality—a phenomenon of which we have met numerous examples.

These sacramental meals, therefore, were not sacramental in the primitive magical sense. They rather signalized the reception of the neophyte communicant as a member of the religious guild or Mystery-church, and served as a token of the communion of the Mystery-saints, forming the main bond[1] of brotherhood among the cult members. They were also in some way not merely the symbol but the outward means or sacrament of union with the patron god.[2] They secured communion between the *mystae* of the same god [3] and magnified by an obvious symbolism the faith of the communicant in the Divine as the source of spiritual nourishment [4] for the tasks of his daily life. Through these sacraments men caught glimpses and premonitions as through a glass darkly of the light of God. Doubtless the degrees of spirituality and vision were as varied among these ancient worshippers as among those who in Christendom approach the table of the Lord.

The ancient communicant, whether pagan or Christian, did not enquire profoundly into the theological question of the nexus between the magical-ritual sacramental act and the spiritual experience.[5] There was, therefore, as wide scope for variety in the theology of the Mystery-sacraments as exists

---

[1] Cf. *collegae et consacranei*, *C.I.L.* III. 2105 ; and *fratres carissimos* of Jupiter Dolichenus, *C.I.L.* VI. 406.

[2] Cf. Clemen, *Primitive Christianity*, p. 260.

[3] " The frequent observance of sacred meals maintained the communion among the *mystae* of Cybele, Mithras, or the Baals " (Cumont, *Relig. orient.*, p. 64, Engl. tr. p. 41).

[4] " Towards the close of the empire moral ideas were particularly associated with the assimilation of the liquids or sacred foods from the tambourine or cymbal of Attis. These became the nourishment of the spiritual life, and were considered as sustaining the initiate in the trials of his life " (Cumont, p. 104 ; Engl. tr. 69 ; cf. also p. 224).

[5] Cf. Holtzmann, *N.T. Theologie*, II, p. 196.

about the central rite of our worship. The *How* in sacramental operation was never answered, consequently the nature of the fellowship was very vague, the same cult act producing different emotions in different people and suggesting various modes of interpretation. Perhaps some celebrants retained antiquated notions of semi-physical fellowship, though this is doubtful in the later Mysteries. At the other extreme were those who found in the fellowship a spiritual experience. But the fellowship was generally not viewed either so literally or so purely spiritually. The average communicant believed that in some realistic, hyperphysical sense the sacrament was an occasion on which or means by which he was privileged to enter into fellowship with the divine life, by which he was reborn or endowed with immortality. What mystical *ex opere operato* virtue may have lain therein escaped his attention or concern. In a world where it was possible for an educated Christian man like the author of the *Clementine Homilies* to assert that ' evil spirits gain power by means of the food consecrated to them, and are introduced by your own hands into your own bodies ; there they hide themselves for a long time and unite with the soul,' [1] or where a respectable Church father could view the Eucharist as ' the medicine of immortality, an antidote against death, and a means of everlasting life in Jesus Christ,' [2] we must hesitate to ascribe a highly spiritual or symbolic efficacy to the Mystery-sacraments.[3] Further, pagans and Christians alike observed no strict boundary-lines between the physical and hyper-physical, between the symbol and the resultant or concomitant experience. Neither their science nor their philosophy necessitated

---

[1] IX. 9.

[2] Ignat. *Eph.* **XX.** Cyril of Jerusalem speaks of ' partaking of the body and blood of Christ, that you may become *con-corporate* and *con-sanguineous* (σύσσωμος καὶ σύναιμος αὐτοῦ) with Him ; for thus we become Christophori, his body and his blood entering into our members ' (Dieterich, p. 107).

[3] Excluding those two great *Spirituals* Paul (of whom Morgan has well said, " Of the sacraments he might have said what he said of circumcision, that neither their observance not their non-observance avails anything," p. 227), and the writer of the ' spiritual gospel,' who affirms in a communion address : ' the flesh profiteth nothing ; it is the Spirit which quickens.'

a strict delimitation. Examples lie to hand in the gospel narratives of the Resurrection and in Paul's doctrine of the *pneumatic* body and of that *metamorphosis* which Christians through the possession of the Spirit of Christ are undergoing from glory to glory in conformation to the image of God's Son. The Christian church of Corinth saw no difference in kind between the Lord's table and the table of the neighbouring heathen temple. Such considerations point to the conclusion that the Mystery-sacraments were conceived with a large amount of realism, but a realism through the denseness of which the light of riper spiritual experience continued to break, and by which men learned that the things that are seen are temporal, but the things that are unseen eternal. In those pagan sacraments, as in the whole course of religious history, man's spirit marched painfully from sacramentarianism through symbolism to that goal to which the external symbol pointed in the truth of God.

(*g*) Contemplative Adoration, or Meditation, represents the more private and personal aspects of communion in the Mysteries, and was practised as a means of ἕνωσις, or identification. In the cult of the Egyptian deities silent prayer and contemplation played an important part both before and subsequent to initiation. So characteristic was this attitude of Egyptian worship that a Roman writer speaks of the Egyptians as ' a people always seated in their temples,' [1] and Porphyry [2] states that the Egyptian priests devoted their whole lives ' to the contemplation and adoration of the deity.' There are frequent literary references to the seats found in the Egyptian temples of the Roman world. In the Isaeum of Pompeii, built about 150 B.C., there has been discovered a bench evidently designed from its position for such worship.[3] The Serapea probably stood open between Matins and Vespers, like Catholic churches of the present day, to receive those who desired to ease their conscience or secure that quiet of heart that comes to many

---

[1] Julius Florus, *Epitomae*, cited by Lafaye, p. 119.
[2] *De Abst.* IV. 6: τῇ τῶν θεῶν θεωρίᾳ κ. θεάσει.
[3] Described in Mau, *Pompeii*, p. 171 ff.

in a holy place. Apuleius describes his boundless delight (*gratissimum mihi*) and 'unspeakable pleasure' (*inexplicabili voluptate*) in such prolonged contemplation before the statue of the deity as an act of piety and stage in preparation for initiation.[1] Some worshippers hired a compartment within the temple in order to indulge uninterruptedly in devotion during the day, and, by means of incubation, to be vouchafed a vision or optical revelation of the deity during the darkness. Such was Apuleius, who testifies : ' There was never one night nor a sleep unvisited by a vision or admonition of the goddess, but by her repeated holy commands she decreed that I should at length be initiated into the holy rites for which I had long since been set apart.' Arrangements for prolonged meditation or incubation could be made through the priesthood for members of either sex. Juvenal speaks of the wife devoted to Oriental rites *cum qua di nocte loquantur*,[2] and Josephus has recorded the notable case of Paulina. Propertius' Cynthia had spent ten nights of the holy season in vigil before the altar of Isis,[3] where Corinna also evidently spent the hours of the day frequently.[4] Others—without doubt the majority—were more sporadic in their practice of contemplative devotion.

Some peculiar atoning efficacy in wiping out the stains of the past was attributed to such silent musing, as we learn from Ovid.[5] This silent worship seems to have appealed most to women, with their more aesthetic sensitiveness, as it does to-day in Catholicism, and in some non-Roman churches. With what different eyes was the Egyptian Madonna gazed upon ! In that silent devotion the none too scrupulous *amatae* of the Roman poets met their sisters of higher rank and purer morals.

Reference has been made to the two main awe-inspiring objects of contemplation in the Mithraic chapels, the Tauroctony and the *agape* of reconciliation. There were

---

[1] *Metam.* XI. 17, 19, 24.   [2] VI. 531.   [3] II. 33, 2.
[4] Ovid, *Amores*, II. 13, 7;   cf. XIV, Tibullus, I. 3
[5] *Ep. Ponto.* I 1, 51–2.

also symbolic objects representative of the elemental forces of nature which affect man's life, the alternation of light and darkness, the decay of winter and rebirth of spring, and such things as made the mystery of the universe less perplexing to the Roman legionary and exiled slave.[1]

III. Epopteia of the Mystery-God and Blessedness

1. The immediate result of initiation was to behold an epiphany of the deity. It was an act of faith that the deity was present to grant a theophany,[2] and great importance was attached to the vision. The ancient mind, pagan and Christian, was predisposed to such visions, whether vouchsafed in dreams, trances, ecstasy, or hypnotic conditions. As examples may be cited the Christophany to Paul on the road to Damascus, the *Apocalypse*, the *Apocalypse of Peter*, or the dream of the Pamphylian Er,[3] to whom was revealed in ecstasy the fate of the wicked and the destiny of souls, or that of Thespesius.[4] Aristides records an experience in which ' there came from Isis a Light and other unutterable things conducing to salvation. In the same night appeared Serapis and Aesculapius himself, both

[1] Lafaye has well described the power of the Egyptian priesthood in its appeal to the emotional life: " When the ceremonies of the daily office, the adoration of the holy objects, the representation of the mysteries no longer sufficed, the devotee might still remain there, silent and impassible, his eyes wandering vacantly, his spirit enraptured with calm and profound reveries. In order to remove the harsh feeling of exterior reality and to detach him from the life of the world a means was discovered in inviting him to sit before the idol" (p. 119). Dill has equally well described the effect of contemplation in the Mithraic chapel: " Before him was the sacred group of the Tauroctonus, full of so many meanings to many lands and ages, but which to his eyes probably shed the light of victory over the perilous combats of time, and gave assurance of a larger hope. Suddenly, by the touch of an unseen hand, the plaque revolved, and he had before him the solemn *agape* of the two deities in which they celebrated the peaceful close of their mystic conflict. And he went away, assured that his hero-god was now enthroned on high, and watching over his faithful soldiers on earth " (p. 608).
[2] Cf. Aristophanes, *Clouds*, 262 ff.
[3] Plato, *Repub.* X. 13 f., 614.
[4] Plutarch, *De sera num. vind.* 22.

marvellous in beauty and stature and in certain aspects resembling each other.'[1] All ancient *epiphaneiae* were of the character of a dazzling light. Porphyry knows that 'the eye of the body cannot bear' the brightness of divine apparitions.[2]

The experience of Apuleius, 'I saw the sun shining at midnight,' and 'adoravi de proxumo,' refers to such an epiphany. In the Attis cult 'Hail, Bridegroom, Hail, new Light' announced the epiphany. In the *Liturgy of Mithra*[3] we read, 'Thou shalt see a youthful god, lovely in form, with red locks, wearing a white tunic and scarlet mantle, and holding a bright crown.' In the fragment of Themistius the soul in death 'as in the great Mysteries,' after fear and shuddering, 'is confronted by as it were a marvellous light.' The most explicit testimony is given by Proclus[4] : 'In all these [initiations and Mysteries] the gods reveal many forms of themselves, and manifest themselves changing their modes of apparition. There issues from them a light, sometimes formless, sometimes in human shape, and again transmuted into other shapes.'

In the tense emotional exaltation of initiation the ancients believed it possible to see God. This was not viewed as a condescension of the deity to earth but as the ascension of man through death and the elements to heaven, for 'none of the heavenly gods will leave the bounds of heaven and descend on earth, but man ascends to heaven.'[5] Of the nature of these visions there is the same uncertainty as about all religious visions. But the collection and sifting[6] of visionary phenomena has lessened the distance between Proclus and ourselves, so that the experiences of the Mysteries no longer sound incredible. The initiand was predisposed by fasting, the suggestions and promptings of the priest, the awful reverence of the sacramental drama, the contagion

[1] *Orat. Sac.* III (Dind. I), p. 500.
[2] *De Mysteriis*, II. 8 (Parthey, p. 86), III 2, p. 104.
[3] Dieterich, p. 10, l. 27.
[4] *In Plat. Remp.* I, p. 110 ; Kroll ; cf. De Jong, p. 379 ff.
[5] *Corp. Herm.* X. 25.
[6] Cf. Delacroix, *Étude d'hist. et de psychologie du mysticisme*, Paris '08.

of collective emotion, the magical effect attached by antiquity to the repetition of cult formulae, the hallucinatory contemplation of the *sacra*, or by *enkoimesis* to behold what he expected. How suggestion could operate is patent in the paintings of the Villa of the Mysteries. To aver that the phenomena were in every case genuine, induced by natural psychopathic means, would demand too much of priestcraft. It is possible that hierophants had ways of assisting or imposing upon the imagination of unpromising candidates, so that robed acolytes or statues sometimes did duty for deity. As in every religion, such cases would be the counterfeits of the genuine. That initiands were not equally susceptible to the vision seems to be suggested by the distinction made by Psellus [1] between *autopsia*, whereby the initiand himself beholds the divine light, and *epopteia*, in which he beholds it through the eyes of the hierophant. But the testimony of the initiated, the corroboration of such experiences in other religions, and the salutary effect attached to the vision, prove its reality in general.

Blessedness and Salvation in General

2. To the question why did such multitudes, especially in the first Christian centuries, rush eagerly into the Mystery-communities, which were at first despised dissenters, sometimes bitterly persecuted, maintained by the offerings of the faithful, when a state church, with the prestige of "establishment" behind it, offered them an inexpensive religion, the answer will in the main be found in what the Mysteries promised. All the Mystery-gods were primarily saviour-gods. To initiation was ascribed a sacramental efficacy which atoned for a man's past, gave him comfort in the present, a participation in the divine life, and assured to faith an hereafter of such dazzling splendour that the trials and conflicts of this earthly existence were dwarfed into insignificance. The Mysteries held out to men the salvation

---

[1] *Exp. orac. chal.* (Migne), p. 1135.

which was so eagerly and pathetically sought [1] by those intensely religious centuries—salvation as it was then understood in its various aspects, more religious than ethical, physical and spiritual. " The deity of the society was a θεὸς σωτήρ, and the society sought through fellowship with him to reach a state of σωτηρία, safety or salvation, a salvation belonging alike to the present life and that beyond the grave. . . . It was the deities of the Mysteries who were in an emphatic sense the saviours of those who trusted in them, and they saved by allowing the votary to have a share in their lives." [2] The other traditional or still surviving deities might afford a specific or partial salvation, e.g. the ' greatest lover of men,' Aesculapius, or the ' Gods manifest ' of the imperial cult, but the Mystery-gods offered what the heart of the ancient worshipper yearned for. It is another matter whether they promised more than they could fulfil ; but they did promise generously, and many of the believing worshippers were persuaded that the promises of the Mystery-god were not like those of Mephistopheles to Faust. The ' regenerated ' initiate believed that his God put a new song in his mouth, and that he could go on his way rejoicing through life. Such at least is their surviving testimony. The salvation imparted in the Mysteries embraced deliverance from the physical ills of life, from bodily ailments, from the sense of alienation, from the galling power of Fate, and the reckless caprice of Fortune, from the ubiquitous terrors of the demons, from the fears of superstition, and lastly from the gloom of death. No other forms of pagan religion could enter into successful competition with the Mysteries in such a comprehensive evangel.

---

[1] " In der Zeit, wo das Christentum auftrat, erlebten die alten griechischen Mysterien eine Art von Renaissance. Das wundersame tiefe Sehnen jener Zeit nach einem ' Heile,' einem heilenden, rettenden Gotte, nach einer σωτηρία, einem σωτήρ, dem jene Mysterien entgegenkamen, schuf ihnen neues Interesses," F. Kattenbusch, Sakrament, in Herzog-Hauck, Real-Encyc. 3rd ed. XVII, p. 351. Cf. Gardner, in Hastings' E.R.E. IX, p. 81 b.

[2] Gardner, Relig Exper. of St. Paul, pp. 82-4.

Specifically, Immortality

3. Multitudes, never touched by the reasonings of Platonism for the immortality of the soul, found in life a new value as a probation for a blessed hereafter. 'As truly as Osiris lives, so truly shall his followers live ; as truly as Osiris is not dead he shall die no more ; as truly as Osiris is not annihilated he shall not be annihilated,' says an Egyptian text.[1] This immortality was acquired by assimilation with Osiris-Serapis, or by becoming Osiris and receiving the new name of ' Osiris.'[2] The member of the Isiac church could carve on the tomb of his departed ' brother' εὐψύχι μετὰ τοῦ 'Οσείριδος.[3] ' May Osiris give thee the water of refreshment,'[4] ' May Isis bestow on thee the holy water of Osiris '[5] are also found. Egypt, that had for millennia brooded upon the mystery of death, offered in Isis and Serapis life and immortality to the dwellers in the Roman Empire. Conspicuous among the symbols of the Isiac faith appears the lotus, emblem of immortality, out of the calyx of which comes forth the youthful god Harpocrates, who had overcome death. Isis, the ' eternal saviour of the race of men,' promises her votary : ' Thou shalt live in blessedness ; thou shalt live glorious under my protection. And when thou hast finished thy life-course and goest down to the under-world, even there in that lower world thou shalt see [6] me shedding light in the gloom of Acheron and reigning in the inmost regions of Styx : thou thyself shalt inhabit the Elysian fields and shalt continually offer worship to me, ever gracious.'[7]

Initiation made all the difference between the saved and the unsaved of the ancient worshippers. In the *Hymn to*

[1] Cf. Cumont, *Rel. orient.* 2nd ed. p. 149.

[2] Cf. Reitzenstein, *Poim.* p. 369, who cites a text in which the dead says : " je deviens nouveau, je deviens jeune, je suis Osiris." Cf. also Wiedemann, *Relig. der alten Ägyptern*, p. 128 f.

[3] *Insc. Graecae*, XIV. 2098.

[4] *Rev. des Ét. grecques*, 96, p. 435 ; *C.I.G.* 6562.

[5] Dieterich, p. 258.

[6] Reading *videbis* for Helm's *vides.*

[7] Apul. *Metam.* XI. 6.

Demeter [1] the Goddess-mother asserts : ' Happy is he of men
on earth who has seen those Mysteries ; but the uninitiate,
who has no part in these holy things, cannot, when dead
and down in the murky gloom, have like portion of such
blessings.' The uninitiate not only die without hope [2]
but have apportioned them all ills by the chthonic powers.[3]
Whereas an Eleusinian hierophant, Glaucus, can triumphant-
ly declare : ' Beautiful indeed is the Mystery given us by
the blessed gods: death is for mortals no longer an evil,
but a blessing.' [4] Of the same rites the scholiast on Aristophanes (*Frogs*, 158) asserts : ' It was the common belief
in Athens that whoever had been taught the Mysteries would,
when he died, be deemed worthy of divine glory. Hence all
were eager for initiation.' Another scholiast [5] records, ' The
Greeks told how those who had been initiated into the
Mysteries found Persephone benign and gracious in Hades.'

The cruder rites of Phrygia also met in their sacraments
the demand for immortality.[6] Attis, in his death and
resurrection, became the prototype of the Cybele-votary
triumphing over death.[7] Attis also played the part to the
dying that the ' Saviour and psychopomp ' Serapis [8] did
to the faithful of the Isiac church. The priests of the
Syrian religion likewise promised the believer a share in the
life of the deathless gods and the ascent of his soul to its
place among the sidereal gods in the realm of light. Many
a legionary from the bleak hills of Caledonia to the burning

---

[1] Lines 480-2.

[2] Cf. Cicero, *De Legg.* II. 14, 36: ' Nihil melius illis Mysteriis quibus ex
agresti immanique vita exculti ad humanitatem et mitigati sumus,
initiaque, ut appellantur, ita re vera principia vitae cognovimus, neque solum
cum laetitia vivendi rationem accepimus, sed etiam cum spe meliore
moriendi.'

[3] Sophocles, *Frag.* 719 (Dind., 348 Didot). In another fragment (Nauck
753) death is, for the initiated, life.

[4] Inscription [b] found at Eleusis, published in Ἐφημ. ἀρχ., '83, p. 82,
thus : ἦι καλὸν ἐκ μακάρων μυστήριον, οὐ μόνον εἶναι τὸν θάνατον θνητοῖς οὐ κακὸν
ἀλλ' ἀγαθόν.

[5] On Aristides, Dindorf, III, p. 314.

[6] Cumont, *Rel. orient.* 2nd ed., p. 89.

[7] Cf. Frazer, *Adonis, Attis, Osiris*, I, p. 272.

[8] Aristides, *Or. sacrae*, VIII. 54 (Dind. I. 93).

sands of Mesopotamia was sustained in his last hours by the conviction of a deathless life which he had learned in the Mithraic chapel.   The emperor Julian closes his satire, *The Caesars*, with the following confession of his own faith : ' As for thee, I have given thee to come to the knowledge of thy father, Mithra.   Keep thou his commandments, and so procure for thyself during life a cable and sure anchorage ; and when it is necessary for thee to depart hence, thou shalt go with a good hope, having rendered thy tutelar god gracious to thee.' [1]   Orphism continued its stern preaching that man is a fallen being who can escape eternal punishment only by initiation into the Orphic life, a strain which entered into every form of Mystery-religion.   The religion of Thrice Greatest Hermes held out deification as the ultimate goal to the true Gnostic.

A few hours spent upon the marvellous symbolism of the underground basilica on the Via Praenestina or upon the beautiful frescoes of the Villa Item will give some idea of the sense of joy and victory experienced by the ancient initiate in his chapel.   On entering the former one is impressed by the other-worldly character of the imagery and by the spirit of hope.   The numerous winged Victories proclaim the initiate's triumph over death.   Mythological scenes— the rape of Ganymede, of a Leucippid, the liberation of Hesione by Hercules, Orpheus and Eurydice—symbolize the rape of the soul or the attainment of apotheosis.   The palaestra scenes, with the crowns and fillets and palms for the victors, confirm the faith of the initiate.   Memorable is the stucco of the apse [2] representing a scene of apotheosis by water.   Into a stormy sea beating between two rocky promontories an Eros (Love) gently assists a veiled figure (the soul, or the initiate herself) holding a lyre (signifying salvation and participation in the Choir of the Blessed), while underneath a Triton is waiting to receive her in a boat-shaped veil or sheet, and another is blowing his horn.   On a third promontory Apollo, the God of Light, is holding out his hand graciously to receive the soul after passing through

[1] 336, C.   [2] E. Strong and N. Jolliffe, *J.H.S.* XLIV, p. 103 f.

the last ordeal, and a Victory is proffering the crown. Love,
Light, and Grace were the portion of the purified soul in the
Isles of the Blessed, as contrasted with the deep dejection
of the pensive male figure on the left of the scene, typifying
the uninitiated to whom blessedness is denied. In the
recently discovered [1] Mithraeum of Capua a white marble
plaque, carved in beautiful relief, represents Eros holding
Psyche by the left hand while encouraging her by gentle
entreaty.

The task of the ancient Mysteries would seem to have been
the education of men in the doctrine of a future life—no
mean service to the ancient world in its despair. Unhappily,
the content of the immortality proffered was attenuated in
comparison with that deeply spiritual idea of eternal life
found in the Fourth Gospel or with the Pauline mystical
conception of a life ' hid with Christ in God,' but in the
purpose of Him who reveals Himself ' in many portions and
in many manners ' these ancient Mysteries whetted the
appetite of men for the larger life which Christians were to
proclaim as found in a knowledge of God through Jesus
Christ. The means of attaining that immortal life in the
Mysteries were for the most part ceremonial and often too
external to touch the springs of conduct,[2] so that a saved man
was not necessarily a moral man; but Paul himself discovered
that it was easier to secure converts than to reform their
morals.

It would run counter to our evidence and to what we
know of human nature to deny that there were conversions
and transformations of character among the members of
the Mystery-brotherhoods. Many a woman among them
was as chaste as the Paulina of Josephus' story, or as
her namesake, the wife of Praetextatus. Doubtless the
evil lives of the thyrsus-bearing votaries attracted more
public attention than the virtuous, as is unfortunately the
case with scandals in our own day. That many of these
ancient *mystae* did ' taste the powers of the world to come '
is beyond dispute. The glowing religious language of

[1] Cf. *Times*, March 31, '24.　　　　[2] Cf. Gardner, *ib*. p. 87.

Pindar and Sophocles, the emphatic testimony of Cicero and Plutarch, the mystic chorus of the *Cretans*, the thanksgiving prayer of Apuleius, the Hymn-book of the Orphic communities and the *Hymn of Regeneration* in the Hermetic literature are only examples that might be multiplied from literature and corroborated from inscriptions. E.g. Vincentius, a believer of Mithra, has on his sepulchral stone [1] carved a relief representing his deceased wife, Vibia, being led through an arched doorway into the unknown by a draped figure to which the name ' Good Angel ' is given. Or we may refer to the notable epitaph [2] of Paulina on her gifted husband, Praetextatus, in which she thanks him beyond the tomb for having saved her from death by initiation into the mysteries of the Great Mother, and Attis, Hecate, and Demeter of Eleusis. She closes the epitaph with an assertion of faith that she will be his again beyond.

[1] *C.I.L.* VI. 1, 142.   [2] *C.I.L.* VI. 1, 1779.

CHAPTER IV

THE APPEAL OF THE MYSTERY-RELIGIONS

A. Conditions Favourable to the Spread of the Mysteries

λαμπρῷ βλέπομεν τοῖς δ' ὄμμασιν οὐδὲν ὁρῶμεν.—ORPHIC VERSE.

At first sight it seems inexplicable that the Oriental mystic and even orgiastic cults, so humble and barbarous in their origin, frowned upon on their first entry by the governments, winning the majority of their followers from the lower, slave and artisan, classes, supported for centuries by private contributions,[1] often exacting austerities and maintaining customs which exposed the votary to the derision of the crowd, and even endangered his health, should have exercised such an increasing sway over the Graeco-Roman world, and, but for Christianity, would have conquered. They did not afford the only religious refuge of the age : why did they afford a refuge to so many ? There were intellectual systems like Greek philosophy, and Gnosticism ; there were ethical forces like Judaism, while state-religion asserted itself in repeated pagan revivals and most conspicuously in the imperial cult. These entailed practically no outlay on the part of their adherents. But the mystery-cults demanded that self-sacrifice which has always distinguished Free Churches as contrasted with Established Churches or philosophic schools. Reflect on what it cost to be a regular adherent of the Isiac cult. There were the austerities and fasts, which could not be agreeable to the flesh. Festal white robes had to be procured in honour of the deity, and would

---

[1] It would seem that Sir William Ramsay's statement (*Hist. Com. on Galatians*, p. 457) concerning voluntary liberality in ancient religion requires some modification : " The duty was one that was quite novel in ancient society. It was something that no convert from Paganism had been accustomed to."

regularly demand the fuller's services. The well-equipped
Isaea had to be erected and the cost of maintenance met by
those who used them. An elaborate and expensive priesthood had to be maintained by the offerings of the faithful.
On an ostracon [1] in the Berlin Museum, bearing date August
4, A.D. 63, a priest of Isis gives a receipt to a working man
thus : ' I have received from you four drachmae, one obol,
as collection of Isis for the public worship.' Devotion to the
Egyptian Madonna resulted in costly statues adorned with
abundance of precious stones.[2] Even the inventory of the
articles [3] in one small shrine of Isis proves amazing liberality.
An inscription from Delos [4] of about 200 B.C. tells how
Serapis in a dream-oracle objects to the continuance of his
cult in hired premises and demands the building of a
temple.[5] Although Apuleius was the son of a rich municipal
official, from whom he and his brother inherited the large
fortune of two million sesterces,[6] he was obliged to sell his
scanty wardrobe to procure funds sufficient for initiation into
the rites of Osiris after having been admitted to those of
Isis.[7] The frescoes of Herculaneum give some idea of the
sacerdotal college attached to any regular Isaeum. There
were the senior or high priest and assistant priests and
acolytes. These *sacerdotes*, unlike the semi-civic priests of
Greece and Rome, devoted all their time to their ecclesiastical
offices, and did not generally earn their living by practising
a craft or speculating in a business. The altar fires had
to be supplied and tended, and the morning sacrifices to be
provided. In the statutes of the Iobacchoi of Athens are
regulations as to the contributions of each member and the
penalty for default of payment.[8] The museum of Thebes

---

[1] Wilcken, *Gr. Ostraka*, II. 413 : photo in Deissmann, *Licht*, 4th ed., p. 84.

[2] E.g. *C.I.L.* II. 3386.

[3] Lafaye, *Hist. du Culte*, p. 135.

[4] *I.G.* XI. 4, no. 1299.

[5] Cf. Weinrich, *Neue Urkunden z. Sarapis-religion*, p. 19 ff.

[6] *Apologia*, 23.

[7] *Met.* XI. 28—' veste ipsa mea quamvis parvula distracta sufficientem
conrasi summulam.'

[8] L. 36 ff. Maas, *Orpheus*, p. 20 f.

contains an inscription [1] detailing the offerings to the Kabiri for one season (*cir.* 332 B.C.). In special cases long pilgrimages were made, which entailed absence from the ordinary means of earning a livelihood, in addition to costly fares paid to greedy ship-masters, and the still more costly land travelling. Moreover, some eager souls [2] in pursuit of salvation sought initiation into several Mysteries, though how the cost was met by any but the rich is difficult for us to conjecture, for men had to earn their bread then as now. The prosperous Syrian merchant, the Jewish banker, the Roman landlord, the successful Greek physician, the speculating freedman could afford to indulge in any expenditure for religion ; but these upper classes constituted a smaller minority then than nowadays. Of course there was much voluntary service given by slaves, artisans, and soldiers ; but all this was rendered outside the long hours of toil, and is itself a testimony to the deep conviction on the part of candidates that there was something worth while in the Mysteries. It is true that in the religious guilds the rich members laudably realized their brotherhood with their poorer ' brethren,' and often bore the whole or the chief part of the expenses incurred in the maintenance of the cult and in furnishing the sacred meals. In the regular offerings the poor contributed their mite, and they that were rich brought much. Unselfishness and generosity were by no means unknown virtues among the pagans, and were not invariably conspicuous in Christian guilds, as we may infer from Paul's description of the abuses in connexion with the *Agape* in Corinth.

The *taurobolium* cannot have been other than costly. The officiating priest's stipend had to be paid, the labour supplied, the timber prepared for the trench, the bull, doubtless of exceptional quality, had to be purchased ; the

---

[1] To which the Ephor, Kyr. N.G. Pappadakis, drew my attention.

[2] E.g. Tatian, Lucius' three initiations in the *Metamorphoses*, and his statement in *Apologia* 55 ' sacrorum pleraque initia in Graecia participavi' ; also Tertullian, Clement of Alexandria, Pausanias, Aurelius Antonius (*C.I.G.* 6206 ; *I.G.S.I.* 1449), Praetextatus and Paulina, Tertullian, Proclus (*In Plat Theol.* I. 19, p. 53 ; VI. 11), Pythagoras, and others.

sacramental garments, saturated in blood, were either fulled or kept as souvenirs of the baptismal rebirth, and so rendered economically valueless.

Some idea of the demands made upon the generosity of votaries in the construction and upkeep of the Mithraea may be gathered from the fact that the second largest Mithraeum discovered, that of Sarmizegethusa, had accommodation for a maximum of 100 members, while the majority of the chapels could not accommodate a half of this number.[1] Upon this limited *sodalicium* fell the cost of the excavation of the grotto, the arching of the roof, the chiselling of stone benches for the worshippers, the altar with its sacrifices, the carving of the Tauroctony and the Mithraic *agape*, the sacred meals and initiations, the holy lights, and all the other cult apparatus. The 'brethren' were generally legionaries whose *stipendium* was small, or oriental slaves whose *peculium* was modest indeed.

Enough has been said to make it clear that votaries in the Mysteries were not—generally speaking—prompted to seek initiation with a view to material gain, or to find a cheap religion, or to escape tithes. Indeed, these ancient initiates had recourse to religions which were costly because those religions which were provided free failed to lay hold of their imagination or satisfy their religious cravings.

As the Mysteries themselves presented a good and a bad side, so there were among their adherents and priests good, bad, and indifferent. Human nature being what it is, some initiates lived in the high latitudes of spiritual exaltation, enjoying religious serenity, while others remained content with the external pomp and symbolism, only vaguely intelligible to them, and never surmounted a superstition which saw in religion a magic or means of compulsion to be applied to the deity for selfish ends. Doubtless entrance into the Mysteries was sought from base motives by some. For the ordinary members initiation entailed financial loss

---

[1] Cf. Cumont, *T. et Mon.* I, pp. 65, 328 ; *Mysteries of M.*, p. 170 Toutain, II, p. 143 ; Legge, II. p. 269. The largest known Mithraeum is that of the Baths of Caracalla, discovered 1912.

rather than gain, but unscrupulous priests had abundant opportunity of using their holy office for self-aggrandizement. The sordid transaction of the senior priest of Isis, as told by Josephus, though an extreme case, is hardly solitary. The zeal of highly organized priesthoods, like that of Isis, for donations and endowments probably corresponded to a similar zeal on the part of the abbots and friars of the Middle Ages, such as is exposed, e.g. in Scott's *Fair Maid of Perth.* It is quite clear from Apuleius' account of the repeated initiations of Lucius [1] that the Egyptian priests at Cenchreae and Rome took advantage of his credulity to enrich their cult and so benefit themselves. The initiatory fee was fixed by the goddess herself (chs. 21, 22). A list of things required was furnished by the priest, which Lucius provided with even greater liberality than was necessary (23). At his initiation he was clad in 'the cloak of Olympus,' very richly embroidered, in which he was presented to his fellow-worshippers, after which followed feasts and banqueting, for which doubtless Lucius himself had paid in hard cash (24). A year later the goddess's grasping priests advised a further initiation into the rites of Osiris (27), for which it was necessary to sell his clothes to procure the necessary fees (28), and shortly thereafter the goddess required a third initiation (29), in the preparation for which he was 'guided by the enthusiasm of my faith rather than the measure of my fortunes,' relying on his earnings as a professor of rhetoric at Rome (30). The priesthood might be sought because of the secured income attached to its functions, because of the powerful influence wielded by it over the initiates, or because of the opportunity for influencing public opinion, or even, in later days, for interfering in politics.

In the history of every religion there are cases of flagrant abuse of holy offices on the part of the ecclesiastics, to which charge even the Christian Church is unable to plead Not guilty. Into the ordinary ranks of the initiates some were drawn by curiosity, some by the habit of that age of forming

[1] *Met.* XI. 21–30.

guilds, some by the love of elaborate ritual and pompous ceremonial, some from a desire to share in the sacred meals and participate in the doles made to the destitute members from the coffers of the society, or in order to be assured of religious interment.

A further obstacle to the success of the Mysteries—an item to be placed on the credit side of their long list— was the repeated and severe persecutions which their adherents suffered from pagan and Christian governments.[1] Some of these repressive measures were due to the de- linquencies rather than to the virtues of the *mystae*. But if some Mystery-Church historian had left behind an authentic account of all the persecutions endured by many generations of Mystery-believers, who have passed off the scene without an advocate, it would have been an interesting document for the history of the human spirit in its Godward strivings ; it would have filled up many of the lacunae in any enquiry as to the enthralling power of this type of religion for a thousand years.

It is generally agreed among students of the history of religion that a religion should be judged by its ideals and positive achievements rather than by its sordid aspects and failures. The necessity for such a criterion will be obvious if we reflect what a distorted history of Christianity a Mithraic or Orphic historian might have composed if he dwelt upon conspicuous instances of uncharitableness, abuse, and ambition on the part of Christian ecclesiastics, the intense hatred of Christian teachers towards heretics, the violations of the Christian sacrament, as at Corinth, and the superstitions of the lower orders of Christian believers. When he had said his worst, perhaps, Christianity would compare not unfavourably with the Mystery-Religions ; but it would be a debased Christianity.

There were many favouring circumstances, positive and negative, in the conditions of the Greek world of Alexander and the Diadochi, and in the Roman Empire, which furthered Orientalism in the West, and prepared the way for the

[1] Cf. p. 60.

Mysteries. The most decisive of such factors may be enumerated :

I. The Greek revival of the sixth century B.C. and the subsequent influence of Orphism. Two or three centuries before Alexander Orphism had invaded the Greek world,[1] and sown the seeds of the mysticism to which the Mystery-Religions appealed, and to which they gave a new impetus, and had also turned the minds of men to another world. Orphism might be termed the harbinger of the Mystery-Religions and Christianity in the West,[2] and its success regarded as the first promise of the long dominance of Oriental religious thought in the Mediterranean world.

Orphism, the greatest revival in Greek religion,[3] proved a force of far-reaching importance through its influence on Heraclitus, Plato, Pythagoreanism, Greek Mysteries, Neo-Platonism, and on such writers as Aeschylus, Sophocles, Euripides, Pindar, and Virgil.[4] It appeared at a time of great social upheaval when the very foundations of life seemed to be tottering. It confronted the situation by shifting the centre of interest from mere earthly existence, and making life here but a preparation for a life beyond.

---

[1] For its increased activity in the Hellenistic era (third cent. B.C. onwards) v. Macchioro, *Zagreus*, p. 265.

[2] " On parle beaucoup aujourd'hui de l'importance qu'a eue l'Orphisme pour la préparation du Christianisme, mais on affirme plus qu'on ne prouve : on ne peut cependant nier que ce fut une étape. . . . Il est vrai, en tout cas, que les idées chrétiennes et le rituel chrétien ont pris beaucoup aux mystères et à l'Orphisme, encore qu'on ait souvent exagéré ces emprunts."— C. de la Saussaye, p. 566 f. Macchioro (*Zagreus*, p. 269) answers the question, " What was the historic action of Orphism throughout the centuries ? " thus : " A primordial mystical activity of the human spirit, originating in a very remote age through an unconscious and immanent activity of our thought, Orphism accompanied the Greek people along all the stages of their evolution from magic to philosophy, from mysticism to rationalism, until at length, in its ultimate conquest, it was transformed and spiritualized in passing into Christianity (*diventando cristianesimo*)— a wonderful example of that aspiration by which humanity has been raised from the formless thought of the savage to the sublimest heights of the spirit."

[3] Cf. Gruppe, *Griech. Mythologie*, II, p. 1016 ff.

[4] For influence of Orphism on poetry, philosophy, and plastic art cf. Macchioro, *Zagreus*, pp. 248 f., 260 f. ; *Eraclito (passim)*.

Orphism introduced a theology of redemption. It taught a doctrine of original sin. Man's nature was dualistic, composed of the *titanic* elements closely associated with the body, and the *dionysiac* elements which were allied with the soul. By an ascetic morality the former must be repressed and the latter cultivated, to the end that the soul may escape ' from the body as from a tomb,' and may cease to be subject to the weary κύκλος τῆς γενέσεως, 'cycle of reincarnation.' ' I have flown out of the sorrowful wheel,' says the Orphic initiate on the Compagno tablet.[1] Orphism stood opposed to the calm Hellenic religion by giving to life a more sombre colour and by introducing such a conception of sin as entailed atonement. On the Dionysiac type of Greek religion it laid hold and remodelled it to its purpose. This Dionysiac religion, like Orphism, was of northern Thracian provenance, and was fraught with orgiastic-mystic elements,[2] on which Orphism fastened, adopting its emotionalism, its doctrine of *Enthousiasmos*, and of possession by the deity, rejecting its wild frenzy, and transforming its savage ritual into a sacramental religion.

Asceticism, ' the Orphic life,' was the primary condition of the attainment of salvation, the means by which the true Orphic delivered his soul from the pollution of the body and escaped the long series of purificatory punishments in Hades. This stern religion, with its anthropology uncongenial to the Greek world-affirming ethic, its emphasis on sin and the need of a cathartic ritual, its relative indifference to civic as compared with personal righteousness, must have appeared to Greek theologians somewhat in the light in which Puritanism appeared to Elizabethan politicians.

The Orphic note was one that never died out of all subsequent Greek and Hellenistic-Roman religion. The prestige of Orphism is well attested in the numerous counterfeits by the Orpheotelestae (of whom Plato speaks so scathingly, while he speaks respectfully of Orpheus) and

---

[1] G. Murray in Harrison, *Proleg.* p. 670 ; Olivieri, p. 4.

[2] " Der Quellenpunkt aller griech. Mystik liegt in der Dionysischen Religion " (Rohde, *Religion der Griechen*, p. 332).

metargyrtae, mendicant magic-mongers, and other charlatans who traded on the fair name of Orpheus. Orphism broke new ground and prepared the West for the Mystery-Religions and for Christianity in some important respects. (1) It was the first factor that successfully disturbed the Hellenic serenity of worship by introducing into the religious consciousness the conception of sin, never since eradicated in the West, and influencing all European thought, and by demanding rigid penances and purifications. Contrary to the prevalent Greek idea of a life according to nature, the body was viewed as a ' prison ' or ' tomb ' of the soul. Life became a grim struggle between the Titanic and the Dionysiac elements in man's nature, by which the Orphic became increasingly Dionysiac or divine till he reached the goal, ' Happy and blessed one, thou shalt be god instead of mortal.' (2) Hence purity received a new emphasis which was " destined to make an ever-widening appeal, and to rank as one of the most impressive factors in the evolution of Hellenic religion." [1] A new ideal was put before the mind of the West, that of ὁσιότης or Holiness, by the path of ἄσκησις rather than that of happiness by self-expression. Unfortunately the Orphics in this, as in so many other details, endeavoured to pour their new wine into old bottles, very much to the detriment of their evangel of Holiness. Their remedies for defilement were too ceremonial. There was the higher Orphism which could feed on spiritual mysticism [2] and derive its incentives from the future prospect of divinity or a divine humanity. But there was the lower and popular Orphism which used the machinery of future punishments,[3] such as that referred to by Plato [4]

---

[1] Kennedy, *St. Paul*, p. 16.

[2] Miss Harrison (*Proleg.* 587) speaks of the higher Orphism as " a faith so high that it may be questioned whether any faith, ancient or modern, has ever out-passed it," while recognizing its lower and magical side.

[3] On the strong predilection of the Orphics for descriptions of the pains of hell compared with their reticence as to the nature of the blissful existence of the divine life into which the initiated entered, cf. Macchioro, *Orf. e Paol*, p. 261 f.

[4] In the Orphic myth of Er., *Repub.* X 614 B.

and described in the Homeric *Nekyia*,[1] and by Pseudo-
Plato in the *Axiochus*,[2] by Virgil, and by Plutarch in his
De Occultim Vivendo, to persuade men to live ' the
Orphic life ' and undergo Orphic initiation, incidentally
paying the fees. The Orphics themselves confessed that
many are called but few chosen. (3) Orphism did a lasting
service to Greek and subsequent religion by rescuing the
orgiastic Dionysiac [3] cult from the extravagances, savagery,
and crudities which would have disgusted the Greek spirit,
the sympathy of which was necessary for the success of any
religion in the Graeco-Roman world,[4] and thus gave free
scope to the enthusiastic and mystical tendencies of Dionysiac faith. Orphism was built on Dionysiac ritual and
mythology. The god of their ritual was Dionysos, especially
in the mystic and chthonic form of Dionysos-Zagreus, while
the esoteric God was *Eros*, or Love. The principle of the
Orphic Reformation was the sound one of using to the
utmost the old material to hand, a principle which, however,
Orphism observed too strictly by conserving naturalistic
practices from Dionysos and the earlier Pelasgic animism
which might with greater profit have been surrendered in
spite of the facility with which they lent themselves to the
imaginative symbolism of the age. Orphism spoke through
the commonplace and familiar ; many simple rites took on
a new mystic value. In primitive sympathetic magic could
be discovered organs of spiritual mysticism. Telluric rites
could be raised to eschatological. Dionysiac divine possession could be theologized into incarnation or identification
with the divine. " The great step which Orpheus took
was that, while he kept the old Bacchic faith that a man
might become a god, he altered the conception of what a
god was, and he sought to obtain that godhead by wholly

[1] *Od.* XI. 34 ff. ; cf. Wilamowitz-Möllendorf, *Hom. Unters.* p. 199 ff.

[2] Cf. *Les Enfers selon l'Axiochus* in *Comptes rendus de l'Acad. des Inscr.*
1920, pp. 272–85.

[3] Cf. Harrison, *Proleg.* p. 474 ff.

[4] Harnack (*Mission and Exp.* II, p. 317) finds the chief cause of the
failure of Mithraism in the fact that " almost the entire domain of Hellenism
was closed to it." Cf. Vollers, *Weltreligionen*, p. 127.

154 THE APPEAL OF THE MYSTERY-RELIGIONS

different means. The grace he sought was not physical intoxication, but spiritual ecstasy; the means he adopted not drunkenness, but abstinence and rites of purification." [1] The flute and maddening cymbals of the Wine-god were superseded by the Orphic lyre. By thus informing the savage rites from Thrace with the spirit of order the Dionysiac, i.e. mystic-ecstatic, means of union with the divine was preserved for Greek religion, Neo-Platonism, and Christianity. (4) Such a religion was inevitably concerned primarily with the salvation of the individual soul—a startlingly new religious conception, enhancing the ideal of personal responsibility and making religion essentially a matter of a man's own moral choice. The incongruity of this doctrine with the absolute rights of the State was to appear in exaggerated form when the subjects of the Roman Empire flocked into the Oriental individualistic cults. (5) In another respect the Orphics prepared for the " free church " principle of the Mysteries and of Christianity. The Orphic cult-brotherhoods established the practice of voluntary association for religious purposes which became pronounced from the days of Alexander the Great. (6) Orphism was steeped in sacramentarianism which flooded the later Mysteries and flowed into Christianity. Salvation was by sacrament, by initiatory rites, and by an esoteric doctrine. [2] Rites performed religiously on earth affected the lot beyond, as is clear from the language of the Orphic tablets. One such sacrament is referred to in the confession from one of the Compagno tablets: ' I have sunk beneath the bosom of Persephone, Queen of the Underworld.' [3] But the sacramental was all too easily confused with the archaic, so that exalted religious feeling and nonsense often lay close together, as in the mystic confession of identification with Dionysos in a fragment of Euripides' *Cretans*, preserved by Porphyry :

[1] Harrison, *ib.* 477. We should write *Orphism* where Miss Harrison writes *Orpheus*, who is to her " a real man, a reformer, and possibly a martyr."

[2] The Orphics were ' the Wise '; cf. Adam. *Repub. of Plato*, II, p. 378.

[3] *V.* Olivieri, *Lamellae aur. orph.*, p. 7.

' There in one pure stream

My days have run, the servant I,
Initiate of Idean Jove ;
Where midnight Zagreus roves, I rove ;
I have endured his thunder cry ;

Fulfilled his red and bleeding feasts ;
Held the Great Mother's mountain flame ;
I am set free and named by name
A Bacchus of the Mailèd Priests.

Robed in pure white, I have borne me clean
From man's vile birth and coffined clay,
And exiled from my lips alway
Touch of all meat where life hath been.' [1]

The tablet of Caecilia Secundina also shows how readily Orphic sacraments could degenerate into magic rites. (7) Orphic Purity, by which man attained divinity, could not be secured by mere self-reliance. Special divine help was requisite, a sacramental grace communicated by initiation. Thus, the optimistic or anthropocentric religious view of the West retreated before the humbler and theocentric view of the helplessness of man.[2] This conviction quickened the yearning for redemption and created a demand for the sacramental grace of the Mysteries and Christianity. (8) The Orphic movement was the most potent and pervasive of the early syncretistic forces which reached their strength in the heyday of the Mysteries. (9) It was also the first promise of that later wide-spread and influential phase of religion known as Gnosticism—in its esoteric doctrines, elaborate cosmogonies and theogonies, and its fundamental dualism. (10) The Orphics were apparently the first to introduce the allegoric method into theology. This innovation arose from their desire to retain the maximum of primitive ritual and from the consequent necessity of reconciling the archaic with the modern, and of mysticizing the commonplace.

[1] G. Murray's tr.
[2] Cf. Gruppe, II, p. 1016. Rohde well remarks : " Das Selbstverlass des alten Griechentums ist hier gebrochen ; schwachmüthig sieht der Fromme nach fremder Hilfe aus ; er bedarf Offenbarungen u. Vermittlungen ' Orpheus des Gebieters,' um den Weg zum Heil zu finden, u. ängstlicher Beachtung seiner Heilsordnung, damit man ihn gehen könne " (II, p. 124).

II. The collapse of the wonderful city-state system of the Mediterranean world, dating in Greece intellectually from the rise of Sophism and politically from the Peloponnesian War, and in Rome from the second Punic War. With it collapsed the religion of which it was the expression. The State religions of Greece and Rome suffered the fate of every religion which allies itself with a political system : it shared their glory in their halcyon days, and it shared their disaster in their disintegration.[1] The fall of the *polis* and the rise of the Greek Kingdoms and the Roman Empire ruined the prestige of state religions, while the commotion and insecurity of the period undermined the faith of the populace in their ancestral gods. The religious instinct in man drove him to look elsewhere for religious support. The Northern and Western hinterlands of Graeco-Roman civilization lay in barbarism : where else could men look save to the immemorial home of religion—*ex oriente lux* ? The Oriental religions were not limited to one language, nor bound up with any one definite political system, or, if with any, with that toward which Rome drifted steadily for centuries— despotism. The Mysteries had in them a power of expansion and the germ of universalism which were lacking in the Olympian or Capitoline theologies.

The breaking up of the city-state conduced to individualism and at the same time catholicity in religion, created a social vacuum to be filled by the religious guilds, gave the masses a freer hand to assert their *superstitio*, and immensely facilitated religious syncretism.

III. The unification of mankind inaugurated by Alexander and consummated by Rome made the religion of each people or race of interest to all, and so inaugurated a process which would issue in the survival of the fittest. If all men were theoretically equal their religions were on an equality and the path of access from one to the other was facilitated. Where men of every degree of culture, of every civilized race, and representative of every ancient religion met

[1] Cf. Kaerst, II. pt. I, pp. 204–8 ; W. Fowler, *The City-State of the Greeks and Romans*.

together under the rule of one man there was ample room for the interchange of thought.   The trend was toward universalism, and the only religion which had promise of a future was that which could disentangle, or had disentangled, itself from particularism of caste or creed or government.   This unification found expression in the " marriage of East and West," and in eclecticism in philosophy and syncretism in religion, whereby men were lifted above the prejudices of nationalism and the narrowness of state churches.

IV.   The powerful reflex action of the East upon the West in those respects in which its genius was superior to that of Greece and Rome, viz. religion, industry, and commercial enterprise.   And not in these only, for some departments in which Greece and Rome considered themselves specialists were contested by Eastern talent with considerable success. As the Orient has at all times devoted itself to religious contemplation with the zeal with which the West has developed political life the growing religious preponderance of the East is not to be wondered at.   But in other respects the East entered upon that career of ascendancy over the West which culminated in the establishment of the imperial cult, in Aurelius' institution in A.D. 263 of the official cult of *Sol Invictus*, in the absolutism of Diocletian, the declaration of Diocletian and his colleagues at Carnuntum in 307 of Mithra as patron (*fautor*) of the empire, the transference of the centre of gravity from Rome to the East by the founding of Constantinople, and lastly in the victory of the religion of Galilee.   As the Greeks, when they turned eastward to hellenize Asia, themselves learned Asiatic ways, so the Romans fell under the spell of the riper and richer culture of the East.   Cumont has done much to dispel " cette illusion d'optique "—the traditional belief in the superiority of the West to the East and in the senility of Oriental life.[1]   The penetration of the East into the West occurred in many ways, and was at last so complete that the Orontes and the Nile were pouring their waters into the Tiber.   Alexander gave

[1] " Ils excellent dans toutes les professions hormis celle de soldat " (*R. Or.* 2nd ed., p. 3).

the weight of his authority to the military policy of strengthening the army by levies of Oriental recruits, and of making the Orientals feel proud of service with the Greeks, as Indian troops have been proud to fight side by side with British comrades on many a field. In the constantly engaged armies of the Diadochi there was a similar opportunity for Orientals to mingle with Europeans. Rome adopted the same policy, and drew recruits from nearly all the eastern provinces. These soldiers were devoted to their religions and became propagandists for it. Greece and Rome had neither the faith nor the enthusiasm of which the missionary spirit is born. The thousands of Oriental slaves who were transported westward from second century B.C. onward contributed their share toward the subjugation of Rome to the East. Under the *Roman Peace* the merchants, bankers, and exporters were largely Oriental. Industrially the East supplied the manufactured articles which Italy and the West needed. It was the wealth of the Orient that first under Alexander introduced luxury and extravagance into the West, and again during the Republican wars of conquest. And it was Oriental treasures that stimulated the taste and paid for Oriental articles of luxury—unguents, atars, tapestries of Damascus, silks of China, spices of Arabia. The large and numerous Greek-Asiatic cities throughout Asia enjoyed great prosperity in catering for the taste of the West, and with their material wares their merchants carried also the things of the spirit. Greek philosophy, which went forth so splendidly equipped to educate the world, was semi-orientalized after Aristotle, really the last Greek philosopher. The founders of Stoicism, Zeno and Cleanthus, came from the East, and with Stoicism Greek thought became as much Oriental as Greek. Posidonius, who adapted Stoicism to Roman character, came from Apamea in Syria. Neo-Pythagoreanism was more Oriental than Greek, and Neo-Platonism was founded by Plotinus of Alexandria. Cumont, in supporting his thesis that "the history of the empire during the first three Christian centuries resolves itself into a pacific penetration of the Occident by the Orient,"

points out that " le mirage d'un empire oriental" became
the directing thought of the dictator Caesar and the triumvir
Antony, while Nero meditated transporting his capital to
Alexandria, and in his last moments deliberated on begging
the province of Egypt from his victorious rival. Rome was
organized by Augustus after the fashion of an Egyptian
capital, and the fiscal reforms of the Caesars were inspired by
the financial system of the Lagids. In the domain of law,
in which the Romans were most original and successful,
Oriental customs were virile enough to withstand or modify
Roman usage. Many of the famous jurists were Syrians, such
as Ulpian of Tyre and Papinian of Hermesa. The law
school of Beyrout increased in prestige from the third until in
the fifth century it was the leading centre of juristic study.
In the realm of science we find the Orientals prominent :
" the majority of the great astronomers, mathematicians,
physicians, as of the great founders or defenders of metaphysical systems, are Oriental." [1] In literature, art, and
architecture the Orientals competed successfully with the
West, and modified Western ideas. All this facilitated the
spread of the Mystery-Religions, for the peoples of the
Orient, unlike those of Greece and Rome, were proselytizers.
The penetration of the politically subject but otherwise
dominant Orientals had set the fashion for things Oriental
which was enhanced by the prestige arising from the
antiquity of Oriental institutions. The fascination
of the Orient, refined and humanized by Hellenism,
gave rise to a long-dominant romanticism in Greece and
Italy.

V. Another factor deserves attention in the changing
circumstances of the age as conducive to the spread of the
Mystery-Religions—the growing influence of the masses and
the concern which their demands caused the government
circles. The Graeco-Roman age was a popularizing age,[2]
during which the lower orders had to be humoured, amused
and fed, and their religious needs satisfied. This holds true

[1] Cumont, p. 9 (Eng. tr., p. 6).
[2] Angus, *Environment of Early Christianity*, p. 11 f.

of the post-Aristotelian period, but this aspect of social life came into prominence chiefly from the days of the Second Punic War, and reached its climax in the second and third centuries A.D. We can trace these popularizing tendencies in several directions, though more conspicuously in religious matters. The *lingua franca*, the vehicle of religious propaganda, was not the Greek of Periclean Athens, but the Greek of the market-place and the port and the field. Classical or Attic Greek had to stoop to conquer; it took on the less precise and more direct character of the language spoken by and ' understanded of ' the people, and received into its *wortschatz* vernacular and even alien elements. One might compare the victory of the native English tongue over the Norman-French court speech, or, in later centuries, both in Romance and in the Teutonic countries, the rise of the vernaculars in opposition to ecclesiastical Latin and their ultimate adaptation to literary purposes.

After Aristotle Greek philosophy was popularized so far as philosophy may ever be said to be popular. The post-Aristotelian philosophy is not that of the secluded schools of Athens; it is that which can be discussed by the average intelligent man on the highways of life. The main philosophical ideas had filtered down among the masses, and the chief results of systematic thinking had been reported to those to whom the results were of more direct interest than the processes. With Socrates philosophy first turned its attention upon man as a thinking subject; with the post-Aristotelian schools it abandoned the speculative sphere and directed its main attention to the practical questions of human conduct in which the ordinary man was interested. When, in the next century, from the second century B.C. onwards, Rome fell under the spell of Greek philosophy, she gave a more decidedly popular and practical turn to it. Cicero says that Socrates first brought down philosophy from heaven to earth, but it was Cicero himself who, through his translations and paraphrases of Greek philosophers and his outlines of the history of Greek philosophy, and by the discovery of a vocabulary, first popularized philosophy in the Western world.

But in the religious life more than in any other department we hear the lower classes knocking at the doors of the ruling classes with a persistency that does not brook refusal. This was observed by Roman writers themselves, who lament the rise of *superstitio* as against respectable *religio*. The uneducated are spiritually less independent than the reflective, and are less able to bear the burden of sin and the guilt of conscience. To them something corresponding to the Roman confessional is an imperative necessity. State religions in their heyday might repress this tendency, but in their decay, when the beautified temple and the elaborate ceremonial only testified to the splendour that had departed, the populace went its own way in search of religion. The history of the Second Punic War first brings into relief the religious policy of the Roman government— whether republican or imperial, pagan or Christian—of endeavouring to control the religion of the masses, or rather of controlling the masses by the instrumentality of religion. It is an interesting spectacle to observe how the governing class furnished a ready-made state religion to the masses and made it attractive in cult, and how, when this failed, the same class cleverly adopted and gave official recognition to whatever alien worship was for the moment popular and likely to restrain the fears of the people and keep them quiet. " Good order first " was always the keynote of Roman administrative policy. In the introduction of the Magna Mater the hands of the government were really forced by the people, a fact which the government was shrewd enough to conceal from the excited people, assuming the rôle of bestowing a new religious boon which they had no power to withhold. Like many wise statesmen, the Roman rulers pretended to lead where they were in truth being led. From the days of the advent of the Great Mother from Pessinus till the adoption of Christianity by Constantine, we observe on the one hand the steadily increasing ascendancy of the religious cults and customs adopted by the populace and on the other the authorizing by the government of what in most instances it could not arrest.[1] Before these popular strivings all the glory of the lovely gods of the Graeco-Roman pantheon paled, and the splendour and patriotism of the imperial cult. Neither official indifference nor restrictive measures could prevent the long-submerged views of the masses from coming to the surface. The cult of Isis-Serapis, though the most persecuted, became the most imposing because the populace willed it. The government vainly endeavoured to gain a monopoly of the current means of utilizing the supernatural, but the superstition of the people thwarted all their efforts. The government recognized an official *divinatio*, but the populace had recourse to their own private *divinatio*. The *Chaldaei* and *mathematici* were repeatedly banished from Rome, but returned as often because they drove a lucrative trade with the masses. All the acrimony of the Roman satirists and the scorn of the Roman historians could not stay the spread of Judaism among the people.

The masses were beginning to come to their own, and they brought with them those forms of religion—chiefly Oriental, chthonic, and archaic—which appealed to them ; the upper classes were compelled at different stages to acknowledge as *fait accompli* the progress of their rivals.

To this popular striving there was a bad as well as a good side. On the debit side we may write the word *superstitio* and on the credit side mysticism. To the former belong many remains of naturalism which had never become extinct among the ignorant classes when the city-state was in its apogee, and these beliefs were resurrected with renewed power, and finally some of them commended themselves to all classes. Such was the practice of magic to compel the deity to one's will, and the belief in the horoscope which spread with the practice of astrology. On the other hand, the people had no ulterior political motive in their search for religious support ; they went in search of a new religion or new religions for religious purposes, and

[1] Cf. Boissier, 7th ed. II, pp. 238–304.

we may venture to say that on the whole they were divinely guided to look in the right direction.

The Oriental cults, affected by this popularizing tendency, stooped to conquer. Nearly all the religions of the Graeco-Roman world aimed at popularity, and, though never negligent of an opportunity to secure recruits among the upper and influential classes, strove to enrol the greatest number of adherents among the masses, as if conscious that in the end the *vox populi* would be the *vox dei.*

This emergence of popular tastes and self-consciousness, together with the correlative retreat of aristocratic influence, is a phenomenon forcibly borne in upon one in reading the records of the Graeco-Roman world; but it is easier to register the phenomenon than to confidently assign adequate causes. In the main such causes would be found in (1) the intellectual disintegration, the rationalism and scepticism of the upper classes, who, having lost faith in their orthodox religion and state-church, could not hope to maintain their hypocritical dissemblance for the sake of the masses ; (2) the decay of the city-state civilization which was favourable to the upper and leisured classes ; (3) the economic results of the Roman wars of conquest which, like all great upheavals, tended to impoverish the poor and enrich a few, with the result of a partial or complete disappearance of the middle classes. The *Latifundia* drove out the peasant proprietor, while the slave system imperilled the competition of the independent artisan and bourgeois. (4) Imperial proscriptions and decimations by exile, confiscation, and death of the upper,[1] especially the senatorial, classes weakened the prestige of the aristocrats and made the masses more conscious of their own power. The whims of the populace could place power in the hands of irresponsible dictators. The vote of the army, including provincials, could dispose of the purple. The importance of popular sentiment in deciding the fate of an empire or a religion was forced upon an emperor like Julian. (5) The

---

[1] Cf. Ferrero, *Ruin of Ancient Civilization*, chs. I and II ; Dill, *Rom. Soc.* Bk. I, ch. I.

increasing trend of the principate of Augustus into a despotism which cannot tolerate an influential aristocratic class, but humours and contents the masses. (6) The increasing proportion and influence of provincials and foreigners in the empire. (7) The rise and spread of the religious and trade guilds, composed mostly of the lower orders.

The strength of this plebeian movement is indicated by the tribute paid to it by loftier movements. The great weakness of the Orphic reform lay in its lack of courage to abandon the popular basis and rituals of religion. Stoicism compromised with the populace by taking over its myths and treating them esoterically by allegorical exegesis. Neo-Platonism did not escape the spell of superstition; it degenerated into an unlovely theurgy or occultism. Monarchy, Diadochian and Roman alike, frowned upon spiritual movements [1] which endangered the peace of the masses. The Mystery-Religions catered for popular tastes. Even Christianity retains to this day traces of some popular beliefs and practices from the Mysteries.

VI. Another circumstance highly favourable to the success of the Oriental religions was the dominance of astrology, or astralism, the nature and influence of which in the ancient world have been revealed within this generation by scholars like Usener, Bouché-Leclercq, Reitzenstein, Cumont, Kugler, Boll. In Greece and Italy there was a primitive and deeply-implanted mystic element [2] which, like chthonic theology, could not come to its own in the heyday of classic faith, but which revitalized later paganism and lent a new energy of faith in its closing struggles. Such was the ' divine Mantic ' among the Greeks, and a somewhat different phenomenon, *Divinatio*, in Italy, the belief in both arising out of the instinctive desire to hold intercourse with the deity and out of a conviction that for the purposes of life the

[1] Cf. Dieterich, *Kl. Sch.*, p. 460. " Erst mit dem Erstehen der Monarchien beginnt eine planmässige Rücksichtnahme auf das religiöse Empfinden breiterer Massen, die ja auch auf orient. Boden von Anfang an politische Notwendigkeit ist " (Reitzenstein, *Hell. Mysterienrel.*, p. 3).

[2] Cf. Bouché-Leclercq, *Hist. de la Divination*, I. pp. 2–5.

deity vouchsafes revelations of his will and of the future. Herein lay a point of contact for astralism in the Graeco-Roman world, in which it antiquated hitherto accepted methods of enquiring into " the future and its viewless things."

In regard to the relations of astral religion to the Oriental cults, Cumont says [1]:

" Its success was connected with that of the Oriental religions, which lent it their support, as it also lent them its support. . . . Astrology was religious in its origin and its principles : it was religious also in its close alliance with the Oriental cults, particularly those of the Syrian Baals and Mithra : it was also religious in the effects which it produced."

It cannot be an accident that Oriental cults and astrology increased in power *pari passu* and simultaneously. But astrology affected not only the church-like cults of Syria, Egypt, and Persia, but also semi-philosophical religions like Hermeticism and Gnosticism. Astrology had its home in Babylonia, where it was cultivated by the original Sumerians and bequeathed as a science and faith in one to the Babylonians, from whom it passed to the Persians, in whose religion it played a long and important rôle in Mazdaeism and Mithraism. It began its successful career westwards as a result of Alexander's conquests.

" In the first place, from the break-up of the Euphratean priestly colleges . . . and the driving out of the lesser priests therein to get their own living, and then from the fact that the scientific enquiry and mathematical genius of the Greeks had made the calculation of the positions of the heavenly bodies at any given date and hour a fairly simple matter." [2]

This alliance of Chaldean sacerdotalism and Greek science

---

[1] *Rel. Or.* 2nd ed. pp. 241, 258 (Eng. tr., pp. 163, 174).

[2] Legge, II. 235 ; cf. Bouché-Leclercq, *Divination*, I, p. 206 ff.; Toutain, *Cultes païens*, II, p. 181.

continued to characterize astral religion through the later centuries, especially under the empire.[1] Astrology, generally allied with magic, was from its nature a highly specialized art, at first an essentially aristocratic [2] faith-science, but because of its practical bearings on life it soon appealed to the populace, and, in spite of police regulations and imperial persecutions against the practitioners of the *ars mathematica damnabilis*, it won its way to universal acceptance and was as firmly believed in by the educated and ruling classes as by the lower orders.[3] The Stoics, generally speaking, accepted it, and it was mainly through the teachings of Posidonius that the astral religion became domiciled in the West.[4]

There are several respects in which astralism abetted the spread of Oriental cults both by way of alliance and in the results produced by it.

The practice of astral lore necessitated the diligent contemplation of the shining heavenly bodies, which never have failed to inspire awe and awaken a religious sentiment of some kind. The beauty of the Eastern night, the long and silent contemplation, the intense practical religious purpose of the gazers—all conspired to induce that spirit of mystic ecstasy or cosmic emotion to which the Mysteries made their appeal [5] and which they in turn magnified.[6] In this lifting of man above himself, in prompting the desire for communion with the divinities of the shining constellations, in diminishing the sense of distance between heaven and earth, and in turning man's thoughts to the future, astrology was working in the same domain as the Mystery-Religions.

Astrology was also the foster-mother of that regnant Element-Mysticism, according to which the soul becomes part of that which it contemplates, and its elements bear affinity to the elements of which the cosmos is constituted.[7]

[1] Dill, p. 93: " Astrology was a Greek as well as a Chaldean art."
[2] Cumont, *R. Or.* p. 244 (Eng. tr., p. 165).   [3] Cf. Dill, 447.
[4] Cumont, *ib.* p. 243 (Eng. tr. 164) ; Bouché-Leclercq, *ib.* I, p. 274 f.
[5] Cf. Kennedy, p. 6 f.   [6] Cf. Gardner, *St. Paul*, p. 61.
[7] Cf. Dieterich, *Abraxas*, p. 58 f. ;   Kennedy, p. 204 ; Cumont, *R. O.* 2nd ed., pp. 254, 264 ; Eisler, *Weltenmantel u. Him.* II, p. 664.

It thus offered a synthesis or bond of unity, which ancient philosophers sought in vain, in a religious sympathy or homoeopathy of the elements of the universe.

Astrology brought its adherents into connexion with Oriental priests because astrology was a religious science which had been practised from time immemorial by the sacerdotal colleges of the Eastern temples. It was sacerdotal in origin, and its adherents did not forget that it came from the temples of Chaldaea and Egypt. The " Bible of Astrology " was an Egyptian-Greek product,[1] the books going by the name of Nechepso and Petosiris [2] of the second century B.C. To the end it remained as much a faith as a science. " Even in the West it never forgot its sacerdotal origins, and never more than half freed itself from the religion which had given it birth : and it is in this respect it attaches itself to the Oriental cults." [3] Astrology thus enhanced the prestige of Eastern priests in the West because it viewed them as specialists in a hieratic science which had to do with a man's affairs here and affected his whole destiny. It lent them a dignity and authority such as that with which the fear of excommunication clothed the mediaeval priest.

It should also be noted that astrology—because of its immemorial antiquity and boasted scientific method—drew men away from the Western religions by antiquating Greek and Roman methods of enquiry into the future. Augury was practically abandoned, and haruspicy shared the same fate. The oracles, though they revived under the empire,[4] could not vie with the *Chaldaei* and *mathematici* in the number of enquirers. No longer the venerable Delphi was consulted with the same confidence [5] in important political and military affairs, but the soothsayers and horoscope-readers of the East.

Astrology benefited religion by casting its influence

---

[1] Boll in *N. Jahrb f. d. Klass. Alt.* XXI, p. 106.
[2] V. *Cat. Astrolog. Graec.* VII, p 129 ff.
[3] Cumont, *ib.* pp. 251–2 (Engi tr. 170).
[4] According to Plutarch, *De Def. Orac.*
[5] On the temporary revival of Delphi cf Dempsey, p. 176 ff.

on the side of the monotheistic tendency which was also favoured by Oriental cults. Though the *Chaldaei* paid most attention to the host of stars, they could not but recognize the premier place of the Sun among the seven planets and the stars. The Sun, as the source of heat and light, became the chief deity of the heaven, and Sun-worship was the ultimate result of astralism. From being the chief among all the heavenly bodies, the Sun became the representative of all by the familiar path from henotheism to monotheism. Sun-worship became an essential feature and indeed the centre [1] of all non-Christian religions in the closing empire. The Mystery-gods, like Serapis, Attis, and Mithra, were brought into most intimate relation with the Sun and finally identified with him. Thus astrology directed men's attention to the heavens, among the luminaries of which the Sun was recognized as the chief and the source of life and light, then acknowledged as the supreme symbol of deity as embracing within his sphere all other lights, and finally the gods of the Mysteries were obliged to become assimilated to the supreme Sun. This solar monotheism, one of the latest aspects of paganism, arose in Syria, the chief centre of which was Palmyra, the ruins of which to this day eloquently attest the august character of solar worship. In the person of Heliogabalus, a high-priest of the Sun-god ascended the imperial throne and promoted the cause of the *Sol invictus Elagabal* more zealously than his subjects were prepared for; in the closing quarter of the third century Aurelian, son of a priestess of the Sun-god, proclaimed *Sol invictus* as protector of the empire and the imperial house, and equipped his worship with a college of Pontiffs. In the first decade of the fourth century (307) Diocletian proclaimed Mithra as *Sol invictus*, patron-god of the empire—*fautori imperii sui.*

Such were the main services [2] rendered by the astral

---

[1] Cf. art. *Zodiacus* in Daremberg-Saglio, V, p. 1056; Reville, p. 286 ff.

[2] I.e. for religion. Astrology supported by magic was helpful to scientific knowledge. " Their counterfeit learning has been a genuine help with the progress of human knowledge Because they awakened chimeri-

religion of the Eastern world. But there were *two baneful* results not wholly but mainly attributable to astrology. In its very nature astrology could not escape being a religion of fatalism,[1] and more than any other factor it made Fate a terrible and crushing power such as we can scarcely believe. Astrology also allied itself with, and conduced to, the practice of magic, a curse from which the non-Christian religions of the Greek and Roman world never entirely escaped. In the former respect, by fostering determinism, astrology produced a disease to discover a remedy or alleviation for which many fled to the Mystery-Religions,[2] which promised sacramental grace, divine sympathy and participation in the victory of the deity, and finally sidereal immortality, by which the soul ascended through the spheres whose constellations proved all-powerful for man's weal and woe. In the latter respect, by encouraging magic, the acts of the Mystery-cults were often degraded into means of compelling the deity for selfish and even immoral ends. Unfortunately the Mystery-Religions, in their proselytizing zeal, were none too scrupulous in the choice of their allies, with whose fortunes they bound themselves. Some of these allies, such as imperial favour, proved broken reeds ; others continued faithful to their Oriental affinities to the end, but sapped the life and finally arrested the progress of the tolerant cults which had enlisted their sympathy. At the close of the long struggle that religion was destined to win which relied on its intrinsic merits, and participated in the world-conquering faith of its Founder.

VII. Resurgence of Chthonian Theology. In the re-

cal hopes and fallacious ambitions in the minds of their adepts, researches were undertaken which undoubtedly would never have been started or persisted in for the sake of a disinterested love of truth. The observations, collected with untiring patience by the Oriental priests, caused the first physical and astronomical discoveries. . . . The occult sciences led to the exact ones " (Cumont, *R. or.*, Eng. tr. p. 194)

[1] Cf. Reitzenstein, *Poim.* pp. 77–9 ; Cumont, *ib.* p. 264 ff. (Eng. tr., p. 178) ; *Fatalisme astrale et les religions antiques, Rev. d'hist. et de lit. rel.,* '15 N.S. III. 6) ; Boll, *ib.* p. 108 ff.

[2] " Der Fatalismus hat als sein Gegenbild den Mystizismus " (Reitzenstein, p. 79).

surgence of chthonian theology an interesting movement took place in Greek religion which changed its whole subsequent outlook and character,[1] and gave to it an eschatological direction which ultimately led to the facile acceptance of Oriental Mystery-cults.[2] This was a democratic movement in which the rustic deities of the populace increased while the Uranian and aristocratic gods decreased. From the earliest period of Greek religious history there are traces of the existence of the twofold worships[3] of the Olympians, or deities of the sky, and of the chthonian or katachthonian deities of the earth and underworld. But the origins of the chthonic cults and the steps by which they attained distinctive prominence in the history of a people like the Greeks, who were freer from superstition and stood less in awe of the supernatural than their neighbours, are hidden from us. Somewhat parallel phenomena are found in the religious revolution by which the Eastern cults adopted by the people were forced upon the Roman government from the Second Punic War, in the coming to the surface of popular methods of consulting or utilizing the supernatural, and in the spread and persistence of the gloomy faith in the *Manes* and *Lemures* in Roman religion.

In the Minoan-Mycenaean civilization, which the invading Aryans from the North confronted, there obtained the conception of a great Mother, or Earth-goddess,[4] with whom was associated a lesser male deity, representative of the power of reproduction, which deserved prime attention in the primitive struggle for existence. The Earth was so intimately connected with the life and death of its inhabitants that Earth-cults were inevitable, the goddess and the satellite being variously represented in each local cult. Further, when the problem of death presented itself, the dead were con-

---

[1] Cf. Dieterich, *Kl. Sch.* p. 437 ; Moore, *Hist. of Religions*, I, p. 432 : " In the great social revolutions of the subsequent centuries these gods and cults came into prominence ; they gave a distinctive character to the later religion of Greece."

[2] Cf. Kennedy, *Vital Forces of the Early Church*, p. 86.

[3] Farnell, *Outline Hist. of Gk. Religion*, p. 34 ; Harrison, *Prol.* p. 8 ff.

[4] Cf. on Earth-mother cults Dieterich, *Archiv f. Relig.* '04, p. 10 ff.

ceived as returning to the domain of the Chthonians, or Earth-spirits, who therefore required tendance or worship from the living, that they might be found to be *Theoi Meilichioi* (propitious deities) in the underworld. This Earth-mother cult was accepted by the conquering Hellenes, and, as Demeter, was held in the greatest honour beside the more aristocratic worship of the Olympians. No god was held in greater repute throughout Greece than Dionysus, of purely chthonic origin. Throughout the centuries of the disintegration of the Olympian religion the secret and mysterious chthonic cults gained in influence, and survived the classic faith. Indeed, from the fifth century B.C. the history of Greek religion is largely that of the victory of the Chthonians over the Olympians, especially by means of Mysteries. The Chthonians were gradually defined by the giving of names. The most universal was Demeter, ' Earth-mother,' an invader from the North, who with her daughter Persephone attained an ecumenical authority.[1] Beside these appear Zeus Chthonios or Trophonios, and Hades or Pluto, and Hecate, the goddess of witchcraft.

These chthonic cults differed from the Olympian or Uranian cults in several particulars which it is important to note in relation to the spread of the Mysteries. (1) They were secret or close cults, restricted to a family, a tribe, or a locality, the rites of which would suffer profanation and lose efficacy by disclosure to outsiders. People refrained from speaking of them, and this secrecy enhanced their prestige by that strange religious phenomenon by which "the irrational and the horrible have in fact a fascination of their own, and it has often been noted that the rites of uncivilized peoples, in proportion to their strangeness, seem to more cultivated neighbours to embody a mysterious wisdom or a peculiarly efficacious magic."[2] (2) Hence

---

[1] Rohde, *Psyche*, I, p. 211 : " Der Glanz u. die weite u. dichte Verbreitung ihres Cultes über alle griechischen Städte des Mutterlandes u. der Colonien beweist mehr als irgend etwas Anderes, dass seit homerischer Zeit eine Wandlung auf dem Gebiete des religiösen Gefühls u. des Gottesdienstes vorgegangen sein müss." [2] Moore, I, p. 441.

arose the necessity of a solemn initiation which marked off
the religious from the irreligious. This lent a significance to
sacramental acts which has reacted strongly on subsequent
theologies, pagan and Christian. (3) They were local cults
each one originally with its own shrine and geographical
boundaries. According to circumstances—the successes
of the worshippers, trading facilities, accessibility, the reputation of the local tutelar—some grew in prominence while
others declined. Thus the Eleusinia, originally merely a
local agrarian cult, became under Athenian suzerainty an
Attic cult, which developed into a pan-Hellenic Church, and
finally an ecumenical religious centre—' a common sanctuary
of the whole world.' [1] In the same fashion the local earth-
daemon, Aesculapius, extended his sway until under the
empire his temples were among the most august and most
frequented. Only less famous became the Mysteries of
Andania in Messenia. (4) The deities of the chthonic cults
had a twofold function,[2] agrarian and eschatological. The
Chthonians granted fertility of the earth on which depended
the life of men and their cattle, and so were givers of
life. Their baneful powers are attested in the *Hymn to
Demeter*, in which Demeter is represented as taking
vengeance on gods and men by sending famine by which
Zeus was finally forced to recall Persephone from the underworld. But the Chthonians, who were likewise Katachthonian (Nether-world gods), received back again to their
abodes the souls of the dead who became *Demetreioi* [3]
(' belonging to Demeter ') or *Chthonioi*. (5) The Chthonians
were gods of gloom contrasted with the splendid Olympian
deities. This was recognized in the distinction observed in
sacrifices to the gods of the Upper and those of the Lower
World. To the former was raised a high altar on which was
burned the god's portion of the sacrifice ; the victim devoted
to the powers whose habitat was air or sky was lifted off the
ground, his head turned towards heaven, and in this posture

[1] Aristides, *Eleus.* (Dindorf, p. 415).
[2] Cf. Rohde, I, p. 205.
[3] Plutarch, *De Facie in Orbe Lunae*, 28.

his throat was cut. To the nether deities the victim's throat was cut with the head earthwards over a hole which received the blood, after which the whole victim, a devoted holocaust, was burned as piacular on a low altar or mound of earth. The formulary of the Olympian ritual was *do ut des*, that of the Chthonic *do ut abeas*.[1] Further, these gloomy divinities were most frequently addressed under conciliatory euphemisms as 'gracious gods' (*Meilichioi*). Zeus Chthonios is 'Zeus of good counsel' (*Eubouleus, Bouleus*), or *Klymenos*. Persephone is 'holy one' and 'mistress'; even dread Hecate is 'most lovely one,' and the Erinys become Eumenides. It was also in connexion with the Chthonians that the cult of the dead arose.[2] To chthonic practices and theories we may also probably relate the demonology, magic, and necromancy which were in vogue during the sway of the Mysteries. (6) Lastly, while literature has much to tell us about the Olympian gods, it maintains a baffling silence respecting the Chthonians, who were rescued from oblivion by the tenacity of the popular faith. Thus once more the lower orders asserted themselves and through them practices which were once a despised and obscure *superstitio* took on the character of a respectable and catholic *religio* acknowledged by the adherents of the Mystery-cults and in some forms by the early Christians.

Further, the dark ritual of the Chthonians formed the model for the Greek ritual of the dead. The surprising emergence of these chthonic cults was not the least important education of the Greek world for the Mysteries and for sacramental religion. Antigone's emphatic declaration[3]—so unlike the Hellenic religion—about the burial of her brother, 'since there is a longer period during which I must please the nether divinities than those here, for there I shall always be,' reflects the conviction of Sophocles' day and is rooted in a religious sentiment which could find satisfaction only in the Mystery-Religions.

[1] Harrison, *ib.* p. 7.   [2] *Ibid.* 215; Farnell, *Gk. Hero Cults*, p. 343 ff.
[3] Soph. *Antigone*, 74 f.

The chthonic cults of the Greek world, or the most vigorous of them, were transformed into Mystery-churches [1] by the coming of the Dionysiac religion, the influence of the Orphic revival, and by contact with the Oriental cults which had more faithfully preserved the primitive autochthonic elements of religion. Thus the chthonic cults, while retaining telluric associations, assumed a more mystic and eschatological character. From Dionysos they acquired enthusiasm and ecstasy ; from Orphism their initiations derived sacramental grace and cathartic efficacy for both here and hereafter, and from the Orient they received that accession of prestige and venerable antiquity by which the popular religion came to the front. The progress of the Chthonians is most obvious in the Eleusinian mysteries. Dionysos was identified with Hades and from about the sixth century B.C. occupies a place of honour with Demeter and Persephone as son of the former goddess by a miraculous birth. As Dionysos-Zagreus he was further identified with the infant god Iacchos. The Orphics provided a theology for the Eleusinian rites whereby the initiate, purged from all sin, was brought into mystic reunion with the deity, and delivered from the terrible lot awaiting those who had neglected the sacraments. The *Hymn to Demeter* is a valuable document enabling us to form some idea of the way in which, even prior to the introduction of Dionysos, the local secret society of Eleusis was assuming the character of a Mystery-church whose sacraments secured a happy lot beyond death.

[1] " L'adoration des divinités chthoniennes et productrices est le fond de tous les mystères grecs et en particulier de ceux d'Éleusis " (Lenormant and Pottier, *Eleusinia* in Daremberg-Saglio, *Dict.* II, p. 544).

CHAPTER V

THE APPEAL OF THE MYSTERY-RELIGIONS (*continued*)

Les grands mouvements d'idées sont généralement précédés d'une période obscure où, à l'insu de tous, ils se préparent. L'esprit nouveau est en gestation. Il se manifeste par des symptômes que l'on ne comprendra que plus tard, à la lumière des événements. L'âme des temps imminents semble s'essayer d'abord en des ébauches qui avortent. Puis, tout à coup, c'est l'explosion—E. DE FAYE, *Gnostiques et Gnosticisme*, p. 451.

B. RELIGIOUS NEEDS OF THE AGE AND THEIR SYMPTOMS

IN enquiring into the success of the Mystery-Religions (as into their ultimate failure) it is difficult to disentangle cause and effect, and to discriminate between favourable circumstances and the positive principles to which they owed their success. The difficulty is further increased because of two tendencies which come to view in a study of the history of the Mystery-cults: first, their marvellous power of adaptation to the varying conditions and ideas of different generations, so that it is impossible to determine in some particulars whether they led the way or only followed in the van; and, secondly, their penchant for seeking alliances which enhanced their popularity.

The rapid spread of the Mystery-Religions constitutes an historical phenomenon for which there must have been an adequate cause. Many reasons have been assigned to account for this phenomenon. Anrich[1] gives the following: (1) the Mysteries possessed the authority of a venerable and immemorial antiquity: in religion *vetustas adoranda est*; (2) their symbolism and vagueness, in which votaries might apprehend the deepest religious truths; (3) they satisfied the yearning for union with the deity; (4) their response to the sense of sin and their sacramental cathartic; (5) promise of a blessed immortality.

[1] P. 35 ff.

An investigator like Sir Samuel Dill, as sympathetic as thorough, would discover the special power of Orphism in its rites of cleansing, its assurance of immortality and its system of mediators and divine helpers; [1] the attraction of the religion of the Great Mother in the appeal of the dying and resurrected god, the solemn sacrament of the *taurobolium*, and in the figure of the great goddess as the universal mother, full of tenderness and grace, and giving peace through her cleansing rites. [2] In regard to the success of the Isiac cult, he indicates its power in the appeal to the many orders of intellect, the sense of atonement, the " impressive ritual, the separation of the clergy from the world, and in the comradeship of the guilds," the assurance of immortality, and the tenderness of Isis. [3] The fascination of Mithraism lay " partly in its ritual and clerical organization, still more in its clear promise of a life beyond the grave." [4] Cumont has accounted for their superiority :

" These religions gave greater satisfaction first of all to the senses and emotions, in the second place to the intelligence, and finally and chiefly to the conscience. They offered, in comparison with previous religions, more beauty in their ritual, more truth in their doctrines, and a superior good in their morality." [5]

To a proper understanding of the success of the Mystery-Religions a knowledge of the religious *milieu* in which they were planted and of their environment is essential. If we would account for the appeal they made to the Graeco-Roman world we must know the religious needs of that world. They succeeded in so far as they

---

[1] Pp. 427, 516.   [2] *Ib.* pp. 554–9.   [3] *Ib.* pp. 569–83.
[4] *Ib.* 597.   Cf. Canon Bigg's words on the Isiac legend : " What elements of beauty does it enclose !   Here we have a divine humanity, a god who suffers a cruel death out of love for man, and a divinely human wife and mother, Isis the compassionate and merciful, who loves her husband with a love stronger than death, yet sets his murderer free, bidding him go and sin no more. Many a stricken spirit found comfort in the adoration of Isis " (*Church's Task*, p. 45).
[5] *Relig. Or.* 2nd ed. pp. 43, 67–8 (Eng tr, pp 28, 44) ; Glover, *Progress*, pp 265 ff., 323.

were capable of adaptation to the religious sentiment of a particular period, and consequently the characteristic expressions of that religious sentiment are of supreme importance. The Mystery-Religions were the seed, the Graeco-Roman world the soil. Having examined the seed in enquiring into the nature of a Mystery, we purpose to examine the soil.

The religious spirit sought expression in multifold ways according to every variety of religious experience and racial outlook. We can register only the most clamant religious needs and the most characteristic and general expressions of this ancient religious spirit relevant to the success of the Mystery-Religions and Christianity.

I. Individualism. No feature in the life of the Graeco-Roman age is more conspicuous or more important for the history of the Mysteries and Christianity than the emphatic individualism which revealed itself in every department of ancient life in economics, politics, art, morality, and religion. Every aspect of the history of this ancient period is dominated by the presence of restless individualism, and the rebellion of the individual against the corporate body.[1]

Individualism arose on the ruins of nationalism. The individual survives every catastrophe of history, rescues himself from the wreckage, and finds new bonds of social cohesion, weaker or stronger according to his tastes. The universal theory of ancient social life was that man was a citizen of a particular State, a member and the property of a particular clan, rather than a member of humanity. His first and almost whole duty was to seek the good of his tribe, or race, or nation, or city, and subordinate every individual interest to the collective welfare. The unit was the corporate body, not the individual. While the tribe or clan or church-nation or city-state maintained equilibrium the theory worked tolerably well, and proved a splendid discipline

[1] Cf. Kaerst, I, p. 78: "So stehen die beiden grossen Grundmächte des antiken Lebens, die Polis u. das Individuum, einander gegenüber, nicht sich gegenseitig befructend u. vertiefend, sondern in einem immer tieferen, unvermittelten Gegensatz zu einander tretend."

in training men to recognize that they are members one of another, and that without the community the individual cannot be made perfect. But this ancient collectivism was a phase of human history which must pass or at least undergo drastic modification because it was an imperfect and one-sided system. It embodied an important half-truth which our generation has taken up in its social outlook. The ancient system was doomed to fall because it educated and developed the citizen to be less dependent on the State, and because it did injustice to personal strivings and aspirations. Our period opens with the transition from the too exclusive collective ideal to the too exclusive individualistic ideal, and is marked throughout by an excessive individualism which acted as a corrective to the evils of the previous corporate regime, but itself engendered just as great evils, because it was as partial and extreme a theory as that which it suppressed.

Individualism became ubiquitous both in the ancient Orient and in the more restless West. Oriental life had not been so severely collective as that of classic Greece and Rome. The Oriental bonds of cohesion were external and therefore weak—that despotism which was exterminated by Alexander the Great. The Orientals had never formed a truly political unity, understanding neither freedom nor self-government in the Western sense. They fought, not for laws which they had themselves made, nor for the freedom which was the spontaneous expression of their social life. The central restraining power, which but distantly influenced the individual, being weakened, each went his own way. The Orientals then found their chief activity in industrial and commercial life, and sought their satisfactions in individualistic religions which were divorced from national concerns and into the fellowship of which new members were admitted irrespective of race or social status.

Nowhere is individualism so unexpected as among the Jews,[1] who developed a tenacious social conscience such as no people of antiquity or of modern times has ever attained.

---

[1] Cf. Fairweather, *Background*, 2nd ed. p. 30 ff.

The problem of individualism presented itself to Israel early, remained with her, sometimes acutely, throughout her history, especially in the problem of divine providence raised by the prosperity of the wicked and the oppression of the righteous, and in that of eschatology in attempting to reconcile the destiny of the pious individual with that of the messianic people—an antinomy which Jewish theology never quite superseded.[1]

The problem of the individual was first thrust upon the attention of Jewish thinkers by the destruction of the Jewish State culminating in the Babylonian Captivity, and accentuated by reflection on the experiences of the Exile. The problem at first concerned individual retribution. Hitherto the holy nation had been the religious unit and in a less degree the family. But the question arose : was the humiliation of the Exile the result of their fathers' unfaithfulness or their own ? In the former case, was it just that innocent descendants should bear the evil consequences of others' sins ? in the latter, was it just that the pious individual should be involved in the penalities of the sinful majority ? Jeremiah came forth to Israel with a message which proved epoch-making in her religious experience. He did not, like his great disciple Ezekiel, thrust the nation as the religious unit into the background, nor did he seriously attempt to reconcile the collective and the individual aspects of relation to God, but he set forth the rights of personal religion in a twofold fashion, first by proclaiming personal responsibility—' they shall say no more, The fathers have eaten sour grapes, and the children's teeth are set on edge. But every one shall die for his own iniquity ; every man that eateth the sour grapes, his teeth shall be set on edge ' (XXXI. 29–30), and ' I try the heart, even to give every man according to his ways ' (XVII. 10); and, secondly, " Jeremiah was the first to conceive religion as the communion of the individual soul with God "[2]— most clearly expressed in the wonderful passage, XXXI. 31–4, which has been without sufficient reason denied to

[1] Charles, pp. 363–4.   [2] Ib. 61.

Jeremiah. He prophesies a new covenant of grace and forgiveness, in which even the least shall know Jehovah, and in which religion will be an inward and therefore personal experience : ' I will put My law in their inward parts, and in their heart will I write it.'

Ezekiel took up and developed one-sidedly Jeremiah's message of a personal relation to God, by emphasizing without qualifications and without observation of *all* the facts of life Jeremiah's doctrine of personal responsibility and God's care for the individual. No prophet has ever given nobler expression to the worth of the individual soul before God than is found in chapter XVIII.

The individualism of Jeremiah and Ezekiel had in view only retribution and reward in this life. But the facts of human experience would not allow men to be satisfied with such a doctrine. It remained only too painfully patent that the righteous man, in spite of his personal relation to God and God's care for him, was involved in the calamities of the wicked, and suffered from calamities of his own from which the godless seemed exempt. The scene of retribution had therefore to be shifted from earth and the date postponed. Job first gave expression to this yearning of the individual for a reward sometime consonant with his merits, and dimly adumbrated a future of personal immortality. In some of the Psalms, e.g. 49 and 73, the hope of personal immortality comes to expression. But the social consciousness of Israel could never be satisfied with a personal immortality like that of Greece,[1] and individual immortality gave way to a doctrine of Resurrection of the righteous Israel, which attempted to blend the social and the personal eschatologies. This doctrine gained the ascendancy because " the common good was still more dear to the faithful in Israel than that of the individual ; the Messianic kingdom was a more fundamental article of their faith than that of a blessed future life to the individual." [2] But the doctrine of a

---

[1] Charles, p. 80 n: 1, 155, describes Plato's doctrine as " the glorification of an unbridled individualism."

[2] *Ib.* 79.

Resurrection never wholly ousted that of personal immortality, the latter asserting itself in the Judaeo-Alexandrine literature under Greek influence. Charles maintains that this synthesis of the personal and the collective eschatologies in a doctrine of Resurrection maintained itself only throughout the third and second centuries B.C. and that in the apocalyptic and apocryphal writers of the first century B.C. " the belief in a personal immortality has thus dissociated itself from the doctrine of the Messianic Kingdom." Thus the synthesis of the two eschatologies achieved two centuries earlier is anew resolved into its elements, never again, save once (1 Enoch 37–70), to be spiritually fused together within the sphere of Judaism. Their true and final synthesis became the task and achievement of Christianity [1] ; Judaism perished in the attempt to translate theocratic conceptions into terms of personal religion.

Throughout the *Wisdom* Literature there is ample expression of individualism. This is due partly to its universalism, which treats life in its general aspects, in which all men are on equality. In spite of the writers' attachment to Jewish institutions and their fundamental dogma that the knowledge of Yahwe and acquaintance with the Law are the beginning of Wisdom, the nationalist outlook has given way to the universal and human. The writers are generally as detached from the nationalistic as the contemporary and subsequent apocalyptic literature is attached to it. Hence this literature is characterized by an ethic which is at once individualistic and cosmopolitan. It is a partial reply to the problems of individualism which had arisen out of the previous experience of Israel, and deals with the *summum bonum* of the individual life.

It was in the Greek world that individualism first assumed a menacing form. This solvent of society entered Greek life in the fifth century, disintegrated it in the fourth, infected the Romans in the third and second centuries, and through its action in Roman life contributed to the establishment

[1] Charles, p. 249; cf. also pp. 299, 362 f.

of the empire. The Sophists are credited with having first inoculated Greek life with the germs of individualism ; in reality the germs were only nurtured by them. By questioning the authority of the *polis*, enquiring into the validity of law, pointing out that what was law at Megara might be unlawful at Athens, by rejecting tradition, by contrasting natural with conventional right, by asserting the subjectivity and relativity of all truth in the words of Protagoras, ' man is the measure of all things,' they threatened to reduce society to atoms. Socrates saw the menace and stepped forward to save and reform the city-state. But he indirectly undermined its authority by calling attention, like Jeremiah and Ezekiel, to the eternal value of the individual, and by finding the ultimate basis of moral action neither in the laws nor the religion of the State, nor in tradition, but in man's own reason and consciousness. In the Athenian law-court he advocated the right of private judgment even against the State by reminding his judges that he must obey God rather than man. Plato made the last heroic attempt to stay the encroaching individualism and buttress the *polis*. Aristotle would also fain preserve the *polis* modified to meet new conditions. The Minor Socratics and the post-Aristotelian schools took up the individualistic aspects of Socrates' teaching, abandoning the *political*. " Stoic apathy, Epicurean quietism, Academic *ataraxia*, have all in common the principle that they direct the moral activity from the outer upon the inner world, and seek the ethical ideal in the independence and release of the individual from all external conditions of life, in isolation from the community." [1] All post-Aristotelian philosophy is marked by detachment from the requirements of the city-state and concentration on the practical concerns of life.

In the West the progress of individualism kept pace with the decay of the city-state, but it would be difficult to say whether the fall of the *polis*, which first occurred in Greece, was an effect or a cause of individualism. Both statements would be equally true, since it was the passions of individuals

[1] Wendland, *Hell.-röm. Kultur*, p. 20.

that undermined the *polis*, while the fall of the *polis*, by releasing the citizen from all-absorbing demands, promoted the growth of individualism. The conflict of individual and *polis* dominates Greek history till the fall of the *polis*. Then the Greeks, unable to rise to any true sense of nationalism, became carriers of a new cosmopolitanism. Alexander's personality and conquests gave a mighty impetus to the development of individualism by inaugurating a cosmopolitanism the necessary corollary of which was individualism. The eyes of the civilized world were also now directed to *one* individual, whose personality was such as to appear a superman, standing nearer to the divine than to humanity.[1] This prominence of individuals and the dependence of the weal of mankind on them led to the practice of deification in the case of Alexander, the Diadochian kings, and finally of Roman emperors. The release of millions of bullion from Oriental coffers by Alexander caused a scramble by fortune-seekers in which the ablest came to the top, and gave rise to capitalism,[2] which was hitherto scarcely known to the Greeks, and which was to work evil among the Romans. The circulation of this new coin and treasures of the East stimulated commerce, opened up new avenues to wealth, encouraged private greed, speculation, and individual enterprise. There were other indications of Greek individualism. The mercenaries long before Alexander's day were a factor in Oriental campaigns. These soldiers of fortune were apostles of cosmopolitanism and individualism. The habit of emigration to better one's lot became common among the Greeks ; they settled in the most distant Greek-Asiatic cities of Alexander's foundation, in the great centres of trade along the Asiatic coast, and at the courts of Hellenistic princes, and later throughout the Roman Empire. The individual was now at home in the world wherever ambition was gratified.

During the Second Punic War even the patriotic Roman was overtaken by individualism, which, if not introduced by Hellenism, was at least fostered by Greek culture. When the

---

[1] Cf. Wendland, p. 20   [2] Kaerst, I. 63

Greeks became Rome's schoolmasters they were men without a country, or rather their country was the world ; their professors had left impoverished Greece to seek personal interests. The literature, and especially the philosophy, of Greece which came to Rome was strongly individualistic. In the second century B.C. Roman character underwent a strange transformation. The individual rebelled against a crushing patriotism. The spoils of conquest engendered selfishness in their division. The degeneration of parties into cliques led by ambitious leaders, the gambling for office, the decay of the state religion and growth of Oriental cults, the multiplication of dictatorships, the sanguinary civil wars, the rise of the empire, were simply the products of unrestrained individualism. Henceforth the individual looked upon the State as a field to be exploited for his aggrandizement. As in the Hellenistic age, so in the Roman, outstanding personalities arose whose crimes or merits placed them above the level of their fellow-men, and the welfare of mankind became more and more dependent upon one man. Everything contributed to the exaltation of the individual ; " the constant wars, conquests, and revolutions threw the powerful man into ever greater prominence, and the poverty and distress of the Graeco-Roman world disposed the humbler folk to adore any leader who could and did procure them decent comfort and adequate bodily maintenance." [1]

The Eastern campaigns of Rome greatly accelerated the development of individualism. New fields were opened for personal ambition. When Rome first entered on the conquest of the East she could not boast of any thorough education or genuine civilization ; she looked upon her conquests as legitimate objects of exploitation. Under the republic provincial governors indulged their greed upon the hapless lands and amassed immense fortunes, which were usually squandered in reckless luxury. Individuals vied with each other in costly display. Throughout the empire the capitalist class increased, and, in Italy especially, there arose landlords who with their retinue of slaves displaced the

[1] Fowler, *Roman Ideas of Deity*, pp. 102–3 ; *Relig. Exper.* pp. 266, 340.

former peasant proprietors—*Latifundia perdidere Italiam.*
There were numberless thousands of slaves with no national
or political loyalties and thousands of once prosperous
artisans and farmers pauperized by Roman wars of confiscation. Such individuals, resenting the injustices of society,
pursued their personal interests.

Individualism invaded every sphere of life and affected
rich and poor, East and West, especially in the closing
republic and early empire. It asserted itself in art, in
literature, in politics and society, in morality and religion.
Greek art in its glory dealt with the ideal and the universal,
whereas Roman art was individualistic and realistic. Among
the Romans portrait-busts (not idealistic) became fashionable. " This is the age [second century B.C.] in which we
first hear of statues and portrait-busts of eminent men," [1]
though Alexander the Great was said to be one of the first
to have his likeness cut in stone.

In society individualism took the form of selfishness and
the cultivation of private interests. Cut loose from the
civitas, men were not yet educated to the new functions of
society. The empire was too large, the family too small :
other intermediate fields in which our corporate and individual life meet were as yet little cultivated. Public life
lost interest, and was abandoned to the demagogue or the
aspirant to power. The domestic virtues and charities
received more attention, which resulted in the emancipation
of women and their prominence in this age. Social instincts
found expression in the multiplication of guilds. The
literature of the Hellenistic and Roman age is individualistic.
The passion of love becomes more acute and modern as found,
for example, in the erotic poetry of Theocritus or Catullus.[2]
Roman literature, being only in its infancy when the tide
of individualism began to sweep over East and West, is
more individualistic than the Greek both in its subject-
matter and in the strong sense of personality which marks
Roman writers. Sellar [3] says of Roman poetry : " in no

---

[1] Fowler, *Relig. Exper.* p. 340.   [2] Wendland, p. 19.
[3] *Rom. Poets of the Repub.* p. 16 f.

other branch of ancient literature is so much prominence given to the enjoyment of nature, and the joys, sorrows, tastes, and pursuits of the individual." The genius of Roman writers is personal and self-conscious, as compared with the self-forgetful and more impersonal Greek genius. The later Greek literature responds to the individual taste of the Romans, as e.g. Plutarch and Polybius. In historical writing the personality of the author comes out more strongly in his prefaces, excursus and attitude of judgment or commendation to his characters.[1] The importance of individuals found expression in the rise of biography, which became fashionable in Greek and Latin, e.g. Plutarch's familiar *Lives*, Diogenes Laertius' *Lives of the Philosophers*, Philostratus' *Apollonius of Tyana*, Sallust's *Jugurtha* and *Catiline*, Tacitus' *Agricola*, Cornelius Nepos' *Lives*, and Suetonius' *Lives of the Roman Emperors*. The writing of *Memoirs*, as by Ptolemy I, Aratus, Caesar, is a further attestation of individualism ; in autobiography the Latin genius excelled and reached its zenith in Augustine's *Confessions* and in the beautiful *De Consolatione Philosophiae* of Boethius.

Much more evidence might be adduced to prove that individualism was one of the most marked features of this age and a factor which dominated all life and the whole religious outlook as collectivism had once done. Enough has been said to show how extensive was the preparation made for the Mystery-Religions and Christianity by individualism. It was a phase in the unfolding of the conception of personality to which Socrates had first called attention, and in doing so had revealed to man the riches of his spiritual being and needs for which he must find satisfaction. The individual became the unit, and the Mystery-Religions held out salvation for the individual soul. The Mysteries magnified the individual by treating him as a man irrespective of his political or social connexions and by endowing him with divine powers. In the religious

---

[1] Cf. Bruns, *Die Persönlichkeit in d. Geschichtschreibung der Alten ;* Wendland, p. 22.

fraternities of these cults, slave and master, artisan and capitalist, met as equals. Men had to pay for individualism in a greater sensitiveness to suffering and loss in which the Mysteries offered consolation and comfort. With the inward direction given to life arose a consciousness of sin and need of reconciliation, to meet which the Mysteries offered a cathartic and assured divine grace with the forgiveness of sins.

II. Another force affecting all Graeco-Roman history and most active in religion was syncretism, or *Theocrasia*,[1] which was the inevitable concomitant of cosmopolitanism and individualism. " In the religious development of the Hellenistic period," says Kaerst,[2] " there are chiefly two moments which illustrate for us the peculiar character of this development and at the same time explain its peculiar significance for the entire religious development of the later period of antiquity, . . . the cult of the Rulers and the religious Syncretism," a statement which is even more applicable to the Roman era. All the pre-conditions for an all-round syncretism obtained in the Graeco-Roman world— the decline of constructive originality and the advent of criticism, the fall of the city-state and the correlative rise of universalism, the international policy of Alexander, the breaking up of national faiths and philosophies, the spread of the *Koiné*, the intermingling of diverse populations[3] at a high stage of culture, the success of Stoicism with its *cosmopolis* and unifying allegorical interpretation, the rise of the Roman Empire, Roman law, roads which joined together the ends of the earth, the passion for novelty in religious matters, the tolerance of paganism, the rise of proselytism, and the continuous convergence of East and West.

Nor does this list exhaust the factors which rendered *theocrasia* inevitable. Intermarriage between members of

---

[1] Cf. *Synkretismus im Altertum* (*Relig. in Gesch. u. Geg.* V. 1043 ff.) ; Kaerst, II, p. 246 ff. ; Toutain, *Cultes païens*, II, p. 241 ff. ; Wendland, *Hell.-röm. Kultur*, pp. 77, 21 ff., 161 ff. ; Dill, pp. 558, 581 ff.

[2] II. 248.

[3] Cf. H. Leclercq, *Colonies d'Orientaux en Occident* (in Cabrol-Leclercq, *Dict.*).

different races and adherents of different religions had much the same results then as now. The historic festal scene of ' the marriage of Europe and Asia ' at Susa on Alexander's return from India was but the beginning of what subsequently became quite frequent. On that occasion Alexander himself married a second Oriental queen—Statira, and about a hundred of his officers married Asiatic brides of rank, and ten thousand of his soldiers followed their example.[1] Timothy was the son of a Jewess by a Greek father (*Acts* XVI. 1). Intermarriages between Christians and pagans or Jews were frequent enough to cause trouble in Paul's Gentile churches. The Roman legionaries, wherever stationed, probably married local women. A bilingual sepulchral inscription in Latin and Aramaic discovered at South Shields records the death of a young British woman, Regina, of the Catuvellaunian tribe, the young wife of a Palmyrene named Barates.[2]

Migration, forced and voluntary, accelerated the intermixture of peoples which conduced to *theocrasia*. Quite possibly one of the contributory causes of Greek migration was the prevalence of malaria on the Greek mainland. W. H. S. Jones[3] contends that before 430 B.C. malaria was either unknown or not dangerously prevalent in Greece, that it broke out as a severe epidemic during the Peloponnesian War, and in the absence of prophylactic measures it became henceforth endemic.

Alexander's campaigns gave the first powerful impetus to universal syncretism which confounded the nationality of gods as well as of men. The breaking up, as a result of his conquests, of the long-established and exclusive priestly colleges of the Euphrates Valley which drove hosts of priests out to earn their livelihood by trading their esoteric knowledge westward, had consequences as far-reaching as the

---

[1] Arrian, *Anab.* 7 IV,; Plut. *Alex.* 70.

[2] 'D. M. Regina, liberta, et, conjuge. Barates. Palmyrenus natione. Catuallauna. A, **XXX.**' (*Proc, Soc. Bib. Arch.* '78, p. 11 f.; *Jour. of Rom. Studies,* 12, pl, VII.).

[3] *Malaria and Greek History*, Manchester, '09.

capture of Constantinople by the Turks in 1453, which drove Greek scholars westward to bring in the Renaissance in Europe. Alexander threw open the world to all. The period of racial exclusion was over ; no nation could live by and for itself and no system could maintain its integrity in competition with other systems. Alexander's unification of mankind and of culture led of necessity to mutual borrowing and lending and conduced to a unity of religion. He adopted the Persian policy of tolerance toward foreign religions. Restraining barriers were thrown down, so that diverse religious usages and cults subsisted side by side. In the world made new by him all movements became co-extensive and consequently coincident. His Graeco-Oriental cities were permanent centres for the amalgamation of culture and religion. Of these foundations the most successful in fulfilling Alexander's policy of blending the nations was Alexandria, which remained for centuries the headquarters of syncretism. The Diadochian kingdoms promoted syncretism in their armies, their capitals, and their libraries. The Roman Empire completed the work commenced by Alexander, and in it syncretism reached its apogee in the third and fourth centuries A.D.

The Greeks were specially gifted as missionaries of syncretism in the larger world opened up by the Macedonians and the Romans. Intellectually curious and fond of innovations, living under a system in which all thought was free and never trammelled by clerical conservatism,[1] they were ready to examine the merits of whatever object of interest was presented to them. Innovations, chiefly in the way of mysticism, had been introduced into the Greek world in the sixth century B.C. and in the fifth Oriental cults began to penetrate Attica and grew in influence and numbers from the fourth century onwards. The Greeks always remembered that their older divinities, acclimatized among them and idealized in art, came from abroad—from the North. Greek mercenaries had brought back intelligence of foreign customs and religions ; the Greek cities of Ionia had

[1] Butcher, *Aspects of Gk. Genius*, p. 25.

already been a gate-way into the life and the thought of the East. With the fall of the city-state went a depreciation of its parochialism and institutions. The Romans were the greatest borrowers and most skilful adapters. Their syncretistic tendencies were accentuated by their Greek education and the influence of Greek literature. Into their pantheon they admitted Etruscan, Italian, Greek and Oriental deities. Between the Second Punic War and the rise of the empire Roman religion was completely hellenized in cult and in mythology [1]; the taste for Oriental cults developed, which finally drew the people away from Greek and Roman deities, though it left them Greek mythology.

Polytheism was tolerant and hospitable to foreign deities : it never disputed the existence or reality of other deities, and the addition of a new member to the Pantheon was a matter of indifference. The Greeks had early adopted a process of *theocrasia* [2]; from Greece *theocrasia* spread and became fashionable, resulting everywhere in *theoxenia*, or hospitality afforded to strange deities. The nationality of deities being lost and the walls of national pantheons thrown down, the deities must be identified or equated, or there must result a survival of the fittest [3]; but Paganism preferred the conciliation principle. Mutual borrowings and co-ordinations resulted. The Romans took over wholesale the Greek pantheon by rebaptizing their own gods with Greek names. Deities with similar attributes or functions were regarded as identical, or, according to the monotheistic trend of the age, all deities of all peoples were regarded as but manifestations of the one supreme deity. Generally this was accomplished by means of what Max Müller designated henotheism, i.e. by the selection of a supreme deity in a pantheon to which the others were but satellites. This facilitated the identification of the chief deities of different nations as representing one supreme unity. Obsolete or unsuccessful gods were relegated to oblivion or

[1] Wissowa, p. 54 ff. ; Aust, p. 106.   [2] Legge, I. 16.
[3] Kaerst, II. 250.

reduced to the rank of *daemones*. A curious evidence of the consciousness of the unity of the divine is afforded by the amalgamation of different deities into a θεὸς πάνθεος, or θεὰ πάνθεος,[1] which might be regarded either as an abstract conception or a new deity according to the fluidity of pagan theology. Usually one deity was chosen, prominent for his merits in the votary's estimation, and the epithet *pantheus*, 'all-God,' added to the personal name [2] as representative of the totality of the divine. Thus we find in Latin inscriptions *Serapis pantheus, Liber pantheus, Fortuna panthea*. Sometimes, without specifying any representative deity, the whole pantheon was summarized in a *deus pantheus*.[3] The more usual method was to select a deity and attach to the god, or goddess, all the names and attributes of other gods, a most conspicuous example of which is 'Isis of the thousand names,' who reveals herself as—

'Parent of nature, mistress of all the elements, the first-born of the ages . . . whom the Phrygians adore as the Pessinuntian Mother of the Gods, the Athenians as Minerva, the Cyprians as Venus, the Cretans as Dictynian Diana, the Sicilians as Proserpina, the Eleusinians as Demeter, others as Juno, or Bellona, others as Hecate or Rhamnusia, while the Egyptians and others honour me with my proper name of Queen Isis.' [4]

With which should be compared a much longer and more inclusive list in an *Invocation to Isis* preserved in the *Oxyrhynchus Papyri*, vol. XI, no. 1380.

Another method was to select a deity as embracing the totality of divinity, e.g. Isis is addressed as 'una quae es omnia, dea Isis,' and Attis as 'Attis the Most High and Bond of the Universe,'[5] which recalls the Christological language of *Colossians*.

Worshippers were most catholic in their tastes in giving

[1] Cf. Kaerst, II. 250.   [3] *C.I.L.* VI. 557 ff.
[2] Wissowa, p. 82, n. 3.   [4] Apul. *Met.* XI. 5.
[5] Kaibel, *Epig. gr.* 824, 2 : Ἄττει θ' ὑψίστῳ κ. συνέχοντι τὸ πᾶν.

recognition to as many deities of diverse origin as they fancied. The emperor Alexander Severus honoured in his private chapel Orpheus, Abraham, Apollonius of Tyana, together with Christ.[1] Ancient tombstones testify to this mingled devotion to deities of Greece and Rome and the Orient. Out of religious restlessness men pried into the secrets of all the cults. Apollonius of Tyana visited many temples and oracles within and without the Roman Empire. Apuleius sought initiation into several Mysteries. Plutarch's Clea was an attendant on the Delphic Dionysus and an initiate of Isis.[2] Tatian[3] in his search for the truth, sought initiation into several Mysteries. Praetextatus and his wife had taken the sacraments in various Mystery-Churches.[4] Even the priesthoods are not exclusive ; the same individual might be a priest of the Phrygian and Persian cults as well as an official in the state cult. A priest of Isis might even be named Mithra or Iacchagogus.[5] Among the deities there was no jealousy ; several might be accommodated in one temple, or the deity to whom a temple was dedicated might admit lesser deities who had some hold on the affection of his votaries. In the Isium of Pompeii stood statues of Dionysus, Venus, and Priapus.[6] In a Mithraeum of Ostia Italian and Greek deities were admitted.[7]

The Jews, because of their wonderful power of adaptation, played no small part in the history of syncretism, in spite of their attempted exclusiveness behind the ' fence of the Law.' During the Exile their religion was for the first time affected to any considerable extent by syncretism—from Persian sources. But it was in the post-Alexandrian period that the Jews became most exposed to, and on the whole the most receptive of, foreign ideas, especially those of Hellenism. So subtle and powerful was the process of

[1] Lampridius, *Alex. Severus*, 29.　　[3] *Ad Graeces*, 29.
[2] Plut. *De Is. et Os.* 35.　　[4] *C.I.L.* VI. 1, 1779.
[5] Apul. *Met.* XI. 22.
[6] Mau. *Pompeii*, p. 169 ; Lafaye, p. 190.
[7] Taylor, *Cults*, p. 68 ff.

hellenization from Alexander to Antiochus Epiphanes that the Jews of Palestine were in danger of becoming thoroughly hellenized.   This danger was arrested by the madness of Antiochus, who, in his desire to achieve religious uniformity in his contest with Egypt, resolved to accelerate the helle- nizing process by wholesale compulsion which drove the Jews into rebellion.   For a time they secured their independence, but could not entirely banish Greek culture.   The Diaspora which produced Paul and Philo was always more liberal in its outlook than the homeland, and more exposed to the contagion of foreign ideas.   It proved a potent factor in the philosophical and religious syncretism of the age. The Diaspora was the strongest bond between East and West, and the chief medium of intercommunication of ideas.   The Jewish-Greek school of Alexandria, represented chiefly by Philo, made the first serious attempt to harmonize the religion of the East and the culture of the West.   In the synagogues of the Diaspora, Greeks and Romans, Syrians and Persians and islanders of the archipelago were attracted ; there they learned to know each other and the people who were the intermediaries between East and West.   The synagogues were fruitful seedplots of syncretism, as were the religious associations of Paganism.   The God-fearers conveyed to the synagogue the best ideals of Paganism and to the non-Jewish world the ideals of righteousness. In this intercourse the Greek version of the Seventy was an important syncretistic instrument.

This syncretism worked hand in hand with the Mysteries, which, freed from all racial and cultural exclusiveness, offered their blessings to all.   By disposing men to seek truth wher- ever found and religious support wherever offered, it made the path into foreign religions easy.   By fostering the religious tendency to monotheism, it convinced men that all cults brought men into relationship with the same divine unity, so that a man would choose that cult which facilitated his approach to God.   All the Mystery-Religions were deeply affected by syncretism, and indeed afford the best field for the study of syncretism.   They formed as it were a religious 'trust' by which they assisted each other. They borrowed in cult, ritual, symbols and mythology. The *taurobolium*, the outstanding sacrament of the Great Mother, was (probably) taken over by the Phrygian priests from the Persian worship of Anahita of Cappadocia, a goddess associated with Mithra in the religion of the Achaemenidae, and had also been practised in the sanguinary cult of the Commagenian Ma.[1] From the religion of the Great Mother it was probably borrowed by the Mithraists, as maintained by, e.g., Reville, Dill, and Legge,[2] though contested by Cumont.[3] The influence of Judaism upon the cult of Sabazius is indisputable.[4] Cumont surmises that Judaism affected the cult of the Great Mother.[5] The priesthoods of these Mysteries were quite catholic. The Mystery-Religions showed their tolerant spirit in the protection which one authoritatively established or popularized cult extended to a sister cult in its propaganda. The Great Mother went sponsor for other Oriental cults, which to the eyes of outsiders looked more or less similar because of certain general features, just as primitive Christianity grew up *sub umbraculo religionis licitae* of Judaism.

Three forms of Mystery-Religion were pre-eminently syncretistic—Orphism, Hermeticism and Gnosticism. Orphism introduced a levelling tendency in religious views which struck at the very roots of nationalism, and so prepared the way for the individualistic Oriental cults and made all religions of equal value to the true Orphic. Possessed of the knowledge of his own secret rites and fortified by his formulae, the Orphic found no difficulty in conforming outwardly to any religion in vogue. Orphism bequeathed to later Gnosticism and Hermeticism the selective principle in religious matters :

" It went a great way towards weaning the minds of men

---

[1] Cumont, *R. or.*, 2nd ed. pp. 98 f., 333, n. 34 ; Toutain, II, pp. 84–8 ; Wissowa, p. 81 ; Boissier, I, p. 368.

[2] Reville, *La Religion à Rome*, p. 95 ff ; Legge, II. 259 ; Dill, pp 609, 556.

[3] *T. et M.* I, p. 334, n. 5 ; *Mithras* (in Roscher, I, p. 3064).

[4] Cf. Cumont, *R. or.* 2nd ed. p. 96 ff.   [5] *Ib.* p. 98.

from the idea of separate gods for the different nations, and towards teaching them that all national and local deities were but different forms of one great Power. . . . By their readiness to identify him [Dionysus] alike with the chthonian god of Eleusis, and with all the foreign gods—Adonis, Attis, Sabazius, Osiris, . . . they showed how far they were willing to go in the path of syncretism ; and, but for the rise of Christianity and other religions, there can be little doubt but that the whole of the Graeco-Roman deities would continually have merged into Dionysus." [1]

The Hermetic religion is an amalgamation of Chaldaean, Egyptian and Greek religious, cosmological, and philosophic theories, in which the Egyptian and the Greek elements predominate. The *Corpus Hermeticum* reflects nearly every phase of religious ideas and practices obtaining in the Graeco-Roman era, ranging from the loftiest spirituality to vulgar magic. This syncretism [2] brought immense popularity to the Mysteries and pressed into their service many auxiliaries such as Magic, Demonology, Astralism, and Philosophy, notably in the case of Iamblichus and Proclus. If syncretism attained its height in the alliances formed to oppose conquering Christianity it should also be ranked historically as one of the greatest movements in the preparation for Christianity. By fostering religious interests, by antiquating exclusivism, by bringing religious systems into comparison and competition, by predisposing men to accept salvation wherever most effectively offered, by reopening the question of authority, by unfolding to the West Love as the secret of the East,[3] and to the East Will as the secret of the West, Graeco-Roman syncretism not only made ready the way of the Lord, but in a real sense assured the victory of His cause.[4]

---

[1] Legge, I, p. 145 f.

[2] The attempt must be renounced to follow syncretism into the realms of Magic, Astrology, and Philosophy, the material for which is abundant.

[3] Cf. F. Anderson, *Liberty, Equality, and Fraternity*, p. 6.

[4] " Die neue durch den Synkretismus aufgenommene Religiosität mit ihrer schwärmerischen Innigkeit, gestattete eine völlige Hingabe an Christus, ein Sichversenken in das Einzigartige seines Wesens, das schliesslich seiner Religion zum Siege verhelfen musste " (*Relig. in Gesch. u. Gegenw.* V, p. 1055).

III. Of great moment for both ancient and modern religious history was the universal and ever-increasing tendency in the Graeco-Roman world to form private brotherhoods [1] or guilds of a more or less religious character. Such associations generally arose at first in the great sea-ports, like the Peiraeus, and in important island *entrepôts*, such as Rhodes, Delos, Thera, etc., where foreigners congregated to preserve their religion and render mutual assistance. The clientele consisted mostly of foreign-born, and the deities were those who chiefly attracted by their Mystery-cult,[2] or who, such as Aesculapius, were saviour and healing deities. Inscriptions of the imperial period testify to the ubiquitous existence of clubs formed by members of every craft that catered to the tastes of a luxurious age, guilds of fishermen, fullers, bakers, bargemen, wood-cutters, smiths, butchers, workers of the mint, of trades such as perfume vendors, wine-merchants, financiers, of ex-soldiers [3] and sailors, and of convivial idlers. These *thiasoi, collegia,* or *sodalitates* were in every town, sometimes several on the same street.

In Greece and Rome private associations were of great antiquity, bearing the character of trade-guilds and cult-brotherhoods in one, for, as ancient life was constituted without a sharp cleavage between secular and sacred,[4] these associations cannot conveniently be classified as industrial and religious. An ancient chamber of commerce could equally well be a religious society. *Thiasoi, Eranoi,* or *orgeones* were evidently in vogue in Attica as early as the beginning of the sixth century (594) B.C., since the legislation of Solon acknowledged and enforced their by-laws.[5] From

---

[1] Cf. esp. Mommsen, *De Collegiis* ; Boissier, II, pp. 247–304; an excellent chap. "The Colleges and Plebeian Life" in Dill, *Rom. Soc.* ; art. *Collegia,* by J. P. Waltzing in Cabrol-Leclercq, *Dict.* ; Foucart, *Des associations religieuses.*

[2] Kaerst, *ib.* 281.

[3] Cf. A. Müller, *Veteranvereine in d. röm. Kaisarzeit* (*N. Jahrb. f. d. Klas. Alt.* XXIX. ('12) p. 267 ff.).

[4] Boissier, II, p. 247.

[5] Jevons, *Introd.* 334 ; Foucart, pp. 49, 57.

the fourth century there is abundant inscriptional evidence of the spread of *orgeones*, which multiplies in the third century B.C. Throughout the Greek world—in Attica, in the islands of the Aegean and in the Seleucid and Attalid territories— religious guilds existed devoted to the cults of the Great Mother, Isis, Attis, Serapis, Sabazios, etc.

Private unions, semi-industrial, semi-religious, belong to a primitive stage of Roman history, some being carried back to the foundation of the city and the days of Numa.[1] For long they multiplied without being molested by the government, which only intervened to prevent excesses in the interests of social order. An impetus was given to the formation of religious clubs by the introduction of Cybele. Livy records the prominence of clubs of Bacchus-worshippers early in the second century B.C. By the days of Sulla (first quarter of first century B.C.) *collegia* of the Egyptian gods are in existence in Italy. In this century such guilds become so conspicuous as to arouse the suspicions of the Senate, which endeavoured to suppress the most dangerous in 64 B.C. About the middle of the first century B.C. these clubs had proved themselves so influential with the populace that ambitious aspirants, such as Clodius,[2] conceived the idea of forming *collegia, sodalitia,* or *compitalia* for political purposes. This abuse of religious associations caused them to fall deservedly under the suspicion of the emperors. For two centuries and a half (from the days of Julius Caesar to the reign of Alexander Severus) imperial legislation aimed at the suppression, and, where this was impossible, at the regulation of *collegia*, and subsequent to Alexander Severus the right of private association was zealously guarded.[3] Caesar and Augustus forbad private associations except those of high antiquity or of a specifically religious character.[4] Pliny, during his governorship of Bithynia, about A.D. 112, requested authorization from Trajan for the establishment

---

[1] Plut. *Numa,* 17 ; cf. Boissier, II, 248.
[2] Mommsen, p. 76.
[3] Boissier, p. 249.
[4] Suet. *Caes.* 42 ; *Octav.* 32 ; Boissier, p 249.

of a club of firemen at Nicomedia numbering 150, to which the answer of the far-seeing Trajan is characteristic : ' Whatever name they may call themselves, or for whatever motives they are established, they will be certain as soon as united to become a partisan association.' [1] Previously Pliny had been compelled, on arrival in Bithynia, to put into operation the law against right of private association.[2] The Roman legal code sternly punished illegal associations, and forbad or restricted the formation of new guilds. Caius asserted the unconstitutional nature of private clubs, though permitting those of the most necessary trades [3] ; and Ulpian attached the severest penalties to the offence of illegal association.[4] Yet, in spite of legislation and penalties, this irresistible popular movement steadily advanced, so that the government had gradually to recognize the existence or formation of guilds of necessary crafts ; before the middle of the second century A.D. the right to establish burial clubs was accorded by the Senate, a concession which facilitated the formation and registration of all kinds of clubs which could shelter themselves under the title of funerary clubs, and which legalized regular association and the levying of contributions. Under Marcus Aurelius another concession was won in the grant of the right to receive bequests. Finally, Alexander Severus accorded official recognition to all guilds of crafts and trades, and appointed patrons (*defensores*) of each.[5] Soon after the middle of the third century legal right to accept and hold property was granted to another class of private association, the Christian Church.

The intense craving for private association is evidenced by the survival of numberless inscriptions from every corner of the Graeco-Roman world, by the anxiety caused to the authorities for centuries and the gradual recognition wrung from them, the universal prevalence of clubs in spite of every

---

[1] Pliny, *Ep.* X. 43 and 97.
[2] *Dig.* III. 4, 1 : Boissier, II, p. 250.
[3] *Dig.* III. 4, 1 ; Boissier, p. 250.
[4] *Dig.* XLVII. 22, 2 ; Boissier, p. 250.
[5] Lamprid. *Alex. Sev.* 33. " Était-ce," asks Boissier, " un acte de faiblesse ou un calcul de politique ? " (II, p. 251).

police precaution, by the testimony that every class of workmen and traders formed guilds, of which many of the aristocracy did not hesitate to become patrons or honorary members, or even ordinary members of associations in which foreigners and plebeians predominated.

The prevalence of the spirit of association corresponded to some imperious human need indicated in Aristotle's dictum that ' man is a political [social] creature.' He cannot realize himself apart from society ; something in his nature calls for fellowship. The Greeks felt this need keenly, and, stimulated thereby, created the city-state, which proved of such historic value to the Mediterranean civilization. The Roman felt this need even more than the Greek.[1] Nothing the Roman feared more than oblivion, and nothing he craved more than the kindly remembrance of his friends. Against the solitariness of death he requested, with deeply human pathos, the passer-by to stop to read his name and age and rank. If a man of means, he established an endowment for a guild of friends and their successors to memorialize him in common meals on the anniversary of his death,[2] or at stated intervals. But the city-state had disappeared, and man left to himself discovered the disadvantages of his newly won freedom, and paid the penalty of individualism. The social instinct survived the city-state which had cultivated and informed social instincts for centuries. Political disasters coming thick and fast, the crises of history falling with a crushing suddenness and weight, men felt the need of individual support. " The empire, which had striven to prevent combination, really furnished the greatest incentive to combine. In face of that world-wide and all-powerful system, the individual subject felt ever more and more his loneliness and helplessness. The imperial power might be well-meaning and beneficent, but it was so terrible and

---

[1] Boissier II. 248 : " Le besoin de se réunir et de se fortifier en s'associant était au moins aussi grand dans l'antiquité qu'aujourd'hui, et parmi les peuples anciens, les Romains sont peut-être celu qui l'a le plus vivement éprouvé."

[2] Cf. Les repas funèbres (in Cabrol-Leclercq, fasc. III. coll. 775-9).

200 THE APPEAL OF THE MYSTERY-RELIGIONS

levelling in the universal sweep of its forces that the isolated man seemed in its presence reduced to the insignificance of an insect or a grain of sand."[1] The religion into which he had been born, and which had rendered its highest service as a social bond, having suffered in the fall of the *ancien régime*, the individual must seek a religion of his own. The ancestral gods being estranged and national cults being unavailing, he must seek other means of purification and atonement.

The State had become too large for the self-realization of the individual and too unwieldy to those accustomed to the compact *polis*. There was another social unit which suggests itself to us—the family. But the family was too circumscribed to engage the main energies of the social instinct.[2] Moreover, the family had not yet assumed the prime importance it occupies with us, partly because the city-state had overshadowed every other social form, and partly because the family had not become the school for public life, as with us, owing to the low position assigned to the woman in Greek social life. We do not forget that it was in the family that Roman piety survived longest, nor that the sweet sanctities of domestic life were by no means uncommon, as the pages of Pliny and Plutarch tell.

The student of the Greek and Latin inscriptions may recall another form of social life which seems to have been particularly active in that age—the municipal life. The frequent mention of municipal elections and honours and decrees and acute rivalries should not blind us to the fact that this municipal life was but a pale reflection of the healthy and all-absorbing life of the city-state. In the self-government and mutual rivalries of the cities and townships the lords of the Graeco-Roman world found a safety-valve for political energy and social ambition. The Greek-Oriental cities of Asia and Egypt enjoyed a liberal measure of home-rule

[1] Dill, p. 256.
[2] Cf. Dill, p. 267: " Probably no age, not even our own, ever felt a greater craving for some form of social life, wider than the family and narrower than the State."

and spent their time in encouraging trade and manufacture, beautifying their streets and amusing the citizens. Their honours, though empty, satisfied local ambition. Their *Boulè* met with all ceremony as if there was no superior or imperial over-lordship. A surprising amount of local patriotism was fostered. Successful men made generous bequests to their native city to make it rank beside or above a neighbouring city.

The *Municipia*, enjoying a liberal constitution, were the glory of the imperial period. Each was a replica of Rome. Each had paved roads, public baths, a theatre, even an amphitheatre, temples, law courts, and places of public assemblage and porticoes for loungers. The remains of Pompeii convey a vivid impression of the competitive eager life that pulsated there. A visit to Timgad will convince one that centuries elapsed after the fall of the Western Empire before Europe recovered to any degree the amenities of the life that had gone. But all this municipal life had much unreality in it. It owed its existence partly to the conservative instincts of the Romans in continuing institutions of proved historic or sentimental worth. It differed from the life of the normal city-state in that its independence was unreal, there being a supreme authority above it, and in that it could not, because of individualism, compel the citizen.

There remained the other chief phase of social life which we know as the Church, or private and voluntary association for religious purposes. Industrial guilds had from the beginning borne a religious character in Greece and Rome. After Alexander the Orientals made great progress in multiplying private associations in the great *entrepôts* of the Mediterranean, into which members of all nations were admitted. A variety of objects could be served by banding together in clubs, and doubtless the motives which increased the membership were as varied as those which bring new members into the masonic brotherhood or into the Christian Church. Men clubbed together from purely human and social instincts, drawn by a sense of solitariness in a world that was too large for the individual, to protect their trade against undue competition or against fiscal greed, to find diversion from the monotony and relaxation from the toil of their daily lives, to benefit by such advantages as accrued from the fellowship, to worship a patron deity, to share in the common meal, to be assured of a resting-place in their club cemetery. The religious instinct was one of many, but the religious motives multiplied when the individual sought a sustaining religion for himself. The way for private religious associations had been prepared by a variety of coefficients [1]—the religious upheavals of the sixth century B.C., the spread of Judaism, migrations of Oriental merchants and slaves. The overthrow of the Delphic oracle early in the sixth century B.C. and its reconstruction as a spiritual power contributed to the formation of *orgeones* and *thiasoi*,[2] by means of which henceforth religious convictions were to be spread independently of political control. Orphism was the most potent solvent ever introduced into Greek religious life. Though its members never constituted themselves into an organized church, they formed *collegia*, or cult-associations,[3] characterized by a distinct theology of Orphic life, observing the cult of the state gods while undermining it. The Orphics sowed the seeds of distrust toward the national and hereditary principle in religion, and made the salvation of the individual soul of first importance. In this way Orphism had enormous influence upon the subsequent history of religion : by making religion a private and personal matter which led to voluntary association, by preaching a doctrine of divine grace, by requiring initiation in the interests of salvation, by concentrating attention upon personal endeavour and holiness, by indifference to state religion, by destroying the nationality

[1] " This transference of the social consciousness from a city or a state to a religious society was no new thing in the history of mankind " (Gardner, *Eph. Gosp.* p. 126).

[2] Gruppe, II, p. 1020.

[3] *Per contra*, Monceaux, art. *Orpheus* in Daremberg-Saglio, *Dictionnaire ;* Gruppe, II, p. 1031 ; Legge, I. 139 f ; Rohde, II, p. 111 ; cf. Macchioro, *Zagreus*, p. 268.

of gods, by the tolerant syncretism of its theology which would identify all gods with its Dionysus, it did much to prepare men for that revolutionary change in the history of religion when men abandon a religion into which they are born as citizens and voluntarily associate themselves in religious congregations. For the past twenty-two centuries these voluntary religious associations have been the decisive factors in history. The way was opened for such religions as were universal and could at the same time satisfy the needs of the individual and win his loyalty so that he became a missionary for his faith.

The Orientals, whose genius had never created a cohesive political unity, but only unwieldy and incoherent absolute empires, were more given to form private religious associations. When such associations become prominent in the Greek and Roman world we invariably find they owed their inception to Eastern slaves, freedmen, merchants, and adventurers ; the majority of their members, originally probably all, bear foreign names, and these associations appear and are most numerous in sea-ports and trading centres, which attracted foreigners. In Greece, for example, they appear first in the harbour of the Peiraeus.[1] These associations gradually attracted converts from the centres in which they operated, increased their prestige socially, and established the voluntary self-supporting principle in religion. The co-mingling of different races, the unification of mankind, and the religious syncretism gave an immense impetus to the formation of religious confraternities : " We see for the first time in history bodies of men and women banded together, irrespective of nationality and social rank, for the purpose of religious observances, and religion becoming recognized as an affair of the individual rather than of the State, while each member of the association was directly interested in its extension." [2] But these associations had found a footing in the West before the days of Alexander, and the Jews had during and subsequent to the Exile discovered a bond of unity in the worship maintained by the

---

[1] Foucart, p. 84 f.　　　　　[2] Legge, I, p. 21.

synagogues, which may be viewed as a conspicuous and successful species of religious confraternities.[1]

From what has been said the importance of the principle of private association both for the spread of the Mysteries and for the religious history of mankind will be evident. As in all the affairs of men, there was a—sometimes incongruous—mingling of heaven and earth ; the industrial clubs were not wholly secular, nor the religious clubs wholly sacred. Associations of crafts and trades met under religious auspices: they often assembled in a temple or were closely associated with a temple ; they had their patron-deity and their sacrifices and holy days. The more religious clubs, on the other hand, had to do with mundane affairs in the collection and administration of funds, the provision of sacrifices, and payment of officials, the discipline of members, the furnishing of the common meals, and the rendering of assistance.

The innumerable *collegia*, founded by workers and craftsmen throughout the empire, did the duties, partly of trades-unions, partly of freemasonry, partly of free churches, and partly of chambers of commerce. They afforded support to the individual, and gave him a sense of security through association with his brethren. They dignified labour, and gave to the toilers a sense of self-respect as servants of society.[2]

The social value of these associations was very great in an age when individualism had triumphed over collectivism as affording a new bond of social cohesion and containing the germs of a new and better social order. They contributed toward the equality of the sexes in assigning to woman her rightful place.[3] Both in pagan and in early Christian religious guilds women appear as the equals of men in

---

[1] Cf. Fairweather, *Background*, 2nd ed. p. 21.

[2] " When the brotherhood, many of them of servile grade, met in full conclave, in the temple of their patron-deity, to pass a formal decree of thanks to a benefactor, and regale themselves with a modest repast, or when they passed through the streets and the forum with banners flying, and all the emblems of their guild, the meanest member felt himself lifted for a moment above the dim, hopeless obscurity of plebeian life " (Dill, p. 256). [3] Cf. Farnell, *Cults*, III, p. 155.

worship, in administration and in cult, and their influence was for good. The members were ' brothers,' a term which had acquired a religious sense before it appeared on the pages of our New Testament. The Mithraists were styled ' brothers ' and ' soldiers,' and had an officer called *pater* and *pater patrum*. Adherents of Jupiter Dolichenus are ' most loving brothers ' (*fratres carissimos*).[1] Others are ' colleagues and participators in holy things ' (*collegae et consacranei*).[2] These voluntary associations were a symptom and a cause of the passing away of the old order, and marked the beginning of new social values [3] and the rise of an elevating ideal that " a man's a man for a' that and a' that." The slave could meet his master with self-respect and the consciousness of being an equal. The poorest and humblest had a new outlook on life. Unity gave to the lower classes the power to confront the upper classes and finally to undermine their exclusiveness.

Equally far-reaching were the effects of this irresistible movement in religious matters. The cravings and needs of the individual, never catered for by the state religions, now found means of satisfaction. The principle was asserted that religion is an affair of the soul with God in a union voluntarily entered into by the individual rather than a mere accident of birth by which a man is furnished with a religion for the good of the community irrespective of his personal needs. No racial or national or class barriers could henceforth intervene between a man and the full exercise of that religion which appealed to his nature. The rights of conscience in religion for which Socrates had died in the Athenian

[1] *C.I.L.* VI. 406.

[2] Boissier, II, p. 269.

[3] Mithraism was essentially a religion of soldiers, and had little to offer to women : the wives of Mithraists attached themselves to the more feminine cults of the Great Mother and Isis. In early Christianity women were not chosen to the highest office, as was possible e.g. in the august Eleusinian Mysteries. Paul, though proclaiming that Christ has blotted out the distinction of Greek and barbarian, male and female, requires women to veil themselves in the church meetings, but rather for the sake of modesty than from a belief in their inferiority. He speaks also of man as the ' head ' of the woman, as Christ is head of the Church.

prison, and the privilege of private judgment, were granted and respected. In the development of individuality these confraternities proved a school for the evolution of personality. This religious individualism brought as its corollary universalism, and in this respect prepared the way for world-religions.

In parting with these ancient *collegia* we regretfully remark how no human institution, however beneficial to mankind, as these *collegia* indisputably were, can escape abuses or ensure against degeneration. In the first place, these ' colleges ' sometimes exemplified the aberrations of mass psychology by encouraging mob-rule. Tacitus records how, in the days of Nero, an *atrox caedes* broke out, at a gladiatorial exhibition in Pompeii between the Pompeians and the neighbouring Nucerians, in which the colleges were evidently implicated, since by the Senate *collegia (que) quae contra leges constituerant dissoluta*.[1] More serious disorders were caused in the reign of Aurelian by the guild of the workmen of the mint, which resulted in the massacre of 7,000 people.[2] Moreover, these very guilds, which first vindicated for the lower orders their freedom and represented the dignity of labour, degenerated in the closing empire into a caste-system of hereditary trades [3] whereby guild-members were bound to their occupations from generation to generation. This stereotyping of the guilds restricted personal freedom and condemned thousands by the accident of birth to trades for which they had no taste. Hence the " go-slow " policy was sometimes resorted to. Even intermarriage among the guilds was forbidden by law.

IV. A developing Sense of Sin. In the Hellenistic and Roman periods we hear distinctly and emphatically a note of sadness and human weakness that sounded only faintly and sporadically [4] in the literature of the West during its

---

[1] *Annales*, XIV. 17. [2] Vopiscus, *Aurel.* 38 (*Scriptores hist. Aug.*).
[3] Cf. Dill, *Rom. Soc. in the Last Cent.* 2nd ed. p. 232 ff.: " It was the principle of rural serfdom applied to social functions " ; and *Rom. Soc. fr. Nero*, p. 254.
[4] Cf. Farnell, *Higher Aspects*, pp. 131–4 ; Glover, *Progress*, pp. 139, 169 ; B. A. G. Fuller, *The Problem of Evil in Plotinus*, p. 27 ff.

classical prime. There is a brooding consciousness of failure, of the futility of human effort, of the load of human sin, the ineluctability of penalty, of gods estranged, and the need of reconciliation and purification. " The Graeco-Roman world had reached a point from which Judaism had started. From generation to generation rose a louder wail over the frailty of human nature, the weakness of mortals, the natural sinfulness of man, who can in no way please the gods, and on whom, therefore, the anger of the gods weighs heavy. The complaint raised by Hebrew conscience in the dawn of history becomes the evening invocation of Hellenic philosophy." [1] Self-sufficiency had given way to a mood of pessimism. Again the spirit of the East was conquering the spirit of the West, and succeeded in bringing it under a conviction of sin,[2] which turned men's thoughts eastwards in search of cathartic sacraments. This painful discovery increased in intensity to the Western spiritual experience until it culminated in the contrition of Augustine's *Confessions*. The self-sufficient Greek believed that he could of himself attain all that was implied in the ideal of manhood —" Hellas, the nurse of man, complete as man." The ceremonious Roman looked upon his religion as a contract with the supernatural powers, the terms of which he could perfectly fulfil. The disillusionment came. The too-careless optimism gave way to a moral despair, a failure of nerve. Like many other psychological phenomena of the Graeco-Roman world, the emergence of this sense of sin is explained by efficient causes ; there had been a long period of preparation, during which thought was turned inwards to plumb the deeps and mysteries of individuality. With individuality came personality, and with personality, conscience—a word which the Stoics coined and popularized. The reign of collectivism was at an end, but the emancipated individual discovered that he now stood alone, cast upon his own resources against the universe. The discomforts of contemporary subjectivity were felt as contrasted with an

---

[1] Hausrath, *Apostles*, Eng. tr. I, p. 42.
[2] Cf. Gardner, *St. Paul*, 23–4.

era of more irresponsible objectivity.[1] A great lacuna was caused in man's life by the elimination of his once absorbing public activities. Leisure for the affairs of the private life was left to him, and this leisure was increased by the paternal imperial policy and the security of the *pax Romana.* The individual, then as now in quest of freedom, discovered a somewhat in himself that must be overcome, something that rendered the ideal difficult of achievement, that tinged the blithesomeness of a bye-gone epoch with sadness. In the isolation of individualism man discovered a rift within his nature. This subjectivity caused an analysis of character and motives which reveals itself partly in the rise of autobiography, but chiefly in the habit of self-examination, which became a regular requirement of the moralists of the age.[2] The necessity of self-examination had been affirmed and self-examination practised by Socrates, who commenced a new era in human thought by diverting investigation from physics to morality, from the external world to man.[3] It was also practised by the Pythagoreans and commended itself greatly to the Stoics. Sextius, a professor of Stoicism, encouraged it among his followers by example and precept, and one of his pupils diligently cultivated it : [4]

' Every day I plead my case before myself. When the light is extinguished, and my wife, who knows my habit, keeps silence, I examine the past day, go over and weigh all my deeds and words. I hide nothing, I omit nothing : why should I hesitate to face my shortcomings when I can say, " Take care not to repeat them, and so I forgive you to-day " ? '

Epictetus commends Socrates for maintaining that a life without self-examination is not a worthy life for man.[5]

---

[1] Cf. Bussell, *School of Plato,* p. 212 ff.

[2] Cf. C. Martha, *Les Moralistes sous l'empire romain,* p. 173 ff.

[3] Cf. his words about Delphic inscription : ' It seems absurd while ignorant of that [self-knowledge] to investigate external things. . . . I investigate not these things, but myself' (*Phaedrus,* 230 A).

[4] Seneca, *De Ira,* III. 36.

[5] Epict. I. 26, 3 ; III. 12, 4 ; Plato, *Apol.* 38 A.

Plutarch asks men to turn their analysis upon themselves. Marcus Aurelius, amid the burdens of imperial power and political anxieties, passed his life in searching introspection.

From the sixth century B.C. there commenced a gradual religious transformation in the Western world which would ultimately cause it to accept the Eastern anthropology, based on the creaturely weakness and sinfulness of man. Orphism had by the sixth century B.C. taken root in Magna Graecia, the islands of the Levant, and in the Greek mainland. It proclaimed a purer mysticism, individualism, asceticism, a dogma of original sin, and cathartic doctrines. Orphism did not commence, but it certainly advanced, the education of the Greeks in the consciousness of sin and the need of reconciliation ; it offered rites of purification,[1] and promised forgiveness and salvation through initiation into its Mysteries. Sin was met by sacramental grace. By securing influence in the Eleusinian Mysteries Orphism modified the character of these Mysteries into a cathartic rite of sacramental efficacy for sin.[2] The rise of the Pythagorean movement in the sixth century and especially the break-up of the Pythagorean schools [3] in Magna Graecia at the beginning of the fifth century, and their adoption of the outstanding moral doctrines of the Orphics are events of prime importance in the education of the Mediterranean world in the consciousness of sin. As Orphism reformed the Dionysiac religion, Pythagoreanism revived and reformed Orphism and adapted it to the demands of the age. Asceticism with severe self-examination was even more rigorously enjoined by the Pythagoreans, who deepened the sense of sin in two ways : first, by emphasizing the metempsychosis of souls according to moral progress—a doctrine borrowed from the Orphics ; and, secondly, by popularizing the doctrine of moral retribution in a future life which radically altered the

[1] Pausanias, IX. 30. 12.

[2] " The mode in which the Mysteries were regarded by the Greeks in general materially altered after the introduction of the Orphic teaching, and this also can hardly be attributed to anything else than the direct influence of its professors " (Legge, I, p. 131 f.).

[3] Cf. Legge, I. 122.

character of the Homeric Hades. As an ethic-religious reform movement [1] it so closely allied itself with the preparatory and kindred Orphic movement that many of the Orphic hymns were attributed to Pythagoras and most of them could be used by Pythagoreans; but it excelled Orphism as a teaching force in popularizing its doctrines, and also in its better organization in cohesive brotherhoods.

The religious spirit of Plato wrestled with the problem of evil rather than with sin in the religious sense. He recognized that something rendered the ideal tantalizingly afar off from man, but could not really diagnose the cause. He found the main obstacle in the body, which acted as a weight upon the soul, and in ignorance. He could not, with his Greek anthropology, convince himself that evil is seated in the will, much less that men are so misguided or wicked as to choose evil instead of good. Sin consisted in ignorance, for no man could fail to love and practise virtue when once he learned what it is. The doctrines of metempsychosis and transmigration of souls taken from Orphic-Pythagorean teachings show that he recognized the possibility of moral deterioration. In the strict system of penance exacted in the next life he recognized clearly the power of sin. Aristotle contributed in at least two conspicuous ways to the evolution of the consciousness of sin. First, in his original and searching analysis of human nature in *The Metaphysics* [2] and *Nicomachean Ethics*—textbooks to the present day—he started men in the path of scientific introspection which was certain sooner or later to discover in our being the presence of the psychic phenomenon known as consciousness of sin. Secondly, he took a step beyond his master in observing that men may be voluntarily wicked, choosing the lower instead of the higher when both are presented. Sin, for Aristotle, consists in either excess or defect, the missing of

[1] Zeller, *Pre-Soc. Phil* Eng. tr. I. 516.

[2] Sir Henry Jones, in *Idealism as a Practical Creed*, p. 15, speaks of Hegel's *Phaenomenology of Spirit* as " a work which, with Aristotle's *Metaphysics* ranks as one of the most adventurous voyages ever made in the world of mind."

the proper mean, righteousness being μεσότης.[1] In later writers the question of Sin occupies an increasingly conspicuous place. Philo's examination of the powers of the soul called the attention of the Jewish-Greek world to the moral disease seated in the flesh which mars the vision of God, a doctrine in which he is at one with Paul.[2] Sin is innate in each by birth : ' each of us is numerically two persons, an animal and a man.'[3] In Plotinus' treatment of evil there appears a further aspect of the convergence of Eastern and Western thought in anthropology, though the treatment is surprisingly scant.[4] Much attention was given to the problem in Stoicism, especially Roman Stoicism,[5] which viewed sin as a necessity in the nature of things as shadow to light, or as madness or ignorance, or even weakness, or as serving the purpose of revealing the good. Plutarch accounted for evil by assigning it to the demons. It was not from an isolated case of a burdened conscience that he had depicted the superstitious man wishing to suffer his punishment, sitting out of doors, wearing sackcloth or filthy rags, wallowing naked in the mire, making public confession of his sin.[6] The parodies of hypersensitive consciences by the satirist of Samosata and by Theophrastus in his *Superstitious Man* would lose all force if they did not stand in a recognizable proportion to contemporary views. Quite modern in Theophrastus' essay is the expectation of the monthly absolution of sins from the Orphic salvationists. Epictetus[7] dwells upon the fact that men do evil voluntarily, but under the persuasion that it is advantageous or that it bears the appearance of good : ' All the great and terrible deeds done among mankind have no other cause than appearance '—that is, the

[1] Cf *Eth. Nic.* VI. 9.
[2] Cf. Kennedy, *Philo's Contribution*, p. 98 ff.
[3] *Quod. det. pot. insid. sol.* XXII.
[4] Cf. B. A. G. Fuller, *op. cit.* chaps. III, IV ; Inge, I, p. 131 ff., II, p. 231 f.
[5] Cf. Arnold, *Roman Stoicism*, p. 330 ff.
[6] *De Superst.*, VII. 12.
[7] I. 28, 2 f.

objects appeared desirable. In another remarkable passage [1] he says : ' Any sin implies a conflict ; or, since the sinner does not wish to sin but to do right, it is clear that he does not do what he desires '—a sentiment parallel to the experience of Paul (*Romans* VII. 15).

The worldly Horace gives expression to this inner conflict :

'Quae nocuere sequar, fugiam quae profore credam,'

and the licentious Ovid [2] in the familiar verses :

'Sed trahit invitam nova vis, aliudque cupido,
Mens aliud suadet. Video meliora proboque,
Deteriora sequor.'

The two pagan writers who are most conscious of the sinfulness of man's nature are Seneca and Virgil. The former recognizes the universality of sin, its downward tendency, and its infectious character. Thus [3] :

' Do we not perceive the need of some advocate to teach us differently from the pagan ideas ? . . . No one sins to himself alone, but diffuses the madness upon those with whom he comes in contact, and in turn receives it himself again. And so the faults of all are in each because the mass has imparted them. While a man makes his neighbour worse he becomes worse himself. First, he learns what is base (*deteriora*) and then becomes a teacher of it. Hence, there results such immense wickedness (*ingens illa nequitia*) because there is gathered in one the worst that is known to each one.'

Again,[4] he complains that we have all sinned and been affected with vice, that vices may change with the fashion, but will remain and even grow worse. The prevalence of wickedness and the deterioration of human affairs, which we lament, was lamented by our ancestors, and shall be lamented by our descendants. Vice is co-extensive with humanity ; when you see the forum crowded with people,

[1] II. 26, I.
[2] Hor. *Epist.* I. 8, xi.; Ovid, *Metam.* VII. 18 ff. Cf. other interesting citations in Wetstein, *Novum Test.* ad Rom. VII. 15.
[3] *Ep.* XC. 52.   [4] *De Benef.* I. 10.

hoc scito, istic tantundem esse vitiorum quantum hominum.[1]
Statements as to the prevalence of sin might be multiplied
from the pages of Seneca.[2]

Virgil, who has never been surpassed by any prophet in
his tender, universal sympathy with the cravings and
strivings of man, holds together in wonderful poise what
might be called the Hebraic and the Hellenic anthropologies.
His " poetry throbbed with the sense of man's grandeur
and his sanctity,"[3] while at the same time no spirit was
more sensitive to man's failures and none felt more oppres-
sively the load of human guilt. His religious and mystic
spirit imbibed from Orphism and Pythagoreanism the doctrine of the perfectibility of human nature by the practice
of virtue, together with that of a system of penances for the
sinful and purgatorial experience for those who had soiled
their souls with the things of sense. Like Goethe, he believed

" Es irrt der Mensch so lang er strebt."

His hell is not so gloomy or hopeless as that of his great
disciple, Dante, but to human wrong-doing there must be
meted out a just penalty. " What," asks Professor Conway,[4]
" is the tremendous machinery of punishment after death
which the Sixth Book describes in the most majestic passage
of all epic poetry (*Aen*. VI. 548–627), but the measure of
Virgil's sense of human guilt ? '

This growing sense of sin in the Graeco-Roman world was
akin to the pessimism which, about the commencement of
the Christian era, gave rise to the belief that history was a
process of degeneration, that the times were out of joint,
and that a saviour was needed to put the world right. The
Jews alone in antiquity were conspicuous for an outlook
which comes nearest to our modern view of an " increasing
purpose " in world-history. The Jew was buoyed up with
a religious optimism that " the best is yet to be." The
opposite view is often expressed in Greek and Roman

---

[1] *De Ira*, II. 8, I.
[2] Cf. *De Clem*. I. 6 ; *Ep*. XXIX. ; *Nat. Quaest* III. 30.
[3] Glover, *Conflict*, p. 31.
[4] *Virgil's Mess. Eclogue*, p. 37.

writers. Thus, Seneca holds that after the destruction of the world by fire, the new race of men will lose their innocence.[1] Sin will increase in quality and quantity.[2] In his *Consolation to Marcia* (XXIII) occur such expressions as ' omne futurum incertum est et ad deteriora certius ' and ' quicquid ad summum pervenit ab exitu prope est ' and ' Indicium imminentis exitii nimia maturitas est ; adpetit finis ubi incrementa consumpta sunt.'

It is important to note that the Greeks, though less sensitive to the disharmony of sin than the Jews and the Romans (whom Sallust calls *religiosissimi mortales*), indicated to the Graeco-Roman world the three main directions in which the doctrine of sin developed and affected Christian theology : (1) What we may term the gnostic-philosophic view, of which Plato may be taken as representative and his ' no one is willingly bad '[3] the watchword. Sin is ignorance and blindness to reality. Virtue is so attractive and rational that no one can look upon her without obeying her behests. Men are not such irrational beings as to choose what they know to be hurtful in their pursuit of the Ideal. The way of salvation lies, therefore, in enlightenment, the reception of the ' holy light ' of divine Truth. Plato's dualism gives to evil an illegitimate *raison d'être* as the necessary antagonism to the Good, with its seat in our fleshly nature. Hence ' our safety is to become like God as far as possible, and to become like Him is to become righteous and holy.'[4] The soul, like the charioteer in the *Phaedrus*,[5] beholding ' the vision of Love,' is guided by Reason above passion to the source of Love.

(2) What we may term, somewhat inaccurately, the Orphic-mystic view, of which Plotinus may be representative in words which laid hold of Augustine,[6] ' we must fly to that dear, dear Fatherland ; there is the Father, there is all . . . to be like God.' Man is a creature fallen from a high estate,

---

[1] *Nat. Quaest.* III. 30.   [4] *Theaetetus*, 176 A.
[2] *De Benef.* I. 10, i.   [5] 253 D f.
[3] *Timaeus*, 86 D.   [6] *D.C.D.* IX. 17 ; cf. *Enn.* I. 6, 8.

a wanderer or exile from the true Home of the soul. He is immersed in the world of sense, oblivious of, or painfully struggling towards, the spiritual world. Salvation will come by the revelation of the One, the Supreme Good, which the soul will gladly embrace in the flight of the ' Alone to the Alone.'

(3) The ethical view, represented by Aristotle, who first, in the seventh book of the *Nicomachean Ethics*, challenged Plato's interpretation [1] of evil by affirming that men do act wickedly in the face of knowledge. ' Sin is not a matter of knowledge,' he says expressly. ' Sin is wickedness,' having to do with the will. It is at once an intellectual and a moral act. Knowledge may be obscured by appetite. This view is also conspicuous in Philo.[2] As a school the Stoics [3] are the best type of this ethical emphasis.

Finally, it may be said that in the Graeco-Roman world the conviction of sin became intensified and the need of atonement more imperious in at least four respects : (1) The communal conception of sin, common to all primitive culture, retreated before that of personal guilt, thus making the question of salvation of immediate interest to each moral unit in his dislocation from corporate religion. (2) The scene of rewards and retribution was increasingly shifted from the visible sphere of earth—where punishments were sometimes perplexingly inadequate and at others perplexingly unjust—to a future world where imagination could riot in inventing means of torture commensurate with the deeds done in the body. The future life, being a continuum of the present, intensified the flagrance of sin here, of which the Orphic tablets furnish an excellent example. (3) The ceremonial or taboo sin began to part company with the ethical sin. Intention and motive, independent of consequences, entered as a new factor. The unconscious sin, done with a good will or in ignorance, might, under the

---

[1] Cf. A. W. Mair, *Sin* (Greek), Hastings' *E.R.E.* XI. 555.
[2] Cf. Kennedy, p. 102.
[3] Glover, *Progress*, p. 18 ; Arnold, *Rom. Stoicism*, XIV.

Hebrew code or ancient Greek religion, entail death and defilement. But the cult word ' holy ' was gradually charged with moral content in the passage from the ritualistic to the moral. (4) The means of reconciliation became correspondingly spiritual. Piacular sacrifices no longer sufficed. A change of mind was necessary, a repentance which would raise its *Miserere Domine* ; the sinner must undergo a rebirth. Plato inveighed vehemently [1] against cheap remedies for sin. The cynic asked,[2] ' Shall Pataikion, the highwayman, have a happier lot after death because of having taken the sacrament than Epaminondas ? ' Epictetus scoffs at the popular sacramentarian view of the venerable Eleusinia apart from inward purity.[3] Ovid [4] derides Greece for introducing cheap ritualistic means to peace of mind. Celsus' statement, accepted by Origen,[5] of the mystagogues' proclamation at the Mysteries for cleansing from sin, ' He who is pure from all stain, whose soul is conscious of no sin, and who has lived a good and upright life,' shows how far the Mysteries had moved from the days when ' Greek speech and clean hands ' admitted aspirants.[6]

V. Asceticism. In the centuries preceding and subsequent to the Christian era there is a remarkable prevalence of ascetic tendencies and practices which seem quite strange to us who have learned from Christian philosophy that to the pure all things are pure and that all things are ours. In the Graeco-Roman world asceticism was as universal and as indifferent to race and creed and nationality as were the syncretistic and individualistic tendencies. It pervaded philosophy and religion. Like a mighty tide it swept onwards, especially from the first century B.C., from the East over the West, gathering momentum as it forced its way into every serious view of life. Every great teacher from Plato to John the Baptist, from Paul to Plotinus, axiomatically accepted asceticism as an essential of and qualification for

---

[1] Cf. *Repub.* II. 364–5 D.
[2] Diog. Laert. VI. 39.
[3] *Diss.* III. 21.
[4] *Fasti,* II. 35 f.
[5] *C. Celsum,* III. 59.
[6] Cf. Farnell, *Cults,* III. 166.

religious life. Only One rejected this method, and 'came eating and drinking.'

There were several factors operative in the origin and spread of asceticism. (1) Asceticism is another conspicuous example of the all-pervading influence of Oriental contemplation, another instance in which the resisting power of the West was overcome by the spirit of the East. Renunciation for religious purposes was little in prominence to the more sober peoples of the West.[1] The Greek, trusting to reason, aimed at self-culture rather than self-repression, and an equipoise of the moral faculties which could not admit the predominance of one faculty over another. Aristotle, with the possible exception of Sophocles the most typical Greek, made the golden mean the rule in ethics. To the genuinely Greek spirit of 'nothing in excess' asceticism was abhorrent as an extreme incongruous with " man *complete as man.*" Hellas could not in her classical prime admit a view of life which set limitations and restrictions upon human effort, which could not be justified to reason, nor be shown to be contrary to nature. The more sober Roman piety did not require asceticism in its discipline ; the world and the fulness thereof were the Roman's. The people who could appropriate the sentiment of their poet Terence—

'Homo sum: humani nihil a me alienum puto,'

were not, while left to themselves, likely to become a nation of ascetics. But the days came when Greece and Rome, in their political pride of place, looked down upon a prostrate Eastern world only to learn, *victi victoribus leges dederunt.* A voice from the mystic East rose even louder upon their ears bearing the sentiment—

" Entbehren sollst du, sollst entbehren."

(2) Asceticism was the inevitable recoil from the excesses

[1] Asceticism was not absent even in the earliest periods of Greek and Roman religion, but occupied a minor place and lacked the later elaborate theological justification. Cf. J. W. Swain, *Hellenic Origins of Christian Asceticism,* p. 6 ff. ; Capelle, *N. Jahrb. f. d. Klass. Alt.* XXIII, p. 681 ff.

of naturalistic religion to which the creed *naturalia non sunt turpia* conduced. In earlier non-moral stages the worshipper was not offended by any incongruity, and the religious sanction given to natural instincts degenerated into dangerous excess. When the reaction came it recoiled to the other extreme, which denied the right of way to what was natural and innocent in itself. Students of the history of human institutions and ethics are familiar with this phenomenon ; the pendulum swings to the other extreme. The reformers reasserted the right of private judgment with an emphasis which has made non-Roman churches conspicuous for their fissiparism. The Puritans failed because they denied " the uses of the flesh " which the next age took up with a zest which degenerated into a cult of the flesh. The convert who abandoned the revolting excesses of paganism found no resting-place except in the excessive position of asceticism. A similar phenomenon is observable in the mediaeval world. The monastic life seemed the only alternative to that of the battle-field or dissoluteness. The liberty of our modern personal autonomy was hardly visible in the practical ethical sphere of antiquity. The mean had not been discovered between antinomianism and asceticism.

(3) The most conspicuous cause of asceticism was the prevalent Graeco-Oriental Dualism which dominated all thought. " Dualism, with the asceticism inseparable from it, was, so to speak, in the air ; it was the strongest spiritual tendency of the time, almost equal to Christianity in power."[1] Dualism was as much a postulate for philosophical and ethical and religious thinkers of the Graeco-Roman age as evolution or the unity of the universe is to us. The more seriously a man devoted himself to religious affairs, the more thoroughly he accepted dualism : witness the two most philosophic religious thinkers of our era, Philo and Plotinus. The fascination of the dualistic systems may be shown by the difficulty with which Paul escaped Greek dualism to adopt a view of *flesh* and *spirit* which is akin to Oriental dualism. We cannot touch Graeco-Roman life or thought at any point

[1] Dobschütz, *Christian Life*, Eng. tr. p. 112 ; cf. also p. 40 f.

without detecting the presence of dualism, to which asceticism is the necessary concomitant. Dualism was introduced into Greek thought by Anaxagoras,[1] who, in opposition to the preceding materialistic monism, segregated spirit and matter. With Plato it made its home in Greek thought, the course of which it distorted to the close of Greek philosophy in Plotinus, who made the last heroic effort to surmount it, confessed his failure, and pointed to the refuge of mysticism. Ethical dualism came in from the Orient—the dualism between two eternally hostile principles of Light and Darkness, Good and Evil, and made its alliance with the Greek metaphysical dualism. Asceticism is the ethical code which arises inevitably from a dualistic opposition between the spiritual and the natural. These are represented as absolutely irreconcilable and mutually antagonistic [2]; if a man is to escape the natural he must renounce the rights of his physical nature in the interests of his spiritual,[3] forgetful of the moral value of the interrelation and interaction of these two elements which constitute a unity of personality. (4) The deepening consciousness of sin, spoken of above, gave new impetus to asceticism in the absence of a moral *via media*. In the desire to surmount this oppressive consciousness and to escape from pollution the ancient devotee, a child of his age, could seek cleansing only in accordance with the contemporary rigorous and dualistic tendencies. The most flagrant sins of paganism were those of sensuality ; hence sin seemed to be identified with the flesh, which, as evil, must be mortified and to which no concessions must be made. The passions must be extirpated, not regulated. To save the soul, we must wholly escape from sense ; ' the body is a tomb of the soul ' was a common watchword of ancient asceticism. The inadequate conception of sin and equally inadequate conception of personality exaggerated the practice of asceticism. The aim of the penitent was not to attain salvation of man's

---

[1] Cf. Angus, *Environment*, pp. 176, 192 f.
[2] Cf. Watson, *Phil. Basis of Relig.*, p. 293.
[3] Cf. Plato, *Timaeus*, 69 ff. ; *Phaedo*, 66 ff. ; *Cratyl.* 400 C.

whole being, but of that portion which seemed of supreme worth. He endeavoured to act as if he were pure spirit and not a spirit in an animal body with physical cravings and wants for which there was ample justification. Only one gospel proclaimed : ' all are yours . . . the world, or life, or death, or the present, or the future ; all things belong to you, and you belong to Christ, and Christ belongs to God.' Men who for the sin of their soul were prepared to practise mortification of the body were naturally disposed to the Oriental religions—including Christianity,[1] especially that primitive Christianity which, even with Paul, began to lose touch with the moral poise of Jesus' own life, and to have recourse to asceticism, which expressed itself in the asperities of the Pannonian father [2] and in the absurdities of the anchorites Antony and Simeon Stylites.

(5) The post-Aristotelian philosophy, which exercised a profound influence East and West, adopted asceticism as a means of moral reform in an age that was pre-eminently occupied with the problem of conduct, and when the combination of ethics with religion was proceeding apace. We are not thinking of Epicureanism nor of Scepticism, but of the religio-philosophic systems of Platonism, Stoicism, Judaeo-Greek philosophy, Neo-Pythagoreanism and Neo-Platonism. The moral earnestness of Stoicism encouraged the spirit of asceticism, as e.g. in Seneca, Epictetus, and Marcus Aurelius. Seneca compares life to a severe struggle : *omnia illi cum hac grave certamen est.*[3] The Stoic doctrine of ' the flesh ' or ' the body,' found e.g. prominently in Seneca and Epictetus, could exist only with an ascetic ideal. Such morbid sentiments as ' this body is but a weight and punishment of the soul,'[4] *inutilis caro et fluida, receptandis tantum cibis habilis*[5]; *nos corpus tam putre sortiti,*[6] could issue only in a philosophy of asceticism. But Stoic asceticism was saved

---

[1] Cf. Swain, *op. cit.,* p. 146 : " The only form of redemption then possible was through an ascetic idealism. It was only because it presented just such an asceticism that Christianity was able to save civilization."

[2] Cf. e.g. his *Ep. ad Eustochium* (XXII), and *ad Heliordorum* (XIV).

[3] *Ad Marc.* 24.   [5] *Ep.* XCII. 10.

[4] Seneca, *Ep.* LXV, 16.   [6] *Ep.* CXX. 17.

from the extreme Oriental forms of self-mutilation through its union with a high sense of the value of man which persisted by the side of the deprecatory doctrine of 'the flesh' and retained the primacy over the latter.[1]

Post-Aristotelian ethics favoured asceticism in concentrating attention on the conduct of the individual. Asceticism, like mysticism, is a creed of solitude which thrives in individualism. The ascetic life aims at the good of the personal, out of relation to the corporate, life. Arnold[2] rightly speaks of the " asceticism and resignation which spread over the whole Graeco-Roman world about this time, resulting from exaggerated attention to the individual consciousness at the cost of social and political life."

The ascetic tendency affected all classes and systems. It found a firm footing in the systems of Orphism, Pythagoreanism, Platonism, Neo-Pythagoreanism, and Neo-Platonism, in the Jewish sects of the Essenes and Therapeutae, and to a considerable degree in Pharisaism ; in Gnosticism of every variety. One of the higher philosophic influences making for asceticism was the theology of astralism. The devotee of this system, 'the contemplator and exegete of heaven,' as Posidonius[3] styled man, impassioned with cosmic emotion, impressed by the immensities of the universe, the brightness and purity of the constellations, the celestial harmonies, was inclined to despise the petty interests of earth and its pleasures.[4] Nearly every heresy of primitive Christianity was imbued with asceticism : Gnosticism, Docetism, the systems of Simon Magus and Marcion, the Encratites, Montanists, Manichaeanism. Christianity itself could not escape the contagion, and departed in this respect from the moral equipoise

[1] Arnold, *Rom. Stoicism*, pp. 258–9 ; Seneca repudiates the practice of self-mutilation : *Nat. Quaest.* VII. 31, 3.

[2] P. 409.

[3] Capelle, *Die Schrift v. d. Welt*, p. 6 ; *N. Jahrb. f. d. Klas. Alt.* VIII p. 534.

[4] " Thus the devotion to knowledge is crowned in a sidereal devotion of a religious nimbus and becomes a holy calling which releases from all terrestrial passion. The exaltation of the intellectual life conduces to asceticism" (Cumont, *Acad. roy. d. Belgique* ; *Lettres*, '09, p. 270).

of the teachings of its Founder, who, unlike His ascetic forerunner, was reputed a wine-bibber. His greatest apostle, Paul, did not escape the ascetic tendency, though he escaped the excesses of asceticism.[1]

Every department of ancient life was affected by ascetic principles—questions of food and drink, property, the nature of matter, sex relations, the observance of days, the use of the baths, and other questions affecting cleanliness. Marriage and the procreation of children were strictly inhibited by the Essenes, Ophites, and the stricter Gnostics. Copulation in itself became a sin in revulsion from naturalism and antinomianism.[2] Hence sexual intercourse was forbidden both within and without the marriage state. Virginity became a virtue superior to that of motherhood. Matter was looked upon as evil or as the seat of the evil principle ; the whole business of life was to release the soul from the contact and pollution of matter, from the body, its bane. The tenure of property for private use was discouraged ; communism was practised by the Essenes and by the Neo-Pythagoreans, who traced the practice back to Pythagoras himself, and attempted by the Christians at Jerusalem. Even baths were omitted because the Oriental connexion between filth and sanctity had seized upon devout minds. Wallowing in mud, covering the body with dust, habiting oneself in sackcloth or in dirty garments, became symptoms of piety—the hall-marks of sincerity to some species of asceticism. Unfortunately for the Northern races, Christianity early fell into similar excesses of asceticism, by failing to serve itself heir to the Greek gospel of health, as witnessed by Greek statuary, and to the Roman gospel of cleanliness,[3] to which the colossal remains of baths in many

[1] Dobschütz, p. 41.

[2] Dobschütz, p. 127 : " The demoniacal mystery with which the act of procreation was surrounded by the ancients, who either deified it or held it accursed " ; also p. 40.

[3] Partly no doubt because of the abuses of the public bathing establishments, in which even Christian women seemed to the Church fathers to lose their modesty and become incentives to evil. The abuses attracted the attention of pagan emperors and Church Councils (e.g. Laodicea, 320). Cf. H. Dumaine's art. *Bains* in Cabrol-Leclercq, *Dict.*

cities of the empire bear testimony, together with the sane teachings of the Founder.[1] In regard to food and drink many fine points were raised by ascetics. Some were total abstainers from wine, some from flesh, some from pork. Vegetarianism was much in vogue not only for valetudinarian reasons but also for religious motives. Asceticism also required the observance of special days as fast-days or penitential days. Social life was on the whole decried by the ultra-religious in favour of some form of monasticism. An interesting papyrus from the site of the Serapeum of Memphis tells of a body of recluses attached to the Serapeum whose seclusion was of the most rigorous kind.[2] If the complete religious history of the Oriental temples were extant we should probably find that this was no isolated case : it was too much in keeping with the tendencies of the age to be such.

(6) Mysticism fostered asceticism, and was in turn fostered by asceticism. A whole volume could be filled with the rise, development, results, and varieties of mysticism in the Graeco-Roman world. Here it is necessary only in a few words to point out the alliance of mysticism with Asceticism. Although " Mysticism was a foreign ingredient in the Greek blood," [3] the entry of mysticism was facilitated by the pantheistic character of Greek religion and the pantheistic trend in all Greek thought. There is a certain affinity between pantheism and mysticism : it has always been difficult for mystics to escape pantheism. Mysticism was one refuge from the dualism which proved so insuperable to ancient thought, and which rendered asceticism a necessity for serious men. Since the days of Plato the idea of the ascent of the soul to a higher spiritual world had become prevalent, an idea which gave a relative insignificance to the

[1] Dobschütz (Eng. tr. p. 251) notes " two influences which worked with disintegrating effect " in early Christianity, viz. " the divergence between the intellectual and the moral side of Christianity," and " the effect which the ascetic tendencies of the age had on its moral ideas."

[2] Bouché-Leclercq, *Les reclus du sérapeum de Memphis* (Paris, 1903); Preuschen, *Mönchtum u. Serapiskult* (Giessen, 1903).

[3] Rohde, *Religion der Griechen*, p. 27 (*Kl. Sch.* p. 338).

affairs of this world. The whole business of man was to imitate God in order to increase in likeness to Him, who was conceived as the Absolute or as pure Spirit. This process of imitation involved the suppression of the natural and physical in the interests of the intellectual and the spiritual. Mysticism presents a positive and Godward side which consists in becoming godlike or a god, and a negative or man-ward side which involves an ascetic life of self-suppression. Sense cannot be silenced without much self-torture, and quietism cannot be attained until the passions are eradicated and the body loses its power over the soul.[1]

(7) The prevalence of asceticism on any large scale has invariably been coincident with social upheavals and economic confusion, and such conditions as drive men out of the old ways and discredit the working theories of a corporate life. In such periods the burden of family and social ties becomes oppressive.[2] The birth-rate declines. Men eschew marriage in the bitter struggle against hunger, and because of the universal sorrow over the sufferings and loss of children which makes celibacy desirable, which again often conduces to the *perversio vitae sexualis*. The comforts of life are denied and the world is given up to despair. The result is either flight from the world on the part of individuals or such ascetic discipline as promises victory over the world by inuring to pain and transiency. The discrediting of fundamental preconceptions necessitates a fresh rethinking of life and the world ; the contemplative, which favours asceticism, secures the right of way over the practical because of the apparent futility of effort. The despair or conviction of the badness of the phenomenal world projects the mind into the suprasensual, a projection which, where dualism is axiomatic, demands asceticism. The emotional excitements, ethical confusions, and failure of nerve in baffling crises furnish a fruitful occasion for the pathological outbreaks and fanaticism, which are the concomitants of asceticism, especially of the religious-mystical variety.

[1] Cf. Denis, *Idées morales*, II, pp. 204-5.
[2] Cf. Paul's discouragement of marriage 1 *Cor.* VII. 8, 40.

Men do not, with the even pulse of the day of comfort, gash themselves with knives, emaciate themselves with fasting, expose themselves to the rigours of a northern winter, or abandon wife and child for an ideal of life. In such crises, too, it is well known that religion is generally remade in its effort to overtake life and interpret the new situation. These revivals produce asceticism in milder or extremer forms according to the preconceptions of the age.

The Graeco-Roman world was no exception to these phenomena in the agonies of history. It is noteworthy that asceticism secured its first firm hold on Greece through the immense dislocations of the seventh and sixth centuries B.C., which made ' the Orphic life ' of renunciation for a time a veritable gospel.[1] Further, to Plato was due in no small degree the permanence of the ascetic movement, and this through his attempts to meet the bewildering challenges to authority and orthodoxy in his day. Still more in the Graeco-Roman period proper do we find the rapid growth of asceticism [2] from the second century B.C. to the fourth and fifth A.D. in the pagan Mysteries and Hellenistic philosophies, and in the Christian Church, evidenced in the increasing indifference to civic duties and desertion of social life, and decline of the birth-rate, so lamented by Polybius.[3] The republican wars of conquest, the subsequent civil wars, devastating earthquakes and frequent famines, the gradual extermination of the steadying middle class, the misery so universal (with the possible exception of the early Antonine era), new theories of holiness, deepening reflection, the brutality of individualism, the rapid vicissitudes of social life, atrocious systems of taxation, repeated political crises, the barbarian invasions of the empire, contributed to that world-weariness and pessimism which react to the extremes of self-indulgence or asceticism.

VI. The Craving for Salvation. The phrase of Seneca,

---

[1] In opposition to Cappelle, Miss Harrison, Kennedy, de la Saussaye, Gomperz, and others, Rohde contests this (*Psyche*, II, p. 125 f.).

[2] Cf Murray, *Four Stages*, p. 181 ; Bigg, *Church's Task*, p. 122.

[3] XXXVII. 9.

ad salutem spectat, might well characterize the attitude
of the Graeco-Roman world, especially about the dawn
of Christianity.[1]   The cry for salvation was loud, per-
sistent, and universal.   In a bewilderingly new age, when
venerable systems had collapsed, when the customs and
conventions that had regulated human intercourse were
rudely cast aside, when property was rapidly changing
ownership, when life was unsafe because of conspiracies and
jealousies, there arose in all hearts a longing for a more settled
state of affairs, for social stability and political permanency.
During such epochs of transition, when men are driven
out of their old ruts and compelled to fresh thinking,
the evil of the world and the ills that infest human life
become more intolerable ; the pain and sorrows of the
individual become more intense through the consciousness
of his isolation.   When the *nouveaux riches* rise to lord it
over families which for centuries had been cradled in the lap
of ease, when the man who was the ornament of society
to-day might to-morrow be on the way to the scaffold or to
an island place of banishment, when the " slings and arrows
of outrageous fortune " baffled the best, when parting with
friends added bitterness to death, when the heretofore
available and orthodox means of consolation failed, a cry
arose for deliverance from the present order of things, for a
Saviour.   Men sought deliverance from the uncertainties
of social life, the upheavals of political life, from the
burden of grief and sorrow, from the reign of death, the
universal power of demons and the malefic astral deities,
from the oppressive tyranny of fate, the caprice of *Sors,*
or *Fortuna,* the pollution of matter, the consciousness of
guilt, the wasting of disease, from the *taedium vitae,* and
from all the ills that " made human life a hell."   ' The
fulness of the times ' was marked about the beginning of our
era by a universal demand for salvation, by an *Erlösungs-
sehnsucht,* such as has perhaps never been equalled except

---

[1] " In the time of Augustus the feeling of guilt and longing for communion and renewal emerge prominently " (Wendland, *Am. Jour. Theo.*
'13, p. 346).

in the pre-Buddhistic India.[1]   Men began to call their gods
' Saviours,' or to add ' Saviour ' as a surname to such
deities as retained some authority, or to new deities that
had come into vogue—Zeus, Apollo, Aesculapius.   Living
rulers were lauded as gods who saved the race when the
gods of theology were asleep.   Thus, e.g., the Athenians
addressed Demetrius the Besieger as ' the only true god,'[2]
and Julius Caesar as ' their Saviour and Benefactor.'   The
same Caesar was spoken of by the cities of Asia Minor around
Ephesus as the ' god manifest, the common Saviour of
human life ' (48 B.C.)   An inscription of Halicarnassus[3]
terms Augustus σωτῆρα τοῦ κοινοῦ τῶν ἀνθρώπων γένους
(' Saviour of the universal human race '), and even Nero
is addressed, on an altarpiece of the year 67, as ' Nero,
God the Deliverer ('Ελευθερίῳ) for ever.'   Among all
classes and races this desire—now more articulate, now
less articulate—was felt.   Some looked for the means of
salvation in philosophy—those lofty souls of Stoicism and
Neo-Platonism.   The Hermeticists sought in revelation the
pathway to salvation by illumination and ' the beauty of
true religion and knowledge.'   Their spiritual kindred, the
Gnostics, were tireless in their speculations as to the
' Mediator and Redeemer.'   In the antiphonal ritual hymn,
preserved in the *Acts of John,* the candidate, probably in a
sacred dance of initiation, prays ' I would be saved,' to which
Christ, the initiator, responds ' And I would save.'   The ideal
wise man, by following whom the faithful Stoic would be led
into the larger liberty, was sought for with increasing earnestness.   But this ideal personage in flesh and blood was very
difficult to discover.   We even detect the note of despair :
' Where will you find him whom we have been seeking so
many ages ? ' asks Seneca.   Eclectics such as Cicero culled
from every accessible philosophy those elements which were
regarded as most healthful and helpful for the higher life.   The

---

[1] Cf. Rittelmeyer, art. *Erlöser* in *Relig. in Gesch. u. Gegenwart,* II, coll.
473 : cf. Anrich, p. 55.

[2] Athenaeus, *Deip.* VI. 62.

[3] Kenyon, *Gk. Inscr. in Brit. Museum,* No. 894.

Platonists continued their efforts to raise the soul above the pollution of the body, and by means of imitation of God and through love to bring it finally to its dear homeland in the Ideal, which was God. The masses sought salvation in the Mystery-Religions, which promised sacramental grace here and a blessed future. The Jew was expectantly awaiting the Messianic salvation.

All races of the empire were looking for some kind of deliverance from the present order—from finitude, sorrow, confusion, pain, and sin. They, however imperfectly, felt a need which was more clamant than they were conscious of. Salvation was conceived rather negatively as deliverance from ills than positively as communion with God : it was conceived in terms of the natural and material and even political. But there were higher aspirations which in no age dominate all classes but emerge in the hearts of the spiritually-minded who are prophetic of a better future and who focus in their experience the needs of their age. It was this sense of need and this desire for salvation that disposed men and women towards the Mystery-Religions, and that in the breakup of ancient society drove them into the Christian Church.

Ever more and more concrete and personal became these longings and premonitions of salvation. The conception of salvation developed into that of a Saviour just as Jewish Messianism evolved into the conception of a personal Messiah. If gods were to be esteemed by their deeds and power to influence humanity Alexander the Great would stand such a test. His personality made the impression of a superman or god. From this time onwards the vague Oriental God-man became increasingly necessary in a living religion and more human in his features. Whether Alexander,[1] or the Diadochian kings, or the emperor, or the deliverer from the terrors of superstition such as Epicurus,[2] or the

---

[1] Cf. Plut. *Alex.* 27 ; *Apophth. Alex.* 15.

[2] Epicurus was honoured by his disciples on the 20th of each month and on his birthday, and was hailed as *Lord* and *Saviour* (von Arnim, Pauly-Wissowa, *R.E.* VI. 135).

Righteous man [1] of Plato, or the Wise man [2] of the Stoics, or the Hermetic Revealer of Truth, That,[3] or the Gnostic Perfect Man, or the Hellenistic-Jewish Logos, a great mystic like Apollonius of Tyana, or the Jewish Messiah, or the resurrected god of the Mysteries, each form of the idea suggested a mediator, an epiphany of the divine, a redeemer from falsehood and finitude and death, a personage acquainted with our grief.[4]

The writer of the *Epistle to Titus* (III. 4) reflects the religious needs of his day and has emphasized the chief quality in the character of the God-man when he speaks of ' the kindness and *philanthropy* of God our Saviour,' the need of a humanized God—a stage in religious progress which the Mystery-Religions accelerated. Practical sympathy with men was demanded of God. " In the honorific inscriptions and in the writings of the learned *philanthropy* is by far the most prominent characteristic of the God upon earth." [5] By such activity Hercules had been enrolled among the immortals, and in the *Dream of Scipio*[6] the highest heaven was opened to service to one's country. Euhemerism knew no gods except such as in their incarnation had conspicuously assisted mankind. In a similar strain Pliny [7] asserts ' that mortal should assist mortal is to be a god ; this is the way to eternal glory.' Antipater [8] makes ' well doing ' (τὸ εὐποιητικὸν) an essential connotation of deity.

This demand for divine *philanthropy* facilitated the propaganda of the Mysteries with their humanized suffering gods. Serapis was to his worshipper φιλανθρωπότατος.[9] Isis was generous in bestowing ' a tender mother's affection on the ills of mortals.' Aesculapius was ' the great lover of men,'

---

[1] Cf. *Repub.* II. 362 A, where the Righteous Man ' will be scourged, tortured on the rack, bound, will have his eyes burned out, and finally, after enduring much suffering, he will be crucified ' (cf. Cicero, *De Repub.* III. 17).

[2] Cf. Hirzel, *Untersuchungen*, II, p. 273 ff.

[3] Cf. *Poim.* XIII (XIV).

[4] Cf. Plut. *De Def. Orac.* 415 A.   [7] *H.N.* II. 7, 18.

[5] Murray, *Four Stages*, p. 136.   [8] *Frag.* 33–4 (ref. Murray, p. 139).

[6] *Tusc. Disp.* I. 14, 32.   [9] Aristides, *Or. Sacr.* VIII 54.

the divine physician who heals because he loves,[1] whose cult could call forth the warmth of prayer preserved on an Attic stone of the second century A.D. :

' These are the words of thy loving servant, O Asklepios, child of Leto's Son. How shall I come into thy golden house, O blessed one, O God of my longing, unless thy heart is favourable to me and thou art willing to heal me and establish me again in thy shrine, that I may behold my God who is brighter than the earth in spring time ? Thou alone, O divine and blessed one, art mighty. Thee, that lovest compassion, the Supreme Gods have granted as a mighty boon to mortals, as a refuge from their sorrows.' [2]

VII. Yearning for Immortality. In the Graeco-Roman age, particularly in the Christian centuries, one of the religious symptoms was a profound craving for immortality,[3] the *appetit d'un monde meilleur*. The new inwardness of the religious spirit quickened the universal human interest for continuity of the personality. ' The hope of immortality, and the hope of existence, is the most venerable and mightiest of all affections,' says Plutarch,[4] who clung with avidity to the hope in the absence of all demonstration. This attitude of the serious minds of the ancient world finds exquisite expression in Virgil, the interpreter of his age :

' Tendebantque manus ripae ulterioris amore.'

The minds of men were engaged upon the problem of their future. With little faith but with much pathos Euripides clearly envisaged the situation :

> But if any far-off state there be
> Dearer than life to mortality,
> The hand of the Dark hath hold thereof,
> And mist is under the mist above ;

[1] Julian, *Ep.* 40.
[2] *C.I.A.* 3, 171. Farnell's tr. *Greek Hero-cults*, p. 277.
[3] Denis, II, p. 253 ff.
[4] τῆς ἀϊδιότητος ἐλπὶς καὶ ὁ πόθος τοῦ εἶναι πάντων ἐρώτων πρεσβύτατος ὢν καὶ μέγιστος. *Non posse suav.* 26. Cf. *De Sera Num. Vind.* 18.

> So we are sick for life, and cling
> On earth to this nameless and shining thing,
> For other life is a fountain sealed,
> And the deeps below are unrevealed,
> And we drift on legends for ever.'[1]

And in the same century the official memorial inscription[2] over those who fell at Potidaea could offer nothing better than ' the ether received their souls, the earth holds their bodies.' Some denied the possibility of continued existence after death, some treated it with ridicule, some left it an open question, but *all* were compelled by the circumstances of the age to consider the perennially interesting question of immortality. ' Which of these opinions is true, some god may know ; what is probable is the great question,' says Cicero of the nature of the soul, confessing *in his est enim aliqua obscuritas*.[3] Though there was much scepticism, much indifference, there was a yearning in most hearts for another life.[4] The religions of Greece and Rome offered little to satisfy this human longing. The gods of Greece differed from men in little except that, though not eternal, they were themselves immortal.[5] The *di immortales* of Rome were never considered by their worshippers as conferring immortality.

It is singular that the majority of the astral theologians, whose influence was so pervasive in later paganism, had little interest[6] in or even denied immortality. Though Posidonius[7] was an ardent believer in future felicity, and Seneca could look for a sidereal immortality[8] to satisfy the *in mentibus nostris insatiabilis quaedam cupiditas veri videndi*,

---

[1] *Hippolytus*, 191 ff., G. Murray's tr.

[2] *C.I.A.* 442 ; Kaibel, *Epig. gr.* 21.

[3] *Tusc. Disp.* I, 11, 23; 32, 78.

[4] " La destinée d'outre-tombe était alors la grande préoccupation," says Cumont (*R. Or.* 2nd ed. p. 327).

[5] Rohde, *Relig. d. Gr.* p. 322.

[6] " D'une façon générale, les espérances eschatologiques n'occupent aucune place chez les astrologues " (Cumont, *Acad. Royale de Belgique, Cl. d. Lettres*, '09, p. 275).

[7] Cumont, *ib.* p. 273.

[8] *Cons. ad Marciam*, 25 ; *Nat. Quaes.* prol. 17.

and Julian had bright hopes for the future, Vettius Valens was very hesitant (' if there is any retribution of good and evil after death ') [1] and the great Ptolemy [2] viewed himself merely as ' a mortal and creature of a day.' Generally, like Manilius and Ptolemy, they were content in directing their *sidereos oculos* to the shining heavens to be enraptured in cosmic ecstasy and to find the highest bliss in transporting communion with the celestials here, and in death to restore their souls, sparks of the cosmic fires, back to their eternal source without the conservation of individuality.

The mysteries of Orphism provided an alternative to the eternal process of the ' sorrowful weary wheel.' The hope was eagerly embraced by Plato and given a firm place in his philosophy. To him man is ' a heavenly plant and not of earth,' [3] the ' spectator of all time and all existence ' [4] with an innate knowledge of the heavenly patterns, who in self-examination [5] can adorn his soul, which is by nature immortal, [6] in her proper jewels so as to face any future, for ' fair is the prize, and the hope great, the venture glorious,' [7] not in a sensuous continuity of existence, [8] but in increasing godlikeness in a differentiated eternity. This great hope could never perish from the earth. The chief tenets of Plato's faith filtered down to the masses during the subsequent centuries. But Platonism could never be conceived as a popular religion : it was too high for the multitude. Contact with the East, the spread of Orphic doctrines which inspired the world-weary Virgil, the rise of Neo-Pythagoreanism, [9] the apparent worthlessness of life, the isolation of the soul, the development of self-consciousness and the dread of extinction, such projected the thoughts to another order of things in which the all too patent inequalities and injustices of life would be remedied, and men raised above pain and finitude. The worst sceptics and materialists were obliged to deal with the desire for immortality which they

---

[1] Ed. Kroll, p. 14.
[2] *Anth. Pal.* IX. 577.
[3] *Tim.* 90 A.
[4] *Repub.* II. 486 A.
[5] *Apol.* 38 A.

[6] *Phaedrus*, 245 C f.
[7] *Phaedo*, 114 C.D.
[8] *Repub.* II. 363 B.
[9] Dill, p. 501.

attempted to eradicate. Stoicism, with its lofty sense of duty and resignation to the will pervading the universe placed the scene of man's moral life in this world. Such a stern Stoic as Epictetus and so loveable a Stoic as Marcus Aurelius seem satisfied with this creed. But there was no message for the heart in a return to ' the dear and congenial elements.' [1] Other Stoics are divided between loyalty to their dogma and a hope for a better world. Thus Seneca, who oftener doubts than believes in immortality, writes to Lucilius characteristically for himself and for his age :

' I was pleasantly engaged in enquiry about the eternity of souls, or rather, I should say, in trusting. For I was ready to trust myself to the opinions of great men, who avow rather than prove so very acceptable a theory. I was surrendering myself to his great hope . . . when I was suddenly aroused by the receipt of your letter, and this beautiful dream vanished.' [2]

Writing to his mother Helvia to console her and himself on his exile he concludes, after referring to the advantages of the mind being free to consider its own faculties and contemplate nature and the gods : ' (animus) aeternitatis suae memor in omne quod fuit futurumque est vadit omnibus saeculis.' [3]

What the records of the age reveal is rather the prominence of the question of man's future and the insatiable yearning for an immortal life than any uniform or universal belief. Faith probed the deep mysteries of life and death. The best philosophic array of arguments for a life beyond the grave could only make this *bellum somnium* probable, while those philosophers who denied immortality, particularly the Stoics, Sceptics and Peripatetics, could by no arguments, however plausible, eradicate the instinct of man for a life which gave to human love and sorrow its full dignity

---

[1] Epict. III. 13.1 ; cf. I. 14.   [2] *Ep.* 102. 2.
[3] *Ad Helv.* 20 (' The soul mindful of its own eternity investigates all that has been and shall be throughout all ages ') ; cf. *Nat. Quaest. Praef.* 12 : [1] The soul has this argument of its divinity, that divine things delight it, nor does it address itself to such as irrelevant but as relevant.'

and meaning. Religion was content to believe in " that undiscovered country from whose bourne no traveller returns " as a working hypothesis. A Platonist like Plutarch [1] could say so finely : ' It is one and the same argument that establishes the providence of God and the persistence of the human soul : you cannot take away the one and leave the other.'

This desire for immortality turned men's minds to those Eastern religions which were pre-eminently religions of authority rather than reasoned theologies, and which, with the authority of immemorial antiquity, supported by the texts and liturgies of their scriptures, defended by an exclusive priesthood, asserted man's immortality and supplied sacraments of initiation by which mortals might become godlike or even gods. Plotinus, with his firm hold on the realities of the unseen, could on his deathbed at Pozzuoli declare to his friend Eustochius, ' I am striving to restore the Divine within us to the Divine in the All,' [2] but the ordinary man could contemplate the viewless things of death only in sacraments of a dying and resurrected god. These sacerdotal creeds did not renounce all attempts at proving their doctrine, but their proofs consisted rather in symbols, sacraments, and allegorical interpretations of their mythology, and in natural analogies. But the important thing was the certainty granted by the revelation on which the Mystery-Religions based themselves. It was only the religions of the East that could satisfy this instinctive yearning for immortality among the masses. Their doctrines constituted a veritable gospel to men who stood anxiously before the mysteries of the grave, as many of the mystery-believers testify.[3] Another Oriental religion emanating from Galilee was to announce a fuller and more satisfying gospel : ' This is the life eternal, to know Thee, the only true God, and Him whom Thou didst send, Jesus Christ.' It was the message of the Living Lord that gave men a new confidence " to sail beyond the sunset."

---

[1] *De Sera Num. Vind.* 18. [2] Porphyry, *Vita Plotini*, 2.
[3] Pages 139 ff., 238 ff.

CHAPTER VI

ULTIMATE FAILURE OF THE MYSTERY-RELIGIONS

Τίς ἐπιχεῖ τοὺς ἱεροὺς κυάθους τῆς πρὸς ἀλήθειαν εὐφροσύνης ὅτι μὴ ὁ οἰνοχόος τοῦ θεοῦ καὶ συμποσίαρχος Λόγος.—Philo, *De Somniis*, II, Cohn-Wendland, 249; M. I. 691.

SUCH a striking phenomenon as the rapid spread and persistence of the Mysteries can be accounted for only by their adaptation to the needs of the age. They offered to the masses and to many of the educated what neither Greek ethics nor Greek philosophy could give, something required by human nature but lacking in the state religions. If the Salvation Army, the Y.M.C.A. and the Masonic brotherhoods were to take away the prestige of the historic churches and ecclesiastical institutions of the English-speaking world and draw to themselves their membership, or if the deeply religious spirit of the Indian people, with their yearning through millennia to find God, were to gain predominance over Western Christendom, the result could not be more unexpected nor more revolutionary in the history of religion than was the victorious sweep of the Oriental religions over the ancient Mediterranean world.

The Mysteries conveyed an evangel to their age. Yet they failed. Another gospel, concerning a ' gibbeted sophist,' preached by unlettered and ignorant men and by learned and cultured men, proved God's power unto salvation ; it outstripped all its competitors, though it entered the Graeco-Roman world last in the race. They decreased ; Christianity increased. To-day the Vatican stands where the last sacrament of the Phrygian *taurobolium* was celebrated. Constantine is said to have been encouraged, at a critical time in his struggle with Maxentius before the battle of the Milvian bridge, by seeing at noonday in the sky a vision of a flaming cross bearing in Greek the inscription ' Conquer by this.' To the noble but misguided Julian ' the Apostate,' as he poured out his life-blood on the battle-field against Rome's inveterate enemies, the Persians, are attributed the words, ' Thou hast conquered, O Galilean.'

That the sacraments of the Mysteries were veritable means of grace to multitudes of initiates cannot be denied in view of the abundant testimony to the blessed issues of initiation. Neither ancient writers [1] nor modern investigators are agreed as to the religious value of the Mysteries. In estimating ancient testimony we should remember that religious abuses in every age attract more attention than the virtues of every-day life ; that the testimony of eye-witnesses and initiates deserves credence over that of outsiders ; that the ancient *mystae* observed their vows of secrecy with provoking fidelity ; that these believers have been mostly judged on the evidence of their most prejudiced and often ill-informed opponents, with their own lips sealed. We should remember too—what the church fathers sometimes forgot—that the many ancient Mysteries cannot be reduced to one common denominator, and that all, therefore, cannot be indiscriminately included under one sentence of commination.[2] Demosthenes knew better. There were Mysteries as lofty as the Eleusinia, while numerous private Mysteries by their charlatanry disgusted the religious pagans. While good and evil are mixed as they are in human life aberrations and inconsistencies on the part of professors of religion need not surprise. He that is without sin in his own religious creed may cast the first stone at the ancient worshipper. An Orphic verse, ' Many are the thyrsus-bearers, but few the *mystae*,' [3] shows that the Orphics, of the nobler side of whose system Plato had a high opinion,

---

[1] Lobeck, *Aglaophamus*, I. p. 67 f; Creuzer, *Symbolik*, p. 849 f. ; Hatch, p. 291 ; Farnell, *Cults*, III, p. 359.

[2] Farnell, *Cults*, III, p. 128.

[3] *Phaedo*, 69 C.

recognized the presence of hypocrites in their numbers.   The strolling mendicant *Orpheotelestae* gave Orphism a bad name, but its prevalence proves that it met a need in reference to the nascent sense of guilt.   In the *Republic* Plato scorns Musaeus (popular Orphism) for promising in the Mysteries 'eternal drunkenness as the fairest meed of virtue,'[1] and ridicules Musaeus and Orpheus for proclaiming absolutions and purifications through sacrifices and self-discipline to both living and dead.[2]   Plato would look upon the purveyors of Orphic charms in the same light in which a bishop would view John Wesley's itinerant and in many cases uneducated preachers in the eighteenth century.   Demosthenes[3] gives a vivid description of his opponent, Aeschines, assisting his mother, Glaucothea, in the nightly purifications of the Phrygian mysteries of Sabazios in which there appears an elaborate symbolism and ceremonial :

'When you grew to be a man, you used to read the scriptures and arrange other matters for your mother at initiations. By night you donned the fawn-skin, prepared and cleansed the candidates, wiping off the bran and clay, raising them up from the purifications with the password " I have shunned evil : I have found good," affecting a solemn air of secrecy that no one should publish such a watchword. . . . By day you conducted fine fraternities through the streets, crowned with fennel and poplar leaves, squeezing the broad, red-brown snakes and waving them over your head to the cry, *Euoi Saboi*, and dancing to *Hyes Attes*, *Attes Hyes*, while you were acclaimed by the old women as leader of the procession, chief, chest-carrier, sieve-carrier, and other such appellatives. You took in pay for these services sops and twisted loaves and fresh cakes.'

Not an edifying procedure, nor suggestive of anything uplifting : but Demosthenes' aim was twofold : to present the worst side so as to discredit his adversary, and to contrast favourably his own membership in a rival Mystery-church,

---

[1] *De Repub.* 363 C.D. [2] *Ib.* 364 E–365 A.
[3] *De Corona*, 259 f.

the Eleusinian.[1] Religious tastes vary. Roman poets frequently refer to the devotion of their *amatae* to the Mystery-cults,[2] though doubtless the chaste Paulinas were as numerous at the shrines. Livy [3] dwells on the scandals connected with the Dionysiac brotherhoods in Rome in 186 B.C., but he has, despite his bias, left in his narrative evidence of the better and more serious side of the Bacchanalia—the propagandist zeal of the *Graecus ignobilis sacrificulus et vates*, the *sacramentum* of initiation by which the candidates became ' soldiers ' of the deity with symbolic armour of their ' holy warfare,' the vow of secrecy, the ten days' fast, the baptism, prophecy, and the fidelity of the great majority. Besides, no one would fairly judge the early Christian Churches by the unlovely picture of 1 *Cor.* XI. The recently published decree [4] of Ptolemy Philopator, aiming at regulating private Dionysiac initiations throughout Egypt, might be cited against the Mysteries ; it is interesting as showing an Egyptian monarch called upon to deal with a psychopathic problem similar to that which the Corinthians submitted to Paul.

But ancient testimony is on the whole favourable as to the worth of the Mysteries, especially with reference to future beatitude. Pindar, a fervent Orphic, speaks thus [5] of the Mysteries :

> ὄλβιος ὅστις ἰδὼν ἐκεῖνα
> κοῖλαν εἶσιν ὑπὸ χθόνα.
> οἶδεν μὲν βιότου τελευτὰν
> οἶδεν δὲ διόσδοτον ἀρχάν.

Sophocles [6] :

' How thrice-blessed are they of mortals who, having

---

[1] Such is the obvious meaning of the words ἐτέλεις, ἐγὼ δ'ἐτελούμην of *ib.* 265 ; cf. Foucart, *Assoc. religieuses*, p. 68.

[2] Cf. Catullus, X. 26 ; Ovid, *Ars Amat.* I. 75 ff. ; Juvenal, VI. 511–52 ; Propertius, II. 33 ; Tibullus, I. 3, 33.

[3] XXXIX. 8.

[4] See Bibliography of Ancient Sources.

[5] *Threnoi*, frag. X. Bergk, 137 ; Boeckh, 102 ; Christ, 137 : ' Blessed is he who hath seen these things before he goeth beneath the earth ; for he understands the end of mortal life, and the beginning (of a new life) given of the gods ' (Sandy's tr.).

[6] Frag. 719 Dindorf, 348 Didot ; cf. *O.C.* 1050 ff.

beheld these mysteries, depart to the house of Death. For to such alone is life bestowed there : to the others fall all ills.' Cicero[1] affirms of the Greek Mysteries that, in addition to a civilizing influence[2] and a philosophy of the beginnings of life, ' we have received from them not only good cause why we should live with joy, but also why we should die with a better hope.' Plutarch, in his *Consolation to his Wife* (ch. x) on the death of their little Timoxena, comforts her with the faith in immortality learned through their becoming communicants in the Dionysiac Mysteries. The initiate of Sabazios cried in religious exaltation, ' I escaped evil, I found the good.' The *taurobolium* effected ' rebirth for eternity.' To the initiated Orphic dead the goddess of death declared ' a god thou shalt be instead of mortal.' On the tombs of the devotees of the Alexandrian cult might be inscribed, ' Be of good cheer,' or ' May Osiris give thee the water of refreshment.'

If it can be said with some truth that the Mysteries were more emphatic on immortality than on ethical demands it is also true that they were obliged to become increasingly ethical[3] in a practical bearing upon life. The orator Sopatros soberly claims, ' On account of initiation I shall be quite prepared for every moral demand.'[4] The exquisite ode in Aristophanes' *Frogs*[5] implies a moral life on earth as a qualification for the Happy Meadows : ' for to us alone

---

[1] Cf. *In Verrem*, V. 72, 187 ; *De Legg.* II. 14, 36 ; *N.D.* I. 42, 119.

[2] This claim is well substantiated in the famous Amphyctionic decree from the second century B.C. discovered at Delphi about twenty years ago, which declares of the Athenians :

> ὧν ὁ δῆμος ἁπάντων τῶν ἐν ἀνθρώποις ἀγαθῶν
> ἀρχηγὸς κατασταθείς, ἐγ μεν τοῦ θηριώδους βίου
> μετήγαγεν τοὺς ἀνθρώπους εἰς ἡμερότητα, παραίτιος
> δ' ἐγενήθη τῆς πρὸς ἀλλήλους κοινωνίας.

> *Bull. Cor. Hel.* 1900, p. 96.

[3] " The fifth century B.C. was ripe for that momentous development in religion whereby the conception of ritualistic purity becomes an ethical idea. . . . By the time of Aristophanes the Mysteries had come to make for righteousness in some degree " (Farnell, *Cults*, III. p. 191 f.). Cf. testimony of Diod. V. 49. 6.

[4] Walz, *Rhet. Graeci*, VIII. 114.

[5] 455 ff.

there is sun and cheerful light, who have been initiated and lived piously in regard to strangers and private individuals.' The stern moralist of Hierapolis sees in the Eleusinian sacraments a means of moral betterment : ' One should come, after purification, with sacrifices and prayer, possessed of the conviction that he is approaching sacred and venerable rites. Thus the Mysteries become edifying ; thus we attain the idea that they were established for discipline and for reformation of life.' [1] In a well-known passage of Diodorus [2] initiation in the rites of the Cabiri is claimed to issue in an increase of righteousness. Initiation fitted men to discharge more conscientiously their duties as jurymen.[3] ' Righteousness ' was a recognized attribute of Isis.[4]

Special mention should be made of some of the beautiful prayers addressed to the mystery-deities. Lucius addresses the following thanksgiving [5] to Isis on his initiation :

' O Thou holy and eternal Saviour of the human race, ever lavish in thy bounties to mortals of thy choice. Thou bestowest a sweet mother's affection upon the misfortunes of wretched men. Nor day nor night, nor even a moment of time passes which is not replete with thy benefits. By sea and land thou protectest men. Thou dispellest the storms of life and stretchest forth Thy right hand of salvation, by which Thou unravellest even the inextricably tangled web of Fate. Thou dost alleviate the tempests of Fortune and restrainest the harmful courses of the stars. Thee the heavenly ones worship and the gods infernal reverence. Thou turnest the earth in its orb ; Thou givest light to the sun ; Thou rulest the world ; Thou treadest Death underfoot. To Thee the stars are responsive ; by Thee the seasons return and the gods rejoice and the elements are in subjection. At Thy command the winds blow ; the clouds bestow their refreshing ; the seeds bud and the fruits increase. The birds that range the heaven, the beasts on the mountains, the serpents lurking in their den, the fish

[1] *Diss.* III. 21.
[2] V. 49.
[3] Andocides, *De Myst.* 31.
[4] Plut. *De Is. et Os.* 3 ; cf. Lafaye, p. 123.
[5] *Metam.* XI. 25.

that swim the sea, are awe-inspired by Thy majesty. But, as for me, I am too feeble to render Thee sufficient praise, and too poor in earthly possessions to offer Thee fitting sacrifices. I lack the eloquence to express what I feel about Thy majesty ; no, nor would a thousand lips, nor a thousand tongues, nor a perpetual uninterrupted prayer suffice. But, a pious though poor worshipper, I shall essay to do all within my power ; Thy divine countenance and most holy deity I shall guard and keep for ever hidden in the secret place of my heart.'

Compare also the prayer of invocation in the so-called *Liturgy of Mithra* [1] :

' O Lord, if it please thee, announce me to the greatest God, . . . I, a man, son of A. and born of the mortal womb of B. and of spermatic substance, that he to-day, having been born again by thee, out of so many myriads rendered immortal in this hour according to the good pleasure of God in his surpassing goodness, seeks to worship thee, and prays to thee to the utmost of his human powers,'

and the Hymn of Regeneration in the same liturgy [2] :

' Lord, hail, potentate of the water, hail, ruler of the earth, hail, potentate of the spirit. . . . Lord, having been regenerated, I depart in exaltation, and having been exalted I die. Born of that life-producing birth and delivered unto death I go the way, as thou hast established, as thou hast decreed, as thou hast created the sacrament.'

In the Hermetic literature [3] Tat learns from his father Hermes the Hymn of Praise for the Regenerate :

' By Thy blessing my spirit is illumined. . . . In the spirit, O Father, what I see I utter. To Thee, O God, author of my birth, I, Tat, offer spiritual sacrifices. O God and Father, Thou art the Lord, Thou art the Spirit. Accept from me the spiritual sacrifices which Thou desirest, for of Thy will is all accomplished,'

---

[1] Dieterich, *Eine Mithrasliturgie*, 2nd ed. p. 10, l. 34 ff.

[2] *Ib.* p. 14, l. 27 ff.

[3] *Poim.* XIII. 21,22, Reitzenstein, pp. 347 f. ; cf. Kennedy's tr., *St. Paul and the Mystery-Religions*, pp. 108–9.

the answer to which prayer presented 'through the Logos' is 'Thou hast come to a spiritual knowledge of thyself and of our Father.'

At the close of the *Poimandres* the Hermetic believer gives thanks for the *Gnosis* of salvation revealed to him by Poimandres :

'This happened to me as I received from the Spirit, that is, from Poimandres, the Word (Logos) of Authority. I became inspired of God and arrived at the Circle of Truth. Wherefore, with my soul and all my strength I give thanks to the Father, God :

> Holy is God, the Father of all the universe ;
> Holy is God, whose Will is accomplished by its own energies ;
> Holy is God, who wills to be known and is known of His own ;
> Holy art Thou, of whom all Nature was made an image ;
> Holy art Thou, whom Nature did not form ;
> Holy art Thou, more potent than all power ;
> Holy art Thou, transcending all excellence ;
> Holy art Thou, who surpassest all praises ;

Accept reasonable holy offerings from soul and heart directed toward Thee, O Thou Ineffable, Unutterable, who art named only in silence. Grant to my prayer that I may not miss the knowledge in conformity with our true being ; strengthen me, fill me with such grace that I may enlighten those of my race who are in darkness, my brothers, thy sons.' [1]

The following remarkable thanksgiving prayer [2] of an initiate of the Hermetic revelation-literature, from the *Perfect Word*, will give some idea of the religious enthusiasm which the Mysteries could awaken.

'We give thee thanks, O Most High, for by thy grace we

---

[1] Cf. also Mead's tr. *Thrice-greatest Hermes*, II, p. 19 f. ; Germ. tr. by Jacoby, p. 31 f.

[2] Greek text, discovered by Reitzenstein in the magical papyrus Mimaut of the third century A.D., will be found in his *Hell. Mysterienrel.* 2, pp. 136-7 ; cf. *Archv f. Religionswis* VII ('04) pp. 393-7. The Latin version, somewhat feeble, of the prayer is given in the *Asclepius*, 41. Cf. Mead's Eng. tr. II, p. 389 f. ; Germ. tr. in Jacoby, p. 35, and a partial Eng. tr., Kennedy, p. 109 f.

obtained this light of knowledge, Name ineffable, honoured in addressing thee as God and blessed in the invocation of thee as Father, because thou didst reveal to all men and women a father's piety and love and affection and thy most benign working. Thou hast bestowed upon us feeling and reason and knowledge—feeling that we may apprehend thee, reason that we may reflect upon thee, knowledge that by the knowledge of thee we may be glad. Saved by thee, we rejoice that thou didst show thyself to us completely : we rejoice that even in our mortal bodies thou didst deify us by the vision of thyself. Man's sole thanksgiving to thee is to know thy majesty. We have come to know thee, O thou Light perceptible alone to our feeling ; we have come to know thee, thou Light of the life of man ; we have come to know thee, thou fruitful Womb of all ; we have come to know thee, thou eternal Principle of that which brings forth by the Father's agency. Thus having worshipped thee we have requested no favour from thy goodness, but grant to our entreaty that we may be preserved in thy Knowledge so that we may not fail to attain to this kind of life.'

The power of the Mysteries and their popularity in the early Christian centuries are eloquently attested by strenuous opposition of Christian apologists from Paul to Justin Martyr, and from Tertullian to Augustine. The Mysteries were the last redoubts of paganism to fall.[1] Prior to that their adherents were the educators of the ancient world for a religion which at an early stage departed from the immediacy of Jesus' religion to become strongly sacramentarian. Just because of their similarities (due to demonic inspiration, according to Christian writers) to the central rites of the new faith the Mysteries formed the chief point of attack to Clement of Alexandria, Origen, Firmicus Maternus, Arnobius, Epiphanius, Hippolytus, and other

[1] " They were the embodiment of the whole syncretistic movement, in which nearly all who felt religious needs could find what they wanted . . . in them genuine religion sheltered itself under the forms of paganism " (Inge, *Plotinus*, I, p. 56). "The Eleusinian Mysteries conducted the forlorn hope of Graeco-Roman paganism against the new religion " (Farnell, *Cults*, III, p. 127).

244 THE DEFECTS OF THE MYSTERIES

fathers. It is also noteworthy that the pagan apologists, e.g. Porphyry and Iamblichus, were as sensitive on the question of their sacraments as were their opponents.

There exists considerable diversity of opinion among recent investigators as to the ethical and religious value of the Mysteries. Such scholars as Rohde,[1] Ramsay,[2] and Farnell[3] incline to a deprecatory opinion of the ancient Mysteries. Others, like Glover,[4] Lake,[5] Legge,[6] seem to adopt a neutral or hesitating position, while the great majority hold to a favourable estimate, e.g. Gruppe,[7] Cumont,[8] Kennedy,[9] Anrich,[10] Wobbermin,[11] Dill,[12] Loisy,[13] Jevons,[14] Vollers,[15] Bigg,[16] and Inge.[17] There are the usual extremists—those who maintain that the Oriental cults compare favourably with Christianity, and that Christianity borrowed lavishly from its competitors, and those who would exalt Christianity by decrying everything outside it. Most writers now recognize that the Mysteries had offensive and unwholesome features together with much that exalted man above the limits of ordinary life and its sin and pain and parting. Had they been so intrinsically

[1] *Psyche*, II, p. 293 ff.
[2] Hastings, *D.B.* extra vol. p. 126 a ; but cf. *C. and B.* I, p. 92 f.
[3] E.g. *Higher Aspects*, p. 141 ; *Cults*, III, p. 191.
[4] *Progress*, pp. 320, 323-30.
[5] *Earlier Epp.* 2nd ed. p. 39 f.; *Stewardship*, p. 71 : " they were genuinely religious " but " on the ethical side they were weak."
[6] I, pp. 22, 81 ff., 145 f.
[7] *Gr. Myth.*
[8] *Rel. Or.* 2nd ed. pp. XXV. 43.
[9] *St. Paul*, p. 84.
[10] P. 47 ff.
[11] *Religionsgesch. St.* p. 35 ff.
[12] *Rom. Soc.* 554 f., 569 ff., 581 ff., 623 ff
[13] *Les Mystères païens*, pp. 25-206.
[14] *Introd.* p. 376.
[15] In *Die Weltreligionen*.
[16] *Church's Task*, pp. 45, 53.
[17] *Plotinus*, I, p. 56 ; *Christian Mysticism*, p. 351 : " The evidence is strong that the Mysteries had a real spiritualizing and moralizing influence on large numbers of those who were initiated, and that this influence was increasing under the early empire." For further favourable views cf. also Brückner, Cappelle, Harrison, Lafaye (p. 167 ff.) ; C. H. Moore, *Religious Thought*, p. 291 f.

bad as some assert it is difficult to account for their wonderful success as missionary religions. They lent themselves too easily to externalism by an exaggerated importance of ritual ; they awakened a religious exaltation such as has rarely appeared in religious history, but with which ethical considerations were not of primary interest ; they confused the physical symbol and the religious experience. But they succeeded in an aggressively religious and serious age, which proves that they were able in some degree to satisfy religious longings. Their adherents were doughty propagandists who believed that they had found the truth and therefore spoke. The Mysteries were a curious blend of higher and lower elements, sensuousness and spirituality, sensuality and asceticism, magic and prayer, remnants of naturalism and symbolic mysticism, deafening music and silent contemplation, brilliant lights and deepest darkness. In estimating these cults we must weigh their merits as well as their defects, but we must also finally adjudicate upon them, as we would upon Christianity, by their *ideals*. " The Mysteries," says Professor Gardner, [1] " had a better aspect in that they taught of deliverance from impurity and of a life beyond the tomb, and a worse aspect, in that they opened the way to superstition, to materialism and to magic." " There were elements in some of them from which Christianity recoiled and against which the Christian apologists use the language of strong invective. But, on the other hand, the majority of them had the same aims as Christianity itself—the aim of worshipping a pure God, the aim of living a pure life, the aim of cultivating the spirit of brotherhood. They were part of a great religious revival which distinguishes the age " is the verdict of Dr. Hatch.[2]

These views of Gardner and Hatch are on the whole fair estimates which do justice to the Mysteries and their appeal to bygone centuries. They were evangels which gladdened men's heart, which brought joy and comfort in men's

---

[1] *Ephesian Gospel*, p. 15 ; cf. id. *St. Paul*, p. 63.
[2] *Influence of Greek Ideas*, p. 291 f.

struggle, and which gave to life a new dignity by asserting the principle of private choice in religious matters, with the worth of the individual, and a moral nexus between life here and life beyond.

Yet they failed and the religion of Jesus triumphed. Orphism, which introduced into Greek religion a note that resounded for at least twelve centuries and which by its syncretistic penetration left its mark upon so many other faiths, disappeared. Isis, the mother of tenderness, the goddess ' of a thousand names,' commenced her victorious career in the Greek world in the Peiraeus[1] in the fourth century B.C. and ended it in A.D. 391, when Theophilus and his iconoclasts demolished the Serapeum of Alexandria and destroyed Bryaxis' venerated statue of Serapis. The Great Mother of Pessinus, the first successful Oriental invader of the state religion of Rome, after winning the adoration of the West for eight hundred years, during six hundred of which she had a temple on the Palatine, lost her power. The Syrian goddess (Dea Syria, Atargatis) and her accompanying Baals, in spite of lending themselves so readily to that solar monotheism which became a conspicuous phase of later paganism and their adoption by Nero, Heliogabalus, and Aurelian, never appealed to the sympathies of the ancient world as did the Great Mother and Isis. They perished, though they left more magnificent ruins than their competitors, who strove to supply a universal religion co-extensive with the imperial sway. *Mithras Invictus,* the god of soldiers, though identified with the *Unconquered Sun* lost his sceptre after a reign in the West of over four centuries. The Hermetic religion of Revelation and Regeneration was too akin to occultism and pitched its demands too high for the masses.

It is all too easy to lay bare the fundamental blemishes

[1] Foucart, *Assoc. Relig.* p. 83 ; Lafaye, *Culte de Div. Alex.* p. 31. We have of course important archaeological evidence of a religious contact of Egypt with Greece centuries before this. An Egyptian figure of Isis together with Egyptian scarabs was discovered in 1898 in the cemetery of Eleusis (Skias, 'Εφ. 'Αρχ., '98, p. 108 ff.). Cf. also Miss Davis, *Asiatic Dionysus,* p. 226 ff.

of the Oriental cults and the reasons of their ultimate failure. They won their conquests partly by material and partly by spiritual weapons. They too often catered to, rather than countered, vulgar tastes. Elements of a dangerous character to unspiritual minds were imbedded in their ritual. The main defects conducing to their decadence and rendering them incapable of permanently satisfying the religious instinct were :

I. They were freighted with myths of primitive naturalism :

" All go back to a distant era of barbarism and have inherited from this savage past a multitude of myths, the offensiveness of which might be dissimulated, but not suppressed, by a philosophical symbolism, and of practices of which all the mystic interpretations could but ill conceal the fundamental crassness, the survival of a rude nature-worship." [1]

Nothing testifies more emphatically to the deadness of state religions in the Graeco-Roman world than the distaste for the sobriety and respectability of these and the emergence of hitherto suppressed superstitions which allied themselves with foreign nature-religions. This atavism to primitive naturalism was a feature of the religious life of the Hellenistic-Roman era.[2] The Oriental cults attempted to cast off what was repulsive in order to win the West and conform to the deepening moral conscience, but they retained enough of their past to disqualify them for the present. The cult-legends dating from a non-moral antiquity were explained as symbols of the life of man and of the deity. Such myths might to the pure-minded become symbols of spiritual truth which in its richness often defies articulate expression and comes in image before idea; but to the majority they were apt to be suggestive of evil. Religious processions in which the *membra virilia* were exhibited could hardly conduce to either reverence or morality. The world

[1] Cumont, *Rel. Or.* 2nd ed. pp. 107–8.
[2] Gardner, *Eph. Gosp.* p. 13 f.

had outgrown phallism.[1] Magical formulae, often a meaningless babble, unintelligible to *idiotae* and probably only vaguely intelligible to the initiate, were ingredients of their prayers. Much of the ritual was savage and bloody, requiring extremes of asceticism or degenerating into lubricity. Many were disgusted at beholding the processions along the streets in which self-emasculated priests held the place of honour, in which men in corybantic fashion raved and gashed their flesh with knives until their garments were stained with blood. Seneca, though himself an ascetic, speaks with scorn of these practices. The impressive sacrament of the *taurobolium* was offensively bloody, and carried along with its spiritual symbolism memories of a savage past. Though these Mysteries made a serious effort to keep pace with the needs of every age, they were burdened with an excessive conservatism which contributed to their decadence and thus bequeathed to Christianity an instructive object-lesson. They introduced daring innovations to enhance their attractiveness ; they borrowed from each other in cult and ritual ; they adopted new religious ideas or gave expression to such ideas as were in the air, so that each showed in its vocabulary the same great religious terms —baptism, regeneration, identification with the deity, ecstasy, theophanies, cathartic, salvation, immortality. Yet in this wonderful progression they never succeeded in superseding their original naturalism. Even the less crude forms of Mystery-Religion did not escape the admixture of spiritual and physical, e.g. Gnosticism and the religion of the Hermetic Literature. It astonishes one to read in the *Liturgy of Mithra*, probably based upon Hermetic [2] religion, beautiful prayers interlarded with directions as to the proper breathing, shouting, gesticulation, etc. Evidently in these more enlightened systems there was a physical attitude in prayer as well as a spiritual.

[1] Cf. Gruppe, *Gr. Myth.* I, pp. 886, 1329; Herod. II. 48.
[2] *Per contra* Reitzenstein, who explains it as a strongly hellenized redaction of Iranian ideas under Egyptian influence (*N. Jahrb. f. d. Kl. Alt.* '04, XIII, p. 192 ; *Hell. Myst.-Relig.* 2nd ed. p. 97).

The Mysteries seem to corroborate the unpleasant truism that where ritual abounds the spiritual vision is oftener marred than quickened. The simple publican goes to his house justified when the scrupulous Pharisee has only deceived himself. The Greeks and Romans built their most beautiful temples when the spirit of their city-state religion had departed. If gorgeous ritual, impressive cere-monial, aesthetic cult, artistic edifices, and images, and a costly priesthood could save a religion these Mystery-Religions would have succeeded, especially those of the Great Mother, and Isis, and the Unconquered Sun.

II. The Mystery-Religions linked themselves with a pseudo-science, Astrology, and with a pseudo-religion, Magic, which contributed to their popularity for a time but under-mined their spirituality by fostering debilitating credulity and imposing terror in religion, and rendering them unequal in the contest with Christianity. Magic, " the bastard sister of religion," was the most dangerous ally.

Egyptians, Syrians, Greeks, Samaritans, Romans, Jews, all practised this black art, which was as universally believed in and feared as in the Middle Ages or in the sixteenth century. Oriental priests were regarded as specialists in the art : for long the temples of the Euphrates and later of Egypt retained practically a monopoly of this supernatural science. The burning of the valuable collection of works at Ephesus as a result of Paul's preaching is one evidence of the preval-ence of this belief in Asia Minor. Magic was one of the most lucrative trades of that age ; it flourished in spite of stringent police regulations and punishments far more drastic than those attached to the practice of astrology. Simon Magus offered the apostles a large sum to secure the *pneumatic* endowments of early Christianity, in the belief that he would recoup himself richly in the increased revenue from the practice of exorcism and kindred arts.

Strange to say, the Jews—the most successful mediators between East and West—became adepts in this illicit form of religion, for whatever reasons—their desire for gain, their propagandist zeal to outbid pagan religions in what were regarded as demonstrations of power, as later the Christian exorcists essayed to outbid Jewish and pagan competitors ; their syncretistic capacities, while retaining their own essential character ; the antiquity of their religion, and its prominence among Oriental religions ; the unique eminence of Jahweh, due to an uncompromising monotheism which permitted no goddess nor son nor satellite deities to detract from his grandeur. No deity ranked so high or is found so often in magical incantations as ' Jahweh ' in many corrupt forms ; also as 'the God of Abraham,' ' the God of Isaac,' ' the God of Jacob.' The Jews were noted for their ability to interpret dreams, to extract the power of enchantments, and to manufacture love-potions, which were in enormous demand. Some of those who burned their books of incantations in Ephesus were Jews : Elymas and the sons of Sceva are represented by Luke as Jewish sorcerers. The Jews enjoyed a unique reputation as exorcists throughout the empire.[1]

The magic that prevailed was not the primitive and enchoric sorcery of Greek and Roman superstition, but the professedly scientific semi-religious magic which had been cultivated for millennia on the Euphrates and in the East.[2] The West had as little faith in its magic as in its state religion. Hence the Mediterranean world was invaded by a trinity of Oriental religions or quasi-religious forces which in their alliance threatened to sweep all before them—the Mysteries, Astrology, and Magic. The Mystery-Religions stooped to magical practices because of their unspiritual conception of the deity and the relation of man to God ; the magicians, mostly of Oriental provenance, resorted to the liturgies and religious formulae and divine names of the Mysteries and of Judaism because these were of more august authority than the Western religions. Magic was also in demand as the means of redemption from the omnipresent dualism of the age, which made earth and heaven a scene of

---

[1] Harnack, *Mis. and Exp.* I, p. 156 f.

[2] Cf. Cumont, *Rel. orient.*, Eng. tr. p. 186 ; *Astrology*, p. 74 ; Wendland, *Hell.-Röm. Kultur*, p. 81 ; Maury, *Hist. des Religions*, III, p. 255 ff.

struggle between demonic powers : it became one of the chief weapons in the religious apparatus of that day to deal with the influence of demons. Astrology shackled the ancient world in determinism, from the burdens of which men sought escape in the Mysteries and in magic. In this way the Mystery-Religions sought to provide a way of escape from the capricious acts of fortune, from the unbridled will of demons, and from the oppressive sense of fatalism concomitant with Astralism. Astrology also vindicated its right to member-ship in this Oriental group by directing attention to the heavenly regions of light, in which, among the seven planets (Sun, Moon, Mercury, Saturn, Jupiter, Mars, Venus), the Sun occupied a position of hegemony as the source of light and life. In this way the germs of sun-worship, or at least a marked reverence for the sun, which were present in the religions of Greek and Rome, developed under Oriental teaching into that solar monotheism in which declining paganism sought to give expression to the religious instincts of monotheism. On this tendency of the age, as on so many others, the Oriental cults fastened ; they brought them-selves into line with it, and promoted it as advantageous to their propaganda. The West, while it fell under the spell of astrology, also produced a considerable reaction upon it. Coming in contact with the Greek science of mathematics, astrology began to assume the character of astronomy, and this contact reacted upon both religion and its congener, magic. On religion—

" The effect was much the same as that produced by the discoveries of Copernicus in the sixteenth century and those of Darwin in the nineteenth. Every religion of the Graeco-Roman world which sought the popular favour after the discoveries of Hipparchus took note of the seven planetary spheres which the geocentric theory of the universe supposed to surround the earth, and even those known before his time, like Zoroastrianism and Judaism, hastened to adopt the same view of the universe and to modify the details of their teaching to accord with it." [1]

E.g. the acceptance of the seven stoles of Isis, the seven-

1 Legge, I, p. 117.

252 THE DEFECTS OF THE MYSTERIES

stepped ladder and seven altars of the Mithraic Mysteries, the seven Amshaspands of the Avestas, and the seven days of the Jewish week. On magic—

"The sevenfold division of things which implied that each planet had its own special metal, precious stone, animal and plant, placed at the disposal of the magicians an entirely new mode of compulsion which lent itself to endless combinations; while for the same reason special conjuratives were supposed only to exercise their full influence under certain positions of the stars." [1]

When we consider the powerful and popular combination of the Mysteries, Astrology, and Magic, we realize more vividly the word of St. Paul : ' for we have to struggle, not with blood and flesh, but with the angelic Rulers, the angelic Authorities, the potentates of the dark present, the spirit forces of evil in the heavenly sphere,' [2] also how his triumphant ' I am persuaded that neither the Powers, nor the Ascension of the stars nor their Declinations shall be able to separate us from the love of God in Christ Jesus our Lord' was a gospel which awakened fervent hallelujahs from many a heart. An early apologist [3] declared of Christians, ' We are above Fate. Instead of wandering demons, we have come to the knowledge of one Lord who wanders not.' Christianity alone set its face against astrology. [4] It dared to take the unpopular course, but astrology yielded long before magic, with which the sacramentalism of early Christianity kept too close company, so deviating from the conception of Jesus. The ideas of magical efficacy were deeply rooted in paganism : when pagans began to rush into the Christian Church because her success seemed assured, or because of the superiority of her Redeemer over demonic potentates, they brought with them magical or quasi-magical conceptions which have infected Christian theology and worship. But if Christianity did not come unscathed out of the conflict with magic it rendered the ancient world

[1] Legge, I, pp. 117–18.   [2] Moffatt's tr.
[3] Tatian, *Ad Graecos*, 9 (with play on πλανητῶν) ; cf. also 4, ' The sun and moon were made for us ; how am I to worship what are my servitors ? ' and 10.   [4] Cf. Cumont, *Astrology and Religion*, p. 167.

the immense service of extracting the terrors of the magic
art and of pointing men to a purely spiritual conception of
their relation to the deity : ' God is Spirit, and His worshippers must worship Him in spirit and in truth.' Christianity's
competitors and forerunners took the popular side and
participated in the magical practices of their day. In fact,
the Oriental cults tended to elevate the position of the
magician and to put at his control more efficient weapons.
The result was the same as if Paul had encouraged the desire
for those ecstatic psychopathic phenomena so prized in
Corinth rather than for the experience of a resident Spirit
which made for holiness ; or as if our Lord had congratulated
the disciples who returned flushed with the success of their
exorcisms rather than ' rejoice not in this that the demons
submit to you ; but rejoice because your names have been
written in the heavens ' (*Luke*, X. 20).

Every living religion must take into account the spirit of
the age ; it must interpret the *Zeitgeist*. But a living religion
must not conform to, but transform, the spirit of the age.
Herein Christianity succeeded—not absolutely—far beyond
her rivals that offered too generous terms to prevalent
conceptions and practices. Astrology by its tyrannous
fatalism drove men to magic to combat through the theory
of universal sympathy the baneful influence of the astral
deities, while magic drove men to the Mystery-Religions.
If we could adequately imagine the incubus of astrology
upon, and the constant nightmare of magic to, the Graeco-
Roman age we could better understand the success of the
Mystery-Religions and the appeal of Christianity as *par
excellence* the religion of redemption. But " we probably
realize very inadequately the pernicious effects of astrology
and magic in the last age of pagan antiquity. These
superstitions were all-pervading, and, except for accidentally
stimulating interest in the heavenly bodies, and to a less
extent in physics, they did unmitigated harm." [1] Magic

[1] Inge, *Phil. of Plotinus*, I, p. 50. " We have never been thoroughly
frightened ; the ancient world was frightened : there is the great difference " (Bevan, *Hellenism and Christianity*, p. 81).

did not do its evil work only in the grossest forms, necromancy and the mixing of poison potions and such-like.[1] In relation to religion it did its most harmful work by driving men to religion for ulterior and questionable purposes : they came for the loaves and fishes ; for theurgy and exorcism ; to secure a love conquest or to discover a guilty party ; to see signs and miracles, even to find means of compassing the death of enemies.[2] But magic as a debased form of religion rests upon " the notion that it is possible, instead of propitiating, to compel the spiritual powers." [3] The chief means of accomplishing this is *Gnosis*, or exact knowledge of their proper name, correct formulae and their authoritatively prescribed mode of approach.   This belief gave rise to an esoteric doctrine, or *Disciplina arcani*, restricting the full benefit of the religion to a secret society of initiates, whose knowledge of the deity and his ways cannot be divulged in detail to outsiders.   The usages of the religion became a monopoly of a favoured few who possessed the keys of the kingdom of heaven.

Philosophy must probably pitch its note too high for the masses, but a religion which seeks to become universal by meeting the needs of man must make its redemptive message intelligible to the wayfaring men.   In addition to driving men to religion from ulterior motives the magical conception in any form conduces to formality and externalism.   Prayer, instead of being a communion of the soul with God, degenerates into incantation and intonation independent of the inner condition of the worshipper.   Sacraments, instead of being means of grace conditioned wholly by the spiritual receptivity of the participants, become virtuous in their own right, their efficacy resting upon an *opus operatum*.

It must not be understood that the Mysteries were forms of magic rather than religions of propitiation and redemption,

[1] Cf. Miss MacDonald, *Inscriptions Rel. to Sorcery in Cyprus* (in *Proc. Soc. Bib. Arch.* '90-'91, 160 ff.).

[2] Tacitus narrates that the death of Germanicus was attributed to *carmina et devotiones* and the inscription of his name upon magic lead tablets found on the premises (*Ann.* II. 69 ; cf. Dio Cassius, LVII. 18).

[3] Legge, I, p. 90.

but they linked their fortunes for good and evil with their Oriental sisters, Astrology and especially with Magic. The only appeal of any religion is ultimately its spiritual message ; but association with magic undermined the spiritual power of the Mysteries. " Those [pagan] Mysteries were never able completely to sever themselves from magic ; that is, the *mystae* usually attached a mysterious efficacy to the mere act of partaking, apart from the motion of will and heart which really gave it the possibility of being efficacious." [1] The first Gospel informs us that Magi came from the East to announce the birth of the Messiah and to do obeisance—a prophetic text. Tertullian, referring to the same Magi 'having received a dream oracle returned homeward by another way,' sees in it an allegory ' that they should no longer walk in their old way.' [2]

The Jews, as above mentioned, excelled in syncretistic magic, and particularly in exorcism. This would be a matter of individual taste and enterprise. But the religion of Judaism was by no means free from the magical element. This may be seen in its excessive ceremonialism and meticulous observances of customs and traditions possessing no intrinsic value. To the outsider salvation was offered only by entrance through the gate of circumcision into Mosaism. Not merely a hygienic but a religious significance was attached to washing before meals. Certain foods were taboo regardless of the truth now so self-evident that it is not what enters into a man that defiles him. Prayer in the posture towards Jerusalem or at prescribed hours was supposed to have a right of way to the ears of the Eternal. Ideas such as the supposed defilement from contact with the dead, from eating with those outside the covenant, from partaking of food offered to idols, rest ultimately on a magical basis. When Paul entered the lists

[1] Gardner, *Eph. Gosp.* pp. 206–7 : cf. *Religious Experiences of St. Paul,* p. 67 f: " As the best points in the Mysteries were absorbed by Christianity, so the worst were absorbed by magic—magic, which always appears as the dark shadow cast by religion, and which takes the place of religion in the view of those who have not in them the seed of religious growth."
[2] *De Idol.* 9.

on behalf of a religion of the free spirit as against the cult of legalism he was really opposing magic in religion.

It will increase our sympathy with the Mysteries if we not only avoid the historical blunder of identifying them with magic, but also if we do not unfairly charge them with the many abuses to which magicians converted their liturgies and debased their theological conceptions. It was faith in the potency of the ' name ' of the Mystery-god that dictated these aberrations. Magic laid hold also of Jewish and Christian formulae and holy names. We shall more readily understand the apparent unspirituality of the Mysteries when we recall how easily magic found entry into Christianity, what havoc it wrought through centuries, and with what difficulty it was extruded.[1] The typical ecclesiastic, Cyprian, stands not far apart from any Mystery-priest when he seriously chronicles stories of the deadly efficacy of the elements of the Supper both upon a little girl who had not reached years of moral discrimination and upon adults. One woman who surreptitiously took the elements ' received not food, but a sword,' causing internal convulsions. A guilty man found that the elements received from the priest turned into cinders in his hand.[2] The sober Gregory of Nyssa relates how his namesake, the Thaumaturgus, spent a night in a pagan temple, which resulted in the flight of the gods, much to the discomfiture of the priest, who heaped execrations on Gregory's head until the latter in pity wrote him a parchment ' Gregory to Satan : Enter,' which, when laid upon the altar, immediately attracted back the demons. Novatian discovered a sure prevention against departure from his teachings by making his followers swear ' by the body and blood of our Saviour, Jesus Christ, that you will never forsake me nor return to Cornelius.'

These few examples, out of scores, give some idea of the

---

[1] Richard Baxter declared in the seventeenth century, " A man must be a very obdurate Sadducee who would not believe in it," and as late as 1760 to John Wesley " Giving up witchcraft is in effect giving up the Bible."

[2] *De Lapsis*, 25–26 ; cf. refs. in Bigg, *Church's Task*, p. 83 f., who remarks, " The church-ale was so like the heathen festival that it was really the same thing, though a little better at every point."

forces which Christianity ultimately overcame, but with which the Mysteries made a questionable truce.

III. Another weighty cause of the ultimate failure of the Mystery-Religions was that they represented an extreme type of religion which did not hold the social and the religious instincts of man in equipoise. An extreme movement sooner or later inevitably produces a reaction. The sanity of mankind is permanently attempting to find the equilibrium of the human faculties and aspirations. Each era is sure to discover the " too-much " or the " too-little " of the preceding, wherein lay its weakness and its warning.

There are two [1] clearly marked types of religion, (*a*) the social-ethical, or political, and (*b*) the individualistic-mystic, or personal type. The former might be designated (in Hegel's phrase) religions of utility, and the latter religions of redemption. The one type looks to the welfare of the community, and stresses social duty ; the other stresses the salvation of the individual soul. The one seeks a brotherhood in a particular combination of men such as tribe, clan, race, or nation ; the other aspires to identification with or absorption into the deity. In the political type the nation or clan is the religious unit, for whose prosperity primarily the rites of the religion are practised ; in the personal type the individual is the religious unit. The one type goes " the trivial round " of common life, the other seeks to enjoy the Vision Beatific.

These two types appear prominently in the Graeco-Roman period. The political type is represented in its strength and in its weakness by the city-state religions of Greece and Rome, and in its strength by the religion of Israel. The personal type is represented by the Mystery-Religions and the Greek moral philosophies. In the Mysteries the main bond was that of fellowship in the same patron deity. Into the one men entered by birth, religion being as hereditary as citizenship ; into the other men entered of their own volition through initiation, or rebirth.

[1] Glover recognizes three great stages in religious thought: Magic, Morality, and Personal Relation (*Progress*, p. 15).

The one found its sphere in a given corporate unity ; the other in private and voluntary association distinct from the state and trans-social.

The historical movement of religion is almost invariably from the political to the personal type, while the innate desire of humanity for unity maintains the struggle to find a synthesis between these two extreme types. The city-state religions of Greece and Rome and the Church-state of the Jews were manifestations of a certain extreme position, from which the Mysteries were a wholesome reaction. But the Mystery-Religions reacted to the other extreme— a reaction of epoch-making moment to religion. Each type represented an important facet of divine truth, but for the time of its predominance obscured another equally valuable truth. " The epoch-making transition is the advance of the human mind from that type of religion which, by emphasizing the social ideal, exalts moral obligation, to that type which, by emphasizing the individual ideal, exalts mystical aspiration." [1] The Mysteries proved of inestimable value in introducing the principle of voluntary choice in religious concerns, by stressing the personal aspects which deepened the self-consciousness, by proclaiming need of regeneration, by directing the mind to immortality, and by fostering that mysticism which makes the things unseen real. They failed by neglecting or depreciating other aspects of the life of man upon earth in his social environment.[2]

The Greek and Roman social-ethical religions were easily displaced by the personal Mysteries. But there was one religion of the earlier political type which did not yield to the Mysteries, but entered the lists against them. The religion of Israel was for six centuries, from the days of Jeremiah and Ezekiel to the triumph of Pauline Christianity, agitated by the conflict between the two competing principles of religion—the political and the personal, and this conflict was in no small degree a preparation for the

[1] B. W. Bacon, *Hib. Jour.* April '13, p. 620 ; cf. 622.
[2] Cf. Cumont, *Rel. orient.* 2nd ed. p. 69.

appearance of a daughter-religion which was destined to succeed where Israel failed. Israel handed on the unsolved problem to Christianity—a problem which had rent her own soul, which had produced bitter divisions within the Theocracy, which gave birth to parties of such marked polarity as the Essenes and the Zealots, and which finally caused the large secession from the synagogue into the Ecclesia. The religion of Israel made a notable attempt to combine both principles, and, though it was and always remained a nationalistic religion, it made provision for individualistic aspirations to an extent never dreamed of in Greece or Rome. The social-ethical consciousness, however, had so dominated the thought of Israel that individualistic religion was looked on askance by the authorities, whose dislike of individualism was increased by the obvious fact that the religions of the individualistic type were not conspicuous for ethical requirements.

The appearance of personal in contrast to political religion in the ancient world was a decided advance of the human spirit. The next religious question which presented itself was : Are these two types to be set in juxtaposition or in opposition ? Are they mutually exclusive ? or may not a synthesis be found ? If we accept Hegel's formula of evolution—thesis, antithesis, synthesis—we might say that the Greek and Roman religions represented the thesis (social-ethical religions), the Mysteries the antithesis (individualistic-mystic) ; while Judaism presented both thesis and antithesis, but laboured in vain to discover the synthesis. It was Christianity that found the synthesis. Christianity was compelled to face the problem because of the conflict between the political religions of the West and the personal religions of the East, which was growing in intensity around her, and because Judaism, which had fostered her early years, had suffered much heart-searching on the question. If Christianity was to be what it professed—a genuine universal religion—it must resolve the enigma and find a means of satisfying both the social and the individual instincts of man, of making man at once moral and mystic, of combining the complementary truths 'that we are members one of another' and 'all souls are mine' into an all-comprehensive truth. Justice must be done " to the one [type] interested and influential in the conduct of this life, but failing to meet man's mystical yearnings ; the other fulfilling man's mystic yearnings, but failing to give the life in this world a moral content and meaning." [1] Christianity vindicated its superiority to the city-state religions, the Mystery-Religions, and Judaism in proving a " reconciliation of the two types in a higher synthesis of an ethical religion of redemption which redeems from this world, and yet enables men to find in this world a sphere of moral activity and purpose." [2] It met the whole needs of man both in his personal aspirations and in his social relations on earth. It held together in beautiful equipoise the two sublime ideas of a divine social order, the Kingdom of God, and of the inestimable worth of the individual personality— ' what shall it profit a man if he gain the whole world and lose himself ? ' Religion and morality were indissolubly wedded in Christianity ; faith must be manifested in works.

The way of Christianity towards the reconciliation of the two extreme types of religion had been prepared both negatively and positively by the Mysteries and Judaism. The Mystery-Religions made man conscious of personal needs and taught him to aspire above earth and matter to an identification with God. Unfortunately, this enthusiasm or exaltation was not accompanied by a marked change in conduct ; spiritual aspiration did not of necessity imply a new moral ideal. Surely Professor Gardner [3] exaggerates when he says, " We have no reason to think that those who claimed salvation through Isis or Mithras were much better than their neighbours : they did not, therefore, live at a higher level," whereas Christians were " not merely filled with a spiritual enthusiasm, but that enthusiasm took the form of a self-denying life, a life of holiness and Christian

---

[1] S. Cave, *Christianity the World-Religion, Exp. Times*, April '19, p. 316.
[2] *Ib.*   [3] *St. Paul*, p. 87 f.

love, an ' enthusiasm of humanity.' '' The trouble which
Paul experienced through the moral aberrations of his
Gentile churches which had felt the power of the new
spiritual exaltation and enjoyed ' distributions of the Holy
Spirit ' is sufficient evidence that paganism could be warmly
religious without being conspicuously moral or even while
flagrantly immoral. The reader of Apuleius' *Metamorphoses*—the best single textbook for the study of the
Mysteries—is impressed by the, to him, perplexing juxtaposition of religious fervour and a sensuous and sensual
imagination. Isiac salvation did not necessarily involve a
transformation of character.

It was from Judaism—pre-eminently the ethical religion
of antiquity—that Christianity inherited its lofty ethical
ideal.[1] Judaism was shocked at the gross sins of paganism,
especially those of idolatry and of the flesh. Her own
morality was not faultless, but it was a permanent challenge
to surrounding paganism. In the sanctities of domestic life,
the religious training of children, the duty of brotherly
helpfulness, the relationship of the sexes, the dignity of
manual labour, and in other respects the Diaspora became
' a leader of the blind ' to the Roman Empire. The morality
of Judaism was such that, with the exception of trivialities
of tradition and excessive biblicism, it could be transferred
en bloc into Christianity. The poorer Jewish-Christian
churches more than repaid the Gentile-Christian contributions in money by the wealth of their ethical heritage.
The former were agitated by questions of legalism, while the
latter were endeavouring to restrain libertinism by the
adoption of the ethical code of Judaism and Christianity.
Because Christianity sprang from Judaism its birth-mark was
morality :

" The Jewish Christianity of Palestine trained by the Law
was, so to speak, the backbone, which supported the moral
conscience of the whole. . . . And the Judaistic agitation
in his (Paul's) churches, in spite of the injury that it did, still

[1] Cf. Wernle, *Beginnings of Christianity*, Eng. tr. I, p. 20 f

achieved the result of laying more stress on the moral side of Christianity." [1]

Jewish catechisms and textbooks were adopted by Christianity and incorporated in Christian writings. Ethical superiority was a strong plank in the platform of the early apologists and Christian historians, and was not unobserved by heathen critics. The co-extension of morality with religion, to us a commonplace, was not such to the Graeco-Roman age. Christianity made it a commonplace : it took up the ethical task so well begun by the Greek philosophers and by the religion of Israel. One cannot say that Christianity has yet completed the moral education of the West, but Christianity has made it impossible that a man should any more be regarded as religious whose conduct is inconsistent with his profession. It has enabled us to unite the subjective and the objective aspects of religion ; to rejoice alike in the raptures of the communion of saints and in the exaltation of personal communion with the Father of our spirits ; to balance the centrifugal and the centripetal forces of the soul.

IV. Aristotle shrewdly detected a fatal defect in the Mysteries when he said, ' It is not necessary that the initiates learn anything but that they should receive impressions and be brought into a suitable frame of mind,' i.e. their vagueness [2] and excessive emotionalism, which was accompanied by a cramping traditionalism. The Mysteries made their appeal to feeling primarily rather than to the moral loyalties and spiritual perceptions. Of this there is abundant evidence.[3] Stobaeus [4] has preserved a fragment of Themistios (Plutarch ?) which compares death with initiation thus :

' Then [in death] the soul undergoes an experience like

---

[1] Dobschütz, *Christian Life*, Eng. tr. p. 172, cf. also p. 139.

[2] Cf. Lobeck, p. 113 ff. ; Anrich, p. 32 ff.

[3] Cf. Anrich, p. 33 ; Hepding, p. 195 ff.

[4] *Floril.* 120–28 (Meinike, 107) ; cf. Macchioro, *Orf. e Paol.* p. 128 ff.; cf. well-known passage of Dio Chrysostom, *Or.* XII. 202 M., de Arnim, I. 163, 33.

that of those receiving initiation into the great Mysteries. Wherefore the correspondence of word to word and act to act in *dying* and *being initiated*. First of all, wanderings and painful tortuous ways, and certain uneasy and endless courses in the dark ; then, before the end, all the frightful things, fears, terrors, sweat and stupor. After which a certain marvellous light confronts it, and pure places and meadows receive it, with voices and choral dances and the most august solemnities of sacred sounds and holy sights. Amid this the man, perfect now and initiated, becomes free and goes round, liberated and crowned, performing the rites ; he consorts with holy and pure men, beholding here the uninitiated crowd of the living uncleansed and trodden under by himself in much mud and darkness, and, through fear of death, persisting in their evil in disbelief of the bliss of yonder world.'

' As those who are being initiated,' says Plutarch,[1] ' approach each other at first with confusion and shoutings, but when the holy things are being performed and exposed they give attention with shuddering and silence, so the beginner in philosophy will at first observe much confusion, but, on com- ing to closer acquaintance and seeing the great light, as when shrines are opened, he will assume another character and maintain silence and awe will hold him ' ; and Pseudo- Demetrius [2] affirms ' the Mysteries are delivered in allegories to strike terror and awe.' This *chiaroscuro*, which neither invited nor permitted definition, adapted the Mysteries to the most varied tastes by an elasticity of interpretation which could make them mean anything to the participant : it lent them the attractiveness which hangs round Theosophy and occultism. The disparate, the obsolete, the symbolic, stood in pacific juxtaposition.

" The hazy ideas of the Oriental priests enabled every- one to see in them the phantoms he was pursuing. The individual imagination was given ample scope, and the dilettante men of letters rejoiced in moulding these malleable doctrines at will. They were not outlined

---

[1] *Quom. qui suos in virt. sent. prof.* 82 E.
[2] Walz, *Rhet. Graeci*, IX. 47.

sharply enough nor were they formulated with sufficient precision to appeal to the multitude. The gods were everything and nothing : they got lost in a *sfumato*." [1]

But the mind cannot long live in a fog. What may be interpreted as anything may mean nothing. Intuition is liable to be called to give account of its activities, and psychopathic states to be subjected to cold scrutiny. Rites may be for a time more important than speculation, but speculation has a way of entering unbidden and causing trouble. Mythology may usurp the place of reflection, but only for a season. No religion can permanently take refuge in the glamour of vagueness and fluidity of conception and uncorrelated elements.[2] Socrates had correctly gauged the emotional inlets of inspiration and revelation when he so truthfully affirmed, ' The greatest of our blessings come to us through *mania*, provided it is a gift of God,' [3] and ' Madness coming from God is superior to sanity of human origin.' Well might the Alexandrine father,[4] with his sympathy for the mystic-gnostic type of religion, appeal to his contemporaries, ' Cleanse yourselves from custom by sprinkling with the drops of truth,' comparing the new mysteries, ' O truly holy Mysteries ! O flawless light ! my way is lighted with torches to contemplate the heavens and God ı in initiation I become holy. The Lord is the hierophant who seals while illuminating his communicant.' [5]

A necessary corollary to the vagueness of the Mysteries was their weakness intellectually or theologically, a defect which did not escape one of their strongest protagonists.[6] Sooner or later criticism is turned upon faith, but a religion rooted in the spiritual nature of man has nothing to fear but rather much to welcome from " man's meddling intellect." From the beginning their intellectual inferiority

---

[1] Cumont, *Rel. orient.* Eng. tr. p. 88, 2nd ed. p. 132.

[2] " Fog is religion's vital breath in this period " (Glover, *Progress*, p. 323), who laments " Fancy, ritual, mysticism, unsound science, are triumphant for the time and are united in a tremendous campaign against truth and science " (p. 320 f.).

[3] *Phaedrus*, 244 A. D.

[4] Clem. Alex. *Protr.* 10, 99.

[5] *Ib.* 12 (120, 1).

[6] Julian, *Ep.* 52.

was apparent to the educated, who had recourse to the religious-philosophic systems. The Mysteries never secured the services of Greek philosophy so fully and so loyally as did Christianity, and could not bear its solvent properties upon their faith. Hence as a rule an earnest man had to choose between the vague Mysteries and formulated Greek thought. Consequently, there were two main currents to one or other of which the efforts made to answer the intellectual curiosity and satisfy the yearnings of unhappy souls belonged :

" Those whose interests were primarily intellectual, or, at all events, demanded a theology which was intellectually acceptable, were strongly influenced by the metaphysics of the Neo-Platonists and the ethics of the Stoics. In them they seemed to find a reasonable explanation of the universe, a ' Weltanschauung ' which corresponded to facts, and a rule of life which satisfied the conscience and seemed to offer a lasting happiness. On the other hand, those whose interest was chiefly religious, in the narrower sense of the word, were attracted by the Oriental Mysteries." [1]

As the Mysteries made advances to thinking men there arose apologists like Apuleius, Celsus, Porphyry, Iamblichus, Proclus, and Julian, who attempted to work out a theology to justify the claims of these religions. To our great loss for an historical appreciation of the ancient world only a fragment of this pagan apologetic has survived. The notable essay of Plutarch on *Isis and Osiris* is rejected by Egyptologists [2] as a trustworthy document of the religion of the Nile. This apologetic and allegorical treatise is a fusion of Platonic speculation on a rather uncertain historical basis with Egyptian mythology. The Egyptian cult is seen through the eyes of the syncretistic Alexandrian medium in which naturalism, zoolatry (totemism), and magic are forced by allegorical exegesis to yield a theology acceptable to the Greek mind. Plutarch

---

[1] Lake, *The Earlier Epp. of St. Paul*, 2nd ed. p. 40 ; *Stewardship*, p. 74.
[2] Cf. P. D. Scott-Moncrieff, *De Iside et Os.* in *J.H.S* '09, XXIX, p. 79 ff.

clearly aims to prove that the doctrines of Egypt are consonant with the advancing thought of his day.[1] Isis appears as a mother of sorrows, a goddess of benign sympathy, and Osiris " passes into the eternal Love and Beauty, pure, passionless, remote from any region of change or death, unapproachable in his ethereal splendour, save, as in moments of inspired musing, we may faintly touch him as in a dream."[2] All that devotion and philosophy could do was done by Plutarch for the Mysteries. And yet in—

" Spite of the radiant mists of amiability which he diffused over these Egyptian gods, till the old myths seem capable of every conceivable explanation, and everything a symbol of everything else, and all is beautiful and holy, the foolish and indecent old stories remain a definite and integral part of the religion, the animals are still objects of worship and the image of Osiris stands in its original naked obscenity."[3]

The Oriental gorgeousness of colour, the strained rhetoric, the wild fantasy, and the surcharge of mysticism character-izing the second-century romance of Apuleius cannot conceal the religious enthusiasm with which he describes his partici-pation in the sacraments of Isis and Serapis, nor blind us to the psychological effects produced. The glowing emo-tional language of the eleventh book of the *Metamorphoses* impresses the reader as a powerful plea of this prophet of paganism [4] on behalf of Mysteries dear to him.

Plotinus repeatedly illustrates [5] the purification of the soul in its ascent from the World of Sense to the World of Spirit, the Ogdoad, by language drawn from the Mysteries. Porphyry held that the Mysteries presented in symbolism

---

[1] In ch. 8 he contends that there is nothing irrational, mythical, nor anything prompted by superstition in the rites, but that they serve ethical and useful ends, or rest on historical or physical grounds.

[2] Dill, *Rom. Soc.* p. 575.

[3] Glover, *Conflict*, p. 111.

[4] Cf. P. Monceaux, *Apulée Magicien* in *Rev de Deux Mondes*, LXXXV, pp. 571–608.

[5] E.g. *Enn.* I. 6, 7.

and action the deepest truths of Platonism. Iamblichus
defended the Mysteries against the charge of obscenity and
absurdity levelled against them, and with eloquent passion
appealed to the edifying contemplation of their blessed
symbols on the soul.[1] Reference may be made to Julian's
discussion [2] of ' the myths adapted to initiation,' and his
advice ' to secure initiation into all the Mysteries.' Proclus
maintained that the philosophical doctrines (chiefly of
Platonism) are of the same content as the mystic revelations,
that philosophy in fact borrowed from the Mysteries,
from Orphism through Pythagoras, from whom Plato
borrowed.

Christianity, by construing under the forms of reason
what had first been vouchsafed to faith, stood the test of
criticism which so often resulted in the evaporation of the
vague ideas of ancient Mysteriology. It had nothing to
fear, but rather much to gain, by the application of enquiry.
It possessed its symbols, but they were simple and inoffensive.
It is true that Celsus [3] ridiculed Christianity as a peasant
religion : ' Let no one with education approach, none wise,
none intelligent—such things we deem evil. But if there
is anyone ignorant, stupid, lacking culture, or a fool, let
such come with boldness,' and ' let us hear what kind
of people these Christians invite. Everyone who is a
sinner, unintelligent, or a fool, or in brief any wretch, such
will the Kingdom of God receive. Now whom do you call
a sinner but the wicked, the thief, the house-breaker, the
poisoner, the sacrilegious, the spoiler of the dead ? whom
else would you invite for a company of brigands ? ' Lucian
mocked Christianity as the cult of a ' gibbeted sophist.'
The greatest of pagan philosophers in the Christian era,
Plotinus, did not deign to mention the new way. To the
noble Antonine emperor the new faith was ' sheer obstinacy.'
Porphyry, an even keener critic than Celsus, with all his
respect for Jesus, poured scorn on Christian preaching,
especially on the magical effects claimed for Baptism [4]

[1] *De Myst.* I. 12.
[2] *Oratio* VII.
[3] *Con. Celsum*, III. 44 ; 59.
[4] In Macarius Magnes, IV. 19.

and the Eucharist,[1] though its chief offence lay in the doctrine of the Incarnation [2] which contravened all philosophical ideas about the relation of spirit and matter, God and the world. Paul avers that not many wise accept the Gospel : it is true, too, that Christianity made its first strides among the lower classes.[3] Some Christian apologists were misguided enough to attempt to commend the new religion by asserting ' It is believable because it is absurd ; it is sure because it is impossible.' [4] It is true, too, that the Christian protagonists, instead of planting themselves firmly on the divine personality of Jesus, sometimes betook themselves to the outposts of such propositions as the Virgin Birth, miracles, exorcisms of Jesus, alleged fulfilment of prophecy, the axiomatic infallibility of Scripture with the inviolability of dogmata, the imminent Parousia of their Lord, the corporeity of the Resurrection, on which they exposed themselves unnecessarily to attack, and on which the emphasis altered with the passing centuries. Others there were who ' neither wished to give nor to receive a reason for their faith,' and who invited converts with ' Don't examine, only believe.' [5] But this is not all the truth. It was only natural that Christianity, as a religion of Redemption, should be more readily accepted by the downtrodden classes, among whom conservatism was less hampering; but at no time was Christianity merely a peasant religion. It satisfied the heart and mind of the same subtle thinker who declared that not many wise had accepted ' the offence of the Cross '; it appealed to cultured minds like those of the Fourth Evangelist, the author of *Hebrews* or the author of the graceful *Epistle to Diognetus*. The Christian apologists proved equal to expounding the fundamental Christian truths in the language of Greek philosophy. Under the Antonines a vast apologetic literature was published by

---

[1] *Ib.* III. 15. [2] *Ib.* IV. 22.

[3] Cf. Deissmann, *Das Christentum u. d. Unteren Schichten.* ' We see them in private houses, wool-carders, cobblers, fullers, the most uneducated and peasants, who dare not open their mouths in the presence of their elder and wiser masters ' (Celsus, in Origen, *Con. Celsum*, III. 55 ; cf. 44).

[4] Tert. *De Carne Christi*, 5. [5] *C. Celsum*, I. 9.

writers like Quadratus, Aristides, Tatian, Justin, Athenagoras, Theophilus, Melito, Apollinarius, and Minucius Felix.
Justin retained after his conversion the philosopher's cloak
for his Christian propaganda, in which he won his double
title 'philosopher and martyr.' He endeavoured to
vindicate the truth of Christianity mainly by appealing to
the morality of its adherents, the proof from prophecy,
and the simplicity and dignity of the Christian worship.
Tatian will not surrender philosophy to unbelievers: 'Our
philosophy is older than that of the Greeks,' and 'rich and
poor among us pursue philosophy,'[1] even old women and
youths. Later apologists took up the battle for education
in the Church, chiefly Origen and Clement. Origen boldly
accepts his opponent's contention against a faith without
enquiry: 'We should follow reason and a rational guide,'
and he claims that, without speaking arrogantly, there
is at least as much enquiry among Christians as elsewhere.[2]
More striking still is Clement's defence of the rights of
philosophic enquiry in Christian doctrine and his assertions
of the benefits accruing from its application. In inviting
his countrymen to come to 'the all-sufficient Physician of
humanity,'[3] he invited them likewise to 'the genuinely true
philosophy'[4]: 'It is impossible to find without having
sought, or to have sought without examining, or to have
examined without analysing and asking questions with a
view to lucidity.' Philosophy was to the Greeks the
preparatory discipline for the Gospel which the Law proved
to the Jews.[5] Since philosophy makes men virtuous it must
be the work of God. No one ever more cordially welcomed
enquiry upon faith than this generously educated Greek
father, to whom the true Christian was the true Gnostic.
None, except the Fourth Evangelist, exemplified better
how Christianity may bring forth things new and old,
and while borrowing transmute. 'One indeed is the
way of Truth, but into it, as into an ever-flowing river,

[1] *Adv. Graecos*, 31 f.
[2] *C. Celsum*, I. 99.
[3] *Paed.* I. 6.2.
[4] *Strom.* VIII. 1.
[5] VI. 17; I. 5; I. 16.

streams from everywhere are confluent.'[1] Greek and non-Greek speculation was a ' torn-off fragment of eternal Truth.'[2] Lactantius likewise recognized the strength of Christianity when he maintained that the true religion and true philosophy are identical.

No other religion in such a short time called forth such a theological literature in which its adherents made explicit the truths implicit in their faith. This, of course, produced such a crop of heresy as alarmed Church leaders—Gnosticism, Docetism, Montanism. It was in the Gnostic controversy that Christianity was brought into closest contact with philosophy in the ancient world, by which it gained through a clearer formulation of its faith.

Christianity offered a more profound and spiritual message than the Mysteries to the theosophic mind of the Orient, the speculative mind of Greece, and the legalist mind of Rome. However brilliant the allegorical exegesis of the Mysteries, however remote their boasted antiquity, however imposing their authority, however impressive and often beautiful their symbolism, there remained at last in the Mysteries but evanescent myths, elusive of a theology, and legends repulsive to the moral sense, whereas the Christian apologist could appeal to truth intelligible because enshrined in the Word made flesh in the Divine Humanity.

[1] I. 5.   [2] I. 13.

CHAPTER VII

THE VICTORY OF CHRISTIANITY [1]

Λέγει Ἰησοῦς ἔστην ἐν μέσῳ τοῦ κόσμου καὶ ἐν σαρκὶ ὤφθην αὐτοῖς.

OXYRHYNCHUS LOGION.

'Erecta sermonis libertate proclama : εὑρήκαμεν συγχαίρομεν.'

MINUCIUS FELIX, De Err. Prof. Rel. II. 9.

'Totus Veritas fuit.'—TERT. De Carne Christi, V.

THE appearance of Christianity attracted little attention for some time and received but scanty notice in contemporary pagan or Jewish literature. Seneca, before whose brother's tribunal the Jews brought Paul, makes no reference to the new faith which we know was rapidly spreading in his day. Suetonius [2] refers to Jesus by a misconception as instigator of a riot in Rome. Tacitus,[3] writing early in the second century, speaks of the rise of this ' baneful superstition (*exitiabilis superstitio*) ' and of the death of its originator under Pontius Pilate.

The disputed passage in Josephus [4] concerning Jesus may now be accepted as authentic. Lucian makes mockery of the

---

[1] Cf. A. Dieterich's instructive essay *Der Untergang der antiken Religion* in *Kl. Sch.* pp. 449–539 ; J. Geffcken, *Der Ausgang des griech-röm. Heidentums* in *N. Jahrb. f. d. Klas. Alt.* '18. XLI, pp. 93–124 ; *The Dissolution of Paganism*, by G. Santayana in *Interpretations of Poetry and Religion*, pp. 49–75 ; *The Triumph of Christianity*, by S. Angus in *Review and Expositor*, XVIII, July and October '21 ; Lecky, *Hist. of European Morals*, vol. I, ch. III ; Glover, *Progress in Religion*, ch. XV ; Renan, *Raisons de la Victoire du Christianisme*, chs. XXXI-IV of *Marc Aurèle* ; Harnack, *Mission and Exp.* bks. II and III ; Mackintosh, *The Originality of the Christian Message*, ch. VI ; McGiffert, *Influence of Christianity in the Roman Emp.* (*Harv. Th. Rev.* January '09) ; C. H. Moore, *Religious Thought of the Greeks*, ch. X ; C. W. Emmet, *Primitive Christianity and its Competitors* (*Modern Churchman*, XII, pp. 316–26) ; V. Macchioro, *Paganesimo e Cristianesimo* in *L'Evangelio*, pp. 63–94.

[2] 'Judaeos impulsore Chresto . . . Roma expulit ' (*Claud.* 25).

[3] *Annales*, XV. 44.

[4] *Antiq. Jud.* XVIII. 3, 3; cf. A.Slijpen in *Mnemosyne* N.S. '14, pp. 96–100.

'gibbeted sophist,' and the noble Aurelius, in his one explicit reference [1] to Christianity, terms it 'sheer obstinacy.'

It was the Jews who first raised the alarm against the new faith so akin to, and yet so different from, the parent faith ; it was they too who both in Palestine and in the Diaspora inaugurated the first persecutions. At first the Jews themselves viewed the new way as merely another sect or a prophetic revival within Judaism. The Apostles at Jerusalem for a time evidently took the same view and continued to live as Jews while proclaiming Jesus as Messiah. Soon the implications of the new teaching became apparent to the Jews, and the difficult questions raised by the Gentile mission brought home not only to Paul but to the Jewish authorities the fact that if Christianity was true Judaism was doomed, Christ being 'the end of the Law.' The conservative elements in Judaism then attempted to stamp out the new heresy, for which purpose they called in the aid of the secular arm. Christianity, repudiated by Judaism, became an 'unlicensed religion,' which for a generation had grown and spread, as Tertullian says, *sub umbraculo licitae Judaeorum religionis*. It must have come as a surprise to the vigilant Roman authorities to discover that a new religion, with apparently no past, should suddenly appear upon the stage professing to be a universal religion and disputing the imperial cult. As a result of the great fire in Rome in July 64 Nero, to dissipate the rumour that he was the incendiary, set on foot the first imperial persecution ; henceforth Christianity attracted increasing attention, hostile and friendly. All the persecutions and police supervision of the imperial government were as futile to arrest the spread of Christianity as Herod's slaughter of the Innocents had been to prevent the teaching from which it was born. Christianity waxed stronger while opposed by the State, by other popular religions, by its parent faith, by the science and the philosophies of the time.

The permanence of Christianity is evidence that its victory was due mainly to spiritual means, not merely to the defects

[1] XI 3.

of the Mystery-Religions but to its own intrinsic qualities. By its possession of the Spirit of Christ it was able to quicken and transform the masses who entered it in ignorance or from ulterior motives. To Christianity, as to other religions, many adherents were attracted by what could not be called religious motives. Some saw in Christianity a greater magical potency for the performance of exorcism and thaumaturgy; some accepted out of dread of the judgment threatened at the imminent Parousia; some sought an earthly paradise; some in an age of theosophy coveted the pneumatic charismata. It was not the faith of such adherents that made Christianity mighty.

It is instructive to note the causes assigned by historians for the victory of Christianity. For example, Gibbon [1] attributes it to (1) the enthusiasm of the early Christians; (2) their belief in immortality, with future rewards and punishments; (3) miracles; (4) the high ethical code of its first professors; (5) efficient organization on imperial patterns. It is more surprising that Merivale [2] should miss the true secret in his enumeration of the four factors: (1) the external evidence of the apparent fulfilment of prophecy and miracles; (2) internal evidence as satisfying the spiritual needs of the empire; (3) the pure lives and heroic deaths of Christians; (4) the temporal success with which Christianity was crowned under Constantine. With more truth John Stuart Blackie [3] says: " Christianity addressed itself to the world with the triple advantage of a reasonable dogma, a tremendous moral force, and an admitted historical basis." Renan, discussing the question in some readable chapters of his *Marc Aurèle*, affirms, "It was by the new discipline of life which it introduced into the world that Christianity conquered," [4] and elsewhere [5]: " There is in the teaching of Christ a new spirit and a stamp of originality " (*cachet original*). A French Modernist, A. Loisy, in his *Les*

---

[1] *Decline and Fall*, ch. XV.
[2] *Conversion of the Rom. Emp.* p. viii ff.
[3] *Day-book of J. S. Blackie*, p. 27.
[4] P. 561.
[5] *Études d'Hist. Relig.* p. 188.

Mystères païens et le Mystère chrétien,[1] discovers the superiority of Christianity in its emphasis on monotheism, involving the personality of God, and in its doctrine of the Incarnation.

Lecky[2] points out that Christianity combined more distinct elements of power and attraction than any other religion, such as universalism, a sympathetic worship, a noble system of ethics, an ideal of compassion. " The chief cause of its success was the congruity of its teaching with the spiritual nature of mankind. It was because it was true to the moral sentiments of the age, because it represented faithfully the supreme type of excellence to which men were then tending, because it corresponded with their religious wants, aims, emotions, because the whole spiritual being could thus expand and expatiate under its influence, that it planted its roots so deeply in the hearts of men." Reinach[3] attributes its victory and permanence to its simplicity and purity, while Cumont[4] views its victory merely as " l'aboutissement d'une longue évolution des croyances." With more historic justification than these last two writers, McGiffert maintains : " Ancient Christianity won its victory chiefly because it had far more of the elements of power and permanence, combined a greater variety of attractive features, and satisfied a greater variety of needs than any other system . . . its victory in the Roman Empire was fairly earned by sheer superiority." [5]

Though Christian apologists appealed to the number and nature of Christian miracles, the success of Christianity was not due to anything which was merely of contemporary

---

[1] P. 343 ff. In the *Hibbert J.* X, p. 64, Loisy says that Christianity conquered because " it had the advantage over them [the Mysteries] of a firmer doctrine of God and of immortality ; of a divine Saviour more living, nearer the heart, and possessed of a place in history ; of a stronger unity in belief and in social organization."

[2] *History of European Morals*, vol. I, ch. III (*The Conversion of Rome*), pp. 388–9 in copyright ed. of 1911.

[3] *Orpheus*, p. 108.

[4] *Rel. or.* p. xxiv; cf. also the paragraph in Aust, pp. 115–16.

[5] *Influence of Christianity in the Rom. Emp.* p. 43 ; cf. C. H. Moore, *Relig. Thought of the Greeks*, pp. 292 f., 356 ff.

value, or to what could be put forth by other religions, but, as we shall see later, to that miracle of miracles, the Personality of Jesus. The conversion of Constantine merely completed the material and political success of Christianity and issued in an alliance which was fraught with more bane than blessing for Christianity. The triumph of Christianity was more than the drawing to a focus of a long evolution of beliefs, more than merely the culmination of the Oriental penetration of the West. Christianity did not win because the East was mainly for Christ while the West was for Mithra. Nor did Christianity win merely because it was adopted by the Hellenic spirit by which its *dogmata* were defended in philosophic terminology, and by which it was supplied with a reasoned theology necessary to the permanence of a religion. Celsus [1] rightly maintained that the Greeks excelled in ' criticizing, establishing, and bringing to bear upon practical life the discoveries of the non-Greeks,' who were admitted to excel the Greeks in ability to ' discover dogmata.' It is true that Mithraism was doomed to failure largely because it could not win the allegiance of the Greeks,[2] but it is also true that other contemporary religious systems failed in spite of Greek advocacy. That this marvellously gifted race decided to consecrate its genius to Christ was a large—perhaps the largest—factor contributing to the success of ancient Christianity, but it was not the supreme factor. Neither, as is sometimes represented, did Christianity drive its competitors off the field by its aggressive syncretistic tendencies and a capacity for borrowing lavishly and assimilating organically. The promise of its victory was assured before it reached its most syncretistic stages in the third and subsequent centuries. The advantages of the syncretistic method did not conceal from the Christian apologists the latent perils. Tertullian [3] uttered his protest : ' Viderint qui Stoicum et Platonicum et dialecticum

---

[1] *C. Celsum*, I. 2.

[2] Because Mithraism did not lay hold of Hellenism " the historian at once sees that the former (Mithraism) has to perish, and the latter (Christianity) survive " (Harnack, *Mission and Expansion*, II. p. 318.)

[3] *De Praes. Haer.* 7.

Christianismum protulerint.' Christianity won because of what it was, because of what Jesus was. This does not deny a long historic process of preparation for the fulness of the times. There had been a real preparation, both negatively and positively, by the Mystery-Religions, the Greek religious philosophies, Judaism, and the Roman empire, and by the terrible thirst for love (the *amabam amare* of Augustine) of dying paganism. The Mysteries had brought men together in those religious associations which were the harbingers of the house-churches of primitive Christianity and had ready to hand for the new religion an organization and system of administration. The Mysteries, both Greek and Oriental, had created a favourable milieu for Christianity by making religion a matter of personal conviction ; they had made familiar the consciousness of sin and the need of a redemption ; and by their salvationist propaganda they disposed men to lend a ready ear to the Christian proclamation of Jesus as Saviour ; they had denationalized gods and men in aiming at the brotherhood of mankind ; they had stimulated cravings for immortality which they could only inadequately satisfy ; they had made men zealous propagandists by laying upon them the duty of the diffusion of their faith ; they had fostered monotheism by making their patron deity the representative of the Divine Unity, or by the syncretistic identification of their deity with the still living deities of polytheism, or by that solar monotheism which concentrated adoration on the one source of life and light.

There were also many circumstances quite favourable to the advancement of Christianity. Alexander and Caesar and Augustus had prepared the way of the Lord. Greek and Greek-Oriental philosophies had revealed the needs and aspirations of the human spirit. Plato and Posidonius and Philo had pointed men to Heaven as the homeland of the soul. The Greeks had furnished the missionaries of the Cross with a world-language. In its inception Christianity had a unique advantage in being permitted to take firm root under the protection of the *religio licita* of Judaism. In its missionary activity its way was everywhere prepared by the preachers and teachers of the synagogue. Be it said that no religion ever facilitated the path of another as did Judaism that of Christianity—a debt sometimes grudgingly acknowledged by early Christian anti-Semitism. The Jew was ubiquitous; the synagogue had in every centre prepared the most serious minds of heathenism—the ' God-fearers,' who were the first to abandon the Synagogue to enter the Ecclesia.

" To the Jewish mission which preceded it, the Christian mission was indebted, in the first place, for a field tilled all over the empire; in the second place, for religious communities already formed everywhere in the towns; thirdly, for what Axenfeld calls ' the help of materials ' furnished by the preliminary knowledge of the Old Testament, in addition to catechetical and liturgical materials which could be employed without much alteration; fourthly, for the habit of regular worship and the control of private life; fifthly, for an impressive apologetic on behalf of monotheism, historical teleology, and ethics; and, finally, for the feeling that self-diffusion was a duty. The amount of this debt is so large that one might venture to claim the Christian mission as a continuation of Jewish propaganda." [1]

Having made due acknowledgment of all these historic facts, let us consider the main differential features and factors, and the mode of diffusion which ensured Christianity its success and permanence.

I. Its Intolerance

Narrow indeed was the gate that admitted into the new Society, and broad that of admission into other religions. In the matter of intolerance Christianity differed from all pagan religions, and surpassed Judaism; in that respect it stood in direct opposition to the spirit of the age. It was emphatic in its positive differential doctrines and uncompromising in its stern protests : it had "inherited from Judaism the courage of its disbeliefs." [2] Never was there a

[1] Harnack, *Mission and Exp.* I, p. 15.
[2] Murray, *Four Stages*, p. 178.

more tolerant age than that in which Christianity appeared. As a result of the spread of Greek thought, which had always been that of the layman and never subjugated to sacerdotal control, the break-up of the city-state, and the regnant cosmopolitanism, men had learned to respect each other's opinions.   Racial and religious barriers had been thrown down.   The most exclusive of races, the Jews, had for centuries played a part in world-history ; particularly was the Diaspora generous in its outlook on the surrounding world.   Men were everywhere exchanging religious views. Syncretism was the religious hall-mark of the time.   Throughout the empire were spread religious communities in which men of different races met.   There was no clear line of demarcation among the foreign cults, which showed a marked hospitality in religion.   Different gods agreed to be housed in the same temple ; the same priest might officiate for half a dozen deities.[1]   Men were willing to try every religion and philosophy in the field.   It was now as fashionable to owe allegiance to the gods of the Nile, Syria, Persia, Samothrace, Greece, and Rome, as it had in the previous epoch been to acknowledge only one national pantheon.   Polytheism is naturally tolerant, and the spirit of the age only increased religious tolerance

The Jews stood aloof.   Their uncompromising monotheism and the Law rendered them conspicuously intolerant as compared with the adherents of the Mystery-Religions.   They would accept no compromise on the question of the imperial cult, Sabbath-keeping, or on such rites as appeared essential to the integrity of their faith.   But Judaism was able to temporize to a certain extent.   Within it there were degrees of piety from that of the Pharisees to that of ' the people of the land.'   Judaism desired to influence the maximum number compatible with its tenets.   Those who would enter into the full benefits of the Covenant must submit to circumcision and undertake the obligations of the Mosaic law with superadded traditions.   There was a much larger class of adherents who refused to break with paganism ;

[1] Cf. *C.I.L.* VI. 1, 1779.

these were encouraged to attach themselves to the synagogue and a minimum of requirements was imposed upon them. Christianity intensified the intolerance of the parent faith and sternly set its face against the tolerance in religious affairs which commenced with the Persians, was first made popular by Alexander, and became the settled policy of the Roman Empire.[1] It frowned upon the hospitality of the competing cults. "Christianity stands proudly aloof from the throng of the *thiasi*; and the only likeness to them which she will acknowledge is the likeness which an angel of light might bear to the spirit of darkness."[2] The rites of pagans were in her eyes performed to devils; pagan worship was founded by demons and maintained in the interests of demons. To those who were in quest of salvation and testing each scheme offered Christianity dared to say: ' In no other is there salvation, for neither is there any other name under heaven that is given among men, wherein we must be saved.' To those accustomed to the idea and practice of initiation into several Mysteries it declared: ' You cannot drink the cup of the Lord and the cup of demons; you cannot partake of the table of the Lord and the table of demons.' To those who, according to the religious conceptions of the time, were seeking mediators, it declared ' there is one God; also *one* Mediator between God and man, a man, Christ Jesus.' To those accustomed to address the ' Lord Serapis ' or the *Domina* Isis or the Emperor as *Dominus* Christianity stoutly asseverated that ' there is one Lord ' whose name is above every name.

This intolerance and exclusiveness naturally drew much odium upon the new Society, which opposed the prevalent *rapprochement* of customs and cults. It heavily handicapped it in competition with the syncretistic [3] Mystery-

---

[1] Cf. E. G. Hardy, *Studies in Rom. Hist.* '06, chs. I–IX.

[2] Gardner, *St. Paul*, p. 94; cf. Boissier, I, p. 382 ff.

[3] In which one deity could order the erection of a shrine for another, as the Dea Caelestis of Carthage did for Mercury (Boissier, I, p. 387), or as the Greek Aesculapius honoured the deity of Doliche (*C.I.L.* III. 1614). Even the high-grade *Fathers* of Mithra might be *Prophets* of Isis (*C.I.L.* VI. 504, 846).

Religions, but in the end proved the secret of its strength.
Many a follower of 'my Lord Serapis' and of Isis, 'the
Saviour of men,' [1] and of the Great Mother was turned away
because he could not find the accustomed hospitality for
his gods with this new faith. The Christian cult was an
exclusive cult [2] which required every candidate to break
with his past and separate himself from much of the social
life because it was tainted with paganism. Christians
attracted attention by their separation from the world;
they were οἱ ἅγιοι. They would not crown themselves
with garlands on festal civic occasions. The story of St.
John fleeing from the baths in Ephesus because Cerinthus
entered is characteristic of the uncompromising spirit of
Christianity. No Christian could imitate the tolerance
indicated in such a sepulchral confession of faith as *pater
sacrorum summi invicti Mithrae, sacerdos Isidis, dei Liberi
archibucolus,* [3] or of the child-priest Aurelius Antonios, [4]
'priest of all the gods, of Bona Dea, the Great Mother, Dionysos and *Hegemon* (Leader).' This self-consciousness and
exclusivism was "immensely imposing and impressive in
that age of religious syncretism and easy tolerance of all
sorts of divergent faiths. Here was a movement that
claimed everything and granted nothing. Bitter hostility
was aroused, of course, but also fanatical devotion." [5]

We may regret this hard intolerance of our primitive faith
which sometimes did bare justice to its forerunners and
competitors; which from the second century turned fiercely
upon Judaism as the latter had a century before excommuni-
cated it; which has left but few fragments of a vast liturgy
and religious literature of paganism which would have been
of immense value to students of the history of religion, and
would have cast many a ray of light on the origins of our own
faith; which demolished holy places and beautiful temples

---

[1] ἀνδρασώτειραν in Invocation of *Oxy. Pap.* XI. 1380, l. 55, and σώτειραν,
l. 91; cf. *Isis Salutaris, C.I.L.* III. 2903; 4809.

[2] Cf. Bouché-Leclercq, *L'Intolérance religieux et politique,* p 140.

[3] *C.I.L.* VI. 500.

[4] *I.G.S.I.* 1449.

[5] McGiffert, p. 43.

such as the world shall never rear again. As we stand in awe amid some of these inspiring ruins we more regretfully bewail early Christian iconoclasm than the student of the Reformation does the blindness of our fathers who destroyed cathedrals and abbeys because these had been the centres of ecclesiastical abuses. But we shall less regret this intolerance of primitive Christianity when we reflect upon the nature and necessity of it, and upon the ability of Christianity to transmute what it saw fit to borrow from paganism. Tolerance too often results from indifference or indecision, but the intolerance of the Christian preachers was that of the conviction that they had found *the* all-comprehensive Truth. And in the welter of religions and philosophies intolerance was the most obvious, if not also the only sure, method of self-preservation. Judaism, on the one side, attempted to allure Christianity with the prestige of the Law, the memories of the fathers, and with usages hallowed from antiquity. Greek thought, on the other side, saw in Christianity immense possibilities of speculation and essayed to transform it into an eclectic philosophy in which the metaphysical would predominate over the spiritual. Again, the Mysteries, with their numerous clientele, welcomed Christianity as another religion of their own genus, offering hospitality to its Christ and to its rites. But the Holy Spirit, as the Christians termed the new source of power which they felt better than they could describe, warned the ' new way ' of the perils of holding dalliance with other cults. The event justified them. The hospitality and syncretism of the competitors of Christianity, while greatly adding to their popularity, ultimately compassed their downfall. Together with their loftier elements, that made for spirituality, they weighted themselves with rudiments of nature-worship, allying them with gross superstitions. Christianity would not stoop to conquer. It made claims of seemingly the most extravagant order, from which it would not abate one jot. Its exclusiveness preserved its integrity. It alone had the courage to be exclusive. Those who entered its fold entered under no delusions as to their connexion with their past.

282 THE VICTORY OF CHRISTIANITY

Its converts, required to surrender so much, came with a deeper conviction and with a warmer zeal for the diffusion of the truth.

The cruel intolerance, political and theological, which mars so many pages of the history of the Church showed a failure to understand the spirit of Jesus in His hatred of unreality and sin combined with such a marvellous love for the misguided. He supplemented the apparently harsh logion ' he that is not with Me is against Me,' with ' he that is not against us is for us.' Christianity has suffered much from the excess of this virtue of intolerance, which has often degenerated into unlovely bigotry. Lecky, after stating that there probably never existed upon earth a community whose members were bound to one another by a purer affection and which combined so felicitously an unflinching opposition to sin with a boundless love to the sinner, says, " There has, however, also never existed a community which displayed more clearly the intolerance that would necessarily follow its triumph." [1] Simultaneously with its *political* triumph, it turned persecutor against pagan, Jew, and heretic. Catholic Christianity tried to exterminate heresy not merely by argument but by sword and flame. The repressive legislation of Theodosius, which by heavy penalties forbade the practice of any other religion than Christianity, the closing of the schools of philosophy at Athens by Justinian, the Albigensian crusades, the Dominican Inquisitions, the religious wars of the seventeenth century, the Acts of Supremacy and Uniformity in Elizabethan England, the cruelties perpetrated upon the Anabaptists —these and such deeds are the debasement of that moral intolerance of apostolic preaching which never doubted *Magna est veritas et praevalebit.* The permanence and success of Christianity were not secured by the contentious Nicene and Athanasian Creeds, but by the simple New Testament creed, ' Jesus is Lord,' which permitted no compromise.

The relation of Christianity to the syncretism of the

[1] *Ib.* I p. 424.

first three centuries[1] would carry us too far afield. [While Christianity avoided the dangers of that syncretism which weakened its competitors] it did not escape unscathed. It borrowed, but it transmuted. It baptized every idea or rite, whether borrowed from the Mysteries or from Judaism, into the name of Christ.[2] It was receptive of the truth, but believed that its only Lord was the Way, the Reality, and the Life. Its attitude is best represented in the words of its greatest Apostle : ' Whatever is true, whatever is venerable, whatever is just, whatever is pure, whatever is lovely, whatever is of good report, if there is any virtue or any praise, consider these things.'

II. Christianity was the only genuinely universal religion which could without reservation declare that there is neither Jew nor Greek, male nor female, bond nor free. It was, in Max Müller's phrase, " the religion of Humanity." It has been shown how Christianity united in a higher and comprehensive synthesis the social-ethical and individual-istic-mystic tendencies in religion, a task which rent the soul of Judaism. It was precisely on this question that ' those of the way ' came into conflict with conservative Judaism ; the nationalistic principle yielded to the universalistic. Paul could say, ' He is our peace, having made both one by breaking down the dividing partition.' Herein the way of Christianity had been prepared by the Mystery-Religions and by Greek philosophy, especially Stoicism. If in its intolerance Christianity was diametrically opposed to the spirit of the age, in its universalism it was in line with the tendencies of a world-civilization. The Mystery-Religions

---

[1] " Das Christentum ist eine synkretistische Religion. Starke religiöse Motive, die aus der Fremde gekommen waren, sind in ihm erhalten und zur Verklärung gediehen, orientalische und hellenistische. Denn das ist das Charakteristische, wir dürfen sagen das Providentielle, am Christentum, dass es seine klassische Zeit in der weltgeschichtlichen Stunden erlebt hat, als es aus dem Orient in das Griechentum übertrat. Darun hat es Teil an beiden Welten. So stark auch später das Hellenistische in ihm'geworden ist, so ist das Orientalische, das ihm von Anfang an eignete, niemals ganz verschwunden " (Gunkel, Z. religionsgesch. Verständnis des N.T., p. 95, with which cf. Dibelius, Sitzb. d. Heidelberger Akad. '17, Abh. 4, p. 53).

[2] Cf. Gardner, Growth of Christianity, chs. II–VI.

and religious philosophies, Jewish preaching and the Roman Empire, were all aiming at a universalism co-extensive with the cosmopolitan character of that time. The Mysteries succeeded most signally, but fell short of a comprehensive universalism in the exclusiveness by which their secrets could not be divulged to outsiders.[1] Greek thought was united with Hebrew Revelation and Oriental mysticism to meet the needs of the day, which it did to a remarkable degree, but mostly for the cultivated classes. Jewish propaganda failed by persisting in making men Jews first. The Imperial cult was little more than a political device. Christianity surmounted all barriers. It had in its heroic days no *disciplina arcani*, no secret which could not be divulged to all; it did not pride itself on a *Gnosis* accessible to the few. Though strait was the gate the conditions of entry were such that all could comply therewith, and those conditions were not buried in a secret lore.

No other religion could compete with Christianity in the scope and variety of its appeal and the comprehensiveness of its message. It admitted of diverse interpretations adapting it to every variety of temperament and racial outlook. It could be presented legally or mystically, in the homely terms of the Sermon on the Mount or in the subtlety of a metaphysical system. It could baptize into the name of its Lord everything that was of worth in the convert's past paganism or Judaism. Its appeal was at once religious, social, philosophical, and ethical, so that it could satisfy the threefold demands made of a religion—social needs, personal solace, and justification of its dogmas.[2]

" Christianity made the double appeal, appealing on the one side as a religion with a practical message to every man, low or high, and on the other side as a philosophy, rivalling the great systems of antiquity, supplementing and correcting them, and at the same time assimilating many of their most

---

[1] Lucian makes Demonax (11) justify his abstinence from the Mysteries on the ground that if they were bad he ought to have denounced them, and if good they should be revealed to all.

[2] Cf. Bussell, *Christian Theology and Social Progress*, p. 165.

persuasive features. No movement can spread rapidly and widely unless it appeals to the common man ; and no movement can establish itself firmly and permanently unless it wins the thinking classes, the intellectual leaders of the world. Christianity did both." [1]

Origen [2] had already remarked upon this excellence of Christianity in not ' despising the populace ' but ' carefully seeking to provide food for the great mass of men.'

The Christian Commonwealth into which men entered by one baptism into one Lord accomplished more for the world than did the Utopian Republic of Plato, with its class distinctions and restrictions, or the Jewish conception of the Kingdom of God in which the premier place was assigned to the Jew, or the *Cosmopolis* of the Stoics, which stood nearest to Christianity in its levelling of all distinctions of race, sex, and culture, but remained only an ideal for lack of the personal ideal of Love to which Christianity could point.

Jesus, by the Edict of Comprehension, as Seeley finely calls the Sermon on the Mount, made morality universal and constituted all men brothers under one Heavenly Father. " The words ' foreign ' and ' barbarous ' lost their meaning ; all nations and tribes were gathered within the *pomoerium* of the city of God ; and on the baptized earth the Rhine and Thames became as Jordan, and every sullen desert-girded settlement of German savages as sacred as Jerusalem." [3] The idea of the brotherhood of man was no novelty introduced by Jesus. The idea had fascinated thinkers from at least the day when Socrates,[4] on being asked to which State he belonged, replied that he was a citizen of the world, and Diogenes, the Cynic lecturer, in reply to the same question,[5] stated that he was a ' cosmopolitan.' Hebrew prophecy had dreamed of the day when ' the God of the whole earth

---

[1] McGiffert, *Ib.* p. 45.

[2] *C. Celsum*, VII. 60.

[3] *Ecce Homo*, ch. XII.

[4] Epictetus, *Disc.* I. 9, 1 ; Cicero, *Tusc. Disp.* V. 37, 108 : 'Socrates quidem cum rogaretur cuiatem se esse diceret, mundanum inquit. Totius enim mundi se incolam et civem arbitrabatur.'

[5] Diog. Laert. VI. 63.

shall He be called,' when all should look to Jerusalem as the religious centre and symbol of unity. Many factors had given emphasis to this feeling of a common humanity which demanded a universal religion. The Stoics made of it a religion, the loftiest element in which is the kinship between God and man in which all participate. ' Of His race are we.' Epictetus dwells upon this inspiring thought. Descent from God should be more elevating than kinship with the emperor [1]; we are 'relatives of God, and come from Him.' [2] The good man is the offspring of God.[3] Another bond of union was the all-pervading Logos. For the realization of brotherhood Stoic teachers recognized the need of love to eradicate selfishness : ' In the State Love is God, a fellow-worker for the salvation of the city.' [4]

The religion of Jesus alone proved equal to the task of establishing a true sense of humanity, and did so by the introduction of a purely human and comprehensive principle of Love, which can be best described in Seeley's phrase " the enthusiasm of humanity," a principle first exemplified in Jesus Himself, and from Him caught up by His disciples. Glover has truthfully said :

" No other teacher dreamed that common men could possess a tenth part of the moral grandeur and spiritual power which Jesus elicited from them—chiefly by believing in them. Here, to anyone who will study the period, the sheer originality of Jesus is bewildering. This belief in men Jesus gave to His followers, and they have never lost it." [5]

It is no exaggeration to say that Christian love was a new moral factor in the world. The Apostle Paul put love above all the gifts of the Spirit. Jesus' love to His followers awakened a responsive love in them. Their love to Him produced an attitude of loyalty to a Person hitherto un-

---

[1] *Disc.* I. 3, 1 ; 9, 1.
[2] *Ib.* I. 9, 3 ; 9, 6.
[3] Seneca, *De Prov.* I.
[4] Zeno, Arnim, *Frag. Stoic.* I. 263 ; cf. also Arnold, *Rom. Stoicism*, p. 275, n. 14.
[5] *Conflict of Religions*, p. 130.

known in religion. His belief in the infinite moral and spiritual capacities of the most ordinary of mortals lent enthusiasm to their preaching. The results have vindicated Jesus' optimism about human nature. ' The philanthropy of God our Saviour ' begot the all-pervading philanthropy of early Christianity which so characterized it in the eyes of outsiders.

III. CHRISTIAN FAITH

The apostolic writer shows his appreciation of a fundamental characteristic of Christianity in contrast with the surrounding world in the declaration ' this is the victory that overcomes the world, our faith.' As Christian love was the new moral force that entered the world with Christ, Christian faith was the new religious force. Faith has always been the root principle of Christianity. Christians are those who ' have faith in God through Jesus Christ,' ' those who practise faith,' ' those of faith.' With Christianity the word " faith " may be said to have become "a permanent addition to the moral vocabulary of the world."[1] The word πίστις, like ἀγάπη, by being baptized into Christianity, took on a more comprehensive content, being linked with morality and with a passionate love to a Person. The thing that Christians called faith embraced the noetic quality of conviction, or belief, the moral quality of steadfastness, or loyalty, and the religious quality of absolute trust in a Person. It did not fall a prey to the assumed dualism between the emotional and the intellectual elements in man's life.

Faith was no new thing, having existed in higher and lower forms throughout the history of religion. Men had previously had faith in the deity, in providence, in the power of truth, in the reality of the unseen, and in the victory of good over evil. The polytheistic religions of Greece and Rome had nothing in them to evoke a personal attitude of the soul, though they maintained a conviction in the existence of

---

[1] Seeley, *ibid*. ch. **VI.**

national deities, and in their ability to send bane or blessing, and in the efficacy of ritual.   The primary purpose of worship was not the good of a man's own soul so much as for the sake of the body politic.   The citizen's conduct was determined by custom and tradition, rather than by personal choice grounded on conviction.   To men of religious aptitudes, of course, the reality of the unseen would be a factor in their lives, and the consciousness of the help of the deity would sustain them in trouble.   There was much diversity of opinion in paganism as to the efficacy and nature of prayer.   Lucian finds abundant material for sarcasm in the unspiritual prayers that ascend to God.   But there were men of prayer like Socrates [1] who laid stress on the subjective attitude of the worshipper, and Maximus of Tyre to whom prayer is ' talking to God,' [2] and the author of the *Epinomis*, who says ' pray to the gods with faith.'   We cannot deny to the loftier pagan souls an element of that passionate abandonment which rose above orgiastic mutilations to the contemplation of Love, the *amor Dei intellectualis*. True *Gnosis* was a passion with the spiritual Plotinus, and Porphyry speaks with awe of his own sublimation.   There is a ring of genuine religious experience in Plutarch's testimony that ' the highest of our initiations in this world is only the dream of that true vision and initiation, and the discourses [of the Mysteries] have been so carefully framed as to awaken the memory of the sublime things above.'   These, however, were the exceptions ; faith was not a basic principle in the life of paganism; "faith," according to Hatch, "as a principle of religion, was quite unknown in the state worships.   A man joined in the rites because he was born or lived in a certain place.   He acted as a member of a social or political group, not as an individual, and personal conviction or trust in the gods played no part in determining his action." [3]

The conception of faith is strangely absent from Stoicism. Though this religious system rendered splendid service by

---

[1] Schmidt, p. 6 ff.   [2] XI. 8
[3] *The Pauline Idea of Faith*, p. 68.

emphasizing the unity of the deity, the supremacy of conscience, the duty of ordering life in harmony with the will of God, and by offering the soul a refuge in the Over-soul, or pervading Reason of the universe, it was either unconscious of the lack of a personal bond with its God or unable to supply it. " The Stoic logic had failed to indicate clearly how from the knowledge of the universe as it is men could find a basis for their hopes and efforts for its future ; the missing criterion is supplied by the Paulist doctrine of faith." [1] The word *fides* is found in the Stoic vocabulary, but not the thing we know as faith.[2]

The Mystery-Religions, appealing to the choice of the individual, were more likely to require and evoke faith.[3] Here again we are disappointed to discover what a scanty rôle faith plays, and how far it is from being a principle of the personal religious life. Faith as confidence or assurance,[4] or as belief in dogma, or ritual, or sacrament, is necessarily present, but that distinctively religious character of faith as personal trust in a God conceived as a person is inconspicuous. The psychological and noetic qualities are present, but faith as the link between the soul and God is missing. The phenomenal success of the Mysteries and their stubborn opposition to Christianity were due to their ability to inspire faith of a kind, that is, belief in their superiority, in the efficacy of their sacraments, and in their power to deliver the individual from the evils of astrology, from earthly limitations, and death. Their gods were believed in as Saviours, and worshipped with assurance as providing atonement here and securing a happy lot beyond. The sacramental virtues were such that they produced an

[1] Arnold, p. 415.

[2] Cf. Hatch, *op. cit.* : " Of faith as a principle of religion it made nothing. Faith was not an important factor in the religious life of the Stoics, and hence it played no conspicuous part in their religious teaching " (pp. 75-6).

[3] " A doctrine of justification by faith rather than by works is at the root of all the ancient mystery-religions " (E. Strong and N. Jolliffe, *J.H.S;* XLIV, p. 107).

[4] 'At length, full of confidence (*plena fiducia*), I began to take part in the divine service of the true religion ' (Apul. *Met.* XI. 26.).

ex opere operato effect but little dependent on the subjective estate or faith of the worshipper, though the contrast in the well-known religious proverb between the thyrsus-bearers and the Bacchi warns us against judging paganism by its averages. Participation in the *taurobolium* rendered the initiate ' reborn for eternity.' Initiation into the Orphic-Pythagorean lore secured for the soul identification with the deity. The mystic state, whether of ecstasy or of enthusiasm, superseded faith. It rested on immediate experience, the fruition of faith. The religion of Hermes Trismegistos speaks several times of faith, which, however, occupies a diminutive place compared with *Gnosis*. The Hermetic mystic can say ' wherefore I believe and bear witness ; I am departing to life and light.'[1] Of him it is said ' to know is to believe [have faith] ; to disbelieve is to fail to know [all aorists] . . . and, having reflected on all things and having discovered that they are consonant with the revelations of the Logos, he believed and found rest in the lovely faith.'[2] This Hermetic faith was too vague, and pitched too high for the average man.

It is only fair to the Hermetic religion and to classic Gnosticism to point out that their *Gnosis* was not that intellectual and metaphysical speculation by which they are so often misrepresented, and especially by the bald translation " knowledge." For the true Hermetic believer *Gnosis* had to do with spirit (*nous*) rather than with mind. And Gnosticism itself was born of the new religious aspiration[3] which commenced with the Roman Empire. Its first teachers were seekers after truth rather than mystagogues. But after its classic prime in the second century it lost touch in the third century with Thought and Reason and gave way to fantasy or degenerated into occultism. But, like the only true modern Gnostic, Blake, the real Gnostics believed that, whereas faith is the evidence of things unseen, they should *not* be unseen, but known

---

[1] *Poimandres*, 32 (Reitzenstein's ed. p. 338).
[2] *Corpus Herm.* IX. 10.
[3] Cf. De Faye, *Gnostiques*, p. 434 f.

and seen. The expression 'we shall know as we are known' gives something the longing for which supersedes faith and which the Gnostics claimed to have, and which the writer of the Fourth Gospel, partly in sympathy with, and partly in opposition to, Gnosticism, claimed to find in the present experience of the knowledge of God in Jesus Christ.

There was also present in the Mysteries another function of faith which became conspicuous in Christianity—cult-loyalty, faith in, or fidelity to, the deity which formed the bond of cohesion of the religious guilds and made the members *collegae* et *consacranei*. The religion of Mithra was a *militia*, or warfare, which for the Roman mind implied a *sacramentum*, or oath of allegiance. Faith was struggling for expression when Mithra was addressed as *Sol Invictus*, or Isis as 'thou eternal Saviour of the race of men,' or when the initiate uttered ' I have escaped evil ; I have found good ' ; 'Thou art I, and I am Thou.'[1] The Mystery-Religions thus inculcated faith in their patron deities, in the magical efficacy of rites, in mystic identification with the god, and cult-loyalty. But such faith was not the mainspring of the religious life and conduct of the average *mystae*, but rather, as it were, a by-product : it was not necessarily of an ethical character, whereas the Christian conception was through and through ethical in its inseparable association with works. Neither could faith in its religious aspect as trust in a person thrive when directed to divinities that were the product of a maturer reflection upon a primitive nature-worship.

As in many other respects, it was the Jew who was the true predecessor of the Christian in demonstrating the power and practice of faith, both in its moral and religious character. Hebrew religion was differentiated from all other religions of antiquity by this personal trust in the living God, and by a faith which expressed itself in an ardent desire for fellowship with Him. This faith took its rise from Jewish monotheism and the ethical conception of the holiness of God which demanded holiness in His worshippers.

[1] Dieterich, *Abraxas*, p. 196.

Their personal reliance upon God was the root of all their piety and the secret of their indestructibility. Neither polytheism nor henotheism nor an abstract monotheism could call forth such a faith. Writers of Hebrew history recognized the uniqueness of Israelitish faith. ' Our fathers trusted in Thee ; they trusted and were not ashamed ' : ' Look at the generations of old and see ; who ever put his trust in the Lord and was ashamed ? ' [1] The faith of Abraham was a commonplace in the theology of the synagogue. The Jewish-Christian author of the *Epistle to the Hebrews* encourages believers by calling the roll of Jewish worthies who ' endured as seeing Him who is invisible.'

Two Jews of the Diaspora, Philo and Paul, men of the profoundest religious convictions, took up the Jewish conception of faith and gave to it a premier place in the religious life which it can never lose. Of Philo Bousset has truthfully remarked,[2] " For the first time in the history of religion we find the thought of Faith in the centre of religion : Philo is the first great psychologist of Faith." Faith occupies a conspicuous place in Philo's mysticism : it is ' a perfect good,' ' a true and abiding good,' ' an amelioration of the soul at all points,' ' the most stable of the virtues,' ' the most perfect of the virtues,' the ' prize ' of the virtuous man. As Philo's system is a syncretism of Platonic Idealism, Stoic Mysticism, and Hebrew Revelation, these three elements are held by some to be discernible in his doctrine of faith. The basis is his Jewish faith as personal trust in the living God, upon which is superadded a sublime idealism which looks to God as the homeland of the soul. The provenance of the mystic strain in his faith is disputed. Bréhier,[3] Hatch,[4] and others attribute it to Stoicism, for which certain passages may be cited, but these furnish parallelisms of language rather than of thought ; and

---

[1] *Ecclus.* II. 10.

[2] *Religion des Judentums*, 2nd ed. p. 514. Cf. also his *Kyrios Christos*, p. 174, and H. A. A. Kennedy, *Philo's Contribution to Religion*, p. 121 f.

[3] *Les Idées Phil. et Relig. de Philon d'Alexandrie*, p. 222.

[4] *Pauline Idea of Faith*, pp. 47, 80.

further, the *a priori* probability that this important ingredient in Philo's philosophy-religion could not fail to act
upon his conception of faith. There is the danger of
deriving this mystic strain from one source, when, as Hatch
admits, " the religious atmosphere of the Graeco-Roman
world was laden with mysticism." Kennedy more correctly
holds that it is " far more probable that he speaks funda-
mentally on the ground of his own religious experience." [1]
Sometimes Philo seems to stress the noetic, or Greek
character of faith, as when he speaks of it as ' the work of
an Olympian understanding '; but this is not a dominant
note. He rather inclines to emphazise the other side, thereby
placing faith as the congener or ally of, or preparation for,
the ecstatic state which gives immediate knowledge of God.
This mystic strain, or juxtaposition of faith and mystic
conditions, was of considerable importance in the history
of religion. Herein, as in many other aspects, Philo proved
the mediator between East and West. He demonstrated
how a vital ethical faith in God could unite with and furnish the means of satisfying the universal mystic strivings
of the age for union with God.

Though Philo's doctrine was of such a comprehensive
nature as was unknown to religious experience previously, a
younger contemporary was independently working out a
kindred empiric doctrine. Philo did much for the Judaism
of the Diaspora and for Christianity. Such a vision of the
spiritual world could never be completely lost to mankind.
He embodied the spirit of the age for his countryman—" a
growing consciousness among the Jews of the time of the
worth and efficacy of faith as a means of salvation alongside
of the righteousness attainable by works." [2] In this way
Philo provided a corrective to the hardness of legalism and to
the degeneracy of trust in God to trust in the Law, corresponding to the later degeneration of Christian faith from a

[1] *Ibid.* p. 125.
[2] Thackeray, *Relation of St. Paul to Contemporary Jewish Thought*,
p. 90 ; cf. Bousset, p. 223 ff. ; Excursus by Lietzmann, *Handbuch z. N.T.*
III, 1, p. 24.

religious trust into a credal assent and acceptance of meta-physical formulae.[1] On the other hand, for the many thousands reached by the teachings of the synagogue of the Diaspora Philo made the moral quality indissociable from the religious by declaring that faith conduced to virtue or was the crown of virtue, as Christianity joined faith and works.

It was only in Christianity that faith as a religious principle of life came to its full fruition. Christian faith embraced every worthy element of prior religious experience and aspiration ; while it exalted man above his earthliness, it did justice to all the interests and relations of earth life. In its comprehensiveness it was unsurpassed, while in one important aspect it proved unique—faith in an historic Person, and in the defiant enthusiasm awakened by loyalty to that Person. The Person of Christ was the centre of the new faith. Jews and Christians believed in God, but Christians ' believed in God through Jesus Christ.'

Faith in Jesus thus became a fundamental doctrine of Christianity. Paul, a younger contemporary of Philo, took up the apostolic message, and, influenced by his personal experience on the road to Damascus and his familiarity with the Old Testament,[2] gave to faith a central position in Christianity which it never can lose,[3] a faith awakened and sustained by the Cross of Christ. The Pauline conception of faith has proved even more epoch-making than that of Philo in that it more effectively combined the Hebraic and the Hellenistic elements in a unity which has been a new dynamic in the religious life of mankind. The emotional, the noetic, the ethical, and the religious elements are commingled. Unlike that of Philo, faith is for Paul rather the initiation of the Christian life than the prize won at the end, though of course the Christian life is a growth in faith as in every other grace, so that " perhaps faith must always be viewed under these two aspects, as the clue

---

[1] Cf. Hatch, *Influence of Greek Ideas*, p. 313 ff.

[2] Thackeray, p. 90 f.

[3] Cf. Morgan, *Religion and Theology of Paul*, p. 114 ff

to spiritual progress as well as its crown." [1] Unlike Philo,
faith, in Paul's view, is not something inferior to the ecstatic
or mystic condition which gives a superior Knowledge, but
the mystic state depends wholly on faith as its source.
Perhaps it might be more truly said that in Paul these
two functions of the psychic life are one : his mysticism is
'faith-mysticism,' or ' Christ-mysticism.' To be ' in faith,'
'in Christ,' 'in the Spirit' are synonymous. Paul himself,
as a 'pneumatic,' enjoyed revelations, visions, ecstasis,
pneumatic *charismata*, but while he prized these as *spiritual*
phenomena he held them secondary to the more normal
experiences of Christian living. To be ' in Christ ' or to have
' Christ in you,' it was unnecessary for a man to be transported into that ecstatic condition described by Philo, in
which personality is for the time being in abeyance, or by
Paul himself in the experience of being caught up into the
third heaven. Whence came this faith-mysticism [2] of Paul
which laid hold of the Graeco-Roman world and attracted
initiates from the gods of the Mystery-Religions to Christ ?
Hatch answers :

" Paul's mysticism seems to have been derived from no one
source in particular, as from Philo or some one of the
Mystery-cults. It was rather absorbed, in a perfectly
natural and partly unconscious way, from his Graeco-Roman
environment, in which mysticism was a very prominent and
important factor." [3]

This answer recognizes the fact that Paul's converts were
steeped in mystic ideas and that they could without difficulty
put themselves *en rapport* with Paul's teaching ; also, that
Paul himself, as a son of the Diaspora, must have been
familiar with the main religious ideas of the Mystery-cults and
touched by the mysticism that was " in the air " ; but it

---

[1] H. A. A. Kennedy, *Expositor*, March '19, p. 218.
[2] In *Orfismo e Paolinismo*, published 1922, Prof Macchioro puts forth a
novel view in claiming for Pauline Christology and mysticism Orphic
origin. Cf. F. Anderson, *Paulinism and Orphism* in *Australasian Jour.
of Phil. and Psychology*, September '24.
[3] *Op. cit.* p. 66.

hardly does justice to the fact that one who had 'seen the Lord' did not need to absorb a mystery-atmosphere, and that Paul's mysticism was first-hand and can be shown to date only from that moment when 'it pleased God to reveal His Son in me,' which the three narratives of his conversion in *Acts* bear out ; nor does it do justice to the distance between Paul's 'Christ-mysticism' and that mysticism which clung round the Mysteries. Paul, as a Hebrew of Hebrews, was prior to his conversion too conservative a Jew to welcome mystic ideas, for, though the Jewish race produced the three great mystics, Philo and Paul and the author of the Fourth Gospel, "the Jewish mind and character, in spite of its deeply religious bent, was alien to mysticism." [1] It would be difficult to detect the affinity between the Faith-mysticism of Paul and the surrounding Graeco-Roman mysticism : the differences far outweigh the faint resemblances.[2] In Paul there is a type of mysticism which stands by itself [3] and which differs from the mysticism of the Mystery-Religions and from that of Philo in two important aspects : first, as regards the human factor, there is a conspicuous absence of any idea of absorption in the deity. Paul valued too highly his own personality and individuality. The will is a factor as potent as emotion. Paul's 'life hid with Christ in God' is a life of active fellowship with Christ, but never absorption into Christ. Secondly, as regards the Divine factor, in the mystic fellowship the faith-mysticism of Paul is faith grounded on an historic Personality to whose love faith is the necessary response. The Christian who is 'in Christ' finds himself in fellowship with a Person, and is not lost, as in the mysticism of Philo or Neo-Platonism, in the ocean of the Absolute, nor, as in the Mysteries, does he undergo divinization. He becomes like Christ, but never Christ.

Such was the character of that Christian faith which

[1] Inge, *Christian Mysticism*, p. 39. Cf. Pringle-Pattison, *Ency. Brit.* 11th ed. art. *Mysticism*, p. 124 a ; Gruppe, *Gr. Myth.* II, p. 1608 ff.

[2] For difference between Pauline and Hellenistic mysticism cf. Bousset, *Kyrios Christos*, p. 172 f.

[3] Cf. Kennedy, *St. Paul and the Mystery-Religions*, p. 291.

overcame the world. It took on the features of Jesus' own all-conquering trust in the Father ; it was based on loyalty to His Person ; it furnished the means of fellowship with Him ; and it met the deepest needs of the age as the link between the human soul and God. It was a faith that kept company with knowledge, arising from a knowledge of what Christ was and issuing in a profounder knowledge—and yet the humblest sinner [1] could by the venture of faith find himself in touch with the living God. Herein, as a democratic principle, it differed from the systems of Gnosticism, whether pagan, Jewish, or Christian, which because of their emphasis on an esoteric ' knowledge ' were aristocratic systems to which universalism was denied. Pagan apologists, misunderstanding the true character of Christian faith and viewing it mainly as belief, ridiculed it as inferior to knowledge and akin to ignorance. The path to victory of Christian faith was prepared by the Jewish personal trust in God, to which it had most affinity, and by those mystic aspirations fostered by the Mystery-cults. The idea of faith was " in the air and waiting only for an object worthy of it." [2]   Christ proved to faith the power of God unto salvation to a world crying out for Saviour-gods.

IV. The Greek Bible

Christianity owed a large debt to Judaism, which put in her hands a holy book sanctioned by its antiquity. From Judaism Christianity learned the use of this book in propaganda and finally derived from the parent faith the idea of the formation of a Christian canonical book. Through the synagogue the Greek Bible became familiar to the Jews of the Diaspora, to the proselytes, and to multitudes of God-fearers. This world-book inculcated the

---

[1] Cf. Seeley, *Ecce Homo*, ch. VI : " Other virtues can scarcely thrive without a fine natural organization and a happy training. But the most neglected and ungifted of men may make a beginning with faith. Other virtues want civilization, a certain amount of knowledge, a few books ; but in half-brutal countenances faith will light up a glimmer of nobleness."

[2] Sanday and Headlam, *Romans*, p. 33.

habit and taught the language of prayer, witnessed to a vital monotheism, and required a lofty ethical standard. It was no small advantage to Christianity, both in its incipient and in its later stages, to have ready to hand such an authoritative spiritual weapon.

"The possession of these sacred Scriptures, descended from an antiquity by the side of which the beginnings of Greek philosophy were modern, and derived from divine Revelation, made a doubly profound impression upon an age which turned its eyes to the ancients for wisdom and to heaven for a truth beyond the attainment of reason." [1]

To understand the advantages accruing to early Christianity from Biblicism we must understand the attitude of that age toward authority, which was altogether different from that of the present day. The tendency of the age was to seek authority and rest in it. It would be unsafe to trace this tendency to any one particular cause, but the main cause was the regnant subjectivity which, in recoil from a previous period of objectivity,[2] laid stress on the inwardness of religion and exposed the perplexities of the question of selfhood. In this limitless region there were few or no guide-posts, so that in the bewilderment of inwardness there arose a new disposition to seek external authority and to believe what one cannot prove. In post-Aristotelian thought there set in a reaction against abstract speculation accompanied by a corresponding demand for concrete views to guide conduct. Socrates and the Sophists undermined the authority of tradition and custom. Platonism and Aristotelianism, deriving their inspiration from Socrates, had essayed the contemplation of the universe and man, trusting in "man's unconquerable mind," and had vindicated the rights and privileges of the "meddling intellect." But a new world-order was inaugurated by Alexander, on the threshold of which stood Aristotle. Mistrust in man's

[1] G. F. Moore, *History of Religion*, II. p. 521 f.
[2] Cf. K. Manitius' note, p. 283 of his ed. of Proclus, *Hypotyposis astronom. positionum*, Leip. '09.

capacity for knowledge and in the reliability of that knowledge, never doubted in the heyday of Greek thought, began to find expression. In the later Greek schools there is much discussion as to the criterion of knowledge as well as its relation to conduct. The Cyrenaics despaired of knowledge. The Stoics, following Aristotle, were pure empirics. The Epicureans [1] relied solely on the senses, but doubted whether these give certain knowledge. The Academicians rejected both sense-knowledge and concept-knowledge, and were content to rest in suspense of judgment, or, like Bishop Butler, to accept probability as the guide of life. The Eclectics fell back on the relativity of knowledge, trusting most in the self-consciousness, or in the *consensus omnium*. The various elements of personality had been coming ever more prominently into view since the days of Socrates and Aristotle ; the intellectual had lost its hegemony, or its hegemony was questioned before the volitional and the emotional, as the moral consciousness asserted its rights beside ratiocination. Thought was moving on its way from the concept theories of Socrates to the quietism of Plotinus. Man cannot permanently rest in agnosticism ; if he cannot by himself attain assurance he will flee for refuge to authority. Criteria for knowledge and standards for conduct were sought in every quarter : in the moral consciousness, in the *consensus gentium*, in Nature, in the ideal wise man, in the early traditions of the Greek world or in the ancient cults of the Orient. Denis, speaking of the religious conditions of the Graeco-Roman world, says of the Greeks :

" Grown old in dialectics, tired of uncertainty and scepticism, they were less conscious of the need of arriving by every means at the emancipation of the spirit, than of discovering a norm which should put an end to their discussions and to their doubts. In the letter of a formal and sacred text they would see an alleviation rather than a constraint and inconvenience. It is well known how many philosophers of the first century avoided dis-

---

[1] Cf. Bussell, *School of Plato*, p. 178.

THE VICTORY OF CHRISTIANITY

cussion in order to adopt sacramental formulae, and how, more anxious for self-discipline than for independence, they themselves had recourse to faith, bound themselves to observances and exercises like believers and ascetics who possessed truth rather than like thinkers in search of it." [1]

In the new clamant needs of the spirit men sought direction from every source which promised help. Some laid their burdens before the spiritual directors and private chaplains whose philosophy had become a very practical religion.[2] Some sought incarnate examples, living or dead, that in imitation of them they might guide their steps aright. Thousands entered the synagogue to be instructed in the requirements of the moral law and in the ideals of prophetism. Multitudes sought initiation in the Mystery-Religions whose priests and adherents welcomed every enquirer.

Christianity, emerging within the fold of Judaism and cognizant of the rôle which the Old Testament, and especially the version of the Seventy, had played in Jewish propaganda, adopted the Jewish Scriptures and baptized them into Christ. In the hands of Christians the Septuagint became such a formidable weapon against Jews and heathen that Jewish scholars later denied to it inspiration in favour of ' the Hebrew verity.' From this Old Testament [3] an anthology of Messianic proof-texts was made by Christian preachers to demonstrate that Christ was the fulfilment of Old Testament Revelation. Scriptural proof occupied a prominent place in reasoning and in controversy. By an exegesis, sometimes literalistic, mostly allegorical, sometimes historic, Christians claimed for Jesus a central place in human history, while proving that the roots of their religion went back to an immemorial past—an especial virtue of a religion in that

[1] *Histoire des Théories et des Idées Morales dans l'Antiquité*, II, p. 321.
[2] Cf. C. Martha, *Les Moralistes sous l'empire romain*, p. 16 ff. ; Dill, *Roman Society*, bk. III. ch. I.
[3] Cf. Weizsäcker, *Apostolic Age*, Eng. tr. I, p. 132 f. ; Lietzmann, *Handbuch z. N.T.* III. 1, p. 255.

day. A book which the Saviour prized and into which He read Himself naturally assumed a position of authority. On the pattern of the Greek Bible the Christians began early in the second century the preparation of a specifically Christian collection, the delimitation of which was not completed until the end of the fourth century.

The advantages of having to hand the Greek Bible will be more apparent if we reflect upon the demand of the age for a new supernatural source of knowledge by Revelation [1] rather than by ratiocination. Still in search of a ' strong raft ' or ' some sure word ' of God, hesitating on the brink of knowledge before plunging into the gulf of mysticism, troubled by acute subjectivity and world-weariness, men manifested a readiness to believe which was accentuated by contact with the East, especially with Hebrew Revelation.

" In a period," says Zeller,[2] " in which much greater weight was laid on the practical effect of philosophy than on scientific knowledge as such, in which a deep distrust of man's capacity of knowledge prevailed, and there was a general inclination to accept truth, when found, on the basis of practical necessity, and a direct conviction of it, even at the cost of scientific consistency—in such a period only a slight impulse was needed in order to lead the spirit in its search for truth beyond the limits of natural knowledge to a supposed higher fountain."

The knowledge now sought was of a different order from that of disinterested speculation. There was a change of emphasis with new associations and new methods and channels. To ' know God ' became the universal question to which every living religion addressed itself, and the more pretensions a religion could make to satisfy this knowledge the more success would attend it. Without *Gnosis* salvation was universally conceived as impossible. Every species

---

[1] Cf. Neander, *Church History*, Eng. tr. I, p. 43 ; Zeller, *Stoics, Epicueans, and Sceptics*, Eng. tr. p. 30.
[2] *Outlines*, p. 350. Murray (*Four Stages*, p. 103) notes as marks of the Christian era, in Christian and pagan literature alike, " a despair of patient enquiry, a cry for infallible revelation."

of Gnosticism attempted to supply this needed revelation that the individual might enter into correct religious relations with the deity. In this sense every competing religion of the Graeco-Roman age was a species of Gnosticism [1] professing to possess a priceless revelation to be disclosed to its adherents. Judaism proclaimed that in the knowledge of Jahweh was Life, and that this knowledge had been vouchsafed to Israel through Moses and the prophets and preserved in their Scriptures. The Mystery-Religions, by a sacramental drama of the life of the deity, put the initiates into possession of such a knowledge of formulae, rites, and sacraments as secured salvation. The Hermetic religion professes to be essentially an esoteric religion, a claim which it makes good in a measure far beyond all other forms of the Mysteries. The Revelation therein is of two kinds [2] : first, that given immediately by a god, Hermes, That, or Aesculapius, or the Good Demon,[3] and secondly that given mediately by a gifted prophet who derives his inspiration either from the god within or by ascending by divine assistance to the home of the gods. There can be no salvation, according to this Hermetic religion, apart from true *Gnosis* which comes partly by instruction and partly by intuition. The salvation to which this knowledge conduces is of two prominent types, that of Regeneration and that of Deification.

All the religions whose vitality rendered them competitors against Christianity belonged to the class of " religions of authority," which professed to be in possession of a supernatural revelation as a means of salvation. Christianity entered the lists also as a religion of authority, as was necessary in that age. It claimed to be in possession from the beginning of a special revelation in a book well known to all who were in contact with Judaism, and this written

---

[1] " γνῶσις θεοῦ wird das Losungswort im Konkurrenzkampfe der Religionen " (Norden, *Agnostos Theos*, p. 109 ; Mead, *Quests*, p. 177 ff.).

[2] Reitzenstein, *Hell. Mysterien-Religionen*, p. 179 ff. ; Kennedy, *St. Paul*, p. 106.

[3] On theories of the Agathodaimon as a mystical angel, the good demon of Egypt, Heaven, an Egyptian philosopher, *v.* Berthelot, *Alchimistes*, pt. 2, Greek text, p. 80 (from Olympiodorus).

revelation it later supplemented by a specifically Christian canon.   But it had an incalculable advantage over Judaism and all other religions in that its authority was augmented by the personality of its Founder, who had so revealed the Father that Christians offered to the world ' the knowledge of God in the face of Jesus Christ.'   The Scribe pretended to hold ' the key of knowledge,' to ' bind and loose,' to ' open and shut ' ; but Christians, as a royal priesthood, before the days of cold ecclesiasticism, opened to all men the Kingdom of Heaven by faith.

It does not pertain to our present purposes to dwell upon the abuses of this handy Biblicism, or to show how, what proved to be an initial advantage, became, through a mistaken reverence, a fetter upon Christianity. As Judaism was pre-eminently " the religion of a book," Christianity too began to be regarded as such rather than as the religion of Life and of the Spirit.[1] On the theory inevitable to that age, Revelation was viewed as something static, a quantum given once for all and of unalterably defined content, whereas a living religion must be dynamic and evolutional, capable of adaptation to every form of life and to every age and of expansion by its own inner laws.   The letter which, by its authority, helped Christianity at the beginning, finally became baneful through abuse.   The freedom of the divine Spirit was hampered even by a misuse of a venerable collection of books of sublime worth.   For long centuries Biblicism proved to Christianity almost as grievous a load as legalism had been to Judaism.   Even the Reformation only lightened the burden. As a result of the application of the historic method to biblical study, and more especially from a due recognition, since the days of Schleiermacher, of the continuity and validity of Christian experience, we are in the happier position of being able to prize the classic holy books of Hebrew religion and early Christianity as books of permanent worth, though containing contemporary elements alongside of the perennial. At the same time we can better appreciate Christianity as

---

[1] Cf. Watson, *Philosophic Basis of Religion*, p. 3 ff.

the religion of Jesus which has in it principles of growth, adaptation, and expansion present in every living organism. Sabatier is correct, in the main, in viewing Christianity as pre-eminently the religion of the Spirit and of Life rather than as a religion of authority.   As *the* religion of the Spirit and of Life it is authoritative.   Vast tracts of religious and specifically Christian experience have been traversed since the Old Testament and New Testament were penned ; new reaches of religious aspiration have been attained, while " leagues beyond those leagues there is more sea."   The leaven implanted by Jesus into the mass of humanity has been working silently but persistently since His day.   That Spirit which He promised His followers has through the centuries been leading men into truth and more truth. Christianity is the religion of liberty : ' if the Son make you free, you shall be free indeed.'

V. CHRISTIANITY BROUGHT A SATISFYING MESSAGE TO THE
WIDESPREAD SORROW OF THE ANCIENT WORLD

The real test of any religion is not its attitude to the joys and raptures of life, but its ability to give moral content to the sorrows and perplexities of life.   Christianity stood this test.[1]   No other religion, except pre-Christian Buddhism, ever approached Christianity in dealing with the perennial problem of human suffering, but both the approach and the solution were different.   Buddhism offered an anodyne or a way of escape, while Christianity gave to suffering a profound religious meaning, and, instead of demanding resignation, offered a means of conquest over a world which God loves, and transmuted grief into joy. Stoicism deserved well of that ancient world because of its eminent services in extracting a meaning from pain,[2]

[1] " It seems sometimes as if the Greek thinkers . . . shrank in the last resort from grasping the nettle of suffering firmly.   Nor is there any religion or philosophy, except Christianity, which has really drawn the sting of the world's evil " (Inge, *Plotinus*, II. 208).

[2] " Stoicism throve because, like Christianity, it is a philosophy of suffering ; it fell because, unlike Christianity, it is a philosophy of despair " (Bigg, *Christian Platonists*, p. 288).

but its richest fruit was a passionless resignation rather than an exultant ' joy fulfilled.' The Mysteries, in their blind instinctive way, did point in their symbolism toward the religious solution in a ' fellowship of sufferings.'

Christianity most effectively brought a sustaining gospel to the sufferers of the Graeco-Roman world. It was uniquely fitted to do so because it was from its birth a religion whose ' Lord of Glory ' had been ' the Man of Sorrows ' in an earthly life of conflict culminating in an agonizing death. Jesus, the Son of God, was proclaimed as the *passibilis Christus* who, in the faith of His followers, was the historic fulfilment of the Suffering Servant of Deutero-Isaiah's vision, in which the mysterious redemptive aspects of suffering are so sublimely portrayed. In loyalty to Jesus' example the demands for self-sacrifice and detachment from the world were pitched higher than in contemporary religions. There was no ambiguity about the conditions of entry into the Christian Society ; no easy terms were offered. ' If a man wishes to come after Me, let him deny himself, and let him take up his cross [Luke adds ' daily '] and follow Me. Whoever wishes to save his life shall destroy it, but whosoever shall lose his life for My sake and the gospel's, shall save it.' ' If the world hates you, you know that it hated Me.' ' If any man will live godly in Christ Jesus, he must suffer persecution.' Such preaching of ' resisting unto blood ' was not calculated to attract the thoughtless. Christianity clearly envisaged the suffering and sin of the world. " The general impression that we receive from the records of the New Testament is assuredly that they were written under a prevailing sense of human misery." [1] With the prevalent individualism of the Christian era and its consequent sensitiveness the problem of suffering had been accentuated. ' Life and pain are akin,' Menander had said, and this is a recurrent refrain of the Greek Anthology. Virgil, " majestic in thy sadness," had sung of the *Lacrymae rerum*. Seneca repeatedly gives utterance to such senti-ments as *Omnis vita supplicium*, and *tota flebilis vita*. All

---

[1] Merivale, *Conversion of the Roman Empire*, p. 88.

religions were obliged to deal with the problem and offer salvation. Saviour-gods must be gods of ' sympathy.' Aesculapius was styled ' the greatest lover of men,' as was also Serapis.   Lucius addressed Isis as ' Thou bestowest a mother's sweet love upon miserable mortals. . . . Thou dispellest the storms of life, and stretchest out thy right hand of salvation to struggling men.'   Plutarch [1] lauds the same goddess that she has not become oblivious of her own trials and sufferings so that she can console humanity in its trials.   The Great Mother of Pessinus was by her loss and grief brought near to suffering mothers.   In nearly all the Mysteries there was enacted a symbolic passion-drama representing the trials and sufferings of the deity, in which joy succeeded grief and life was born of death.

The two centuries preceding the Christian era had been a period of uninterrupted misery.   For a time the Roman peace gave the world rest, but after the Antonine days happiness departed from the ancient world.   It is significant that Christianity spread most rapidly in the half-century (closing third century) of the greatest confusion for pagan society.[2]   It is significant, too, that every persecution only strengthened the Church.   When the emperors were anxiously guarding the frontiers, when the results of a vicious fiscal system had worked themselves out, when industry was paralysed, when earthquakes devastated rich and populous regions, when freemen were decreasing, when Goth and Hun and Vandal were swooping down on their prey in the empire, and when the Eternal City itself fell before the Germanic invaders, Christianity lengthened its cords and strengthened its stakes.   Its competitors were overtaken by mortal weakness when ancient society was tottering to its fall—a weakness from which they never eventually recovered in spite of many deceptive revivals. Christianity outstripped all other religions in offering a comfortable message to a distracted world.   Men were invited into the ' fellowship of His sufferings ' that thus

[1] *De Is. et Osir.* ch. XXVII.
[2] Cf. Geffcken, *N Jahrb. f. d. Kl. Alt.* XLI. '18, p. 99 ff.

His ' joy might be fulfilled ' in them. The bitter cries and tears of the agonizing Sufferer in Gethsemane reverberated through the Christian message, making Jesus very real and near to men in their agonies. The eschatological hope made the sufferings of the present time unworthy of comparison with the glory to be revealed. In mutual spiritual fellowship Christians supported one another, bearing one another's burdens. For them the Communion of the Saints was a very real thing, as we learn, for example, from Paul's thanksgiving to ' the Father of all mercies and God of every comfort, who comforts us in our every affliction that we may be enabled to comfort those in every affliction through the comfort with which we ourselves are being comforted of God. Because in proportion as the sufferings of Christ abound toward us our comfort shall abound through Christ.'

The Christian message of the Cross was that of a suffering God in a real incarnation which made effective in life's agonies the full depth of the co-suffering (*sympathia*) of God with His creatures.[1] This was then, as it is to-day, the only evangel for the world's pain,[2] of which the Cross remains the perennial symbol :

" Blazoned as on Heaven's immortal noon,
The Cross leads generations on." [3]

The πάθη of Dionysos were legendary ; the πάθη of Jesus were very real to Himself and His followers. Jesus was preached to the ancient world as the Physician greater than great Aesculapius, and more *philanthropic* than Serapis φιλανθρωπότατος. The reputation which He acquired in Palestine as an efficient physician was immensely enhanced after His death, as seen in the spurious third-century correspondence between Abgar of Edessa and Jesus. One of the most popular and frequent titles of Jesus was Physician, and the Gospel was represented as a therapeutic of body, mind,

---

[1] Contrast the statement in a textbook of Hellenistic theology (Sallustius, *De Diis et Mundo*, 14) : ' God does not rejoice ; for that which rejoices also grieves.'

[2] Cf. Pringle-Pattison, *The Idea of God*, p. 407 ff.

[3] Chorus of the *Hellas*.

and soul.[1] In the early Christian propaganda were united
the functions of the medical profession and the ministry of
preaching. Ignatius writes : ' There is only one Physician,
Jesus Christ.'[2] Clement hails the Logos as ' the only
Paeonian physician of human infirmities, and the holy
charmer of the sick soul, the all-sufficient physician of
humanity.'[3] Tertullian writes *Christum medicatorem*[4] and
Augustine [5] *medicus magnus* and *omnipotens medicus.* The
dispute between Celsus and Origen,[6] with equal conviction,
as to the relative merits of Aesculapius Saviour or Jesus
Saviour, and the less pleasing pleading of Arnobius on the
same theme,[7] are instructive as evidence of the demand
for healing [8] through religion. Eusebius describes Jesus
in a literal quotation [9] from a Greek medical writer, pseudo-
Hippocrates, as ' like an excellent physician who examines
what is repulsive, handles ulcers, and reaps pain for Himself
from the sufferings of others.' An inscription discovered at
Timgad in 1919 records the prayer of an age that suffered
more deeply than has our own : *Sub [veni] Christe tu solus
medicus.*[10] The keen sensitiveness to pain and the widespread
misery in which the Graeco-Roman period ended caused
such a demand for personal consolation and healing through
religion that the god of healing and ' lover of men ' was
one of the last to submit to Christianity, but not without
his cult contributing a salvationist terminology and healing
usages to the Christian Church. Many of the votive inscriptions to Aesculapius could be pressed into Christian
service by the simple substitution of the name of Christ for

[1] Cf. Harnack, *Medicinisches aus d. ältesten Kirchengesch.* in *T. u. Unters.*
VIII, 1892 ; pp. 101–24 in *Mission and Exp.* I.
[2] *Ad Eph.* 7.
[3] *Paed.* I. 2, 6.
[4] *Ad Marc.* III. 17.
[5] *Serm.* 175, 1.
[6] *C. Celsum,* III. 3, 23, 24.
[7] *Adv. Gentes,* I. 38, 41, 49 : VI. 21.
[8] On Pythagoras' reputation as a healer *v.* Aelian, *V.H.* IV. 17 ; cf.
Roscher, II. 521 ff.
[9] *H.E.* X. 4 ; 1.
[10] *Acad. des Inscr.: Comptes Rendus,* 1920, pp. 75–83.

that of His healing rival.   Perhaps, too, it was the figure
of Aesculapius that suggested the model[1] for the gracious
fourth or fifth century figure of Christ.

VI. AN HISTORIC AND PERSONAL CENTRE

Christianity had a unique advantage over all its competitors, including even Judaism, in having an historic Person
as Founder, whose Person was greater than His teachings.
Herein lay its greatest originality and the main secret of its
power.   Christian enthusiasm was awakened and sustained
not by an ideal, but by a Person.   Christianity was the new
spiritual power which entered our humanity from the Personality of one who had been a familiar figure in Palestine.
Christian preachers did not require faith merely in Jesus'
teachings or in His Resurrection, but in Himself.   By a true
religious instinct His followers recognized that the Personality of their Master, which fascinated and perplexed them,
which prompted Christologies, which gained their allegiance,
was the new factor in history.   Other religions might show a
more imposing ceremonial, might offer a liturgy more subtle
than the Disciples' Prayer or the Apostles' Creed ; other
religions and philosophies might with considerable success dispute the originality of Jesus' teachings and furnish parallels
to most of them, but no other religion could ' placard ' a
real Being in flesh and blood who had lived so near to God
and brought men into such intimate soul-satisfying union
with the Father.

" The centre in the new religion is not an idea, nor a ritual
act, but a Personality.   As its opponents were quick to point
out . . . there was little new in Christian teaching. . . .
What was new in the new religion, in this ' third race ' of
men ?   The Christians had their answer ready.   In clear

---

[1] Cf. Harnack, *Miss. and Exp.* I, p. 118 f.   In *Rev. des Études grecques*,
XXIX, p. 78, is a photo of the ' Healer ' with a kneeling woman touching
his garment with her right hand.

speech, and in aphasia, they indicated their Founder. He
was new." [1]

The Christian apologists were conscious of the strength of
their position in having an historic centre. Thus, in the
middle of the second century an Assyrian *fidei defensor* [2]
wrote :

' We do not utter idle tales in declaring that God was born
in form of a man. I challenge you, our detractors, to contrast your legends with our narratives. . . . Your legends
are but idle tales. . . . O Greeks, believe me now, and do
not attempt to resolve your myths or gods into allegory.'

A religion with a personal and historic founder, such as
Judaism boasted in Moses or Ezra, Buddhism in Gotama,
the Persian religion in Zoroaster, and Islam in the prophet
of Arabia, has inevitably an advantage in propaganda over
purely naturalistic and mythical faiths. Ideas must be
incorporated in a person before they can effectively move
mankind. Christianity could boast of a founder of unique
holiness and power. Its sturdy competitors, the Mystery-
Religions, could offer only myths which called for constant
purification and allegorization to meet the moral needs of
the day. The ethics of Jesus defied challenge ; His
character required no burnishing. He was and remained
Leader and Captain to His followers : no modernization nor
allegorization was necessary to remove offence to the moral
consciousness. On the other hand, there never was a
Mithra, and he never slew the mystic-sacramental bull.
There never was a Great Mother of sorrows to wail over
Attis and to become a true mother to the sorrowing daughters
of humanity. Isis, in all her splendour, was but the product,
however idealized by the religious instinct, of Egyptian
Zoolatry. ' Come, thou Saviour ' [3] was addressed to Dionysos,
a creation of Chthonism. Apollo, the special god of the

---

[1] Glover, *Conflict*, p. 116.   [2] Tatian, *Ad Graecos*, 21.
[3] *Bul. Cor. Hell.* XIX, p. 400.

Pythagoreans, who declared, ' I dwell with less pleasure in the resplendent heavens than in the hearts of good men,' was the lofty culmination of a cult which saw in the Sun the image of the Good.[1] The Logos of the Stoics was a pure abstraction, the inspiration of which would touch only the enlightened, and of their ideal Wise Man Plutarch declared, ' He is nowhere on earth, nor ever has been.'[2] The Logos of Philo was merely a Hypostasis, or, at best, never stepped beyond the limits of personification. But for Christians ' the Logos became flesh and tabernacled among us, and we beheld His glory,' an advantage which Augustine declares he could not find in any of the competitors of Christianity.

To appreciate the dynamic which the Person of Jesus supplied to His followers we must remember how on the one hand ideas and ideals not clothed in a personality are unable to raise the masses of men, and, on the other, we must take account of a remarkable moral trait of the Graeco-Roman age—the " ever-increasing tendency to personify the ethical ideal." The sublime teachings of Plato, the Stoics, and Neo-Platonism could not effectively lay hold on the masses so as to become the guide and inspiration of their lives. Educated men found a refuge there, and many of " the martyr-souls of heathendom " faced the last hours with a serene courage because of the spiritual truth and comfort derived from the philosophies which had supplanted the moribund national faiths. Some philosophers and their disciples made attempts to reach the masses. The Stoics, and especially their kindred Cynic preachers and lecturers and directors of conscience, went out into the highways and marts of life to cure souls, much as the Salvation Army does in our day. But the driving power of personality was lacking. " Precepts," says Luther, " show us what we ought to do, but do not impart to us the power to do it." Ideals were held up before men, but these ideals had never been seen incarnated upon earth. An ideal never incarnated was too cold and powerless. Accordingly, the Hellenistic and Roman age

[1] Cf. Plato, *Rep.* VI. 508.
[2] *De Com. Not.* 33.

was emphatic in its demand for examples [1] to supplement precepts and support ideals. We may doubt if in any age morality and religion were more persistently taught by examples. Earnest men wished to behold beings of flesh and blood from whose example they might draw inspiration.[2] All history was searched for patterns by which men might live and die. In an eminently practical age virtues were illustrated from the *dramatis personae* of history. The legendary Orpheus, Pythagoras, Socrates, Apollonius, Epicurus, and others were held before men's gaze to accompany and reinforce precepts. But a perfect example— where was such to be found ? Hence, the Stoic teachers, while drawing upon the records of the good and great of the past, preferred to portray their ideal Wise Man, at the same time frankly acknowledging that he had never lived.[3] No one has given such definite expression to this yearning of the time for a personal ethical ideal as Seneca in his memorable despairing question : *Ubi enim istum invenies quem tot saeculis quaerimus ?* a question to which his creed could furnish no answer, but to which the answer was found in the Christian message.

As another instance to indicate how universal was this personal ideal of perfection the quickened expectation of a Messianic leader among the Jews may be mentioned. Messianism, which was the earliest form of the prophetic confidence in a brighter future, was too vague : it must be achieved by a personal Messiah. The ideal of a Messianic era retreated more and more before that of a Messianic personage. Moreover, among pagans there was a nascent consciousness that the time was ripe for the epiphany of a God-man. This thought is familiar to us in the Latin court-poets.[4] The wish was father to the thought. The most conspicuous literary example of this focusing of religious

---

[1] Cf. Epict. *Disc.* II. 19 ; Seneca, *Ep.* XI. 8.

[2] Cf. Angus, *Environment of Early Christianity*, p. 82.

[3] Cicero, *Acad. Pr.* 145 : ' Sed qui sapiens sit aut fuerit ne ipsi quidem solent dicere ' ; and Plutarch, *De Com. Not.* 33.

[4] Cf. Fowler, *Roman Ideas of Deity*, lect. IV.

and religious-political hopes and longings in a person is found in Virgil's so-called *Messianic Eclogue,* in which, perhaps in reply [1] to the pessimism of Horace's—

'Suis et ipsa Roma viribus ruit,'

and his fantastic solution—

'Arva beata
Petamus arva, divites et insulas,'

there is held forth the hope of the speedy birth of a wonderful child who shall inaugurate a new era and bring back to earth the Golden Age. Nor is this personal ideal found here alone in Virgil. Conway,[2] speaking of this Messianic ideal, says:

" It can hardly, I think, be denied that in both the *Georgics* and the *Aeneid* we continually meet with a conception which in many ways is a parallel to the Jewish expectation of a Messiah ; that is to say, the conception of a national hero or ruler, divinely inspired, and sent to deliver not his own nation only, but mankind, raising them to a new and ethically higher existence."

There was a universal craving in serious circles for a personal ethical ideal as a dynamic in the moral struggles of men and as a guarantee of the successful issue of those struggles and the perfectibility of human nature. This spirit of that age has been caught by Renan and well expressed in his words : " Humanity seeks the ideal, but it seeks it in a person, and not in an abstraction. A man, the incarnation of the ideal, whose biography might serve as a frame for all the aspirations of the time, is what the religious mind sought."[3] This need Christianity alone

---

[1] Cf. Ramsay, *Expositor,* June 1907.

[2] Virgil's *Messianic Eclogue,* p. 31.

[3] *Marc Aurèle,* p. 582, 5th ed. ; cf. Dill, p. 621 : " The world needed more than a great physical force to assuage its cravings ; it demanded a moral God, who could raise before the eyes of men a moral ideal, and support them in striving to attain it, one who could guide and comfort in the struggles of life, and in the darkness of its close, who could prepare the trembling soul for the great ordeal, in which the deeds done in the body are sifted on the verge of the eternal world."

proved able adequately to meet in the Person of Jesus, so truthfully described by James Martineau as " the realized Ideal."   The seething hopes and dreams and premonitory glimpses of this ancient world, pagan and Jewish alike, were realized in the Gospel, " not by borrowing ideas, or decking itself out in ancient symbols, but by the exhibition of a fact within the field of history in which were more than fulfilled the inextinguishable yearnings of the world's desire." [1]

[1] Mackintosh, *Person of Jesus Christ*, p. 533.

SELECTED BIBLIOGRAPHY OF MODERN WRITERS

Aall, A. *Der Logos, Gesch. seiner Entwickelung in der griech. Philosophie u. der Christ. Lit.* (2 vols. Leip. '96–'99).

Abelson, J. *Jewish Mysticism* (Lond. '13).

Abt, A. *Die Apologie des Apuleius v. Madaura u. die antike Zauberei* (Giessen, '08).

Achelis, T. *Die Ekstase* (Berlin, '02).

Adam, J. *Religious Teachers of Greece* (Aberd. '08).

Allard, P. *Le Christianisme et l'empire romain de Néron à Théodose* (3rd ed. Paris, '98).

Amélineau, E. *L'Enfer égyptien et l'enfer virgilien* (Paris, '14) ; *Proleg. à l'Étude de la Religion égyptienne* (2 vols. Paris, '08 f.).

Angus, S. *Environment of Early Christianity* (Lond. and N.Y. '15, '20), *v.s.* Varro.

Anrich, G. *Das antike Mysterienwesen in seinem Einfluss auf das Christentum* (Gött. '94).

Anz, W. *Zur Frage nach dem Ursprung des Gnosticismus* (Leip. '97).

Arnold, E. V. *Roman Stoicism* (Camb. '11).

Aust, E. *Religion der Römer* (Münster, '99).

Baudissin, Count W. W. v. *Adonis u. Esmun* (Leip. '11) ; *Esmun-Asklepios* (Giess. '06).

Baumgarten, Poland, Wagner. *Die hellenistisch-römische Kultur* (Leip. '73).

Baur, F. C. *Zur Gesch. d. alten Philosophie u. ihr Verhältnisses zum Christentum* (Leip. '76).

Beloch, J. *Die Bevölkerung der griech.-röm. Welt* (Leip. '86).

Benn, A. W. *The Greek Philosophers* (2nd ed. Lond. '14).

Berthelot et Ruelle. *Collection des anciens Alchimistes grecs* (Paris, '87–88).

Beurlier, E. *Le culte rendu aux empereurs romains* (Paris, '91).

Bevan, E. R. *House of Seleucus* (2 vols. Lond. '02).

Bigg, C. *The Church's Task under the Roman Empire* (Oxf. '05) ; *Neoplatonism* (Lond. '95).

Bissing, F. W. *Cult of Isis in Pompeian Paintings* (Oxf. '08, Trans. of 3rd Internat. Congress of Religions).

Bloch, L. Art. *Megaloi Theoi* in Roscher's *Lexikon; Der Kult u. d. Mysterien von Eleusis* (Hamb. '96).

Bois, H. *Essai sur l'origine de la philosophie judéo-alexandrine* (Toulouse, '90).

Boissier, G. *La religion romaine d'Auguste aux Antonins* (2 vols. 7th ed. Paris, '09) ; *La Fin du Paganisme* (2 vols. 2nd ed. Paris, '91, 6th ed. '09).

Boll, F. *Sphaera* (Leip. '03) ; *Die Erforschungen der antiken Astrologie* (in *N. Jahrb. f. d. klass. Alt.* XXI, '08, pp. 103-26) ; and C. Bezold, *Sternglaube u. Sterndeutung* (Leip. 2nd ed. '23).

Bousset, W. *Die Religion des Judentums im neutest. Zeitalter* (2nd ed. Berlin, '06) ; *Hauptprobleme der Gnosis* (Gött. '07) ; *Himmelreise der Seele* (in *Archiv f. Religionswiss.* IV, pp. 136-69, 229-73) ; *Kyrios Christos* (Gött. '13) ; *Christentum u. Mysterien-religionen* (*Th. Rundsch.* XV. '13, pp. 31-60, 25-77).

Brandis, C. A. *Gesch. u. Entwick. d. Griech. Philosophie u. ihrer Nachwirkungen im röm. Reich* (2 vols. '62-64).

Breasted, J. H. *History of Egypt* (N.Y. '09) ; *Development of Religion and Thought in Ancient Egypt* (N.Y. '12).

Bréhier, E. *Les idées philosophiques et religieuses de Philon d'Alexandrie* (Paris, '08).

Brillant, M. *Les Mystères d'Éleusis* (Paris, '20).

Brückner, M. *Der sterbende u. auferstehende Gottheiland in d. orient. Religionen* (Tüb. '20).

Budge, E. A. T. W. *The Gods of the Egyptians* (2 vols. Lond. '04) ; *The Book of the Dead* (3 vols. Lond. '98) ; *Osiris and the Egyptian Resurrection* (2 vols. Lond. '11) ; *The Book of Paradise* (2 vols. Lond. '04) ; *The Liturgy of Funerary Offerings* (Eg. texts and Eng. tr. Lond. '09).

Burckhardt, J. *Die Zeit Konstantins der Grossen* (Bale, '80).

Burel, J. *Isis et Isiaques sous l'empire romain* (Paris, '11).

Buresch, C. *Klaros. Unters. z. Orakelwesen d. späteren Altertums* (Leip. '89).

Bussell, F. W. *School of Plato* (Lond. '96).

Butcher, S. H. *Some Aspects of Greek Genius* (3rd ed. London, '04) ; *Harvard Lectures on Greek Subjects* (Lond. '04).

Caird, E. *The Evolution of Theology in the Greek Philosophers* (2 vols. Glasg. '04).

Campbell, L. *Religion in Greek Literature* (Lond. '98).

Capelle, W. *Die Schrift von der Welt* (in *N. Jahrb. f. d. klass.*

Alt. 1905, VIII, pp. 529–68) ; *Altgriech. Askese* (*ib.* XXIII, 1909, p. 681 ff.) ; *Zur antiken Theodizee* (*Archiv f. Gesch. Phil.* '07, XX, p. 180 ff.).

Carter, J. B. *The Religious Life of Ancient Rome* (Lond. '12).

Case, S. J. *The Evolution of Early Christianity* (Chicago, '14).

Caspari, E. *De Cynicis qui fuerunt aetati imperatorum Romanorum* (Chemnitz, '96).

Caton, R. *The Temples and Ritual of Asklepios at Epidauros and Athens* (Lond. '00).

Charles, R. H. *Eschatology, Hebrew, Jewish, and Christian* (2nd ed. Lond. '13).

Chastel, E. *Destruction du Paganisme dans l'empire d'Orient* (Paris, '50).

Cheetham, S. *The Mysteries, Pagan and Christian* (Lond. '97).

Chwolsohn, D. *Die Ssabier u. der Ssabismus* (2 vols. St. Petersburg, '56).

Clemen, C. *Primitive Christianity and its non-Jewish Sources* (Eng. tr. Edin. '12) ; *Die Resten d. primitiven Religion im ältesten Christentum* (Giessen, '16).

Cohn, M. *Zum röm. Vereinsrecht* (Berl. '73).

Colin, G. *Rome et la Grèce de 200 à 146 avant J.-C.* (Paris, '05).

Comparetti, D. *Laminette orfiche* (Florence, '10).

Conybeare, F. C. *Myth, Magic, and Morals* (Lond. '10).

Cook, A. B. *Zeus* (Camb. '14).

Cooper, W. M. *Flagellation and Flagellants* (Lond. n.d.).

Cornford, F. M. *From Religion to Philosophy* (London, '12).

Coulanges, F. de. *La Cité antique* (2nd ed. Paris, '66).

Creuzer, F. *Symbolik u. Mythologie der alten Völker* (ed. by Moser and Mone, Leip. and Darmstadt, 1822 ; 1st ed. 1810. French tr. by Guigniaut, 2 vols. Paris, 1825).

Cumont, F. *Textes et Monuments relatifs aux Mystères de Mithra* (2 vols. Brussels, '96–99) ; *Religions orientales dans le paganisme romain* (2nd ed. Paris, '09. Eng. tr. by G. Showerman, Chicago, '11) ; *Mysteries of Mithra* (Eng. tr. by T. J. McCormack, 2nd ed. Chicago and Lond. '10, 3rd rev. Fr. ed. Paris, '13) ; *Astrology and Religion among the Greeks and Romans* (N.Y. and Lond. '12) ; *Le Mysticisme astral dans l'antiquité* (in *Acad. roy. de Belgique, Classe des Lettres,* '09, pp. 256–86) ; *La théologie solaire du paganisme rom.* (in *Mém. présentés par divers savants à l'Acad. d. Inscr.,* XII, pt. 2, p. 447 ff.) ; *Fatalisme astral et les relig. antiques* (in *Rev. d'Hist. et de Lit. relig.* N.S. Nov. '15) ; *After-Life in Rom. Paganism* (New Haven, '22) ; *Mithras* and *Anahita* (in Pauly-Wissowa) ; *Zodiacus* (in Daremberg-Saglio *Dict.*) ; *La Basilique souterraine de la Porta Maggiore* (*Rev. arch.* '18, pp. 52–77).

Dähne, A. F. *Gesch. Darstellung der jüdisch-alexandr. Religionsphilosophie* (2 vols. Halle, '34).

D'Alton, J. F. *Horace and his Age* (Lond. '17).

D'Alviella, E. G. *Eleusinia* (Paris, '93) ; *La Migration des Symboles* (*ib.* '98) ; *De quelques problèmes rel. aux mystères d' Éleusis* (*Rev. hist. rel.* '02).

Davis, G. M. N. *The Asiatic Dionysos* (Lond. '14).

Decharme, P. Art. *Cybèle* in Daremberg et Saglio, *Dictionnaire* ; *La Critique des Traditions religieuses chez les Grecs des origines au temps de Plutarque* (Paris, '04).

Deissmann, A. *Light from the Ancient East* (Eng. tr. Lond. '19, 4th Ger. ed. '22) ; *Die Neutest. Formel in Christo Jesu* (Marburg, '92) ; *Die Helleniesierung d. semitischen Monotheismus* (in *N. Jahrb. f. d. klass. Alt.* '03, p. 161 ff.).

Delacroix, H. *Études d'hist. et de psychologie du Mysticisme* (Paris, '08).

Dempsey, T. *The Delphic Oracle* (Oxf. '18).

Denis, J. *Hist. des Théories et des Idées morales dans l'Antiquité* (2nd ed. 2 vols. Paris, n.d.).

Deubner, L. *De Incubatione* (Leip. 1900) ; *Zur Entwicklungsgeschichte der altröm. Religion* (*N. Jahrb. f. d. klass. Alt.* XXVII, 1911, p. 321 ff.).

Dibelius, M. *Die Geisterwelt im Glauben des Paulus* (Gött. ' 09) ; *Die Isisweihe bei Apuleius u. verwandte Initiationsrite* (in *Sitzb. der Akad. Heidelberger* ; phil.-hist. Kl. Abh. 4, 1917).

Diels, H. *Elementum* (Leip. '99) ; *Sibyllinishe Blätter* (Berlin, '90).

Dieterich, A. *Eine Mithrasliturgie* (2nd ed. Leip. '10, 3rd ed. '22) ; *Abraxas* (Leip. '91) ; *Nekyia* (Leip. '93, 2nd ed. '13) ; *Kleine Schriften* (*ib.* '11) ; *Die Religion des Mithras* (*Bonner Jahrb.* 108).

Dill, S. *Roman Society from Nero to M. Aurelius* (Lond. '04, '11) ; *Roman Society in the last century of the Western Empire* (2nd ed. Lond. '19).

Döllinger, J. J. I. *The Gentile and the Jew* (2 vols. 2nd ed. Eng. tr. Lond. '06).

Domaszewski, A. v. *Die Religion des römischen Heeres* (Trier,

'95) ; *Abh. z. röm. Religion* (Leip. '09) ; *Magna Mater in Latin Inscriptions* (*Jour. Rom. Studies,* '11, pp. 50–7) ; *Die politische Bedeutung d. Religion von Emessa* (*Arch. f. Rel. Wis.* XI. '08, p. 226 ff.).

Drexler, W. Arts. *Gaia, Isis, Mên,* in Roscher's *Lexikon ; Dei Isis- u. Sarapiskultus in Kleinasien* (*Zeitsch. f. Num.* '89, XXI, pp. 1–234).

Droysen, J. G. *Histoire de l'Héllenisme* (3 vols. Paris, '83–5, French tr. of *Gesch. d. Hellenismus,* 2nd ed. Gotha, '77–8).

Drummond, J. *Philo Judaeus, or Jewish-Christian Philosophy* (2 vols. Lond. and Edin. '88).

Dupuis, C. F. *Origine de tous les Cultes* (3 vols. Paris, 1794 ; new ed. by Anguis, 7 vols. *ib.* 1822 ; *Abrégé* (3 vols. '97–00).

Eisele, Th. *Die phrygischen Kulte u. ihre Bedeutung f. d. griech.-röm. Welt* (*N. Jahrb. f. d. klas. Alt.* XXIII. '09, pp. 620–37).

Eisler, R. *Weltenmantel u. Himmelszelt* (2 vols. Munich, '12).

Erman, A. *Handbook of the Egyptian Religion* (Eng. tr. Lond. '07 ; 2nd Germ. ed. '09).

Eucken, R. *Lebensanschauungen der grossen Denker* (Leip. '09).

Everling, O. *Die Paulinische Angelologie u. Dämonologie* (Gött. '88).

Faber, G. S. *Dissertation on the Mysteries of the Cabiri* (2 vols. Oxf. 1803).

Fairbanks, A. *Handbook of Greek Religion* (New York, '10).

Fairweather, W. *The Background of the Gospels* (2nd ed. Edin. '11).

Farnell, L. R. *The Higher Aspects of Greek Religion* (Lond. '12) ; *Greece and Babylon, Mesopotamian, Anatolian, and Hellenic Religions* (Edin. '11) ; *The Cults of the Greek States* (5 vols. Oxf. '96–99) ; art. *Greek Religion* (Hastings' *E.R.E.*: *Outline Hist. of Greek Religion* (new ed. Lond. '21) ; *Greek Hero-Cults and Ideas of Immortality* (Oxf. '21) ; *The Place of Sonder-Götter in Greek Polytheism* (in *Essays presented to E. B. Tylor,* Oxf. '07) ; *Sacrificial Communion in Greek Religion* (*Hib. Jour.* II, pp. 306–322).

Faye, E. de. *Gnostiques et Gnosticisme* (Paris, '13).

Fehrle, E. *Die kultische Keuschheit im Altertum* (Giessen, '10).

Ferrero, F. *La Ruine de la Civilisation antique* (in *Rev. des Deux Mondes,* Sep. '19 ff. Eng. tr. by Lady Whitehead, *The Ruin of Ancient Civilization and the Triumph of Christianity.* Lond. and N.Y. '21).

Findlay, G. *Greece under the Romans* (2nd ed. Edin. '57)

Fossey, C. *La magie assyrienne* (Paris, '02).

Foucart, P. *Des Associations religieuses chez les Grecs : Thiases, Eranes, Orgéons* (Paris, '73) ; *Recherches sur l'origine et la nature des Mystères d'Éleusis* (*ib.* '95) ; *Les grands Mystères d'Éleusis* (*ib.* '00) ; *Les Mystères d'Éleusis* (*ib.* '14) ; *Le Culte de Dionysos en Attique* (*Mém. de l'Acad. des Inscriptions,* XXXVII. Paris, '04) ; *Les Drames sacrés d'Éleusis* (*Compt. rendus,* '12).

Fowler, W. W. *The Religious Experience of the Roman People* (Lond. '11) ; *Roman Ideas of Deity* (Lond. '14) ; *Roman Festivals* (Lond. '99) ; art. *Roman Religion* in Hastings' *E.R.E.*

Frazer, J. G. *The Golden Bough* (12 vols. 3rd ed. Lond. '11–15), especially parts III, *The Dying God* ('11), and IV, *Adonis, Attis, Osiris* ('14) ; *Psyche's Task* (2nd ed. Lond. '13) : *Taboo and the Perils of the Soul* (Lond. '11).

Freudenthal, J. *Zur Gesch. der Anschauungen über die jüdisch-hell. Religionsphilosophie* (Leip. '69).

Friedländer, G. *Hellenism and Christianity* (Lond. '12).

Friedländer, L. *Roman Life and Manners under the Early Empire* (Eng. tr. of 7th Germ. ed. 4 vols. Lond. and N.Y. '08–13).

Friedländer, M. *Die Religiöse Bewegungen innerhalb des Judentums in Zeitalter Jesu* (Berlin, '05) ; *Der vorchrist jüd. Gnosticismus* (Gött. '98).

Ganszyniec, R. *De Agathodaemone* (*Travaux de la Soc. d. Sciences de Varsovie,* II. 1917).

Gardner, P. *The Growth of Christianity* (Lond. '07) ; *The Religious Experience of St. Paul* (Lond. '11).

Gardthausen, V. *Augustus u. seine Zeit* (2 vols. Leip. '91–6).

Garrucci, R. *Les Mystères de Syncrétisme phrygien dans les Catacombes romaines de Prétextat* (Paris, '54).

Garstang, J. *Burial Customs of the Ancient Egyptians* (Lond. '07).

Gasquet, A. L. U. *Le culte et les mystères de Mithra* (Paris, '99).

Geffcken, J. *Aus der Werdezeit des Christentums* (2nd ed. Leip. '09) ; *Zwei griech. Apologeten* (Leip. '07).

Gennep, A. v. *La Formation des Légendes* (Paris, '10).

Gfrörer, A. F. *Philo u. die alexandrin. Theosophie* (2nd ed. Stuttgart, '35).

Gibbon, E. *The Decline and Fall of the Roman Empire* (ed. J. B. Bury, 7 vols. Lond. '97–00).

Girard, J. *Le Sentiment religieux en Grèce d'Homère à Eschyle* (Paris, '69–79).

Glover, T. R. *The Conflict of Religions in the Early Roman Empire* (5th ed. Lond. '12) ; *Progress in Religion* (Lond. '22).

Gomperz, Th. *Greek Thinkers* (Eng. tr. by Magnus and Berrie, 4 vols. Lond. and N.Y. '05–12).

Graillot, H. *Le Culte de Cybèle, Mère des Dieux* (Paris, '12).

Granger, F. *The Poemandres of Hermes Trismegistus* (*Jour. Th. Stud.* April '04, pp. 395–412).

Griffith, F. L. *Stories of the High Priests of Memphis* (Oxf. '00).

Grill, J. *Die persische Mysterienreligion im röm. Reich u. das Christentum* (Tüb. '03).

Gronau, K. *Poseidonius u. d. jüdisch-christ. Genesisexegesis* (Leip. '14).

Gruppe, O. *Griech. Mythologie u. Religionsgeschichte* (2 vols. Munich, '06) ; *Griech. Culte u. Mythen in ihren Beziehungen zu den orient. Religionen* (Leip. '87).

Gudemann. *Jüdische Apologetik* (Glogau, '06).

Guimet, E. *L'Isis romaine* (Paris, '96) ; *Le Dieu d'Apulée* (*ib.* '95).

Gunkel, H. *Zum religionsgesch. Verständnis des neuen Testaments* (2nd ed. Gött. '10).

Güntert, H. *Der arische Weltkönig u. Heiland* (Halle, '23).

Habert, O. *La Religion de la Grèce antique* (Paris, '10).

Hahn, L. *Rom. u. Romanismus im griech.-röm. Osten* (Leip. '06).

Halliday, W. R. *Greek Divination* (Lond. '12) ; *Hist. of Rom. Religion* (2 vols. *ib.* '23).

Hamilton, M. *Incubation, or Cure of Disease in Pagan Temples and Christian Churches* (Lond. '06).

Harnack, A. *Mission and Expansion of Christianity in the first three Centuries* (Eng. tr. by J. Moffatt, 2nd ed. 2 vols. Lond. and N.Y. '08) ; *Das Mönchtum* (4th ed. Giessen, '95).

Harris, R. *The Ascent of Olympus* (Manchester, '17).

Harrison, J. *Prolegomena to the study of Greek Religion* (3rd ed. Camb. '22) ; *Themis* (Camb. '12) ; *Epilegomena* (Camb. '21).

Hatch, E. *Influence of Greek Ideas and Usages upon the Christian Church* (Lond. '90).

Havet, E. *Le Christianisme et ses Origines* (4 vols. Paris, '71–84).

Heinrici, G. *Hellenismus u. Christentum* (Berlin, '09) ; *Die Hermes-mystik u. d. neue Testament* (Leip. '18).

Heinze, M. *Die Lehre vom Logos in d. griech. Philosophie* (Oldenburg, '72).

Heitmüller, W. *Taufe u. Abendmahl in Urchristentum* (Tüb. '11).

Hepding, H. *Attis, seine Mythen u. sein Kult* (Giessen, '03).

Hicks, R. D. *Stoics and Epicureans* (N.Y. '12).

Hild, J. A. *Étude sur les Démons dans la littérature et la religion des Grecs* (Paris, '81).

Hirzel, R. *Untersuchungen zu Cicero's phil. Schriften* (3 parts, Leip. '77–83).

Holst, J. J. van. *De Eranis veterum Graecorum* (Leiden, 1832).

Hönn, K. *Studien zur Gesch. der Himmelfahrt* (Mannheim, '10).

Hopfner, Th. *Gr.-ägypt. Offenbarungszauber mit. e. eingeh. Darst. d. gr.-syn. Daemonglaubens*, etc. (Leip. '21).

Hubert, H. Art. *Magia* (in Daremberg-Saglio, *Dictionnaire*).

Hubert, H., and Mauss, M. *Esquisse d'une théorie générale de la Magie* (Paris, '04) ; *Théorie générale de la Magie* (in *L'Année Sociologique*, '02–3, pp. 1–146).

Hyde, T. *Veterum Persarum et Parthorum et Medorum religionis historia* (Oxf. 1700 ; 2nd ed. 1760).

Ida, C. *Heavenly Bridegrooms* (N.Y. '18).

Immisch, O. *Kureten u. Korybanten* (in Roscher's *Lexikon*).

Inge, W. R. *Christian Mysticism* (Lond. '99) ; *The Philosophy of Plotinus* (2 vols. Lond. '18).

Jacoby, A. *Die antiken Mysterien-Religionen u. d. Christentum* (Tüb. '10).

James, W. *The Varieties of Religious Experience* (Lond. and N.Y. '02).

Jastrow, M. *Religion of Babylonia and Assyria* (Boston, '98) ; art. Hastings' *D.B.* (ext. vol. pp. 531–84) ; *Aspects of Religious Life and Practice in Babylonia and Assyria* (N.Y. and Lond. '11).

Jequier, G. *L'Enneade Osirienne d'Abydos et les enseignées sacrées* (*Comptes Rendus*, Dec. '20).

Jeremias, A. *Handbuch der altorientalischen Geisteskultur* (Leip. '13).

Jevons, F. B. *Introd. to the History of Religion* (6th ed. Lond. '14) ; *Intr. to the Study of Comparative Religion* (N.Y. '08).

Jong, K. H. E. de. *Das antike Mysterienwesen* (2nd ed. Leiden, '19) ; *De Apuleio Isiacorum Mysteriorum teste* (*ib.* 1900).

Joubin, A. *Scène d'Initiation aux Mystères d'Isis sur un Relief crétois* (in *Recueil de travaux rel. à phil. égypt.* '94, p. 162 ff.).

Juster, J. *Les Juifs dans l'empire romain* (2 vols. Paris, '14).

Καββαδίας, Π. Τὸ ἱερὸν τοῦ 'Ασκληπίου ἐν 'Επιδαύρῳ καὶ ἡ θεραπεία τῶν ἀσθενῶν (Athens, 1900).

Kaerst, J. *Gesch. des hellenistischen Zeitalters* (2 vols. Leip. '01–9).

Kan, I. *De Iovis Dolicheni Cultu* (Groningen, '01).

Keim, Th. *Rom. u. d. Christentum* (Berlin, '81).

Kennedy, H. A. A. *St. Paul and the Mystery-Religions* (Lond. '13) ; *Philo's Contribution to Religion* (Lond. '19).

Kern, O. *Dionysus* (in Pauly-Wissowa *Real-ency.*) ; *Orpheus* (Berlin, '95).

Kiesewetter, K. *Der Occultismus des Altertums* (2 vols. Leip. '95–6).

King, C. W. *The Gnostics and their Remains* (2nd ed. Lond. '87).

Koch, H. *Ps. Dionysios Areop. in s. Bez. zum Neoplatonismus u. Mysterienwesen* (Mainz, '08).

Kornemann. Art. *Collegium* (in Pauly-Wissowa, IV. coll. 380–480).

Krebs, E. *Der Logos als Heiland* (Freiburg, '10).

Kroll, J. *Die Lehren des Hermes Trismegistus* (Münster, '14).

Kroll, W. *Antiker Aberglaube* (Hamb. '97) ; *Die gesch. Bedeutung des Poseidonius* (in *N. Jahrb. f. d. klas. Alt.* XXXIX. '17, pp. 145–57) ; *Aus der Gesch. der Astrologie* (*ib.* VII. '01, p. 559 ff.) ; art. *Hermes Trismegistus* (in Pauly-Wissowa).

Kugler, F. X. *Sternkunde u. Sterndienst in Babel* (Münster, '07 ff.).

Kutsch, F. *Attische Heilgötter u. Heilheroen* (Giessen, '13).

Lafaye, G. *Hist. du Culte des Divinités d'Alexandrie hors de l'Egypte* (Paris, '84) ; *L'Initiation mithriaque* (in *Conf. au Musée Guimet*, XVIII, '06) ; *Isis* (in Daremberg-Saglio) ; *Litanie grecque d'Isis* (*Rev. de Philologie*, XL. '16, pp. 55–108).

Lagrange, M. J. *Études sur les religions sémitiques* (2nd ed. Paris, '08) ; *Attis et Christianisme* (*Rev. Bib.* '19) ; *Les Mystères d'Éleusis* (*ib.* '19).

Lajard, F. *Introd. à l'étude du culte public et des mystères de Mithra en Orient et en Occident* (Paris, 1847).

Lake, K. *Earlier Epistles of St. Paul* (2nd ed. Lond. '14).

Lang, A. *Myth, Ritual and Religion* (2 vols. Lond. '87, 2nd ed. '01).

Lebreton, J. *Les Théories de Logos au début de l'ère chrét.* (Paris, '06).

Leclercq, A. Bouché-. *Hist. de la Divination dans l'Antiquité* (4 vols. Paris, '79–82) ; *L'Astrologie grecque* (*ib.* '99) ; *Hist. des Lagides* (4 vols. *ib.* '03–7) ; *L'Intolérance religieuse et politique* (*ib.* '12).

Legge, F. *Forerunners and Rivals of Christianity* (2 vols. Camb. '15) ; *Names of Demons in the Magic Papyri* (*Proc. Soc. Bib. Arch.* 1900) ; *The Greek Worship of Serapis and Isis* (*ib.* '14).

Lehmann, E. *Mysticism in Heathendom and Christendom* (Eng. tr. Lond. '10).

Leisegang, H. *Der heilige Geist: Das Wesen u. Werden der mystisch-intuitiven Erkentnis in d. Phil. u. Religion d. Griechen* (vol. I. Leip. '19).

Lembert, R. *Der Wunderglaube bei Römern u. Griechen* (pt. I. Augsburg, '05).

Lenormant, C. *Mémoire sur les représentations qui avaient lieu dans les Mystères d'Éleusis* (in *Mém de l'Acad. des Inscr.* N.S. XXIV, pt. 1).

Lenormant, F. *Recherches archéol. à Éleusis* (Paris, '62) ; arts. *Eleusinia* (with E. Pottier), *Baubo, Ceres, Cabiri, Cotytto,* in Daremberg-Saglio ; *Eleusinian Mysteries* (*Cont. Rev.* '80, XXVII, pp. 847–71, XXVIII, pp. 121–49, 412–33).

Lévy-Bruhl, L. Les fonctions mentales dans les sociétés inférieures (Paris, '09).

Liechtenhahn, R. *Offenbarung im Gnostizismus* (Gött. '01).

Lietzmann, H. *Der Weltheiland* (Bonn, '09).

Lobeck, C. A. *Aglaophamus, sive De Theologiae mysticae Graecorum causis* (2 vols. Königsberg, 1829).

Loisy, A. F. *Les Mystères païens et le Mystère chrétien* (Paris, '14. 2nd ed. '21).

Lübbert, E. *Commentatio de Pindaro dogmatis de migratione animarum cultore* (Bonn, '87).

Maas, E. W. T. *Orpheus* (Munich, '95).

Macchioro, V. *Zagreus, Studi sull' Orfismo* (Bari, '20) ; *Eraclito* (*ib.* '22) ; *Orfismo e Paolinismo* (Montevarchi, '22) ; *Orfismo e Cristianesimo* (reprint from *Gnosis,* Naples, '21) ; *Dionysos Mystes* (in *Atti d. Reale Accad. d. Scienze di Torino,* Dec. '18, pp. 126–238) ; *Orphica* (in *Riv. indo-greco-ital.* Naples, 18) ; *Dionysiaca* (*Accad. di Arch.,* Naples, '18).

Macdonald, L. *Inscriptions relating to Sorcery in Cyprus* (*Proc. Soc. Bib. Arch.* '91, pp. 160–90).

Mahaffy, J. P. *Hellenism in Alexander's Empire* (Chicago, '05) ; *Silver Age of the Greek World* (*ib.* and Lond. '06) ; *Survey of Greek Civilization* (Meadville, '96) ; *What have the Greeks done for Modern Civilization ?* (Lond. and N.Y. '09).

Marchi, A. de. *Il culto privato di Roma antica* (Milan, '96).

Mariette-Bey, A. *Dendérah ; Description générale du grand temple de cette ville* (Paris and Cairo, '75) ; *Dendérah, planches,* 4 vols. Paris, '70–73).

Martha, C. *Études morales sur l'Antiquité* (Paris, '83) ; *Moralistes sous l'empire romain* (8th ed. Paris, '07).

Maspero, G. *Histoire ancienne des peuples de l'Orient classique* (3 vols. Paris, '95–9) ; Eng. trs. under titles *The Dawn of Civilization* (Lond. '94), *The Struggle of the Empires* (*ib.* '96), *Passing of the Empires* (*ib.* '90). *Études de Mythologie et d'Archéologie égyptiennes* (Paris, '93 ff.).

Matter, J. *Hist. critique du Gnosticisme* (3 parts, Paris, '43–4) ; *Hist. de l'École d'Alexandrie* (2nd ed. Paris, '40).

Maury, L. F. A. *Hist. des Religions de la Grèce antique* (3 vols. Paris, '57–9) ; *La Magie et l'Astrologie dans l'Antiquité et au Moyen Âge* (*ib.* '60).

McGiffert, A. C. *What did Christianity do for the Roman empire ?* (*Harv. Th. Rev.* April '09, pp. 28–49).

Mead, G. R. S. *Thrice-greatest Hermes* (3 vols. Lond. and Benares, '06) ; *Fragments of a Faith Forgotten* (2nd ed. *ib.* '06) ; *Quests Old and New* (Lond. '13) ; *Apollonius of Tyana* (*ib.* '01) ; *Philo u. d. hell. Theologie* (in *Vierteljahr. f. Bibelkunde,* '08).

Merivale, C. *Conversion of the Roman empire* (2nd ed. Lond. '65).

Meyer, E. *Gesch. des Altertums* (5 vols. Leip. '93–02).

Milne, J. G. *Graeco-Egyptian Religion* (in Hastings' *E.R.E.*).

Möller, E. W. *Gesch. der Kosmologie in d. griech. Kirche bis auf Origines* (Halle, '60).

Mommsen, A. *Feste der Stadt Athen* (Leip. '98).

Mommsen, Th. *The Provinces of the Rom. empire* (Eng. tr. 2 rev. ed. 2 vols. Lond. '09) ; *De Collegiis et Sodaliciis Romanorum* (Kiel, '43).

Monceaux, P. Arts. *Orpheus, Orphici, Sabazios,* in Daremberg-Saglio.

Moore, C. H. *Religious Thought of the Greeks* (Camb. Mass. '16) ;

Greek and Roman Ascetic Tendencies (in *Harv. Essays*, '12, pp. 97–104) ; *Spread of Oriental Religions* (in *Harv. Studies in Class. Phil.* XI, p. 47 ff.) ; *Origin of the Taurobolium* (*ib.* XVII, pp. 43–8) ; *Distribution of Oriental Cults* (*Tr. Amer. Phil. As.* '07, p. 142 ff.).

Moore, G. F.   *History of Religions* (2 vols. Edin. '14–20, vol. 1).

Moret, A.   *Mystères égyptiens* (Paris, '13) ; *Du caractère religieux de la Royauté pharaonique* (*ib.* '02) ; *Le Rituel du culte journalier en Égypte* (*ib.* '02) ; *Rois et Dieux d'Egypte* (*ib.* '11).

Moulton, J. H.   *Early Zoroastrianism* (Lond. '13) ; *The Treasure of the Magi* (Oxf. '17).

Mudie-Cooke, P. B.   *The Paintings of the Villa Item at Pompeii* (in *Jour. Rom. Stud.* III. '13, pp. 157–174, pls. viii–xiv).

Murray, G.   *Four Stages of Greek Religion* (N.Y. '12).

Naville, E.   *The old Egyptian Faith* (Eng. tr. by C. Campbell, Lond. '09).

Naville, H. A.   *Julien l'Apostat et la philosophie du polythéisme* (Paris, '77).

Nicolo, M. S.   *Ägypt. Vereinswesen z. Zeit d. Ptolemäer u. Römer* (Munich, '15).

Nilsson, M. P.   *Studia de Dionysiis Atticis* (Linden, '00) ; *Griech. Feste* (Leip. '06).

Nöldeke, Th.   *Die Selbstentmannung bei d. Syrern* (*Arch. f. Religionswis.* X. '07, p. 150 ff.).

Norden, E.   *Agnostos Theos* (Leip. and Berlin, '13).

Oakesmith, J.   *The Religion of Plutarch* (Lond. '02).

Olivieri, A.   *L'uovo cosmogonico d'Orfici* (*Atti d. Reale Accad. d. Arch.* VII. '20, pp. 295–334).

Otto, W.   *Priester u. Tempel in hellen. Ägypten* (2 vols. Leip. and Berlin, '05–8) ; *Augustus Soter* in *Hermes*, XLV. '10, p. 448 ff.

Perdelwitz, R.   *Die Mysterienreligion u. d. Problem d. I Petrusbriefes* (Giessen, '11).

Petrie, W. M. F.   *Personal Religion in Egypt before Christianity* (Lond. and N.Y. 2nd ed. '12); *Egyptian Religion* (in Hastings' *E.R.E.*).

Pettazoni, R.   *Le Origini dei Kabiri nelle Isole de Mar Tracio* (Rome, '09).

Pfister, F.   *Der Reliquienkult im Altertum* (Giessen, '09–12).

Pfleiderer, O.   *Vorbereitung des Christentums in d. griech. Philosophie* (Tüb. '06).

Philos, D. *Éleusis, ses Mystères, ses ruines, et son musée* (Athens, '96, Eng. tr. '06).

Phythian-Adams, W. J. *The Problem of the Mithraic Grades* (in *Jour. Rom. Studies*, II. '12, pp. 53–64) ; *Mithraism* (Lond. '15).

Pierret, P. *Les Interprétations de la Religion égyptienne* (*Conf. au Musée Guimet*, XX. '06).

Pinches, T. G. *The religious Ideas of the Babylonians* (Lond. '93).

Plew, C. F. Th. E. *De Sarapide* (Königsberg, '68).

Poland, Fr. *Gesch. des griech. Vereinswesens* (Leip. '09).

Prel, C. du. *Die Mystik der alten Griechen* (Leip. '88).

Preller, L. *Demeter u. Persephone* (Hamburg, '37) ; *Griech. Mythologie* (4th ed. by C. Robert, Berlin, '94) ; *Römische Mythologie* (3rd ed. by H. Jordan, *ib.* '81).

Preuschen, E. *Mönchtum u. Serapiskult* (2nd ed. Giessen, '03).

Pringsheim, H. G. *Archaeol. Beiträge zur Gesch. d. eleus. Kultus* (Munich, '05).

Probst, F. *Sakramente u. Sakramentalien in d. drei ersten christl. Jahrhunderten* (Tüb. '72).

Quandt, W. *De Baccho ab Alexandri aetate in Asia Minore culto* (in *Diss. philologicae Halenses*, XXI. '13, 2.).

Ramsay, W. M. *Cities and Bishoprics of Phrygia* (2 parts, Oxf. '96–7) ; *Religion of Greece and Asia Minor* (in Hastings' *D.B.* ext. vol. pp. 109–56) ; *Mysteries* (in *Ency. Brit.* 9th ed.) ; *Studies in the history and art of the Eastern Provinces* (Lond. '06).

Reinach, S. *Orpheus* (Eng. tr. by F. Simmonds, Lond. and N.Y. '09) ; *Cultes, Mythes, et Religions* (2nd ed. 3 vols. Paris, '08, from which a drastic abridgment in Eng. tr. *Cults, Myths, and Religions*, Lond. '12).

Reisner, G. A. *The Egyptian Conception of Immortality* (Lond. '12).

Reitzenstein, R. *Poimandres* (Leip. '04); *Die hellenist. Mysterien-religionen* (2nd ed. *ib.* '20) ; *Hellenistische Wundererzählungen* (*ib.* '06) ; *Hellenistische Theologie in ägypten* (*N. Jahrb. f. d. klas. Alt.* XIII, '04, pp. 177–94) ; *Christentum u. Mysterienreligionen* (*Theo. Rundschau*, XV, pp. 41–60) ; *Das iranische Erlösungsmysterien* (Bonn, '21).

Renan, J. E. *Marc Aurèle et la Fin du monde antique* (8th ed. Paris, '99 ; vol. VII of *Origines du Christianisme*) ; *The In-*

fluence of the Institutions, Thought, and Culture of Rome on Christianity, Lond. '80).

Rendtorff, F. M. *Die Taufe im Urchristentum* (Leip. '05).

Renouf, P. le P. *Lectures on the Origin and Growth of Religion* (Lond. '80).

Reville, J. *La Religion à Rome sous les Sévères* (Paris, '86).

Ribbeck, O. *Anfänge u. Entwickelung des Dionysoscultus in Attika* (Kiel, '69).

Riess. *Aberglaube* (in Pauly-Wissowa).

Rizzo, G. *Dionysus Mystes* (in *Mem. Accad. Arch. Napoli*, III, '18, pp. 1–102).

Rohde, E. *Die Religion der Griechen* (in *Kl. Schr.* '01, II, pp. 314–39) ; *Psyche, Seelencult u. Unsterblichkeitsglaube der Griechen* (6th–7th ed. Tüb. '21).

Roussel, P. *Les cultes égypt. à Délos du III* au I* siècle av. J.-C.* (Paris, '16).

Rubensohn, O. *Die Mysterienheiligtümer in Eleusis u. Samothrake* (Berlin, '92).

Ruhl, L. *De Serapide et Iside in Graecia cultis* (Leip. '06).

Rusch, A. *De Serapide et Iside in Graecia cultis* (Berlin, '06).

Sainte-Croix, G. E. J. *Recherches hist. et critiques sur les Mystères du Paganisme* (ed. by S.de Sacy, 2 vols. Paris, 1817 : 1st ed. 1784).

Saussaye, Chantepie de la. *Manuel d'histoire des Religions* (Fr. tr. from 2 Germ. ed. Paris, '04 ; 3rd Germ. ed. Tüb. '05).

Sayce, A. H. *The Religion of Ancient Egypt* (rev. ed. Edin. '13).

Schäfer, H. *Die Mysterien des Osiris in Abydos unter König Sesostris III* (Leip. '04).

Schiaparelli, G. *I Primordi ed i Progressi dell' Astronomia presso i Babilonensi* (*Riv. di Scienza*, Bologna, '08. III).

Schmekel, A. *Die Philosophie der mittleren Stoa* (Berlin, '92).

Schmidt, C. *Gnostische Schriften in koptischer Sprache* (Leip. '92).

Schmidt, C. G. A. *Essai historique sur la société civile dans le monde rom. et sur sa transformation par le Christianisme* (Paris, '53. Eng. tr. by Mrs. Thorpe, Lond. '07).

Schmidt, E. *Kultübertragungen* (Giessen, '10).

Schnegelsberg, A. *De Liberi apud Romanos cultu* (Marburg, 95).

Schultz, W. *Dokumente der Gnosis* (Jena, '10) ; *Altionische Mystik* (Vienna and Leip. '07 f.) ; *Pythagoras u. Heraklit* (*ib.* '05).

Schulze, V. *Gesch. des Untergangs der griech.-röm. Heidentums* (2 vols. Leip. '87–96).

Schürer, E. *Gesch. des jüdischen Volkes* (4th ed. 3 vols. Leip. '01–11. Eng. tr. from 2 Germ. ed. 5 vols. Edin. '90 ff.).

Schweitzer, B. *Herakles ; Aufsätze zur griech. Religions- u. Sagengeschichte* (Tüb. '22).

Scott-Moncrieff, P. D. *Paganism and Christianity in Egypt* (Camb. '13) ; *De Iside et Osiride* (*Jour. Hel. Studies*, XXIX. '09, pp. 79–90).

Seeck, O. *Gesch. des Untergangs der antiken Welt* (2nd ed. 5 vols. Berlin, '97-13, 3rd ed. '10 ff.).

Showerman, G. *The Great Mother of the Gods* (Madison, '01).

Siegfried, C. *Philo v. Alexandria als Ausleger des A.T.* (Jena, '75).

Simon, J. *Histoire de l'École d'Alexandrie* (2 vols. Paris, '45).

Smith, W. R. *The Religion of the Semites* (new ed. Lond. '94).

Snijder, G. A. S. *De forma matris cum infante sedenits apud antiquos* (Vindovonae, '20).

Söderblom, N. *Tiele's Kompendium der Religionsgeschichte* (4th ed. Berlin, '12, 5th ed. '20).

Soltau, W. *Das Fortleben des Heidentums in d. altchrist. Kirche* (Berlin, '06).

Steindorff, G. *Religion of the Ancient Egyptians* (N.Y. '05).

Stengel, P. *Opferbräuche der Griechen* (Leip. '10) ; *Die griech. Kultusaltertümer* (2nd ed. in I. v. Müller's *Handbuch*, V, Munich, '98).

Stoffels, J. *Die mystische Theologie Makarius des Ägypters* (Bonn, '08).

Stoop, E. de. *La Diffusion du Manichéisme dans l'empire romain* (Ghent, '09).

Strack, H. L. *Das Blut im Glauben u. Aberglauben d. Menscheit* (Munich, '00, no. 14 of *Schr. d. Inst. Judaeum*).

Strong, E. (Mrs. A.). *Apotheosis* (Lond. '15) ; and N. Joliffe, *The Stuccoes of the Underground Basilica near the Porta Maggiore* (*J.H.S.* XLIV. '24, pp. 65–111).

Strong, H. A. and J. Garstang. *The Syrian Goddess* (Lond. '13).

Svoronos, J. H. Ἑρμηνεία τῶν μνημείων τοῦ ἐλευσινιακοῦ μυστικοῦ κύκλου (Athens, '01).

Tambornino, J *De antiquorum Daemonismo* (Giessen, '09).

Taylor, A. E. *Epicurus* (Lond. '10) ; *Plato* (Lond. '08).

Taylor, R. L. *Cults of Ostia* (Bryn Mawr, '12).

Taylor, T. *The Eleusinian and Bacchic Mysteries* (3rd ed. N.Y. '75).

Thackeray, H. St. J. *Relation of St. Paul to contemporary Jewish Thought* (Lond. '00).

Thorndike, L. *Place of Magic in the intellectual history of Europe* (N.Y. '05).

Tiele, C. P. *Religions de l'Égypte et des peuples sémitiques* (Fr. tr. Paris, '81).

Toutain, J. *Les cultes païens dans l'empire rom.* (3 vols. Paris, '11–20).

Toy, C. H. *Judaism and Christianity* (Lond. '90).

Tucker, T. G. *Life in the Roman World of Nero and St. Paul* (Lond. '10).

Turchi, N. *Manuale di Storia delle Religione* (Turin, '12).

Tyler, E. B. *Primitive Culture* (4th ed. 2 vols. Lond. '03).

Uhlhorn, G. *Conflict of Christianity with Heathenism* (Eng. tr. Boston,' 79).

Underhill, E. *Mysticism* (Lond. '11) ; *The Mystic Way* (*ib.* '13).

Usener, H. *Götternamen* (Bonn, '96) ; *Das Weihnachtsfest* (*ib.* '89 : 2nd ed. '11) ; *Religionsgesch. Untersuchungen* (*ib.* '89).

Vacherot, E. *Hist. critique de l'École d'Alexandrie* (3 vols. Paris, '46–'51).

Valeton, J. *De templis Romanis* (in *Mnemosyne*, XVII, XVIII, XX, XXI, XXIII, XXV, XXVI).

Vellay, C. *Le Culte et les Fêtes d'Adonis-Thammous dans l'Orient antique* (in *Annales du Musée Guimet*, XVI. Paris, '04).

Vollers, K. *Die Weltreligionen in ihrem gesch. Zusammenhange* (2nd ed. Jena, '21).

Wachsmuth, C. *Die Ansichten der Stoiker über Mantik u. Dämonen* (Berlin, '60).

Wächter, Th. *Reinheitsvorschriften in griech. Kult* (Giessen, '10).

Wallace, W. *Epicureanism* (Lond. '80).

Wallon, H. *Hist. de l'Esclavage dans l'Antiquité* (2nd ed. Paris, '79, 3 vols.).

Walton, A. *Cult of Asklepios* (Ithaca, '94).

Waltzing, J. P. Art. *Collegia* (in Cabrol-Leclercq) ; *Études hist. sur les corporations professionnelles chez les Romains* (Louvain, '95–00).

Watkin, E. I. *The Philosophy of Mysticism* (Lond. '20).

Weber, W. *Ägypt.-griech. Götter im Hellenismus* (Groningen, '12).

Webster, H. *Primitive Secret Societies* (N.Y. '08).

Weidlich, Th. *Die Sympathie in der antiken Literatur* (*Prog. d. Karls-Gym. in Stuttgart*, '94, pp. 1–76).

Weinreich, O. *Antike Heilungswunder* (Giessen, '09) ; *Neue Urkunden z. Sarapis-Religion* (Tüb. '19).

Weiss, J. *Das Urchristentum* (2 vols. Gött. '14–17).

Wendland, P. *Die hell.-röm. Kultur* (Tüb. '07 ; 2nd ed. '12) ; *Die Therapeuten u. d. philonische Schrift vom beschaulichen Leben* (Leip. '96) ; Σωτήρ (in *Zeit. f. d. neutest. Wiss.* '04, V. pp. 335–53) ; *Hellenistic Ideas of Salvation* (in *Amer. J. Theol.* '13).

Weniger, L. *Über das Collegium der Thyaden* (Eisenach, '76).

Wessely, K. *Spread of Jewish-Christian Ideas among the Egyptians* (*Expositor*, '86, pp. 199–204) ; *Ephesia Grammata* (Vienna, '86).

Westermarck, E. *Origin and Development of the Moral Ideas* (2 vols. Lond. '06–8).

Whittaker, T. *The Origins of Christianity* (2nd ed. Lond. '09).

Wiedemann, A. *The Ancient Egyptian Doctrine of the Immortality of the Soul* (Eng. tr. Lond. '95) ; *Religion of the Ancient Egyptians* (Eng. tr. Lond. '97) ; *The Realms of the Egyptian Dead* (ib. '01).

Windisch, H. *Taufe u. Sünde im ältesten Christentum* (Tüb. '08) ; *Urchristentum u. Hermesmystik* (in *Theol. Tijdsch.*, '18, 4. pp. 186–240).

Wissowa, G. *Religion u. Kultus der Römer* (2nd ed. Munich, '12).

Wobbermin, G. *Religionsgesch. Studien zur Frage der Beeinflussung des Urchristentums durch das antike Mysterienwesen* (Berlin, '96).

Zahn, Th. *Skizzen aus dem Leben der alten Kirche* (2nd ed. Erlangen, '98).

Zeller, E. *Outlines of the history of Greek Philosophy* (Eng. tr. Lond. '95) ; *Pre-Socratic Philosophy* (Eng. tr. 2 vols. ib. '81) ; *Plato and the Older Academy* (Eng. tr. ib. '76) ; *Aristotle and the Earlier Peripatetics* (Eng. tr. 2 vols. ib. '97) ; *Socrates and the Socratic Schools* (Eng. tr. 2nd ed. ib. '77) ; *Stoics, Epicureans, and Sceptics* (Eng. tr. ib. '80) ; *History of Eclecticism in Greek Philosophy* (Eng. tr. ib. '83) ; *Religion u. Philosophie dei den Römern* (*Vortr. u. Abhandl.* 2nd ser.

pp. 93–105) ; *Zur Vorgesch. des Christentums : Essener u. Orphiker* (*Kl. Sch.* pp. 120–84).

Zielinski, Th. *Hermes u. die Hermetik* (in *Arch. f. Religionswis.* VIII. '05, pp. 321–72 ; IX, '06, pp. 25–60).

Zipfel, G. *Das Taurobolium* (pp. 498–520, *Festsch. L. Friedländers dargebracht,* Leip. '95).

Zöckler, O. *Askese u. Mönchtum* (2nd ed. Frankf. '97).

SELECTED LIST OF CHIEF RELEVANT ANCIENT SOURCES

Abercius, Inscription of : *Die Grabschrift des Abercius* (ed. W. Lüdtke and Th. Nissen, Leip. '10 ; ed. A. Dieterich, Leip. '96 ; *id.* Cabrol-Leclercq, I. 85–7).

Achilles, *Isagoge ad Arati Phaenomena* (in Migne, *Patrologia Graeca* ; critical ed. in Maas' *Aratea,* Berlin, '92).

Acta Thomae, Gk. text by M. R. James, Eng. tr. by S. C. Malan, in *Texts and Studies,* V. 1, pp. 28–63.

Aesculapius, Prayer to, *C.I.A.* III, 171.

Almagest, *v.s.* Claudius Ptolemaeus.

Ancient Fragments : Greek and Latin texts with tr. by I. P. Cory (2nd ed. Lond. 1832).

Andania : Mystery-inscription of (Demeter and Kore, and (?) the Kabiri) 91 B.C. (in Dittenberger, *Sylloge,* 2nd ed. 653 ; 3rd ed. 736) ; Cauer, *Delectus,* 2nd ed. 47 ; Sauppe, *Die Mysterien-Inschrift von Andania* (Gött. '60) ; *Inscr. d'Andania,* by P. Foucart (Paris, n.d.) ; Collitz, *Dialect-Inschriften,* 4689 ; Michel, *Recueil,* 694 ; Prott-Ziehen, II. 58 ; *I.G.* V. 1390.

Andros, *Hymn to Isis* in Kaibel, *Epig. Graec.* 1028 ; Abel, *Orphica,* p. 295 f. ; *I.G.* XII, 5, 1, no. 739.

Apollodorus Atheniensis, *Bibliotheca,* ed. I. Bekker, Leip. '54 ; *v. Mythologi Graeci,* ed. R. Wagner, Leip. '94 ; also in Müller, *Frag. hist. gr.* I. ; Eng. tr. by J. Frazer, in Loeb's *Class. Lib.* 2 vols. '21).

Apollonius Rhodius, *Argonautica* (ed. R. C. Seaton, Oxf. ; Eng. tr. A. S. Way, Lond. '01; also by R. C. Seaton in Loeb's *Class. Library,* '12).

Apuleius, *Metamorphoses,* or *Golden Ass,* especially bk. XI. (ed. R. Helm, Leip. '13, Eng. tr. by H. E. Butler, 2 vols.

Oxf. '10 ; also by Adlington and Gaselee in Loeb's *Class. Library*).

De Magia (Apologia), ed. R. Helm, Leip. '15.

De Deo Socratis ; De Platone ; De Mundo, ed. P. Thomas, Leip. '08.

Aratus, *Phaenomena*, ed. E. Maas, Berlin, '93 (Eng. tr. by G. R. Mair, Loeb's *Class. Library*, '21).

Comm. in Aratum reliquiae, col. E. Maas, Berlin, '98.

Aratea, E. Maas, Berlin, '92.

Aristides, *Apology* (Syriac text with Eng. tr. by J. R. Harris, with portion of Greek text by J. A. Robinson in *Texts and Studies*, I. 1, 2nd ed. Camb, '93).

Aristides, Aelius Rhetor, *Orationes Sacrae*, ed. Dindorf, 3 vols. Leip. '29.

Aristophanes, *Nubes*, ll., 223 ff., 382 ff.

Lysistrata, 388 ff.

Vespes, 5 ff.

Ranae, 324 ff., 455 ff.

Thesmae, 134 ff.

Arnim, H. v.   *Stoicorum Veterum Fragmenta* (3 vols. Leip. '03-5).

Arnobius, *Adversus Gentes* (ed. A. Reifferscheid, Vienna, '75. Eng. tr. by A. H. Bryce and H. Campbell in *Ante-Nicene Library*, Edin. '71).

Arrian, *v.s.* Epictetus.

Artemidorus, *Oneirocritica* (ed. Reiff, Leip. 1805).

Asclepiasts, Guild of, in Attica, *I.G.* II. 617.

Asclepius, v. *Corpus Hermeticum*.

Athenaeus, *Deipnosophistae* (ed. G. Kaibel, 3 vols. Leip. '87-'90 ; Eng. tr. by C. D. Yonge in Bohn's *Class. Library*).

Athenagoras, *Apology for the Christians (Legatio)* (ed. J. C. T. Otto, Jena, '57, Eng. tr. by B. P. Pratten in *Ante-Nicene Library*, Edin. '67).

Attis, Hymn to, Hippolytus, *Ref. omn. Haer. (Philosoph.)* V. 9.

Augustine, *De Civitate Dei* (ed. B. Dombart, 2 vols. Leip. '77-92) ; Eng. tr. by Marcus Dods in *Post-Nicene Fathers*).

Augustus, *Res Gestae Divi Augusti ex Monumentis Ancyrano et Apolloniensi* (by Th. Mommsen, 2nd ed. Berl. '83).

Aulus Gellius, *Noctes Atticae* (ed. C. Hosius, Leip. '03 ; Eng. tr. by W. Beloe, Lond. 1795).

Autolychus, *De Sphaera quae movetur* (Greek text with Lat. tr. by F. Hultsch, Leip. '85).

Berossus, *Fragments*, in Mullach, *Frag. hist. Gr. II*, pp. 495–510) ;
  Berossos u. d. Babyl.-Hellenistische Literatur, by P. Schnabel,
  Leip. 23.
Berthelot, M. et Ruelle, E. *Collection des anciens Alchimistes
  grecs* (Paris, '87–8).
Bruns, C. G. *Fontes Iuris Romani antiqui* (6th ed. Freib. and Leip.
  '93).
Callimachus, *Hymns* (ed. Wilamowitz-Moellendorf, Berl. '07 ;
  Eng. tr. by A. W. Mair, in Loeb's *Class. Library*, '21).
Callixenes of Rhodes : *Bacchic procession at Alexandria under
  Ptolemy Philadelphus*, in Athenaeus, V. 25–35 (196a–203b).
Carmen contra Paganos (Anon.) from fourth century, ll., 57–109.
  (Baehrens *Poetae Lat. Min.* III, p. 286 f. ; Hepding, *Attis*,
  p. 61.)
Catalogus Codicum astrologicorum Graecorum, ed. F. Boll, Fr.
  Cumont, W. Kroll, A. Olivieri, and others. I–VIII, Brussels,
  '98-12).
Catullus, *Carmen*, LXIII (ed. of Ellis).
Chaldean Oracles, v. G. Kroll, *De Oraculis Chaldaeis*, in *Breslauer
  phil. Abhandl.* VII, '94, pt. 1. G. R. S. Mead, *The Chaldaean
  Oracles* (Lond. and Benares, '08).
Cicero, Philosophical Works :
  Academica, ed. with commentary and tr. by J. S. Reid, 2 vols.
    Lond. '85).
  De Divinatione (in ed. of J. G. Baiter and C. L. Kayser, Leip.
    '60–69 ; or ed. of R. Klotz or Th. Schiche).
  De Officiis (ed. C. F. W. Müller, Leip. '82 ; ed. H. Holden,
    7th ed. Lond. '91 ; Eng. tr. by G. B. Gardiner, Lond. '99 ;
    by W. Miller, in Loeb's *Class. Lib.*).
  De Finibus (ed. J. N. Madvig, 3rd ed. '76 ; with intro. and
    comm. by W. M. L. Hutchison, '09 ; Eng. tr. by H. Rackham
    in Loeb's *Class. Lib.*).
  De Fato (Müller, '98).
  De Legibus (ed. of Baiter and Kayser, or C. F. W. Müller,
    Leip. '98).
  De Republica (Müller, Leip. '98).
  Paradoxa (ed. M. Schneider, Leip. '91 ; Eng. tr. by C. R. Ed-
    monds, Lond. '74).
  De Natura Deorum (ed. with comm. by J. B. Mayor, 3 vols.
    '80–85).
  Tusculanae Disputationes (ed. O. Heine, '96) ; *v.s.* Hirzel.

Cleanthes (in Arnim's *Stoic. Vet. Frag.* Fragments also by A. C. Pearson, '91).

Clemen, C. *Fontes Historiae religionis Persicae* (Bonn, '20 f.; *v.s. Fontes*).

Clement Alexandrinus, *Paedagogus*.
Protrepticus, esp. II.
Stromateis (ed. G. Dindorf, 4 vols. Oxf. '69). Best ed. of *Paedagogus* and *Protrepticus*, O. Stählin (Leip. '05–9). Eng. tr. of *Stromateis*, bk. VII, by J. B. Mayor, Lond. '02 ; of whole by W. Wilson, in Clark's *Ante-Nicene Library* (2 vols. Edin. '67–9).

Collegia : Roman Legislation re, in Bruns' *Fontes*, pt. II. ch. XIII.

Conon, *Diegeseis* (in Photius' *Bibliotheca*, Migne, *P. Gr.*)

Cornutus, *Theologiae Graecae Compendium* (ed. C. Lang, Leip. '91).

Corpus Haereseologicum, ed. by F. Oehler, 5 parts, Berlin, '56–61).

Corpus Hermeticum :
Poimandres (ed. G. Parthey, Berlin, '54; ed. R. Reitzenstein, Leip. '04).
Asclepius, or *The Perfect Word* (Latin version by (?) Apuleius, ed. P. Thomas, Leip. '08).
Aesculapii Definitiones ad Ammonem Regem (Greek text with Lat. tr. by M. Ficino in Turnebus' ed. of *Poemander*, Paris, 1554).
Numerous Extracts in Johannes Stobaeus.
Minor Fragments in Lactantius, Cyril, Suidas, Psellus; *v.* F. Patrizzi, *Nova de universis philosophia*, Ferrara, 1591.
Eng. tr. of *Poimandres* from Arabic, *The Divine Pymander of Hermes Trismegistus*, by Everard, Lond. 1650 ; reprinted in *Jour. Spec. Phil.* July, '66).
The Theological and Philosophical Works of Hermes Trismegistus, Christian Neo-Platonist, by J. D. Chambers (Edin. '82). Most complete tr. by G. R. S. Mead, *Thrice-greatest Hermes* (3 vols. Lond. and Benares, '06).

Cultores Dianae et Antinoi, the *Lexs Collegi* from inscription of Lanuvium, *C.I. Lat.* XIV, 2112 : Bruns, *Fontes*, 6th ed. p. 345 ff. : Dessau, *Inscr. Lat. Selectae*, 7212.

Curtius, R. Quintus, *De rebus gestis Alexandri Magni* (ed. E. Heidicke, '08).

Cyril, *Contra Julianum*.

Damascius *De primis principiis*, ed. C. A. Ruelle, 2 parts, Par. '89 ; French tr. A. E. Chaignet, Par. '98).

Democritus, *De Sympathiis et Antipathiis* (in Fabricius, *Bibliotheca Graeca*, IV. pt. II, pp. 333–8).

Demosthenes, *De Corona*, 259 ff.

Diels, H. *Fragmente der Vorsokratiker* (Greek text with Germ. tr. 2 vols. in 3 parts, 2nd ed. Berlin, '03–10 ; 3rd ed. '12 ff. ; 4th ed. '22).

Poetarum Philosophorum Graecorum Fragmenta (Berlin, '01).

Doxographi Graeci (Berlin, '79).

Dio Cassius, *Historia Romana* (ed. L. Dindorf, Leip. '63–5 ; ed. J. Melber, Leip. '90 f. ; U. P. Boissevain, 3 vols. Berl. '95–'01. Eng. tr. in 9 vols. in progress by E. Cary in Loeb's, *Class. Lib.*).

Dio Chrysostom, *Orationes* (ed. L. Dindorf, Leip. '57 ; best ed. J. de Arnim, 2 vols. Berlin, '93–96).

Diodorus Siculus, *Bibliotheca Historica* (ed. Vogel, 3 vols. Leip. '83–93).

Diogenes Laertius, *De Vitis Philosophorum* (ed. H. G. Hübner, 2 vols. Leip. '28–'31 ; also by C. G. Cobet, Didot, Paris, '78. Eng. tr. by C. D. Yonge, Lond. '53).

Dionysiac Mysteries : Edict of Ptolemy Philopator on private initiations outside Alexandria (Greek text and Germ. tr. by W. v. Schubart in *Amtliche Berichte aus d. könig. Kunstsammlungen* of Strassburg, XXXVIII, 7, coll. 189–97. Text and Fr. tr. by P. Roussel in *Comptes Rendus*, '19, p. 238. Cf. R. Reitzenstein, *Archiv f. Religionswis.* XIX. '18, pp. 191–14).

Dionysiac Thiasos of Athenians, second cent. B.C. *Insc. Graecae*, II, 623.

Dionysius, *Periegetes* (in C. Müller, *Geographi Graeci Minores*, II Paris, '82).

Dionysius Halicarnassus, *Antiquitates Romanae* (ed. C. Jacoby, Leip. '85–'05).

Dithyramb of the Women of Elis, in Plutarch, *Quaest. Gr.* XXXVI, p. 299.

Epictetus, *Dissertationes* (H. Schenkl, Leip. '04. Eng. tr. by G. Long, Lond. '48, '91).

Epidaurian temple-cures inscribed on slabs, *v.* Cavvadias, Ἐφ. Ἀρχ. '83, p. 198 ff. ; '85, p. 16 ff. Cavvadias, *Fouilles d'Épidaure* (Athens, '91).

Epiphanius, *Panaria* (Greek text with Lat. tr. of Petavius and comm. of A. Jahn, in Oehler's *Corpus Haeresiologicum,* II–III).

Etymologicum Magnum (Oxf. '48 ; ed. Sylburg, Leip. 1816).

Eunapius, *Vitae Sophistarum* (Greek text with Lat. tr. by J. F. Boissonade in Didot's ed., Paris, '73).

Euripides, *Bacchae* (Eng. tr. by G. Murray, or A. S. Way).
   Fragment of the *Cretans* (in *Frag. tragica papyracea,* V., A. Hunt, Oxf. '12). Chorus from *Cretans* in Porphyry, *De Abst.* IV. 19 ; No. 475 in Nauck's *Tragicorum graec. frag.* ; Didot's ed. p. 735. Eng. tr. by G. Murray, *Euripides,* 5th ed. p. 324.
   Phoenissae, 649 ff.
   Alcestis, 962 ff.
   Ion, 1074–86.
   Helena, 1301–68.

Eusebius, *Praeparatio Evangelica* (4 vols. T. Gaisford, Oxf. '43).

Fairbanks, A. *The First Philosophers of Greece* (Fragments, with Eng. tr. and notes, Lond. '98).

Fontes Historiae Religionum ex Auctoribus Graecis et Latinis collectos (ed. C. Clemen, Bonn, '20 f.).

Fragmenta Herculanensia (W. Scott, Oxf. '85).

Fragmenta Historicorum Graecorum (ed. C. and Th. Müller, Didot, Paris, 4 vols. '41–53).

Fragmenta Philosophorum Graecorum (ed. F. G. A. Mullach, 3 vols. Paris, '81–3).

Galenus, *Opera* (ed. Marquardt, Müller, and others, in Teubner, Leip. '84–93. Eng. tr. of *Natural Faculties,* by A. J. Brock in Loeb's *Class. Library*).

Geminus, *Elementa astronomica* (Greek, with Germ. tr. by K. Manitius, Leip. '98).

Gnosticism :
   Codex Askewianus, containing Coptic text of (1) *Pistis Sophia,* (2) Part of the *Texts of the Saviour,* (3) Frag. on *The Mystery of the Ineffable.*
      (French tr. by E. Amélineau, Paris, '95 ; Germ. tr. by C. Schmidt in *Koptisch-Gnostische Schriften,* Leip. '05 ; Eng. tr. by G. R. S. Mead, Lond. '96, 2nd ed. '21 ; by F. Legge in S.P.C.K. Lond. '22.)
   Papyrus Brucianus in Bodleian Library, Oxford, containing according to Schmidt's analysis, (1) *The Books of Jeou*

(entitled by Mead, *The Book of the Great Logos according to the Mystery*) ; (2) Two fragments of Gnostic invocations ; (3) Frag. of the *Passage of the Soul through the Archon of the Middle Region* ; (4) Fragment of an old Gnostic work.

(Coptic text with Fr. tr. by Amélineau in *Notices et Extraits de MSS. de la Bibliothèque nationale et autres Bibliothèques,* vol. XXIX, pt. I, Paris, '91. Text with Germ. tr. by C. Schmidt in *Gnostische Schriften in Koptischer Sprache aus dem Codex Brucianus,* Leip. '92.)

The Akhmim Papyrus, in the Berlin Museum of Egyptian Antiquities, containing (1) *Gospel of Mary Apocryphon* (? Apocalypse) *of John,* (2) *The Wisdom of Jesus Christ,* (3) *Acts of Peter.*

Cf. C. Schmidt, *Ein vor-irenaeisches gnostisches Original-Werk in koptischer Sprache* (in *Sitzber. d. kgl. Akad. preuss. Akad. d. Wiss.* '96).

Excerpta Theodoti (Greek text Clemens Alex. III, pp. 103–33 of *Die griech. christ. Schriftst.* and in C. C. J. Bunsen's *Analecta Antenicaena,* I, pp. 205–78, with Lat. tr. by J. Bernays, Lond. '54).

Letter of Ptolemaeus to Flora (in Epiphanius, *Panaria, Haer.* XXXIII. 3–7 ; Oehler, II, I. 1. pp. 400–12 with Lat. tr. Ed. A. Harnack, 2nd ed. Bonn '12 in *Kl. Texte*).

Naassene Psalm (in Hippolytus' *Philosophoumena,* V. 182–4, Cruice ; Eng. tr. p. 145 in Legge's tr. or II, p. 62 in his *Forerunners,* etc. ; cf. Wendland, *Berl. phil. Woch,* '02 sp. 1324 ; A. Swoboda, *Wiener Studien,* XXVII. 2).

The Hymn of Bardaisan = The Hymn of the Soul.

The Hymn of the Soul in *Acta Thomae,* ch. 108–13. Syriac text by A. S. Bevan in *Texts and Studies,* V. 3. Camb. '97. Also by G. Hoffmann in *Zeitschr. f. neut. Wiss.* IV, p. 273 ff. ; and in Wright's *Apoc. Acts of the Apostles,* I ; Lipsius and Bonnet, *Acta Apost. apocr.* II, 2, pp. 219–24, Leip. '03. (Eng. tr. by F. C. Burkitt, Lond. '99 ; by G. R. S. Mead in *Fragments of a Faith Forgotten,* pp. 406–14, under title *The Hymn of the Robe of Glory,* and separately under same title Lond. '08. Excellent Germ. verse tr. in Schultz, *Dokumente,* pp. 13–21 ; also prose by Hoffmann, *l.c.*)

The Hymn of Jesus, in *Acta Johannis,* XI. Greek text and tr. by M. R. James in *Texts and Studies,* V, I, pp. 10–15.

Heracleon, Extant Fragments, Greek text by A. E. Brooke in *Texts and Studies*, I, 4, Camb. '91.

Basilidis Fragmenta (from VI book of Hippolytus, in Bunsen, *ib*. I. pp. 55–75).

Valentini Fragmenta (from book VII of Hippolytus, in Bunsen, *Analecta Antenicaena*, pp. 77–96).

Basilidis Fragmenta (from book VII of Hippolytus, in Bunsen, *ib*. I. pp. 55–75).

For further fragments cf. A. Hilgenfeld, *Ketzergeschichte des Urchristentums* (Leip. '84).

Harpocration, *Lexicon* (Dindorf, 2 vols. Oxf. '53).

Helbig, W. *Wandgemälde der vom Vesuv verschütteten Städte Campaniens* (Leip. '68).

Heliolatry, *v.s.* Sun-worship.

Heracliti Ephesii Reliquiae, ed. I. Bywater, Oxf. '77 ; and in Diels, *Fragmente d. Vorsokratiker*, *v.s.* Macchioro.

Hermias, *Irrisio gentilium philosophorum*, *v.s.* Otto.

Hermippus, sive De Astrologia Dialogus (Anonymi Christiani, ed. W. Kroll and P. Viereck, Leip. '95).

Herodotus, *Histories* (esp. I. 34–45 ; II. 42, 48, 50–60, 81, 144–6, 156 ; IV. 79–108 ; VII. 6 ; VIII. 65). (Eng. tr. by G. C. Macaulay, Lond. '90, 2 vols.)

Hierocles, *Commentary on the Golden Verses of Pythagoras* (in Mullach, *Fragmenta*, I, p. 480 ff.), Eng. tr. by N. Rowe, Lond. '06.

Hippolytus, *Philosophoumena, sive Omnium Haeresium Refutatio* (ed. P. M. Cruice, Paris, '60, with Lat. tr. Best ed. by P. Wendland in *Griech. christ. Kirchenväter*, 3 vols. Berlin, vol. I, '16).

Eng. tr. by MacMahon in *Ante-Nicene Library*, Edin. '68 ; best tr. by F. Legge, 2 vols. Lond. '21.

Historiae Augustae Scriptores, *v.s.* *Scriptores Hist. Aug.*

Homer, *Odyssey*, XI (cf. U. von Wilamowitz-Möllendorf, *Hom. Untersuchungen*, p. 199 ff.).

Homeric Hymns, esp. II (To Demeter), VII (To Dionysos), VIII (To Ares), XIV (To the Mother of the Gods). Best ed. by T. W. Allen and E. E. Sikes, Lond. '04; Eng. tr. by J. Edgar, Edin. '91 ; A. Lang, Lond. '99 ; H. G. Evelyn-White in Loeb's *Library*, '14.

Hopfner, Th. *Fontes Historiae Religionis Aegypticae* (3 parts, Bonn, '22 f., *v.s.* *Fontes*, etc.).

Horace, *Carmen Saeculare* (cf. Zosimus, II. 5, 6).

Iamblichus, *De Vita Pythagorica* (ed. T. Kiessling, Leip. 1815 ; A. Nauck, St. Petersburg, '84) ; Eng. tr. by T. Taylor, Lond. 1818.

De Mysteriis (ed. G. Parthey, Berlin, '57 ; T. Gale, with Lat. tr. Oxf. 1678 ; Eng. tr. by T. Taylor, Lond. 1821).

Protrepticus, Exhortatio ad Philosophiam (ed. H. Pistelli, Leip. '88).

Inscriptions :

Corpus Inscriptionum Graecarum (A. Boeckh and others, Berlin, 1828–77).

Corpus Inscriptionum Latinarum (by Mommsen and others, 1863 ff.).

Inscriptiones Graecae (in course of publication by the Prussian Academy, Berlin, since 1873) in following main parts :
Corpus Inscriptionum Atticarum (Berlin, '73–97).

Corpus Inscriptionum Graeciae Septentrionalis (ed. W. Dittenberger, Ber. '92).

Inscriptiones Graecae Siciliae et Italiae (G. Kaibel, Ber. '90.

Inscriptiones Graecae Insularum Maris Aegaei (H. v. Gaertringen and W. R. Paton, Ber. '95 f.).

Inscriptiones Argolidis.

Inscriptiones Megaridis et Boeotiae.

Inscriptiones Oris Septentrionalis Ponti Euxini (E. H. Minns, Camb. '13).

Inscriptionum Latinarum amplissima selectarum Collectio (J. C. Orelli and W. Henzen, 3 vols. Turin, 1828–56).

Leges Graecorum sacrae e titulis collectae (J. v. Prott and L. Ziehen, Leip. '96–'06).

Inscrizione greche e latine (by E. Breccia in *Antiquités égypt. du Musée d'Alexandrie*).

Recueil des Inscriptions grecques-chrétiennes d'Egypte (G. Lefebure, Cairo, '07).

Sammelbuch Griechischer Urkunden aus Ägypten (F. Preisigke, I, Strassburg, '15 f. Contains also papyri).

Collection of Ancient Greek Inscriptions in the British Museum (ed. E. L. Hicks, Oxf. '74 ff.).

Defixionum Tabellae (A. Audollent, Paris, '04).

Inscriptiones Graecae ad res Romanas pertinentes (R. Cagnat, 3 vols. Paris, '11–14).

Orientis Graecae Inscriptiones Selectae (W. Ditter berger, 2 vols. Leip. '03–5).

Sylloge Inscriptionum Graecarum (W. Dittenberger, 2nd ed. 2 vols. and index, Leip. '88–91 ; 3rd ed. 4 vols. Leip. '15–20).

Recueil d'Inscriptions grecques, also *Supplement* (Ch. Michel, Paris, '00–12).

Recueil des Inscriptions grecques et latines de l'Égypte (M. Letronne, 2 vols. Paris, '42–8).

Inscriptiones antiquae Orae septentrionalis Ponti Euxini Graecae et Latinae (B. Latyschev, St. Petersburg, '85).

Epigrammata Graeca (G. Kaibel, Berlin, '78).

Fouilles d'Épidaure (P. Cavvadias, Athens, '91).

Inscriptions grecques et latines recueillies en Grèce et en Asie Mineure (P. Le Bas and W. H. Waddington, Paris, '70).

Antike Fluchtafeln (R. Wünsch, Bonn, '07).

Selection in Foucart's *Des Associations religieuses*, pp. 187–243.

Invocation of Isis, early second cent. Greek text, tr. and comm. in *Oxyrhynchus Papyri*, XI, no. 1380, pp. 190–220.

Liturgical text of Isis cult in second or third cent. inscr. from Ios, Dittenberger, *Sylloge*, 3rd ed. 1267, or R. Weil, *Ath. Mitth.* II, '77, p. 81 ff. ; *I.G.* XII, V, 1, no. 14 ; cf. Diodorus, *Bib.* I. 27.

The Burden of Isis : being the Laments of Isis and Nephthys (tr. by J. T. Dennis, Lond. '10).

Iobacchoi, Regulations of a Thiasos of, in Greek inscription published by S. Wide in *Athenische Mitteilungen*, '94, XIX, p. 248 ff. ; No. 46, pp. 132–47 of Prott-Ziehen, *Leges Graec. Sacrae* ; Dittenberger, *Sylloge*, 2nd ed. no. 737, 3rd ed. no. 1109 ; Maas, *Orpheus*, pp. 18–32.

Irenaeus, *Adversus Haereses* (ed. W. W. Harvey, 2 vols. Camb. '57 ; Eng. tr. by A. Roberts and W. H. Rambant in Clark's *Ante-Nicene Library*, 2 vols. Edin. '68–9 ; also by F. R. M. Hitchcock in S.P.C.K. 2 vols. Lond. '16).

Isis, Praises of, found on a tomb of Osiris and Isis, Diodorus Siculus, I. 27.

Poetic dedication to Isis, *I.G.* XII, pt. V. 1, p. 213 f.

Prose dedication to, *ib.* p. 217.

Isocrates, *Panegyric* (ed. J. E. Sandys, Lond. '97).

Isyllos, Paean of, from Epidaurus, late fourth cent. B.C. *Eph.*

Arch. '85, p. 65, *v.* Wilamowitz-Möllendorf, *Isyllos v. Epi-daurus,* '86 (in *Philolog. Unters.*).

Josephus, *Antiquities of the Jews* (e.g. XVIII. 3, 4).

Julian the ' Apostate ' : *Orationes,* esp. IV (*Hymn to the Sovereign Sun*), V (*Hymn to the Mother of the Gods*), VI (*To the un-educated Cynics*), VII (*To the Cynic Heraclius*).
Letter to Themistius (frag.).
Against the Christians (frag.).
Two complete French trs. by R. Tourlet, 3 vols. Paris, 1821, and by E. Talbot, Paris, '63; Eng. tr. of *Hymn to the Sovereign Sun* and *To the Mother of the Gods,* by T. Taylor, Lond. 1793 ; and of *Against the Christians* by same, Lond. 1803; Greek text and Eng. tr. by W. C. Wright in Loeb's *Library,* 3 vols. '13.

Justin Martyr, *Apologies* I and II ; *Dialogue with Trypho ; Oratio ad Graecos ; Cohortatio ad Graecos* (ed. J. C. T. Otto, 3 vols. with Lat. tr. Leip. '76–81 ; Eng. tr. by Marcus Dods in Clark's *Ante-Nicene Library,* Edin. '67).

Kouretes, Hymn of the, Greek text and tr. in J. Harrison, *Themis,* pp. 6–8.

Lactantius, *Institutiones Divinae* (ed. S. Brandt and G. Laubmann in *Corp. Script. eccles. Lat.* ; Eng. tr. by W. Fletcher in Clark's *Ante-Nicene Library,* Edin. '71).

Lampridius, Aelius, in *Scriptores Hist. Aug.*

Libanius, *Orationes* (ed. R. Foerster, 4 vols. Leip. '03–8).

Livy, *Ab urbe condita libri* (esp. X, 47 ; XXIX, 11–14 ; XXXIV, 54 ; XXXVI, 36 ; XXXIX, 8–18 ; XL, 29).

Lucian, esp. *Alexander ; Bacchus ; De Astrologia ; De Dea Syria ; De Morte Peregrini ; De Saltatione ; Philopseudes ; Saturnalia* (ed. J. Sommerbrodt, 3 vols. Leip. '86–99 ; or E. Nilen, Leip. Eng. tr. by H. W. and F. G. Fowler, Lond. '05).

Lucretius, *De Natura Rerum.* Cf. II. 608 ff.

Lycosura, mystery inscr. Dittenberger, *Syl.* 2nd ed. 939, 3rd ed. 999 ; Prott-Ziehen, II. 63 ; *I.G.* V. 2, 514.

Macarius Magnes, *Apocritica* (Greek text by Blondel and Foucart, Paris, '76; Eng. tr. by T. W. Crafer, in S.P.C.K. Lond. '19).

Macrobius, Ambrosius Theodosius, *Commentarium in Somnium Scipionis* and *Saturnalia* (ed. F. Eyssenhardt, Leip. '93 ; Fr. tr. in Nisard's *Auteurs latins,* Paris, '45).

Magi, Hymn of the : Dio Chrysostom, *Or.* XXXVI, 39–54 (de

Arnim, II, pp. 11-15 ; Cumont, *T. et M.* II, pp. 60-64 ; part in Clemen, *Fontes hist. rel. pers.*, p. 44 ff.).

Magic :

Out of a vast literature cf. esp. the following :

Magic Papyrus of A.D. 395 in Museum of Leyden, published by C. Leemans in *Papyri Graeci Musei antiq. pub. Lugduni Batavorum*, 2 vols. '83-5, vol. II, pp. 77-198. Also by Dieterich in *Jahrb. f. d. klas. Philol. Suppl.* XVI, pp. 749-830, and in his *Abraxas*, pp. 167-205.

Berlin Magical Papyri, ed. G. Parthey, in *Abhandl. der Akad. zu Berlin*, Pap. I. in '65, pp. 109-180.

Wessely, *Ephesia Grammata* (Vienna, '86, in XII *Jahresb. über d. kgl.-kais. Franz-Joseph Gymnasium*).

Griechische Zauberpapyri von Paris u. London (Vienna, '88 in *Denkschriften d. kais. Akad. d. Wiss. zu Wien, Phil.-hist.* XXXVI).

Neue Griechische Zauberpapyri (Vienna, '93, *ib.* XLII).

F. Kenyon, *Greek Papyri in the British Museum*, II.

U. Wilcken, *Archiv f. Papyrusforschung*, I, p. 427 ff.

R. Heim, *Incantamenta Magica Graeca Latina* (in *Jahrb. f. klas. Phil.* Suppl. XIX, '93, pp. 463-576).

Griffith, *The Demotic Magical Papyrus of London and Leiden* (Lond. '04).

Apuleius, *Metamorphoses*, and *Apologia, sive De Magia* (ed. R. Helm, Leip. '05).

Cato, *De Re Rustica* (in *Scriptores rei rusticae veteres Latini* ed. I. M. Gesner, Leip. 1773).

Pliny the Elder, *Historia Naturalis.*

Democritus, *De Sympathiis et Antipathiis* (in Fabricius, *Bibliotheca Graeca*, IV, pt. 2, pp. 333-8).

R. Wünsch, *Antike Fluchtafeln* (Bonn, '07) ; *Defixionum Tabellae Atticae* (Berl. '97).

A. Audollent, *Defixionum Tabellae* (Paris, '04).

L. Macdonald, *Inscriptions relating to Sorcery in Cyprus* (*Proc. Soc. Bib. Arch.* '91, pp. 160-90).

Cf. review of material in Hubert's art. *Magia* in Daremberg-Saglio, *Dictionnaire* ; and R. Wünsch, *Antikes Zaubergerät aus Pergamon*, in *Jahrb. d. Arch. Inst.* VI. 19.

Manetho, *Apotelesmaticorum lib. VI* (ed. A. Koechly, Liep. '58).

Manilius, *Astronomica* (ed. J. v. Wagenigen, Leip. '15 ; J. P.

Postgate, Lond. '94–'05. Good ed. with Eng. tr. of Bk. II by Garrod, Lond.).

Marcus Aurelius, *Meditations* (ed. J. Stich, Leip. '82 ; J. H. Leopold, Oxf. Eng. tr. with introd. by G. H. Rendall, 2nd ed. Lond. 'o1 ; also by C. R. Haines in Loeb's *Library*, Lond. '16).

Maternus, Julius Firmicus, *De Errore profanarum religionum* (ed. K. Ziegler, Leip. '07).

Matheseos Libri VIII (ed. W. Kroll and F. Skutsch, Leip.).

Maximus of Tyre (ed. F. Dubner, Paris, '40 ; H. Hobein, Leip. '10. Eng. tr. by T. Taylor, 2 vols. Lond. 1804).

Mendel, *Catalogue des sculptures grecques, romaines, byzantines* (Musée Impérial ottoman, 3 vols., 12 ff.).

Minucius Felix, *Octavius* (ed. H. Bonig, Leip. '03. Eng. tr. by R. E. Wallis in Clark's *Ante-Nicene Library*, Edin. ; by J. H. Freese in S.P.C.K. Lond. n.d.).

Mithra, Liturgy of (so-called), v. Dieterich, *Eine Mithrasliturgie.*

Naassene Psalm, v.s. Gnosticism.

Nechepsonis et Petosiridis Fragmenta magica (ed. E. Riess, *Philologus*, '91, Supp. VI, pp. 327–88).

Nemesius, *De Natura Hominis* (Greek text with Lat. tr. in Migne, *Patrologia Graeca*).

Nonnus Panopolites, *Dionysiaca* (ed. A. Koechly, 2 vols. Leip. '72–3. French tr. by Comte de Marcellus in Didot's *Bibliotheca Graeca*, Paris, '56).

Origen, *Contra Celsum* (in C. and V. de la Rue's ed. Paris, 1733–59, reprinted in Migne ; Eng. tr. by F. Crombie and W. H. Cairns in Clark's *Ante-Nicene Library*, Edin. '72).

Orphism :

Argonautica ; Lithica ; Hymni.

All three in A. C. Eschenbach's ed. Trajecti-ad-Rhenum, 1689 ; Tauchnitz ed. of the *Orphica*, Leip. 1829 ; G. Hermann's *Orphica*, Leip. 1805.

Fragments in *Orphica*, ed. E. Abel (Leip. and Prague, '85).

Nova Fragmenta Orphica, by Vari in *Wiener Studien*, XII, p. 222 ff.

Orphicorum Fragmenta, ed. O. Kern (Berlin, '22).

Orphic Tablets, ed. A. Olivieri, *Lamellae aureae orphicae*, Bonn, '15 ; Diels, *Fragmente d. Vorsokratiker*, 3rd ed. II, p. 163 ff. ; J. Harrison, *Prolegomena* by G. Murray, text and Eng. tr. pp. 660–74.

(Eng. tr. of *Hymns* by T. Taylor, Lond. 1787, reprint 1896.)

Otto, J. C. T. *Hermiae philosophi Irrisio gentilium philosophorum. Apologetarum Quadrati Aristidis Aristonis Miltiadis Melitonis Apollinaris Reliquiae* (Jena, '72).

Overbeck, J. A. *Gesch. d. griech. Plastik* (Leip. '93–4) ; *Griech. Kunstmythologie* (3 vols. Leip. '71–89).

Ovid, e.g. *Pont.* I. 1, 37–51 ; *Amatores,* II. 13, 7 ff. ; *Fasti,* XX, iv, 223 ff., 305–30 ; *Met.* XV. 61–478, 622 ff.

Paean to Dionysus, from Delphi (338 B.C.) : reconstruction of Greek text by H. Weil in *Bull. de Corr. Hell.* XIX. '95, p. 400 ff. ; Eng. tr. in J. Harrison, *Proleg.* pp. 439, 542.

Palaephatus : περὶ ἀπίσων (ed. N. Festa, Leip. '02 ; *Mythographi Graeci,* III. 2).

Panaetii et Hecatonis Fragmenta (H. N. Fowler, Lond. '85).

Papyri :

The *Oxyrhynchus Papyri,* vols. I–XVI, Lond. '98–24.

The *Flinders Petrie Papyri,* 3 parts, Dublin, '91–4.

The *Tebtunis Papyri,* 2 vols. Lond. '02–7.

The *Amherst Papyri,* 2 vols. Lond. '00–1.

Fayum Towns and their Papyri, Lond. '00.

Ägyptische Urkunden aus den kgl. Museen zu Berlin : Griechische, 5 vols. Berlin, '95–19.

Griechische Urkunden des Ägyptischen Museum zu Kairo (F. Preisigke, Strassbourg, '11–).

Selections from the Greek Papyri, 2nd ed. G. Milligan, Camb. '12.

Papyri Ercolanesi (ed. D. Comparetti, Turin, '75).

Papyrus ptolémaïques du Musée d'Alexandrie (G. Botti, Alexandria, '99).

Greek Papyri in the British Museum, ed. F. G. Kenyon, 3 vols. Lond. '93–'07.

Greek Papyri from the Cairo Museum (E. J. Goodspeed, Chicago, '06).

Les Papyrus de Genève (J. Nicole, Geneva, '96–00).

Papiri Grechi et Latini, 5 parts, Florence, '12–17.

Heidelberger Papyrus-Sammlung (ed. A. Deissmann, Heidelberg, '05).

Papyri Fiorentini (3 vols. ed. G. Vitelli and D. Comparetti, Milan, '06–15).

Corpus Papyrorum Raineri (ed. K. Wessely, Vienna, '95).

Papyrus grecs de Lille (ed. P. Jouget, 2 parts, Paris, '07-8).

See also under Magic.

Pausanias, *Description of Greece* (ed. F. Spiro, 3 vols. Leip. '03 ; Eng. tr. and commentary by J. G. Frazer, 6 vols. Lon. '98).

Peter, *Apocalypse of*, Greek text in Robinson and James, *The Gospel according to Peter*, Lond. pp. 89–96 ; cf. A. Dieterich, *Nekyia*, 2nd ed. Leip. '13.

Petosiris, vol. VII, p. 130 ff. of *Catalogus Astrologorum Graecorum*, ed. Fr. Boll. Cf. under Nechepso.

Philo Judaeus, *Opera*, ed. T. Mangey, 6 vols. Lond. 1742 ; Tauchnitz, ed. 8 vols. Leip. '51–80 ; Cohn-Wendland, ed. 6 vols. Berl. '96–15 ; *Fragments*, by J. R. Harris, Camb. '86 ; Eng. tr. by C. D. Yonge, 4 vols. Lond. '51–5.

Philocalus, *Calendarium*, in *C.I.L.* I, part 1, 2nd ed. with comm. of Th. Mommsen, Berlin, '93).

Philostratus, *Opera* (ed. C. L. Kayser, Leip. '70–11 ; also by A. Westermann in Didot's *Philostrati et Callistrati opera*, with Lat. tr. pp. 1–194, 267–318, Paris, '78).

Life of Apollonius of Tyana (Eng. tr. by F. C. Conybeare in Loeb's *Library*, 2 vols. Lond. '12 ; tr. with introd. and notes by J. S. Phillimore, 2 vols. Oxf. '12).

Heroicus (Didot, pp. 267–318).

Photius, *Bibliotheca* in Migne, *P.G.* CIII–IV; Eng. tr. by J. H. Freese in 6 vols. in progress in S.P.C.K.

Pindar, *Paeans* (Greek text with comm. and tr. in *Oxyrhynchus Papyri*, V, pp. 11–110 ; text and tr. by J. Sandys in Loeb's *Library*, pp. 518–51).

Olympic, 2.

Plato, *Phaedrus, Phaedo, Republic, Laws, Timaeus, Symposium, Gorgias*.

Pliny, *Historia Naturalis* (ed. D. Dtelefsen, Berlin, '66–82 ; ed. L. Janus, 6 vols. Leip. '70–'98 ; C. Mayhoff, '92–'09 ; Eng. tr. by J. Bostock and H. T. Riley, 6 vols. Lond. '55–57).

Plotinus, *Enneades* (ed. R. Volkmann, 2 vols. Leip. '83–4; Lat. tr. by Massilio Ficino, 1492 ; French tr. by N. Bouillet, 3 vols. Paris; Germ. tr. by H. F. Müller, 2 vols. Berlin, '78–80 ; partial Eng. tr. by T. Taylor, Lond. 1787–1834. Complete Eng. tr. in progress by Stephen McKenna, Lond. '17 f.).

Plutarch, *Moralia* (ed. G. N. Bernardakis, 7 vols. Leip. '88–96; Eng. tr. of select essays by C. W. King in Bohn's Class. Library, Lond. '82 ; of others by A. R. Shilleto, in Bohn, Lond. '88).

Selected Essays (tr. by T. G. Tucker, Oxf. '13 ; vol. II, by
A. O. Pickard, Oxf. '18; complete tr. ed. W. W. Goodwin,
5 vols. '70).

Vitae (ed. C. Sintenis, 5 vols. 2nd ed. Leip. '89–'12 ; Eng. tr. by
B. Perrin in 11 vols. in progress in Loeb's *Lib.* Lond. '14 ff.).

Polybius (ed. L. Dindorf, Leip. '86–8; Eng. tr. in progress in
Loeb's *Library*, by W. H. Paton, in 6 vols.).

Porphyry, *De Abstinentia* (ed. A. Nauck, Leip. 85 ; R. Herscher,
Paris, '58).

Vita Plotini (ed. R. Volkmann, in ed. of Plotinus).

Vita Pythagorae (ed. A. Nauck, Leip. '86).

De Antro Nympharum (ed. A. Nauck, '85).

Ep. ad Marcellam (ed. A. Nauck, '85).

Ad Anebonem (in Parthey's ed. of Iamblichus, *De Mysteriis*).

Sententiae (ed. B. Mommert, Leip. '07).

    (Eng. tr. of *De Abst.* and *De Antro Nymph.* in T. Taylor's
Select Works, Lond. 1823 ; of *De Abst.* by S. Hibberd,
Lond. '57 ; of *Ad Marc.* by A. Zimmern, Lond. '96 ;
of *Vita Plotini*, by McKenna in tr. of Plotinus ; of
Sententiae by T. Davidson in *Jour. of Spec. Phil.* III. '69.)

Posidonii Rhodii Reliquiae Doctrinae (ed. J. Bake, Leiden, 1810).

Proclus, *Institutio Theologica* (ed. G. F. Creuzer in Didot's ed. of
Plotinus, pp. XLVII-CXVII).

In Platonis rempublicam Commentaria (ed. W. Kroll, 2 vols.
Leip. '99–'01).

In Timaeum (ed. E. Diehl, 3 vols. Leip. '03–6).

In Plat. Cratylum Comm. (ed. G. Pasquali, Leip. '08).

Parmenides (ed. A. E. Chaignet, '00–3).

Hymni (in Tauchnitz' ed. of *Anthologia Graeca*, Leip. '29 ;
E. Abel, Leip. '83 ; A. Ludwich, '95).

    (Eng. tr. *The Six Books of Proclus*, including *On the Theology
of Plato, Elements of Theology, On Providence*, and minor
frags., by T. Taylor, 2 vols. Lond. 1816.)

Prudentius, *Peristephanon*, X. 1006–85 (cited in Hepding, *Attis*,
65–7).

Psellus, Michael, *Quaenam sunt Graecorum opiniones de Dae-
monibus* (J. F. Boissonade, Nuremberg, '38 ; pp. 875–82 in
Migne, *P.G.* CXXII).

De Daemonum energia sue operatione (Migne, *ib.* pp. 82–75).

Expositio in Oracula Chaldaica (after Gallaeus, ed. Migne, *ib.*
pp. 1115–50).

Pseudo-Apuleius, *Asclepius* (ed. P. Thomas, Leip. '08. Eng. tr. in Mead's *Thrice-greatest Hermes*).

Pseudo-Aristotle, *De Mundo*; Eng. tr. by E. Forster, Oxf. '14.

Pseudo-Callisthenes, *Hist. of Alexander the Great* (by E. A. W. Budge).

Pseudo-Dionysius, the Areopagite, esp. *De Mystica Theologia* and *De Coelesti Hierarchia* (Greek text in Migne, *P.G.* vols. III–IV ; Erigena's Lat. tr. in Migne, *P.L.* CIII ; Eng. tr. of former work by A. B. Sharpe in *Mysticism*, Lond. '10 ; also, by C. E. Rolt in S.P.C.K. Lond. '20 ; of latter by J. Lupton, Lond. '69 ; and by Parker, Lond. '94, '97).

Pseudo-Eratosthenes, *Catasterismi* (A. Olivieri, Leip. '97 in *Mythographi-Graeci*, III, 1).

Pseudo-Hippocrates, *De Morbo Sacro*.

Pseudo-Plato, *Axiochus*.

Pseudo-Plato, *Epinomis* (" the first gospel preached to Hellenes of the stellar religion of Asia ").

Ptolemaeus, Claudius, *Opera*, ed. J. L. Heiberg, *Syntaxis Mathematica*, 13 books, in 2 vols. Leip. '98–'03. *Opera Astronomica Minora*, '07).

Handbuch der Astronomie (Greek text with Germ. tr. and comm. by K. Manitius, 2 vols. Leip. '12–3).

Almagest = Syntaxis Mathematica.

Reinach, S. *Répertoire des reliefs grecs et romains* (3 vols. Paris, '09–'12) ; *Rép. des vases peints grecs et étrusques* (2 vols. *ib.* '99–'00).

Ritter, A. H. Preller, L. *Hist. Philosophiae Graecae-romanae*, 9th ed. (Gotha, '13).

Sacred Books of the East (Eng. tr. ed. by M. Müller and others, 50 vols. Oxf. '79–'10. Vol. L, valuable index).

Sallustius, *De Diis et Mundo* (Greek text with Lat. tr. in Mullach's *Fragmenta*, III, pp. 30–50 ; Eng. tr. by G. Murray in *Four Stages of Greek Religion*, pp. 185–214).

Scriptores Historiae Augustae (ed. H. Peter, 2 vols. Leip. '84 ; Eng. tr. by D. Magie in progress in Loeb's *Library*).

Scriptores rerum mirabilium Graeci (ed. A. Westermann, Brunswick, '39).

Scriptorum rerum mythicarum Latini (ed. G. H. Bode, Cellis, '34).

Senatusconsultum de Bacchanalibus (in Bruns' *Fontes*, etc. 7th ed. p. 164 ff. ; *C.I.L.* I. 196 ; Livy, XXXIX. 8 f.).

Seneca, *Epistulae Morales* (ed. O. Hense, Leip. '14) ; *Dialogorum libri* (ed. E. Hermes, Leip. '05) ; *De Beneficiis*, etc. (ed. C. Hosius, Leip. '14) ; *Naturales Quaestiones* (ed. A. Gercke, Leip. '07) ; Eng. tr. of *Epistulae Morales*, by R. M. Gummere, in Loeb's *Library*, 3 vols. : tr. of *Moral Essays* in progress by J. W. Basore ; cf. E. Badstübner, *Beitr. z. Erklärung der phil. Schriften Senecas*, Hamb. '01.

Serapis, *v.* important prose and verse inscr. from Delos about 200 B.C. in *I.G.* XI. 4, 1299 ; Weinreich, *Neue Urkunden z. Sarapisreligion*, pp. 31–3.

Servius, *Commentary to Virgil's Aeneid*.

Sextus Empiricus (ed. I. Bekker, Berlin, '42).

Simplicius, *Commentary on Aristotle* (ed. Heiberg and others, Berlin).

Sopatros (in C. Walz, *Rhetores Graeci*, VIII).

Sophocles, *Antigone*, 944–87, 1115–54.

Oedipus Rex, 211 ff.

Statius, *Silvae* (ed. A. Klotz, Leip. '71) ; *Thebais* (ed. P. Kohlmann, Leip. '84).

Stephanus Byzantinus, *Ethnica* (ed. A. Westermann, Leip. '39).

Stobaeus, Johannes, *Eclogae* (ed. A. Meineke, 2 vols. Leip.) ; T. Gaisford, 2 vols. Oxf. '50 ; *Florilegium* (A. Meineke, 4 vols. Leip.) ; *Opera* (ed. C. Wachsmuth and O. Hense, Berlin, '84).

Strabo, *Geographica* (ed. A. Meineke, 3 vols. Leip. '66–77. Eng. tr. in progress in Loeb's *Library*, by W. H. S. Jones, 8 vols.).

Suetonius, *Opera* (ed. C. L. Roth, Leip. '08. Eng. tr. by J. C. Rolfe, 2 vols. in Loeb's *Library*).

Suidas, *Lexicon* (ed. I. Bekker, Berlin, '54).

Sun-worship. Cf. *In laudem solis* (IV, pp. 433–7 of A. Baehrens, *Poetae Latini Minores*, 6 vols. Leip. '79–86) ; Proclus, *Hymn* I ; Macrobius, *Saturnalia*, I. 23 ; *Orphic Hymns*, VIII ; Julian, *Oratio*, IV (*Hymn to King Sun*) ; Ps.-Plato, *Epinomis*.

Symmachus, *Epistulae* and *Relationes* (ed. O. Seeck, vol. VI. 1 in *Monumenta Germaniae historica—auctores antiquissimi*, Berlin, '83).

Synesius, *Dion* (in Migne, *P.G.* LXVI, coll. 1111–1164).

Tacitus, *Annales* and *Historiae*.

Tatian, *Oratio ad Graecos* (ed. J. C. T. Otto, Jena, '51).

Taurobolium. Cf. e.g. *C.I.L.* II. 5260 ; X. 1596 ; VI. 497–504, 510, 512 ; *I.G.* I. 1019–20 ; *C.I.A.* III. 172.

Tertullian, esp. *Contra Marcionem ; Apologia ; De Praescriptione Haereticorum ; Adversus Valentinianos ; Ad Nationes* (ed. F. Oehler, 3 vols. Leip. '53–61 ; latest ed. by A. Reifferscheid and G. Wissowa, in *Corpus Script. eccles.* '90 f. Eng. tr. by various authors in Clark's *Ante-Nicene Library*).

Testament of Epicteta, inscr. from island of Thera, *C.I.G.* II. 2448 ; H. v. Gärtringen, *Inscr. Graecae*, XII, pt. 3, 330 ; Cauer, *Delectus,* 2nd ed. 148 ; Ziehen-Prott, II, pp. 318–222 ; Michel, *Recueil,* 1001.

Theo Smyrnaeus, *Expositio rerum mathematicarum* (ed. E. Hiller, Leip. '78).

Theocritus, *Idylls,* XV (*Festival of Adonis*) ; XXVI (*The Bacchanals*).

Theophilus, *Ad Autolycum* (ed. J. C. T. Otto in vol. II of *Corpus Apologetarum Christ. Saec. II,* Jena, '61 ; Eng. tr. by Marcus Dods, in Clark's *Ante-Nicene Library,* Edin. '67).

Theophrastus, *Deisidaemon, Characteres,* XXVIII (XVI). Jebb and Sandy's ed. Lond. '09, with tr.

Tresp, A. *Die Fragmente der griech. Kultschriftsteller* (Giessen, '14).

Usener, H. *Epicurea* (Leip. '87).

Valentinus, *v.s.* Gnosticism.

Valerius Flaccus, *Argonautica* (ed. C. Schenkl, Berlin, '71).

Varro, M. Terrentius, *Antiquitatum rerum humanarum et divinarum, libri I, XIV, XV, XVI.* ed. R. Agahd, Leip. '98.

Id. *Liber XVI,* ed. E. Schwarz, '88.

Id. *The Sources of the First Ten Books of Augustine's De Civitate Dei,* S. Angus, Princeton, '06.

Vettius Valens, *Anthologiarum libri* (ed. W. Kroll, Berlin, '08. Also in *Catalogus Codicum astrologorum graec.*).

Virgil, *Aeneid VI* (with Norden's Commentary) ; *Eclogae,* IV.

Zeno, *Fragments of Zeno and Cleanthes* (ed. A. C. Pearson, Lond. '91 ; also in Arnim's *Stoic. vet. Frag.*).

Zosimus, *Nova Historia* (ed. L. Mendelssohn, Leip. '87. French tr. by Cousin, Paris, 1678 ; Eng. tr. anon. Lond. 1684, 1814).

ADDENDA TO BIBLIOGRAPHY

A. Modern Works

Boulanger, A. *Orphée; Rapports de l'Orphisme et du Christianisme* (Paris, '25).

Carcopino, J. *Etudes romaines: La basilique pythagoricienne de la porte majeure* (Paris, '26); *La basilique de la porte majeure* (I in *Rev. des deux mondes*, XXXV, pp. 781-810; II, *ib.* XXXVI, pp. 170-201; III, *Une église pythagoricienne, ib.* pp. 391-425).

Casel, O. *De philosophorum graecorum silentio mystico* (Giessen, '19).

Cerfaux, L. *Influence des mystères sur le judaïsme alex. avant Philon* (*Muséon*, XXXVII, pp. 29-88).

Eisler, R. *Orphisch-dionysische Mysteriengedanken in der christ. Antike* (Leipzig, '25).

Faber, G. S. *Origins of Pagan Idolatry* (Oxf. 1816).

Halliday, W. R. *The Pagan Background of Early Christianity* (Liverpool, '25).

Lagrange, M. J. *Attis et le christianisme* (*Rev. biblique*, '19, pp. 419-80; '27, pp. 561-6).

Mischkowski, H. *Die heiligen Tische im Götterkultus der Griechen u. Römer* (Königsberg, '17).

Nock, A. D. *Studies in the Graeco-Roman Beliefs in the Empire* (*J. Hell. St.* XLV, pp. 84-101).

Otto, R. *West-östliche Mystik* (Gotha, '27).

Poerner, J. *De Curetibus et Corybantibus* (Halle, '13).

Rabes, H. *Das Eleusinische Zehntengesetz von Jahre* 353/2 (Giessen, '24).

Reinhardt, K. *Poseidonios* (Munich, '21).

Reitzenstein and Schaeder. *Studien zum antiken Synkretismus aus Iran u. Griechenland* (Leipzig, '26).

Rohde, E. *Psyche* (Eng. tr. from 8th German ed. by W. B. Hillis, Lond. '25).

Völker, K. *Mysterium u. Agape. Die gemeinsamen Mahlzeiten in der alter Kirche* (Gotha, '27).

Ziehen, L. *Der Mysterienkult von Andania* (*Archiv. f. Religionswiss.* XXIV., pp. 29-60).

B. Ancient Sources

Geden, A. S. *Select Passages illustrating Mithraism* (Lond. '25).

Hermetica. Text, tr., and notes by Walter Scott (Oxf. I, '24 ; II, '25).

Pistis Sophia. Eng. tr. by G. Horner, with intr. by F. Legge (Lond. '24).

Sallustius, *Concerning the Gods and the Universe* (with tr. by A. D. Nock, Camb. '26).

INDEX OF AUTHORS

INDEX OF SUBJECTS

A CATALOG OF SELECTED

DOVER BOOKS

IN ALL FIELDS OF INTEREST

DOVER BOOKS

DRAWINGS OF REMBRANDT, edited by Seymour Slive. Updated Lippmann, Hofstede de Groot edition, with definitive scholarly apparatus. All portraits, biblical sketches, landscapes, nudes. Oriental figures, classical studies, together with selection of work by followers. 550 illustrations. Total of 630pp. 9⅛ × 12¼.
21485-0, 21486-9 Pa., Two-vol. set $29.90

GHOST AND HORROR STORIES OF AMBROSE BIERCE, Ambrose Bierce. 24 tales vividly imagined, strangely prophetic, and decades ahead of their time in technical skill: "The Damned Thing," "An Inhabitant of Carcosa," "The Eyes of the Panther," "Moxon's Master," and 20 more. 199pp. 5⅜ × 8½. 20767-6 Pa. $4.95

ETHICAL WRITINGS OF MAIMONIDES, Maimonides. Most significant ethical works of great medieval sage, newly translated for utmost precision, readability. Laws Concerning Character Traits, Eight Chapters, more. 192pp. 5⅜ × 8½.
24522-5 Pa. $5.95

THE EXPLORATION OF THE COLORADO RIVER AND ITS CANYONS, J. W. Powell. Full text of Powell's 1,000-mile expedition down the fabled Colorado in 1869. Superb account of terrain, geology, vegetation, Indians, famine, mutiny, treacherous rapids, mighty canyons, during exploration of last unknown part of continental U.S. 400pp. 5⅜ × 8½. 20094-9 Pa. $8.95

HISTORY OF PHILOSOPHY, Julián Marías. Clearest one-volume history on the market. Every major philosopher and dozens of others, to Existentialism and later. 505pp. 5⅜ × 8½. 21739-6 Pa. $9.95

ALL ABOUT LIGHTNING, Martin A. Uman. Highly readable nontechnical survey of nature and causes of lightning, thunderstorms, ball lightning, St. Elmo's Fire, much more. Illustrated. 192pp. 5⅜ × 8½. 25237-X Pa. $5.95

SAILING ALONE AROUND THE WORLD, Captain Joshua Slocum. First man to sail around the world, alone, in small boat. One of great feats of seamanship told in delightful manner. 67 illustrations. 294pp. 5⅜ × 8½. 20326-3 Pa. $4.95

LETTERS AND NOTES ON THE MANNERS, CUSTOMS AND CONDI-TIONS OF THE NORTH AMERICAN INDIANS, George Catlin. Classic account of life among Plains Indians: ceremonies, hunt, warfare, etc. 312 plates. 572pp. of text. 6⅛ × 9¼. 22118-0, 22119-9, Pa., Two-vol. set $17.90

THE SECRET LIFE OF SALVADOR DALÍ, Salvador Dalí. Outrageous but fascinating autobiography through Dalí's thirties with scores of drawings and sketches and 80 photographs. A must for lovers of 20th-century art. 432pp. 6½ × 9¼. (Available in U.S. only) 27454-3 Pa. $9.95

CATALOG OF DOVER BOOKS

HOW TO WRITE, Gertrude Stein. Gertrude Stein claimed anyone could understand her unconventional writing—here are clues to help. Fascinating improvisations, language experiments, explanations illuminate Stein's craft and the art of writing. Total of 414pp. 4⅝ × 6⅜. 23144-5 Pa. $6.95

ADVENTURES AT SEA IN THE GREAT AGE OF SAIL: Five Firsthand Narratives, edited by Elliot Snow. Rare true accounts of exploration, whaling, shipwreck, fierce natives, trade, shipboard life, more. 33 illustrations. Introduction. 353pp. 5⅜ × 8½. 25177-2 Pa. $9.95

THE HERBAL OR GENERAL HISTORY OF PLANTS, John Gerard. Classic descriptions of about 2,850 plants—with over 2,700 illustrations—includes Latin and English names, physical descriptions, varieties, time and place of growth, more. 2,706 illustrations. xlv + 1,678pp. 8½ × 12¼. 23147-X Cloth. $89.95

DOROTHY AND THE WIZARD IN OZ, L. Frank Baum. Dorothy and the Wizard visit the center of the Earth, where people are vegetables, glass houses grow and Oz characters reappear. Classic sequel to *Wizard of Oz.* 256pp. 5⅜ × 8.
24714-7 Pa. $5.95

SONGS OF EXPERIENCE: Facsimile Reproduction with 26 Plates in Full Color, William Blake. This facsimile of Blake's original "Illuminated Book" reproduces 26 full-color plates from a rare 1826 edition. Includes "The Tyger," "London," "Holy Thursday," and other immortal poems. 26 color plates. Printed text of poems. 48pp. 5¼ × 7. 24636-1 Pa. $3.95

SONGS OF INNOCENCE, William Blake. The first and most popular of Blake's famous "Illuminated Books," in a facsimile edition reproducing all 31 brightly colored plates. Additional printed text of each poem. 64pp. 5¼ × 7.
22764-2 Pa. $3.95

PRECIOUS STONES, Max Bauer. Classic, thorough study of diamonds, rubies, emeralds, garnets, etc.: physical character, occurrence, properties, use, similar topics. 20 plates, 8 in color. 94 figures. 659pp. 6⅛ × 9¼.
21910-0, 21911-9 Pa., Two-vol. set $21.90

ENCYCLOPEDIA OF VICTORIAN NEEDLEWORK, S. F. A. Caulfeild and Blanche Saward. Full, precise descriptions of stitches, techniques for dozens of needlecrafts—most exhaustive reference of its kind. Over 800 figures. Total of 679pp. 8⅛ × 11. 22800-2, 22801-0 Pa., Two-vol. set $26.90

THE MARVELOUS LAND OF OZ, L. Frank Baum. Second Oz book, the Scarecrow and Tin Woodman are back with hero named Tip, Oz magic. 136 illustrations. 287pp. 5⅜ × 8½. 20692-0 Pa. $5.95

WILD FOWL DECOYS, Joel Barber. Basic book on the subject, by foremost authority and collector. Reveals history of decoy making and rigging, place in American culture, different kinds of decoys, how to make them, and how to use them. 140 plates. 156pp. 7⅞ × 10¾. 20011-6 Pa. $14.95

HISTORY OF LACE, Mrs. Bury Palliser. Definitive, profusely illustrated chronicle of lace from earliest times to late 19th century. Laces of Italy, Greece, England, France, Belgium, etc. Landmark of needlework scholarship. 266 illustrations. 672pp. 6⅛ × 9¼. 24742-2 Pa. $16.95

CATALOG OF DOVER BOOKS

AMERICAN CLIPPER SHIPS: 1833–1858, Octavius T. Howe & Frederick C. Matthews. Fully-illustrated, encyclopedic review of 352 clipper ships from the period of America's greatest maritime supremacy. Introduction. 109 halftones. 5 black-and-white line illustrations. Index. Total of 928pp. 5⅜ × 8½.

25115-2, 25116-0 Pa., Two-vol. set $21.90

TOWARDS A NEW ARCHITECTURE, Le Corbusier. Pioneering manifesto by great architect, near legendary founder of "International School." Technical and aesthetic theories, views on industry, economics, relation of form to function, "mass-production spirit," much more. Profusely illustrated. Unabridged translation of 13th French edition. Introduction by Frederick Etchells. 320pp. 6⅛ × 9¼. (Available in U.S. only)

25023-7 Pa. $8.95

THE BOOK OF KELLS, edited by Blanche Cirker. Inexpensive collection of 32 full-color, full-page plates from the greatest illuminated manuscript of the Middle Ages, painstakingly reproduced from rare facsimile edition. Publisher's Note. Captions. 32pp. 9⅜ × 12¼. (Available in U.S. only)

24345-1 Pa. $5.95

BEST SCIENCE FICTION STORIES OF H. G. WELLS, H. G. Wells. Full novel *The Invisible Man*, plus 17 short stories: "The Crystal Egg," "Aepyornis Island," "The Strange Orchid," etc. 303pp. 5⅜ × 8½. (Available in U.S. only)

21531-8 Pa. $6.95

AMERICAN SAILING SHIPS: Their Plans and History, Charles G. Davis. Photos, construction details of schooners, frigates, clippers, other sailcraft of 18th to early 20th centuries—plus entertaining discourse on design, rigging, nautical lore, much more. 137 black-and-white illustrations. 240pp. 6⅛ × 9¼.

24658-2 Pa. $6.95

ENTERTAINING MATHEMATICAL PUZZLES, Martin Gardner. Selection of author's favorite conundrums involving arithmetic, money, speed, etc., with lively commentary. Complete solutions. 112pp. 5⅜ × 8½.

25211-6 Pa. $3.95

THE WILL TO BELIEVE, HUMAN IMMORTALITY, William James. Two books bound together. Effect of irrational on logical, and arguments for human immortality. 402pp. 5⅜ × 8½.

20291-7 Pa. $8.95

THE HAUNTED MONASTERY and THE CHINESE MAZE MURDERS, Robert Van Gulik. 2 full novels by Van Gulik continue adventures of Judge Dee and his companions. An evil Taoist monastery, seemingly supernatural events; overgrown topiary maze that hides strange crimes. Set in 7th-century China. 27 illustrations. 328pp. 5⅜ × 8½.

23502-5 Pa. $6.95

CELEBRATED CASES OF JUDGE DEE (DEE GOONG AN), translated by Robert Van Gulik. Authentic 18th-century Chinese detective novel; Dee and associates solve three interlocked cases. Led to Van Gulik's own stories with same characters. Extensive introduction. 9 illustrations. 237pp. 5⅜ × 8½.

23337-5 Pa. $5.95

Prices subject to change without notice.

Available at your book dealer or write for free catalog to Dept. GI, Dover Publications, Inc., 31 East 2nd St., Mineola, N.Y. 11501. Dover publishes more than 400 books each year on science, elementary and advanced mathematics, biology, music, art, literary history, social sciences and other areas.

CHRISTMAS CUSTOMS AND TRADITIONS, Clement A. Miles. Origin, evolution, significance of religious, secular practices. Caroling, gifts, yule logs, much more. Full, scholarly yet fascinating; non-sectarian. 400pp. 5⅜ × 8½.
23354-5 Pa. $7.95

THE HUMAN FIGURE IN MOTION, Eadweard Muybridge. More than 4,500 stopped-action photos, in action series, showing undraped men, women, children jumping, lying down, throwing, sitting, wrestling, carrying, etc. 390pp. 7⅞ × 10⅝.
20204-6 Cloth. $24.95

THE MAN WHO WAS THURSDAY, Gilbert Keith Chesterton. Witty, fast-paced novel about a club of anarchists in turn-of-the-century London. Brilliant social, religious, philosophical speculations. 128pp. 5⅜ × 8½.
25121-7 Pa. $3.95

A CÉZANNE SKETCHBOOK: Figures, Portraits, Landscapes and Still Lifes, Paul Cézanne. Great artist experiments with tonal effects, light, mass, other qualities in over 100 drawings. A revealing view of developing master painter, precursor of Cubism. 102 black-and-white illustrations. 144pp. 8¾ × 6⅜.
24790-2 Pa. $6.95

AN ENCYCLOPEDIA OF BATTLES: Accounts of Over 1,560 Battles from 1479 B.C. to the Present, David Eggenberger. Presents essential details of every major battle in recorded history, from the first battle of Megiddo in 1479 B.C. to Grenada in 1984. List of Battle Maps. New Appendix covering the years 1967–1984. Index. 99 illustrations. 544pp. 6½ × 9¼.
24913-1 Pa. $14.95

AN ETYMOLOGICAL DICTIONARY OF MODERN ENGLISH, Ernest Weekley. Richest, fullest work, by foremost British lexicographer. Detailed word histories. Inexhaustible. Total of 856pp. 6½ × 9¼.
21873-2, 21874-0 Pa., Two-vol. set $19.90

WEBSTER'S AMERICAN MILITARY BIOGRAPHIES, edited by Robert McHenry. Over 1,000 figures who shaped 3 centuries of American military history. Detailed biographies of Nathan Hale, Douglas MacArthur, Mary Hallaren, others. Chronologies of engagements, more. Introduction. Addenda. 1,033 entries in alphabetical order. xi + 548pp. 6½ × 9¼. (Available in U.S. only)
24758-9 Pa. $13.95

LIFE IN ANCIENT EGYPT, Adolf Erman. Detailed older account, with much not in more recent books: domestic life, religion, magic, medicine, commerce, and whatever else needed for complete picture. Many illustrations. 597pp. 5⅜ × 8½.
22632-8 Pa. $9.95

HISTORIC COSTUME IN PICTURES, Braun & Schneider. Over 1,450 costumed figures shown, covering a wide variety of peoples: kings, emperors, nobles, priests, servants, soldiers, scholars, townsfolk, peasants, merchants, courtiers, cavaliers, and more. 256pp. 8⅜ × 11¼.
23150-X Pa. $9.95

THE NOTEBOOKS OF LEONARDO DA VINCI, edited by J. P. Richter. Extracts from manuscripts reveal great genius; on painting, sculpture, anatomy, sciences, geography, etc. Both Italian and English. 186 ms. pages reproduced, plus 500 additional drawings, including studies for *Last Supper, Sforza* monument, etc. 860pp. 7⅞ × 10¾.
22572-0, 22573-9 Pa., Two-vol. set $35.90